Capablanca's

HUNDRED BEST

GAMES *of* CHESS

Chosen and Annotated by

H. GOLOMBEK

With a Memoir by

J. du MONT

Capablanca's Hundred Best Games of Chess

chosen and annotated by Golombek

with a memoir by J. Du Mont

ISHI PRESS
INTERNATIONAL

Capablanca's Hundred Best Games of Chess
chosen and annotated by Golombek
with a memoir by J. Du Mont

First Published in 1947

Copyright © 1947 by Harry Golembek and
J. Du Mont

This Printing in November, 2015
by Ishi Press in New York and Tokyo
with a new introduction by Sam Sloan

Copyright © 2015 by Sam Sloan

ISBN 4-87187-575-X
978-4-87187-575-2

Ishi Press International
1664 Davidson Avenue, Suite 1B
Bronx NY 10453-7877
USA
1-917-507-7226
1-917-659-3397
samhsloan@gmail.com

Printed in the United States of America

Capablanca's Hundred Best Games of Chess
chosen and annotated by Golombek
with a memoir by J. Du Mont

Introduction by Sam Sloan

Jose Raoul Capablanca is widely regarded as the strongest chess player who ever lived prior to Bobby Fischer. The authoritative work, "**The Rating of Chess Players Past and Present**" by Arpad Elo, inventor of the modern rating system, **ISBN 0923891277**, rates Capablanca as 2725, higher than any other player in history prior to Fischer.

The great thing about Capablanca's style of play is he tended to play simple, direct moves, moves that even an amateur player can find over the board.

José Raúl Capablanca y Graupera was the third World Champion, reigning from 1921 until 1927. Renowned for the simplicity of his play, his legendary endgame prowess, accuracy, and the speed of his play, he earned the nickname of the "Human Chess Machine".

Jose Raul Capablanca was born in Havana on November 19, 1888. He was a Cuban chess player, world chess champion from 1921 to 1927. Capablanca's ideas are still relevant on the world stage of chess. His images are a powerful aid to the student board secrets.

Jose Raoul Capablanca one of the outstanding players of all time became world's chess champion in 1921 when he defeated Lasker by 4 to 0. During his lifetime he held all the world's major records. In twenty five years of tournament play he lost less than twenty-five games, while between 1916 and 1924 he lost not a single one. He died in New York City on March 8, 1942.

In this volume Harry Golombek, the distinguished chess correspondent of the times and one of Great Britain's leading players, has bought together Capablanca's Hundred Best Games. These will provide the expert as well as the beginner with a new insight into the master's extraordinary grasp of the game's fundamental strategic principles, the brilliance of his tactical development. Golombek's clearly written notes highlight the games most crucial phases and provide the reader with many interesting clues as to possible variations.

Harry Golombek OBE was born on 1 March 1911 in London. He was a British chess International Master and honorary grandmaster, chess arbiter, and chess author. He was three times British Chess Champion, in 1947, 1949 and 1955. He became a grandmaster in 1985. He was famous as an author of many books and magazine articles. During World War II he worked at Bletchley Park deciphering the German enigma codes. He died on 7 January 1995 in the United Kingdom.

Julius Du Mont was a chess player, author and translator best known for "500 Master Games of Chess" and "The Basis of Combination in Chess". He was born December 15, 1881 in Paris and died April 7, 1956 in Hastings, England.

Sam Sloan
Los Angeles California
USA
November 17, 2015

CONTENTS

CHAP.   PAGE

  PREFACE vii

  LIST OF GAMES xi

  MEMOIR OF CAPABLANCA. *By* J. DU MONT 3

  TOURNAMENTS AND MATCHES 21

 I. EARLY YEARS — THE MATCH WITH MARSHALL 23

 II. RAPID DEVELOPMENT — THE VISIT TO EUROPE 41

 III. ON THE WAY TO THE WORLD CHAMPIONSHIP — THE MATCH WITH LASKER 71

 IV. WORLD CHAMPION 106

 V. VICTORY AND DISASTER 142

 VI. ATTEMPTS AT REHABILITATION 183

 VII. 1929 — A RICH YEAR 212

 VIII. PRELUDE TO RETIREMENT 252

 IX. TRIUMPHANT RETURN 272

 X. THE FINAL PHASE 308

  INDEX OF OPENINGS 331

  LIST OF OPPONENTS 332

PREFACE

The games of Capablanca are pervaded by a general feeling quite different from those of other great players. They breathe a serenity, a lucid crystal clarity, a type of model perfection present in no other master. This " splendidior vitro " quality of Capablanca's style has led some critics to assume falsely that he erred on the side of over-safety and that in his preference for the simple line rather than the richly complicated he was inclined to concede too many draws. Nothing could be further from the truth. This simplicity of perfection was the product of supreme art. Playing through a Capablanca game and fully understanding it after close study constitutes a liberal education in the art of chess.

For this reason I have found it necessary to annotate the games as exhaustively as was within my powers. With Capablanca every move is significant and his games will reward the closest study by the freshness and clear beauty of the conceptions they contain. I believe their essential greatness has been somewhat obscured in popular estimation from several causes. Firstly, and though it may seem something like lèse majesté to say it, yet this is my sincere belief and I must out with it, Capablanca was strangely poor at explaining and annotating his own games. Possibly this was because he assumed immediate comprehension on the part of the reader of moves that really demanded considerable explanation.

Then, too, he has suffered a great deal at the hands of his rivals. Too many of these (Tartakower being a notable and happy exception) have allowed jealous prejudice to blind them to the greatness of his games and have consequently joined in creating a myth concerning the aridity and dullness of his style. Those who read the German edition of the New York tournament book of 1927 will find it an excellent illustration of the systematic depreciation employed by one of the world's greatest annotators. To explain away the

hard fact that Capablanca won the tournament several points
ahead of all the leading players in the world every opportunity is
taken, and some occasions that did not previously exist are created,
to show how weakly and with what strange regularity all Capablanca's opponents played below their true form against him. Only
grudging admissions are given, and these rarely, of Capablanca's
great play. This injustice was never repaired since Capablanca
never troubled to reply.

Well, here are the games and the reader can judge for himself.
But when the reader has played through the games I would ask
him to consider this question. Has any other player the chess world
has yet seen produced such a mass of games impregnated by that
inner logical harmony that to my mind constitutes the essential
quality of a great game of chess? Rubinstein, alone, I believe, would
have rivalled Capablanca, had it not been for a regrettable tend-
ency to lapse into grotesque blunders, thereby marring the perfection of many a wonderful game.

It is this harmonious perfection that makes him such a model for
the young and aspiring player. The stormy and attractive genius
of Alekhine, on the other hand, is full of pitfalls for its imitators.
The mention of Alekhine's name brings me to one of the great con-
troversies of the chess world of the present century. Everybody is
fully aware of the quarrel and even enmity that existed between
these two great masters and it is by now generally realized that
faults existed on both sides, though at one time the chess world was
sharply divided into supporters of either camp.

I became acquainted with both towards the end of their careers
and found them equally charming, friendly, and most agreeable
and sparkling conversationalists. But if you once mentioned the
name of their hated rival (it was not done more than once) then a
constrained and freezing atmosphere was immediately noticeable.
There was an amusing illustration of this antipathy at the Buenos
Aires Olympiad of 1939. I was standing in one of the corridors of
the Teatro Politeama, where the congress was held, when Alekhine
came in, and I walked down the corridor with him, discussing a
game he had played the previous day. Suddenly Capablanca
emerged from a side door in the theatre and came up towards us in
the somewhat narrow corridor which would only just take three
abreast. It was extraordinary and indeed comic to observe how they

passed each other by with a supreme obliviousness as to each other's presence.

Now that they are both dead one can only regret the petty nature of the quarrel that prevented a return match for the championship and so probably deprived the world of some great games.

Into the details of Capablanca's life it is unnecessary for me to enter, since this has already been done so capably by Mr. du Mont in his biography, which follows.

I would like to acknowledge here my deep indebtedness to my friend F. W. Allen, who not only submitted himself to the tedium of checking through the proofs but also proffered several valuable suggestions and corrections to the notes, and my grateful thanks are also due to W. Ritson Morry who was so kind as to furnish me with the sources of some games I had been unable to trace.

H. GOLOMBEK

December, 1946.

List of Games

Game
Number   *Page*
   1 Havana, 1900   *Black:* Corzo. Vienna Gambit   24
   2 Havana, 1900   *White:* Corzo. Queen's Pawn   25
   3 New York, 1906   *Black:* Fox. Ruy Lopez, Steinitz Defence   28
   4 New York, 1909   *White:* Marshall. Ruy Lopez, Steinitz
                                     Defence   30
   5 New York, 1909   *White:* Marshall. Ruy Lopez, Steinitz
                                     Defence   33
   6 New York, 1909   *Black:* Marshall. Queen's Gambit De-
                                     clined, Tarrasch Defence   35
   7 New York, 1910   *White:* Jaffe. Queen's Gambit Declined,
                                     Slav Defence   39
   8 San Sebastian, 1911   *White:* Bernstein. Ruy Lopez, Steinitz
                                     Defence   44
   9 San Sebastian, 1911   *White:* Burn. Ruy Lopez   47
  10 Buenos Aires, 1911   *White:* Molina. Queen's Gambit Declined   50
  11 Havana, 1913   *Black:* Corzo. Queen's Pawn   52
  12 St. Petersburg, 1913 *White:* Dus-Chotimirski.   Ruy   Lopez,
                                     Morphy Defence   55
  13 St. Petersburg, 1913 *White:* Alekhine. Queen's Gambit De-
                                     clined, Slav Defence   57
  14 Moscow, 1914   *Black:* Bernstein. Queen's Gambit De-
                                     clined, Queen's Fianchetto De-
                                     fence   60
  15 St. Petersburg, 1914 *Black:* Alekhine. Ruy Lopez, Steinitz
                                     Defence   62
  16 St. Petersburg, 1914 *White:* Bernstein. Queen's Gambit De-
                                     clined   65
  17 St. Petersburg, 1914 *White:* Blackburne. Ruy Lopez, Bird's
                                     Defence   68
  18 New York, 1915   *White:* Kupchik. Ruy Lopez, Morphy
                                     Defence   74
  19 New York, 1915   *White:* Chajes. Ruy Lopez, Morphy De-
                                     fence   76
  20 New York, 1916   *Black:* Schroeder. Queen's Gambit De-
                                     clined, Orthodox Defence   79
  21 New York, 1916   *White:* Janowski. Queen's Gambit De-
                                     clined, Slav Defence   81
  22 New York, 1918   *White:* Marshall. Ruy Lopez, Morphy
                                     Defence   83
  23 New York, 1918   *White:* Janowski. Queen's Gambit De-
                                     clined   87
  24 Havana, 1919   *White:* Kostich. Petroff Defence   89
  25 Hastings, 1919   *White:* Scott. Queen's Gambit Declined,
                                     Slav Defence   94

Game
Number   *Page*
26 Havana, 1921   *Black:* EM. LASKER. Queen's Gambit De-
                          clined, Orthodox Defence   95
27 Havana, 1921   *White:* EM. LASKER. Queen's Gambit De-
                          clined, Orthodox Defence   101
28 London, 1922   *White:* BOGOLJUBOFF. Ruy Lopez, Morphy
                          Defence   108
29 London, 1922   *White:* VIDMAR. Queen's Gambit De-
                          clined, Orthodox Defence   111
30 New York, 1924   *White:* TARTAKOWER. Queen's Pawn, Dutch
                          Defence   114
31 New York, 1924   *White:* YATES. Queen's Pawn, King's In-
                          dian Defence   117
32 New York, 1924   *Black:* BOGOLJUBOFF. Queen's Pawn   121
33 New York, 1924   *Black:* MAROCZY. Ruy Lopez, Morphy De-
                          fence   124
34 New York, 1924   *White:* EM. LASKER. Queen's Gambit De-
                          clined, Slav Defence   128
35 New York, 1924   *White:* JANOWSKI. Réti's Opening   135
36 New York, 1924   *Black:* TARTAKOWER. King's Gambit Ac-
                          cepted   138
37 Moscow, 1925   *White:* MARSHALL. Rétis Opening   144
38 Moscow, 1925   *White:* SUBAREW. Queen's Gambit Ac-
                          cepted   148
39 Moscow, 1925   *Black:* GOTTHILF. Queen's Pawn, Q. In-
                          dian Defence   150
40 Moscow, 1925   *White:* BOGOLJUBOFF. Queen's Gambit Ac-
                          cepted   152
41 Lake Hopatcong, 1926 *Black:* EM. LASKER. Queen's Pawn   156
42 New York, 1927   *Black:* NIMZOVITCH. Queen's Gambit De-
                          clined   159
43 New York, 1927   *Black:* ALEKHINE. Queen's Pawn, Q. In-
                          dian Defence   162
44 New York, 1927   *White:* VIDMAR. Ruy Lopez, Morphy De-
                          fence   164
45 New York, 1927   *White:* SPIELMANN. Queen's Gambit De-
                          clined, Westphalia Variation   166
46 New York, 1927   *Black:* NIMZOVITCH. Caro-Kann Defence 170
47 Buenos Aires, 1927   *White:* ALEKHINE. Queen's Pawn, Q. In-
                          dian Defence   173
48 Buenos Aires, 1927   *White:* ALEKHINE. Queen's Gambit De-
                          clined, Cambridge Springs De-
                          fence   176
49 Buenos Aires, 1927   *White:* ALEKHINE. Queen's Gambit De-
                          clined, Cambridge Springs De-
                          fence   179
50 Bad Kissingen, 1928   *White:* TARTAKOWER. Queen's Pawn, Bu-
                          dapest Defence   185
51 Bad Kissingen, 1928   *White:* MIESES. Queen's Gambit Declined,
                          Orthodox Defence   188
52 Bad Kissingen, 1928   *White:* YATES. Sicilian Defence   190

Game Number			Page
53	Bad Kissingen, 1928	*Black:* BOGOLJUBOFF. Queen's Pawn, Q. Indian Defence	193
54	Berlin, 1928	*White:* RUBINSTEIN. Queen's Pawn	196
55	Berlin, 1928	*Black:* RUBINSTEIN. Queen's Pawn, Rubinstein Variation	199
56	Budapest, 1928	*White:* HAVASI. Queen's Gambit Accepted	202
57	Budapest, 1928	*Black:* MERÉNYI. Sicilian Defence	203
58	Budapest, 1928	*White:* H. STEINER. Queen's Gambit Declined, Orthodox Defence	206
59	Budapest, 1928	*White:* VON BALLA. Queen's Pawn, Nimzovitch Defence	209
60	Ramsgate, 1929	*Black:* WINTER. Queen's Pawn, Nimzovitch Defence	215
61	Carlsbad, 1929	*White:* MATTISON. Queen's Pawn, Nimzovitch Defence	219
62	Carlsbad, 1929	*White:* BECKER. Queen's Gambit Declined, Westphalia Variation	221
63	Carlsbad, 1929	*White:* TREYBAL. Queen's Gambit Declined, Stonewall Defence	223
64	Carlsbad, 1929	*White:* MAROCZY. Queen's Gambit Declined, Orthodox Defence	226
65	Carlsbad, 1929	*Black:* COLLE. Queen's Pawn, Colle System	229
66	Carlsbad, 1929	*White:* MARSHALL. Queen's Pawn, Q. Indian Defence	232
67	Budapest, 1929	*White:* BRINCKMANN. Queen's Gambit Declined, Slav Defence	235
68	Budapest, 1929	*Black:* HAVASI. Queen's Pawn, Nimzovitch Defence	237
69	Barcelona, 1929	*White:* COLLE. English Opening	239
70	Barcelona, 1929	*White:* YATES. Réti's Opening	242
71	Barcelona, 1929	*Black:* MONTICELLI. Queen's Pawn, Q. Indian Defence	245
72	Barcelona, 1929	*White:* TORRES. English Opening	248
73	Barcelona, 1929	*Black:* RIBERA. Queen's Pawn, Q. Indian Defence	249
74	Hastings, 1930–31	*Black:* MISS MENCHIK. Queen's Pawn, Q. Indian Defence	254
75	Hastings, 1930–31	*White:* TYLOR. Queen's Gambit Declined	256
76	New York, 1931	*Black:* KEVITZ. Réti's Opening	258
77	New York, 1931	*Black:* MARSHALL. Queen's Pawn, Q. Indian Defence	261
78	Amsterdam, 1931	*White:* EUWE. Queen's Gambit Declined, Slav Defence	263
79	Amsterdam, 1931	*Black:* EUWE. Queen's Pawn, Q. Indian Defence	265
80	Los Angeles, 1933	*White:* H. STEINER. Four Knights' Game	269
81	Moscow, 1935	*Black:* ALATORTZEFF. Queen's Gambit Declined, Orthodox Defence	276

Game Number		Page
82 Moscow, 1935	*White:* RAGOSIN. Queen's Pawn, Nimzovitch Defence	278
83 Moscow, 1935	*White:* KAN. Queen's Gambit Declined, Orthodox Defence	281
84 Moscow, 1935	*Black:* MISS MENCHIK. Queen's Pawn, K. Indian Defence	284
85 Moscow, 1935	*White:* LÖWENFISCH. Queen's Gambit Declined, Slav Defence	286
86 Margate, 1935	*White:* MIESES. Queen's Gambit Declined, Slav Defence	288
87 Margate, 1935	*White:* SIR G. THOMAS. Queen's Pawn, Bogoljuboff Defence	291
88 Margate, 1936	*White:* MILNER-BARRY. English Opening	293
89 Moscow, 1936	*White:* LILIENTHAL. Réti's Opening	295
90 Moscow, 1936	*White:* ELISKASES. Giuoco Piano	298
91 Leningrad, 1936	*Black:* ALLIES. Queen's Pawn, Q. Indian Defence	302
92 Nottingham, 1936	*White:* ALEXANDER. English Opening	304
93 Semmering-Baden, 1937	*Black:* RAGOSIN. Queen's Gambit Declined, Slav Defence	312
94 Paris, 1938	*White:* ROSSOLIMO. Queen's Gambit Declined, Orthodox Defence	314
95 Paris, 1938	*White:* ZNOSKO-BOROWSKI. Queen's Gambit Declined, Tarrasch Defence	316
96 Avro, 1938	*White:* FLOHR. Queen's Pawn, Grünfeld Defence	319
97 Margate, 1939	*White:* GOLOMBEK. Queen's Pawn, Nimzovitch Defence	321
98 Buenos Aires, 1939	*White:* MIKENAS. Queen's Pawn, Nimzovitch Defence	323
99 Buenos Aires, 1939	*White:* VASSAUX. Queen's Gambit Declined, Slav Defence	325
100 Buenos Aires, 1939	*White:* CZERNIAK. Caro-Kann Defence	327

CAPABLANCA'S

Hundred Best Games of Chess

Memoir of

CAPABLANCA

By J. du Mont

A MAN's importance in the scheme of things is entirely relative. People go through life both cheerfully and successfully without giving astronomy a thought. To them the most famous astronomer is but a name should they happen to have heard of him. To his fellow astronomers he is of paramount interest and importance.

Capablanca, a star of the first magnitude in the chess firmament, was, however, more than a name to the general public. It is not easy to adduce a tangible reason for this remarkable fact; perhaps it is the unerring instinct of the people, which seldom fails to single out the man who makes history.

Be that as it may, Capablanca has done more than anyone to spread the gospel of chess by the glamour of his personality and the brilliance of his achievement and he has the great merit of having raised the status of the chess player by the dignity and graciousness of his intercourse with his fellow men.

He may have had his faults, but they were at the worst some of the minor weaknesses from which genius is hardly ever free. They had, however, nothing to do with his art, and the biographer who gives these more than a passing notice does a disservice to his readers in the presentation of the man. You may as well disparage Beethoven's immortal works because his landladies complained of his being untidy.

Capablanca has frequently been compared with Morphy, and not without good reason. Both were of Latin descent, they learned to play good chess as small children, became masters at the age of twelve. They beat every contemporary American player at the age of twenty, following this up immediately by a visit to Europe, where they beat the foremost European masters with consummate ease.

Here the parallel ends; Morphy retired, unbeaten, at the age of twenty-two, while Capablanca who, had he likewise retired, would also have perpetuated the nimbus of invincibility, went on from success to success, winning the World's Championship, until he met Dr. Alekhine, to whom he lost a long-drawn-out match by 6 losses, 3 wins and 21 draws. He was then thirty-eight, which in Latin races represents a greater age than in the Nordic strain.

This unexpected reverse played havoc with Capablanca's self-confidence, and there is no doubt that his failure to secure a return match preyed on his mind and affected his playing strength. At any rate, he no longer was the odds-on candidate for first prize when playing in a strong tournament. Nevertheless, but for one exception, he invariably came out high up in the lists of the tournaments in which he took part and twice scored a success comparable with his first appearance at San Sebastian, 1911, the great tournaments of Moscow and Nottingham in 1936. His only comparative failure was in the Avro Grandmasters' Tournament in 1937. He was then nearly fifty and suffering from high blood pressure, to which he succumbed a few years later.

The comparative strength of the great chess players is practically impossible to assess, for their powers are no static entity. It seldom happens that both the players taking part in a match are on the up-grade. The reigning champion in particular is not overanxious to play a really dangerous rival until forced to do so by circumstances, a human failing, deplorable perhaps, but not restricted to chess. Who knows what would have happened had Lasker played Tarrasch in 1898, if Lasker had played Capablanca in 1914 or Capablanca had met Alekhine in 1925?

The true criterion of a chess master, as it is also in other walks of life, is whether his work will endure through generations. There is little doubt that Capablanca will prove one of the immortals.

Jose Raoul Capablanca y Graupera was born in the city of Havana on November 19th, 1888. He was in his fourth year when he first showed signs of his exceptional talent for chess, and the following incident is perfectly authentic. One day the child happened to watch his father play a game of chess with a friend. The pieces attracted him, and he watched the players again on the next day. On the third day he noticed that his father moved a knight from a white square to another white square. At the end of the game the child laughed at his father and said he had won by cheating. His father remonstrated with him, saying that he did not even know the moves, whereupon Jose Raoul said he could beat his father and forthwith vindicated his assertion by beating him twice. Thus, without ever having been shown the moves, the boy genius won his first two games of chess. During the next few years, on medical advice, the child was allowed to play chess on rare occasions only.

After his eighth birthday young Raoul was taken to the Havana Chess Club and thus was launched on his chess career.

The Havana Chess Club has long enjoyed the reputation of being one of the most enthusiastic and enterprising clubs in the world. In its fine and spacious premises, many important matches have taken place, as, for instance, Steinitz-Tchigorin, Tchigorin-Gunsberg, Tchigorin-Tarrasch. Many leading players have been the guests of the Club — Morphy, Captain Mackenzie, Blackburne, Pillsbury and many others. The membership has always been numerous, with a high percentage of strong players.

The youthful genius thrived in this atmosphere, and three months after joining the Club he was promoted to the first class and held his own easily with the strongest players in the Club, with the exception of Vasquez and Corzo. His progress was so rapid and his success so sustained that it was decided to arrange a match for the Championship of the Club between the boy, now aged twelve, and the holder, Juan Corzo. Corzo won the first two games, and it seemed as if the youngster was being tried too high. But young Raoul, with a steadiness worthy of an experienced master, was not to be denied and ran out the winner by 7–5.

After this remarkable success, the boy was kept away from chess as much as possible so that he could devote himself to his studies, with special attention to the English language, in preparation for his forthcoming entrance examination to the University of Columbia.

In this connection he visited the Manhattan Chess Club for the first time in 1905, and in subsequent visits he showed such good form that, a year later, he was considered second to none in this famous club. He was easily the best at lightning chess, and in 1906, during a visit by Dr. Lasker, he won a rapid transit tournament, beating the World Champion in their individual game.

In the same year he entered the University of Columbia. In the entrance examination he gained high marks in scientific subjects and as much as 99 per cent. in algebra. After two years devoted to his studies at the University and, incidentally, a great deal of sport, he left the University and gave most of his time to chess.

In that year, 1908, he went on a tour of the United States for the first time and broke all records both by the results and the speed of his simultaneous play. He played 168 games in ten consecutive séances before losing one game out of twenty-two at Minneapolis. As to speed, he could at that time, always be relied upon to complete thirty games in under two hours. Altogether his score during this his first tour was 703 wins, nineteen draws and only twelve losses.

Then came his first real test, his match with Frank Marshall, the undisputed leader of American chess since the death of Pillsbury. With a long list of Continental successes to his credit and his sensational triumph at Cambridge Springs in 1904, no one thought that Marshall had anything to fear from his youthful and inexperienced opponent. As Capablanca said himself, he had never studied a book on the openings, and the result of the match — a win for Capablanca by 8–1 and fourteen draws — was amazing and none was more surprised than Marshall himself.

Shortly after the match Capablanca returned home to Cuba after an absence of five years, during which he had almost forgotten his mother tongue.

On his return to the U.S.A., Capablanca undertook his second tour. This was of a very exacting nature, as a result of which he found that his physical condition made it imperative to postpone his first visit to Europe, where he had accepted an invitation to take part in the International Tournament at Hamburg in 1910. This gave rise to many acid comments, some Continental experts suggesting that fear of the strong opposition was the real reason of the defection.

The following year he undertook yet another very exacting tour of the U.S.A. This was followed by his participation in a tournament in New York which he thought would be good practice for the forthcoming tournament at San Sebastian. The only opponent of real calibre was Marshall but, evidently as a consequence of his strenuous exertions when on tour, Capablanca started the tournament very badly and at the half-way stage he stood fifth in the list. He then found his form and, by winning five consecutive games, he finished second to Marshall.

Shortly afterwards he was on the high seas, making for Europe, hoping to emulate the feat of his great predecessors, Morphy and Pillsbury, by holding his own, at the first time of asking, with the best that Europe could muster.

The San Sebastian Tournament of 1911 was the first contest which could be rightly called a grandmasters' tournament as we know it to-day. A novel condition of entry was that every contestant had to show that he had won at least two third prizes in very strong master tournaments. This resulted in an exceptionally strong entry, the participants being Rubinstein, Vidmar, Marshall, Nimzovitch, Schlechter, Tarrasch, Bernstein, Spielmann, Teichmann, Janowski, Maroczy, Burn, Duras and Leonhardt — the most powerful contingent of masters ever known in one contest up to that time. In view of his sensational victory over Marshall, an exception was made for young Capablanca, who had not yet played in any master's tournament, let alone won two third prizes. There was much shaking of heads, especially in view of his partial failure in a second-rate tournament shortly before, and several of the masters taking part in the San Sebastian fixture objected strongly to the newcomer's entry being accepted. The most vocal were Bernstein and Nimzovitch, and it was but poetic justice that Capablanca should beat Bernstein in the first round in a sensational " brilliancy " and that he should also account for Nimzovitch in decisive fashion. In the end he lost only one game, against Rubinstein, won six and drew seven. The scores of the leaders were: Capablanca 9½, Rubinstein and Vidmar 9, Marshall 8½.

No one expected the novice to win this tournament, in which, with the sole exception of Dr. Lasker, all the leading players of the world took part, and it is safe to say that there has never been a greater sensation in the history of the game. As a consequence there was a tremendous demand for Capablanca's services from clubs throughout Europe, but, as he had accepted a two months' engagement in the Argentine, he only took a short trip through Germany on this occasion. His visit to the Argentine was very successful; playing only the very best players single-handed or in consultation, he won every game but one, a consultation game (versus Illa and Gelly), which was drawn.

Taking in a number of South American cities on his way back, he returned to Europe, where a triumphant tour took him through

Holland, Denmark, Germany, Austria, France and England. The results of his simultaneous play were staggering, for every club he visited took a pride in putting up their strongest possible team, and yet 100 per cent. results were no isolated instances. Quite unusual too were the fees demanded and which clubs paid willingly for such outstanding experience as a visit from Capablanca. There is no doubt that professional chess benefited from this new departure.

After he left Europe in 1912, nothing of any great importance occurred for some time; there were a few small tournaments, some tours in Cuba and the U.S.A. In 1913 in a tournament in New York, Capablanca won all thirteen games and although, of the participants, only Duras could be said to be of his own class, it is nevertheless an unusual feat.

In a double-round tournament in Havana in 1913, Capablanca lost one game to Janowski, in consequence of which he finished second, half a point behind Marshall. Such was the exaggerated view the chess public took of the popular hero that for him to take the second place, half a point behind the winner, was accounted a failure.

During this year, 1913, Capablanca entered the Cuban Foreign Office. This carried a substantial salary and involved a good deal of travelling, which enabled him to meet the strongest players of most countries. This appointment is generally thought to have been a sinecure. This was not so and, although the Cuban Government were fully aware of the magnificent advertisement they were given by the sensational activities in the chess world of their compatriot, he took his duties, such as they were, seriously and certainly in correct diplomatic style and never discussed them with anyone.

His first mission took him to St. Petersburg. On his way he gave simultaneous exhibitions in London, Paris and Berlin. During a short stay in the last-named city, four exhibition games were arranged, two against Mieses and two against Teichmann. He won all four games. Soon after his arrival in St. Petersburg a similar series of six games was arranged, two each against Alekhine, Znosko-Borowski and Dus-Chotimirsky. One of these he lost to Znosko-Borowski, the five others he won.

The following year again brought much travelling and visits to Vienna, Paris and Berlin. Besides simultaneous play, there were many serious games against masters such as Nimzovitch, Dr. Bernstein, Alekhine and others of the same class. Of ten games he won eight and drew two — games never surpassed in accuracy and sheer skill.

Capablanca's next great test was the tournament at St. Petersburg in 1914, where for the first time he met the holder of the World Championship, Dr. Lasker, in a tournament. In point of strength, the entries to this great tournament were on a par with San Sebastian, 1911, but an unusual arrangement was that the first five players were to decide the destination of the prizes in a final double-round tournament. Even more unusual was the fact that the scores in the preliminary tournament were taken over into the second. Capablanca won through his first stage, scoring 8 points without loss, a point and a half ahead of his great rivals, Dr. Lasker and Dr. Tarrasch. Next came Alekhine and Marshall with six points each. It seemed a foregone conclusion that Capablanca, with this substantial start, should come out first, but Dr. Lasker, in one of those bursts of superhuman energy for which he was famous, actually managed to score two more points than his rival and in the end was first with $13\frac{1}{2}$ to Capablanca's 13. At an interval of 3 points came Alekhine, the first great achievement of the future world champion. Dr. Tarrasch scored $8\frac{1}{2}$ and Marshall 8. If the result of this tournament gave no real indication of the relative strength of Dr. Lasker and Capablanca at that time, it at least made it very clear that the two were in a class by themselves and that Capablanca was the only possible challenger for the title. There were indeed several attempts to bring these two great players together, but the War of 1914 intervened and it was not until long afterwards that the match actually took place.

Shortly before the War of 1914 Capablanca left St. Petersburg for Buenos Aires, where he had an engagement. His visit was longer than anticipated. All the steamers carried the British flag and many suffered heavy damage at the time from German raiders. Here his diplomatic status again helped him, as he was allowed to board one of the Argentine transports sailing for Philadelphia, where he landed at the beginning of 1915. The war years very naturally made larger chess fixtures impossible, and all there is to report during that time is the winning of two minor tournaments, a visit to Havana, and the inevitable tour for simultaneous play. In the autumn of 1918 a double-round tournament at New York brought a number of masters together, the result being Capablanca 10½, Kostics 9, Marshall 7, Chajes 6, Janowski 4, Black 3½, Morrison 3. Both the leaders won through the tournament without loss, Kostics drawing both his games against Capablanca. Thereupon Kostics issued a challenge to Capablanca which was accepted, and a match duly took place in the fine surroundings of the Union Club of Havana. Kostics resigned the match after losing five games off the reel.

A study of these five games explains the feeling of hopelessness which befell the loser and justifies his resignation. He played well according to principles recognised at the time, and this match perhaps more than any previous achievement of Capablanca's revealed the fact that his genius had found something deeper and quite individual which formed the basis of his play. These games were at the time quite beyond the understanding of the average student of the game and left him with a sense of wonderment.

Capablanca's style of play never formed the basis of a method, nor were the principles underlying it ever analysed and proclaimed as something new. But there is no doubt that it gave the younger masters food for thought and initiated a general overhaul of the guiding ideas in chess. I feel certain that from this sprang the whole idea of modern play which was later rather blatantly styled " hyper-modern."

At the end of the First World War the famous Hastings Club arranged a tournament in celebration of the Allied victory. The twelve participants were of uneven strength and it is no wonder that Capablanca scored 10½, winning all his games except a draw with Kostics, who was second with 9½ points. The third and fourth prizes were shared by Sir George Thomas and Yates with 7 points. Nevertheless, this overwhelming victory, coming after the hiatus of the war years, reawakened the public interest in chess in general and in Capablanca in particular.

An analysis of his results in the course of eight years in competitive chess showed that during that time, counting only tournament and individual match games as well as exhibition games against front-rank masters, Capablanca won 136 games against only ten losses — ten losses in eight years !

As a matter of interest, after that date, when some critics professed to have noticed a great falling off in Capablanca's powers, he won 187 games and lost twenty-four over a period of twenty years in tournament and individual matches. In addition, there were in the first period only two contests which could rightly be termed full-scale masters' tournaments against fifteen in the second period, which also included his match against Dr. Alekhine.

The long-awaited match with Dr. Lasker for the championship of the world took place at last in 1921. The venue was Havana, and Capablanca proved the winner by four wins, fourteen draws and no losses. Much has been said and written about this result. Dr. Lasker certainly did not appear as the Titan of former days; on the other hand, he could have met his younger opponent at an earlier date, when possibly the result might have been different or at any rate the contest more even. Anno Domini is a hard taskmaster, and possibly the four war years, in which Dr. Lasker practically lost his all, reacted on his stamina and playing strength.

Capablanca had now reached the pinnacle of fame, and the first full master tournament in which he took part after winning the championship, the London Tournament of 1922, was won by him with consummate ease. He scored thirteen out of fifteen, allowing his competitors only four draws. Dr. Alekhine was second with 11½. He also went through the tournament without loss, but scored seven draws. Yet there was noticeable in the new champion's play that something was lacking. One missed his indomitable will to win. He won by sheer skill and not by the exercise of his normal combativeness.

This was accentuated in the next two big tournaments in which he took part, New York, 1924, and Moscow, 1925. In New York he made a really bad start with four draws of a lackadaisical nature and one bad loss against Réti before he pulled himself together and played more like a champion. He went through this heavy double-round tournament without further loss and but five more draws. But in the meantime Dr. Lasker had forged ahead in the style of his best days, and although Capablanca scored one win and one draw against Lasker in their individual encounters, he could not atone for his bad start and the tournament resulted in a win for the grand old man with 16 points, 1½ points ahead of Capablanca. Next came Alekhine with 12 and Marshall with 11.

In Moscow he fared even worse at the start, losing two games to comparatively unknown players, Ilyin-Zhenevsky and Verlinsky, who came out tenth and fourteenth respectively. In the end the tournament was won by Bogoljuboff, who thus scored in his homeland the greatest triumph of his career. His score was 15½, Lasker was second with 14, followed closely by Capablanca with 13½. Capablanca beat the winner and drew with the runner-up, but again could not make good his failure in the early rounds.

At Lake Hopatcong, in the following year, Capablanca took part in a double-round tournament in which Maroczy and Marshall took part as well as Edward Lasker and Kupchik. He won easily with four wins, four draws and no loss. Kupchik surprisingly won the second prize with 4½ points, losing only one game, against the winner.

At this time a number of challenges were issued for a championship match, especially by Nimzovitch and Alekhine, who both had scored important successes since the end of the First World War. A tournament was arranged, the participants being Capablanca, Alekhine, Nimzovitch, Vidmar, Spielmann and Marshall. This was a double-round affair, and should the champion fail to win, the winner was to be the accepted challenger. If the champion won, the runner-up would be entitled to a match.

In this tremendous trial of strength, Capablanca once more deployed the whole of his amazing powers and won with 14 points and not a single loss (nine wins and eleven draws) 3½ points ahead of Alekhine who scored 11½ (five wins, thirteen draws and two losses). This victory probably marked the pinnacle of the Cuban's career, and may in some measure be responsible for the result of the match with Alekhine which took place the same year in Buenos Aires.

There is no doubt that, after this overwhelming triumph, Capablanca did not take the challenge seriously and entered the lists totally unprepared. After losing the first game, playing white in a French defence, he lost after missing a chance of a draw and never recovered from the shock. The new champion, however, did not score a runaway victory, for he won by six games to three with the unprecedented number of twenty-five draws.

For the rest of his life Capablanca tried hard to get a return match and he was more than justified in doing so. In all the tournaments in which both these players took part Alekhine won only one single game.

The total results between them read:

	Wins	Draws	Losses
Tournaments	5	7	1
Exhibition Games	3	—	—
Championship Match	3	25	6
	11	32	7

Omitting the exhibition games, Capablanca's score reads: 8 wins, 32 draws, 7 losses.

There is no shadow of doubt that Capablanca was in truth fully entitled to a return match. The chess world is the poorer for the fact that it never took place. There would be little to be gained at this stage by apportioning the blame, but it would have been a keen encounter, for Capablanca would have prepared himself for the ordeal in a very different way from the almost casual manner in which he usually regarded these things. Of course, nobody could tell what the result would have been.

During the next ten years Capablanca played in many tournaments, trying to establish his claim to a return match. On the whole he was successful, although at times he won a negative success by securing the third or even the fourth prize.

In 1928 he played in three important tournaments. At Bad Kissingen he was second, one point behind Bogoljuboff, who scored 8. In Berlin he was first with $8\frac{1}{2}$, $1\frac{1}{2}$ points ahead of Nimzovitch, and in Budapest he was first, 1 point ahead of Marshall. In 1929 he shared second prize with Spielmann, scoring $14\frac{1}{2}$ to Nimzovitch's 15. He was first in three tournaments in that year, at Ramsgate, Barcelona and Budapest.

During the next five years he seems to have lost heart, taking part in only two minor tournaments, securing the second prize at Hastings, 1930–31, and the first in New York, 1931.

Lack of practice told when he resumed activities in 1935, coming out fourth only in Hastings and fourth again in Moscow, his worst placing so far. He recovered much of his strength in 1936.

After two second prizes in less important fixtures at Margate in 1935 and 1936, he scored a notable triumph in the Moscow, 1936, double-round tournament with 13 points, a point ahead of Botvinnik and no less than $3\frac{1}{2}$ points ahead of the third prize-winner, Flohr!

In the same year he scored another outstanding success in one of the strongest tournaments ever held, that at Nottingham, where, with the champion and three former champions competing, he shared first prize with Botvinnik, the new star from Russia.

This seems to have been his swan song, although his third, equal with Reshevsky in the Semmering tournament of 1935 closely behind Keres and Fine, must be accounted a good performance, judged by normal standards. He won a weak tournament in Paris in 1938, but did badly in the A.V.R.O. double-round tournament of 1938, his only failure throughout his career. At that time he was suffering from angina pectoris to which he was to succumb a few years later. He was then fifty and the conditions of the tournament, in which each round was played in a different town, entailed much uncomfortable travelling. Moreover, besides the champion, his six rivals — Keres, Fine, Botvinnik, Reschevsky, Euwe and Flohr — were all grandmasters, fully fledged contenders for the title and all considerably younger than himself. Dr. Alekhine himself, at forty-seven, found the conditions too onerous, and did almost equally badly, scoring but one point more than Capablanca. Even so, Capablanca finished 2½ points only behind the winner, Keres, scoring two wins, eight draws and four losses.

After the A.V.R.O. tournament, Capablanca took part in but two more events. At Margate, 1939, in which he shared the second prize with 6½ points behind Keres, who scored 7½. He and Keres went through the tournament without loss. In the same year he played in the team tournament at Buenos Aires which witnessed the advent of the Second World War. This, his last appearance, was an excellent one. He played top board for Cuba, and of the ten games he played he won six and drew four.

The World War now put an end for a time to representative international chess.

On March 8th, 1942, Capablanca died of a heart attack. He was taken ill at the Manhattan Chess Club, from where he was taken to the Mount Sinai Hospital, New York. His great rival, Dr. Lasker, had preceded him just over one year before.

The veteran Frank Marshall expressed himself as follows:

" Comparatively little has been written about Capablanca's style of play, and much of what has appeared in the Press was contradictory. Many called his play dull and himself a mathematical precision machine. Yet in his very first game in international chess, that against Bernstein in San Sebastian, 1911, Capablanca deservedly won a first brilliancy prize and the game remains a classic among brilliancies. In tournament after tournament Capablanca gained brilliancy prizes, as many as three in Budapest, 1929. Indeed, the prizes he won for brilliancies in major tournaments almost equalled the number of such events in which he took part.

" The truth is that, a true artist, he felt that the simplest way to win was also the most artistic. He never went in for a brilliancy for the sake of being brilliant. Only when the sacrifice, the combination were the shortest way to a win did Capablanca exhibit his outstanding talent in that direction."

In a lengthy article in the book of the San Sebastian tournament of 1911, J. Mieses, that eminent critic and author, wrote as follows:

" Concerning his type of play, let it be said that it has not, contrary to what one might expect, anything youthful and lacking in development; it is entirely mature. One must not forget that Capablanca as a man is young, but as a player he is quite aged; from the fourth to the twenty-second year of his life he gave practically all his time to his favourite pursuit, and at this period of life eighteen years count double or treble. . . . Many an expert says that there is a certain affinity between his style and that of the world master, Lasker. There may be some truth in it. Lasker's style is clear water, but with a drop of poison which is clouding it. Capablanca's style is perhaps still clearer, but it lacks that drop of poison."

In 1913 Znosko-Borowski gave a lecture on the Cuban master before the St. Petersburg Chess Club and clearly showed that it was Capablanca's play that gave the Russian author the first idea of his theory of time and space, which he later on developed in his remarkable book, *The Middle Game in Chess.*

Like all world champions, Capablanca excelled in the end game, which he played with a precision seldom equalled and never excelled. In the middle game his extraordinary quick grasp of the position gave him a tactical advantage over most of his opponents, so that he seldom needed to go in for deep strategy.

His openings were correct and ably planned, but here his aversion from the extensive study of " the book " put him rather at a disadvantage, which became more marked after he lost the championship, when a great number of eager young players, all of world championship class, made their presence felt, to name but a few besides Dr. Alekhine: Botvinnik, Keres, Reshevsky, Fine, Euwe, Flohr, all of them possible world champions and versed in the intricacies of modern opening strategy.

Nikolai Grekov, in his personal reminiscences, gives an interesting account of Capablanca's reception in Russia. It goes farther than most published accounts in giving sidelights on the character of the man:

" In 1914, on the eve of the First World War, Jose Raoul Capablanca took part in a big tournament at St. Petersburg. An unlucky defeat by Tarrasch deprived him of the first prize. Capablanca came second to Lasker, but received a special prize for the tournament's most beautiful game.

" After the October Revolution I met Capablanca in Moscow in 1925, 1935 and 1936 during the three big international tournaments. In 1925 he arrived there with the title of World Champion added to his other laurels. In the Moscow tournament of 1925 he lost two games, one to Boris Verlinsky and the other to Alexander Ilyin-Zhenevsky, who was killed by a German bomb near Leningrad in the autumn of 1941. Capablanca started badly in the 1925 contest and as a result was placed third, but nobody can forget his brilliant finish: in the last ten games he scored $8\frac{1}{2}$ points, defeated the winner of the tournament and again got the prize for the most beautiful game.

" As Editor of the Soviet chess magazine, I received an article from Capablanca in which he characterised his attitude towards chess. ' Let us depart from science,' he wrote. ' Chess can never reach its height by following in the path of science. . . . Let us, therefore, make a new effort and with the help of our imagination turn the struggle of technique into a battle of ideas.'

" The last words were particularly characteristic of Capablanca, as his success came from his natural gifts and qualities as a tournament player rather than his knowledge of chess theory.

" What Soviet players admired most in the late ex-Champion was his tremendous self-possession. In 1935, after an interval of almost three years, Capablanca was placed fourth in the international tournament held in Moscow. I recall his dramatic encounter with Emanuel Lasker. Capablanca found himself in a difficult position. His opponent was nervous because he was afraid of victory slipping through his fingers. But still more excited was Lasker's wife. After he made his move, Capablanca would calmly pace the hall and beg Mrs. Lasker not to worry, because in his opinion her husband had the better position.

" Capablanca's last appearance in a Soviet chess competition was an impressive one. In the two-round 1936 tournament he won the first prize without a single loss. Taking into account the fact that a number of outstanding players (Botvinnik, Lasker, Flohr, etc.) took part, the result cannot be called anything but brilliant. Again as in the two previous ones, he received the prize for the most beautiful game.

" The following curious episode took place during the 1936 Moscow tournament. In the interval a thirteen-year-old schoolboy, Pavel Pomoschnikov, approached Capablanca and in fluent French challenged the ex-Champion to a game. Not wanting to distress the boy, Capablanca consented. Having lost three games in succession, Pavel Pomoschnikov demanded a handicap of a queen. Capablanca replied that a queen was too much. The boy then solemnly declared that in ten years he would play against Capablanca as an equal and with better success. The Cuban champion advised the young champion to prepare well for the coming match and presented him with an autographed copy of his book on chess.

" Capablanca's literary works enjoy widespread popularity in the Soviet Union. Six editions of his *Principles of Chess* have been published to date. The book has become almost a handbook for a whole generation of Soviet players, and particularly for Mikhail Botvinnik, the present Champion of the U.S.S.R. It is interesting to note that Capablanca was the first to predict a brilliant future for Botvinnik. When during a simultaneous chess match in Leningrad in 1925 Botvinnik won a game from the master, Capablanca said: ' This boy will go far.' The prophecy came true. Ten years later, in the international tournament in Moscow, Botvinnik shared the first prize with Salo Flohr and outstripped his teacher. In the big 1936 Nottingham tournament Botvinnik shared the first prize with Capablanca. In the 1936 Moscow tournament Botvinnik lost to the former champion of the world, but had his revenge in Amsterdam in 1938. The full score of Botvinnik's tournament games with Capablanca is plus one minus one and five draws.

" Capablanca last visited the Soviet Union in 1936. Whenever he came to Russia, Capablanca not only competed in tournaments, but played numerous simultaneous matches with amateurs. He was always willing to study and analyse his games in public, and showed an ability to gauge the positions with an insight that is possessed only by players of genius.

" In 1925 Capablanca took part in a film produced in Moscow and devoted to the international tournament held there at the time. The film was entitled *Chess Fever* and made a great hit throughout the country.

" While in Soviet Russia, Capablanca showed a lively interest in the Soviet system. He liked to go sightseeing in Moscow and frequently visited sports grounds to play various games, especially tennis, which he liked very much. He was also an enthusiastic theatre-goer and expressed his particular admiration for the Russian ballet.

" Those who had the privilege of knowing Capablanca will always remember him as a charming man and a player of genius."

Capablanca wrote three books, *My Chess Career*, *Chess Fundamentals* and a *Primer of Chess*, all three valuable additions to chess literature which were translated into many languages.

I had the privilege of collaborating with the author in the production of the first two and had the opportunity of getting an unusual insight into the character of this great player. His chief characteristics seemed to me to be simplicity, charm and sincerity. After the publication of his *Chess Career* he was severely criticised, especially by English critics, for what they thought to be his overweening conceit. I can vouch for it that there was no trace of this in his make-up. These critics did not allow or had no understanding for the difference between a Southern temperament and our own, between the views of a towering genius and those of the merely gifted. A Britisher, having achieved something great, would say with characteristic understatement, " It was nothing " or, at best, " Not too bad." Capablanca would not hesitate to say, " I played this ending as well as it could be played," and why should exception be taken to this if indeed it was the case. It is a mere statement of fact, made without any trace of vainglorious boasting.

Another criticism levelled against him was that in his *Chess Career* he gave none of his lost games. Why should Capablanca have been criticised for taking advantage of the accepted privilege of selecting his own best games, which are naturally those which he won — his losses were readily recorded by his adversaries? Alekhine's two volumes of some 250 games, Keres' *Best Games*, to name only two, contain none of their losses.

Capablanca was very sensitive to criticism — too much so — and in his *Chess Fundamentals* he gave *the whole* of his lost games up to that time: eight in all out of some twenty-four games given in the book.

His personality was both genial and magnetic, and when he walked unobtrusively, unheralded, into a room full of people, not necessarily chess players, his presence would never pass unnoticed. He would immediately become the centre of interest.

He made innumerable friends by his kindly and genuine manner. I remember his winning a brilliant game from Dr. Vidmar in London, 1922, and, laughingly patting the loser on the back, saying: " He always give me a chance of a brilliancy; he is my meat " — this accompanied by such a charming and good-natured smile that everyone, including Dr. Vidmar, had the impression that he had bestowed the finest compliment on his opponent. Who else could make such a remark to his adversary and convey the feeling of the utmost friendliness?

There are and have been many great chess players and there have been great figures in chess, among the latter Philidor, Morphy, Steinitz, Lasker, Capablanca and Alekhine. Who shall say who was the greatest?

One thing is certain. Capablanca has written pages of indelible glamour in the history of chess and his games will bring joy and happiness to many as long as chess is played. As Marshall said, " His games will be his everlasting memorial."

Tournaments

	Rank	Won	Lost	Drawn	Total
New York State, 1910	1	7	0	0	7
New York, 1911	2	8	1	3	9½
San Sebastian, 1911	1	6	1	7	9½
New York, 1913	1	10	1	2	11
Havana, 1913	2	8	2	4	10
New York, 1913	1	13	0	0	13
St. Petersburg, 1914	2	10	2	6	13
New York, 1914	1	11	0	0	11
New York, 1915	1	12	0	2	13
New York, 1916	1	12	1	4	14
New York, 1918	1	9	0	3	10½
Hastings, 1919	1	10	0	1	10½
London, 1922	1	11	0	4	13
New York, 1924	2	10	1	9	14½
Moscow, 1925	3	9	2	9	13½
Lake Hopatcong, 1926	1	4	0	4	6
New York, 1927	1	8	0	12	14
Berlin, 1928	1	5	0	7	8½
Bad Kissingen, 1928	2	4	1	6	7
Budapest, 1928	1	5	0	4	7
Ramsgate, 1929	1	4	0	3	5½
Carlsbad, 1929	2–3	10	2	9	14½
Budapest, 1929	1	8	0	5	10½
Barcelona, 1929	1	13	0	1	13½
Hastings, 1930–31	2	5	1	3	6½
New York, 1931	1	9	0	2	10
Hastings, 1934–35	4	4	2	3	5½
Moscow, 1935	4	7	2	10	12
Margate, 1935	2	6	1	2	7
Margate, 1936	2	5	0	4	7
Moscow, 1936	1	8	0	10	13
Nottingham, 1936	1–2	7	1	6	10
Semmering, 1937	3–4	2	1	11	7½
Paris, 1938	1	6	0	4	8
Avro, 1938	7	2	4	8	6
Margate, 1939	2–3	4	0	5	6½
Buenos Aires, 1939	—	6	0	4	
		277	26	177	

Matches

	Won	Lost	Drawn
Corzo, 1900	4	2	6
Marshall, 1909	8	1	14
Kostich, 1919	5	0	0
Dr. Lasker, 1921	4	0	14
Alekhine, 1927	3	6	25
Euwe, 1932	2	0	8
	26	9	67

CHAPTER ONE

Early Years—The Match with Marshall

THE amazing precocity of genius evidenced in the early games of Capablanca has no real parallel in the history of chess. The nearest example that springs to mind, that of Reshevsky, cannot compete with the sureness of touch and maturity of technique that are to be found in, for instance, the ending of the second game given here against Corzo. Still more striking is his astonishing victory over Marshall in 1909, over a player who then ranked high amongst the world's best chess masters, who only a few years previously had won the Cambridge Springs tournament above the most outstanding players in the world and who was reckoned as well in the running for the world's championship.

The games themselves are, as one would expect, somewhat crude and lacking in subtlety in the opening. The middle games, however, are characterised by a fine, rich combinative vein full of fresh ideas, and the end games, as always in Capablanca, are impeccable. His games against Marshall are especially interesting for the marked contrast in personality reflected by the opposing styles employed. The same difference will be constantly observed in Capablanca's contests against the American master throughout his career. Marshall's play full of fire and brilliant ingenuity but occasionally, alas, embarking on a dashing combination without testing it thoroughly for flaws ; Capablanca's calm, clear, farseeing and pervaded by that " organized simplicity " that seemed a natural antidote to the élan of his opponent's style.

23

1
MATCH FOR
CUBAN CHAMPIONSHIP,
HAVANA, 1900

Vienna Gambit

White	Black
J. CORZO	CAPABLANCA
1. P — K 4	P — K 4
2. Kt — Q B 3	Kt — Q B 3
3. P — B 4	P × P
4. Kt — B 3	P — K Kt 4
5. P — K R 4	P — Kt 5
6. Kt — K Kt 5	

The Hampe-Allgdier Gambit which sacrifices a piece for rapid development. It is not sound, but White was relying upon his opponent's complete lack of book knowledge and hoping he would go astray in the complications that arise. In a sense he was right, since Capablanca does diverge from the book of the time — but only to find a better continuation for Black!

6.	P — K R 3
7. Kt × P	K × Kt
8. P — Q 4	P — Q 4

Better than 8. . . . . P — Q 3; 9. B × P B — Kt 2; 10. B — B 4 ch with a strong attack!

9. P × P

If 9. B × P, B — Kt 5 is good for Black.

9.	Q — K 2 ch
10. K — B 2	P — Kt 6 ch
11. K — Kt 1	

The White King is only apparently in safety; Black now returns the piece in order to open up the

diagonal K Kt 1 — Q R 7, after which, owing to the presence of the Black Pawn on Kt 6 White is continually harassed by mating threats.

Position after 11. K — Kt 1

11.	Kt × P !
12. Q × Kt	

White must accept the return of the piece for if 12. B × P, Q — B 3 !

12.	Q — B 4
13. Kt — K 2	Q — Kt 3 !

An original and pleasing touch and much more powerful than the humdrum 13. . . . . Q × Q ch; 14. Kt × Q, B — Q B 4; 15. P — B 3. Now Black's threat of B — Q B 4 forces White to exchange Queens thereby allowing Black to bring the Q R into the game at once.

14. Q × Q	R P × Q
15. Kt — Q 4	B — Q B 4
16. P — B 3	R — R 5

This wins another Pawn because of the threat of R × Kt followed by mate.

17. B — K 2   B × Kt ch
18. P × B   R × Q P
19. P — Kt 3

White has been relying upon this manœuvre to pull the game round in his favour by exploiting the risky position of Black's Q R. It soon becomes apparent that Black has seen further into the position than White.

19. ......   Kt — B 3
20. B — Kt 2   R — Q 7

And not 20. .... R × P; 21. B — B 4.

21. B — R 5 ch

Hoping for 21. .... K — Kt 2; 22. B — Q B 3, R — Q B 7; 23. B — K 5 with distinct counterchances but Black now finishes off the game in the best style.

21. ......   Kt × B !
22. B × R   P — B 6
23. P × P

White must exchange Pawns, for if 23. B — B 3, P — B 7 ch; 24. K — B 1, B — B 4; 25. B × R, B — Q 6 mate.

23. ......   Kt — B 5
24. B — K 5

Mate follows after 24. R — K 1, R — Kt 7 ch; 25. K — B 1, R — B 7 ch; 26. K — Kt 1, B — R 6, etc.

24. ......   R — Kt 7 ch
25. K — B 1   R — B 7 ch
26. K — K 1   Kt — Q 6 ch

Resigns. This, and the following game, are indeed astounding in a twelve-year-old player.

2
MATCH FOR CUBAN CHAMPIONSHIP, HAVANA, 1900

Queen's Pawn

White   Black
Capablanca   J. Corzo

1. P — Q 4

When having White against Corzo, Capablanca invariably played P — Q 4, since at that time it was comparatively uncharted ground and the young player's complete lack of book knowledge would not matter so much. Curiously enough, the opening follows the game Bogoljuboff–Capablanca, New York, 1924 (or perhaps it should be put the other way round), for quite a way, and if the reader would like to compare Capablanca's masterly handling of the defence with the antipositional methods adopted by Corzo he should consult Game No. 32.

1. ......   P — Q 4
2. Kt — K B 3   P — Q B 4
3. P — K 3   Kt — Q B 3
4. P — Q Kt 3

Played with the elementary logic of youth; since the Q Bishop is shut in by P — K 3, it must be developed in some other way — hence the text.

4. ......   P — K 3
5. B — Kt 2   Kt — B 3
6. Q Kt — Q 2   P × P ?

Inferior objectively to both 6. .... B — Q 3 and B — K 2, the

text is also bad from a psychological point of view, since it simpli-
fies the opening problem for his
inexperienced opponent.

7. P × P	B — Q 3
8. B — Q 3	Castles
9. Castles	Kt — K R 4

The commencement of a time-
wasting manœuvre which profits
White only. Correct was 9. ....
P — Q Kt 3, followed by B —
Kt 2. As played, Black's Q Bish-
op is left with little future.

10. P — Kt 3	P — B 4
11. Kt — K 5	Kt — B 3
12. P — K B 4	B × Kt
13. B P × B	Kt — K Kt 5

Black hopes to extract more
than a draw out of the position,
otherwise he would have striven
for equality by Kt — K 5. Need-
less to say, the text is much inferior and Black loses a deal of time
in order to find the Kt a peaceful
haven.

| 14. Q — K 2 | Q — Kt 3 |
| 15. Kt — B 3 | B — Q 2 |

Black is still obsessed with the
idea of avoiding a draw. He is
rudely disillusioned by the later
middle-game play. His best move
now was to play for Bishops of
opposite colours by 15. ....Kt
— Kt 5.

16. P — Q R 3

Now White has prevented this
and contemplates an eventual advance of his Q B and Q Kt Pawns.

| 16. ...... | K — R 1 |

Black reorganizes his pieces in
order to obtain some counterplay
on the K side.

17. P — R 3	Kt — R 3
18. Q — B 2	Kt — B 2
19. K — Kt 2	P — Kt 4

He does not wish to remain passive whilst White advances on the
Q side with P — Q B 4, P — Q
Kt 4, P — B 5, P — Kt 5, etc. But
now a weakness has been created
on the long diagonal of which
White takes subtle advantage.

20. P — K Kt 4 !

Throwing a clear light on the
weakness of Black's last move. If
now 20. ....P × P; 21. P × P,
followed by 22. R — R 1, with a
string K side attack, and if 20.
....P — B 5 in an attempt to
block the position, then White can
eventually break it open by P —
K R 4.

20.	Kt — K 2
21. Q — K 3	R — K Kt 1
22. Q R — K 1	

All this is in excellent positional style, worthy of a mature master.

22.	Kt — Kt 3
23. P × P	Kt — B 5 ch
24. K — R 2	Kt × B

If 24. .... P × P ; 25. Kt × P !

| 25. Q × Kt | P × P |
| 26. P — B 4 ! | |

Very strong; White now completely breaks open the position.

| 26. ...... | Q — K 3 |

The alternative was 26. ....
Q — K R 3; 27. P × P, P — Kt
5; 28. Kt — Kt 1, Kt — Kt 4; 29.
P — K 6, Kt — B 6 ch; 30. R ×
Kt! and White wins.

27. P × P   Q × P
28. P — K 6!

This fine winning combination
foreshadows the grand master.

28. ......   B — Kt 4
For if 28. ....B × P; 29.
R × B.

Position after 28. ....B — Kt 4

29. Q × B

A very pretty sacrifice which
Capablanca had in mind when
playing P — K 6. It is true that
29. Q — Q 2 also wins in somewhat simple and quicker fashion
but this hardly detracts from the
merits of the combination.

29. ......   Q × Q
30. P — Q 5 dis. ch R — Kt 2
31. P × Kt   P — K R 3
31. ....R — K B 1 would have
put up a better resistance though

White should still win by 32. Kt
— Q 4, Q × Q P; 33. R — K 8,
Q × B P; 34. R × R ch, Q × R;
35. Kt × P according to Capablanca.

32. Kt — Q 4   Q × R

There is nothing better; if
32. ....Q — Q 2 Capablanca
gives 33. Kt × P, Q × B P; 34.
B × R ch, K — R 2; 35. R — K 7
winning the Queen since 35. ....
Q × P leads to mate after 36.
B — K 5 dis. ch, K — Kt 3; 37.
R — Kt 7 ch, K — R 4; 38. Kt —
Kt 3 ch, K — R 5; 39. R — B 4
ch, P × R; 40. R — Kt 4.

33. R × Q   R × P
34. R × P   R × R
35. Kt × R dis. ch K — R 2

The rest is a matter of technique, but one demanding considerable precision, and Capablanca
takes it all in his stride, as though
already world champion.

36. Kt — K 7 !

Neatly cutting the King off
from the centre.

36. ......   R — K B 1
37. K — Kt 2   P — K R 4
38. P — Q 6   P — Kt 5
39. P × P   P × P
40. B — K 5   K — R 3
41. P — Q 7   R — Q 1
42. Kt — Kt 8 ch R × Kt

Or 42. ....K — Kt 3; 43. Kt
— B 6, K — B 2; 44. B — B 7.

43. B — B 6   K — Kt 3

Black plays on in the hope of a
draw by stalemate and might have

achieved it against a less wary opponent.

44.	P — Q 8 = Q	R × Q
45.	B × R	P — Kt 4
46.	K — B 2	K — B 4
47.	K — K 3	K — K 4
48.	K — Q 3	K — Q 4
49.	K — B 3	P — Kt 6
50.	B — R 4	P — Kt 7
51.	B — B 2	P — R 4
52.	P — Kt 4	K — K 5
53.	B — Kt 6	

And not 53. P × P, which would give a draw, since the queening square is the opposite colour to the Bishop.

53.	. . . . . .	K — Q 4
54.	K — Q 3	K — B 3
55.	B — Kt 1	K — Q 4
56.	B — R 2	K — B 3
57.	K — Q 4	P — R 5
58.	K — K 5	K — Kt 3
59.	K — Q 5	K — R 3
60.	K — B 5 !	

And since White has not fallen into the trap with 60. K — B 6, P — Kt 8 = Q; 61. B × Q stalemate Black resigns.

3

NEW YORK, 1906

Ruy Lopez, Steinitz Defence

White	Black
A. W. Fox	CAPABLANCA
1. P — K 4	P — K 4
2. Kt — K B 3	Kt — Q B 3
3. B — Kt 5	Kt — B 3
4. Castles	B — K 2
5. R — K 1	P — Q 3

By transposition via the Berlin Defence we have now arrived at the Steinitz Defence which demands great patience on Black's part and has the merit of solidity. In addition, there is always the likelihood that White will overreach himself — as he does in the present game.

6. P — Q 4	P × P
7. Kt × P	B — Q 2
8. Kt — Q B 3	Castles
9. Kt (Q 4) — K 2	

Since Black has a somewhat constricted position White does well to avoid exchanges. If, for example, 9. B × Kt, P × B; 10. B — Kt 5, P — K R 3; 11. B — R 4, R — K 1; 12. Q — Q 3, Kt — R 2; 13. B × B, R × B; 14. R — K 3, Q — Kt 1 with equality (Capablanca–Lasker match, 1921).

But a better way of maintaining the initiative is 9. B — B 1 followed by P — Q Kt 3 and B — Kt 2. After the text the exchange of White's valuable K Bishop is inevitable.

| 9. | . . . . . . | R — K 1 |
| 10. | Kt — Kt 3 | Kt — K 4 |

It is not perhaps too fanciful to discern in this freeing manœuvre the germ of Capablanca's later famous method of freedom by exchange in the Orthodox Defence to the Queen's Gambit; the principle is very similar.

| 11. | B × B | Q × B |
| 12. | P — B 4 | |

This move does not suit the nature of the position. It would have

been quite in order if White's
Rooks were placed on K 1 and
K B 1 but as it is it merely loos-
ens White's control of the centre.
Best is still 12. P — Q Kt 3 fol-
lowed by B — Kt 2 and Kt — Q 5.

12. ......   Kt — Kt 3
13. Kt — B 5   B — B 1
Threatening Kt × K P.
14. Q — Q 3   Q R — Q 1
But now 14. ....Kt × K P;
15. R × Kt, Q × Kt; 16. R × R,
Q × Q; 17. R × B ch would lose
a piece.

15. B — Q 2
A miserable square for the
Bishop, but there is now no time
for 15. P — Q Kt 3 when P —
Q 4 would be even more effective
than in the actual game. He might,
however, have prevented the ensuing combination by 15. P —
K R 3.

15. ......   P — Q 4 !
White's opening strategy is
condemned by this strong move
which at once shows up the weakness on the K B file and the hanging nature of White's Kt on B 5.

16. P — K 5
Forced, since 16. P × P, R ×
R ch; 17. R × R, Kt × P will lose
at least a Pawn as would also 16.
Kt — Kt 3, P × P, etc.

16. ......   B — B 4 ch
17. K — R 1
And not 17. B — K 3, Kt
× B P.

17. ......   Kt — Kt 5
18. Kt — Q 1   P — K B 3 !
Black is playing with great energy; now White's Pawns disappear from the centre with alarming rapidity.

Position after 18. ....P — K B 3 !

19. P — K R 3
If, instead, 19. P × P Capa-
blanca would have won by 19.
....Kt × Q (B 5); 20. Kt —
K 7 ch (or 20. R × R ch, R ×
R; 21. Q — Q B 3, Q × Kt; 22.
Q × B, Kt — K 7); 20. ....
R × Kt; 21. P × R, Kt × Q;
22. P × R = Q ch, Q × Q; 23.
P × Kt, Q — R 5; 24. P —
K R 3, Q — Kt 6, a fine combina-
tion.

19. ......   Kt — B 7 ch
20. Kt × Kt   B × Kt
21. R — K 2   P × P !
A merely temporary sacrifice of
the piece in order to gain control
of the centre.

22. R × B   P — K 5
23. Kt — R 6 ch   P × Kt
24. Q — Q 4   Q — Kt 2
25. Q × R P ?

White's game is clearly lost, but this accelerates the end. He should have played 25. B — B 3, Q × Q; 26. B × Q, P — Q Kt 3; 27. P — B 5, Kt — K 4; 28. P — Q Kt 4, Kt — B 5, when the game would last considerably longer.

25. ......   Q × P
26. R — K 1   P — Q 5 !

Cutting off the Queen from the centre and winning more material.

27. P — B 5   P — K 6
28. R (B 2) — K 2 Kt — B 5
29. B — B 1   Q — Kt 3
30. Q — R 4

Not liking to resign when there are prospects of obtaining a check.

30. ......   Kt × R
31. Q — B 4 ch   K — R 1
32. R × Kt   Q — R 3
33. Q — Q 3   Q × Q
34. P × Q   P — B 4
35. P — Kt 4   P — B 5
      Resigns.

4
SIXTH MATCH GAME, NEW YORK, 1909

Ruy Lopez, Steinitz Defence

White	Black
CAPABLANCA	F. J. MARSHALL

1. P — K 4   P — K 4
2. Kt — K B 3   Kt — Q B 3
3. B — Kt 5   P — Q 3
4. P — Q B 3

This restrained move is not so strong as the normal 4. P — Q 4, but at this early stage in his development Capablanca knew practically nothing about the openings. Nevertheless, as soon as the preliminaries of the opening are passed, he intuitively adopts a system of K side attack strongly reminiscent of some of the games of Steinitz.

4. ......   B — Kt 5

This pin is a waste of time, as it will only facilitate White's K side attack by encouraging him to play P — K R 3 and P — K Kt 4.

Not good, however, is the alternative recommended by Capablanca and others, 4. ....P — B 4, since White can treat it on similar lines to the so-called Siesta Defence (but with still greater effect) and play 5. P × P, B × P (not 5. ....P — K 5; 6. Kt — Q 4 and wins); 6. P — Q 4, P — K 5; 7. Kt — Kt 5, B — K 2; 8. Castles, B × Kt; 9. Q — R 5 ch, B — Kt 3; 10. Q × B, Q × Q; 11. B × Q, with much the superior development.

But an excellent, solid defence is to be obtained by the King's fianchetto as in the game Lasker-Speyer, 1909, 4. ....P — K Kt 3; 5. Castles, B — Kt 2; 6. P — Q 4, B — Q 2; 7. B — Kt 5, P — B 3; 8. B — K R 4, Q — K 2; 9. Kt — R 3, Kt — R 3; 10. Kt — B 2, Kt — Q 1; 11. B — B 4, K Kt — B 2; 12. Kt — Q 2, Kt — K 3.

5. P — Q 3

The Steinitz method of making the centre safe before embarking on a K wing attack; better and more aggressive, however, is 5. P — Q 4.

5. ......   B — K 2

Here again Black would have been well advised to fianchetto his K Bishop, thereby counteracting the type of attack contemplated by White.

6. Q Kt — Q 2   Kt — B 3
7. Castles   Castles
8. R — K 1   P — K R 3

With the idea of freeing his K side by Kt — R 2 and Kt — Kt 4. It loses too much time and allows White to develop his K side attack with alarming speed. A better plan was 8. ....P — Q R 3; 9. B — R 4, P — Q Kt 4; 10. B — B 2, P — Q 4 with counter-chances on the Q file.

9. Kt — B 1   Kt — R 2
10. Kt — K 3

A condemnation of Black's 4th move.

10. ......   B — R 4

It would have been better to retreat with the Bishop to Q 2; bad would have been 10. ....B — K 3; 11. P — Q 4 threatening P — Q 5, and if 10. ....P — B 4 Capablanca gives 11. P × P, B × P; 12. Kt × B, R × Kt; 13. P — Q 4 with a winning

game; e.g. 13. ....P × P; 14. B × Kt, P × B; 15. Kt × P or 13. ....B — B 3; 14. B — Q 3.

11. P — K Kt 4!   B — Kt 3
12. Kt — B 5

Achieving his strategic aim. This strong outpost can only be captured by Black at the cost of opening up the K Kt file with attack on his weakened K position.

12. ......   P — K R 4 ?

Black's position was bad, but this weakens the K side still further. The best defence was 12. ....Kt — Kt 4; 13. K — Kt 2, Kt × Kt; 14. Q × Kt, B — Kt 4 with some emancipation by exchange.

13. P — K R 3   P × P ?

Preferable was 13. ....B — B 3. The move played merely opens up the K R file for White's attack. It is true White could have eventually forced this exchange by moving the K Kt but why hasten to provoke this possibility?

14. P × P   B — Kt 4
15. Kt × B   Kt × Kt
16. K — Kt 2

White now prepares to occupy the K R file with his major pieces — the penalty Black has to pay for his ill-advised 12th and 13th moves.

16. ......   P — Q 4
17. Q — K 2   R — K 1
18. R — R 1   R — K 3

Position after 18. .... R — K 3

19. Q — K 3 !

A masterly move; by forcing
19. .... P — B 3 White not only
cuts off the Black Queen from the
K side but also induces a weakness
on the Q R 2 — K Kt 8 diagonal.

White rightly disdains the win
of the exchange by 19. Q B × Kt,
Q × B; 20. P × P, B × Kt; 21.
P × R, B × K P, since then the
attack would pass to Black.

19. ......   P — B 3

If 19. .... Kt — R 2; 20. Q —
R 3 with the threat of Kt --- R 4.

20. B — R 4 !

The Bishop is to be brought to
bear on Black's weakened diagonal.

20.	Kt — K 2
21. B — Kt 3	P — B 3
22. Q — Kt 3	P — R 4
23. P — R 4	Kt — B 2
24. B — K 3	P — Kt 3

To prevent 25. B — B 5.

| 25. R — R 4 | K — B 1 |

White was threatening to triple
on the K R file followed by
Kt × Kt ch and R — R 8 ch winning a piece.

| 26. Q R — R 1 | Kt — Kt 1 |
| 27. Q — B 3 ! | B × Kt |

There is no other way to defend the Q Pawn, but now fresh
lines of attack are opened up.

28. Kt P × B	
29. Q --- R 5	R — Q 3
30. Q — Kt 6	R — R 2
	Kt (B 2) — R 3

Position after 30. .... Kt (B 2) — R 3

White must not be allowed to
play 31. R — R 7 and if 30. ....
Kt — K 2; 31. R — R 8 ch, Kt ×
R; 32. R × Kt ch, Kt — Kt 1; 33.
Q — R 7, K — B 2; 34. B × P.

| 31. R × Kt ! | P × R |

Or 31. .... Kt × R; 32. B ×
Kt, P × B; 33. R × P, etc.

32. B × P ch	K — K 2
33. Q — Kt 7 ch	K — K 1
34. Q × Kt ch	K — Q 2
35. Q — R 7 ch	Q — K 2

36. B — B 8 !   Q × Q
37. R × Q ch   K — K 1
38. R × R   Resigns

5
EIGHTH MATCH GAME, NEW YORK, 1909

Ruy Lopez, Steinitz Defence

White	Black
CAPABLANCA	F. J. MARSHALL

1. P — K 4   P — K 4
2. Kt — K B 3   Kt — Q B 3
3. B — Kt 5   P — Q 3
4. Castles

As mentioned in the notes to the previous game, P — Q 4 is the strongest move here.

4. ....   P — Q R 3

But Black's reply represents the sheer loss of a move, a very important factor at this early stage. Either 4. ....B — Q 2 or 4. ....Kt — B 3 would be far preferable.

5. B × Kt ch   P × B
6. P — Q 4   P × P

Owing to the loss of a move Black is compelled to make this exchange and thereby lose ground in the centre. If instead 6. ....Kt — B 3 then 7. P × P, Kt × P; 8. P × P, P × P; 9. R — K 1, P — Q 4; 10. K Kt — Q 2 and White will win a Pawn.

7. Kt × P   B — Q 2
8. R — K 1   P — Q B 4

Something immediate must be done as White was threatening 9. P — K 5 and if 9. ....P — Q 4; 10. P — K 6 !

9. Kt — K B 3

White is playing on positional lines and retires the Kt in order to keep the threat of P — K 5 dangling over White's head. But still better was the combinational 9. Kt — B 5 ! and now if 9. ....Kt — K 2; 10. Kt — Q B 3 (not 10. Q × P, Kt × Kt, etc.); 10. ....P — Kt 3; 11. Kt — Q 5 ! and Black can resign. The same theme is evident in this variation after an immediate 9. ....P — Kt 3; 10. Kt — B 3 ! P × Kt; 11. P × P dis. ch. B — K 2; 12. Kt — Q 5, B × P; 13. R × B ch, K — B 1; 14. Q — R 5, B — Kt 3 (or 14. .... Kt × R; 15. B — R 6 ch followed by Kt — B 6 mate); 15. B — R 6 ch, Kt × B; 16. Q × Kt ch, K — Kt 1; 17. Kt — B 6 mate.

If, after 9. ....P — Kt 3; 10. Kt — B 3, Black plays 10. ....B — B 3 then 11. Kt — Q 4, P × Kt (if 11. ....B — Q 2; 12. P — K 5 !); 12. Q × P, Q — B 3 (or 12. ....Kt — B 3; 13. P — K 5, P × P; 14. Q × P ch, Q — K 2; 15. B — Kt 5 !); 13. P — K 5, P × P; 14. R × P ch, B — K 2; 15. B — Kt 5, Q — Q 3 (or 15. ....R — Q 1; 16. R × B ch !); 16. R × B ch, Kt × R; 17. Q × R ch, K — Q 2; 18. Q × P and wins.

Position after 9. Kt — K B 3

9. ......   B — K 2

The attempt at a delayed fian-
chetto by 9. ....Kt — K 2; 10.
Kt — B 3, P — Kt 3; 11. P —
K 5 would lead to a lost game for
Black.

10. Kt — B 3   P — Q B 3

If 10. ....Kt — B 3; 11. P —
K 5, P × P; 12. Kt × P, Castles;
13. B — Kt 5, B — K 1; 14. Q —
B 3, R — Kt 1; 15. Q R — Q 1,
Q — B 1; 16. Kt — Kt 4! and
wins.

11. B — B 4   B — K 3
12. Q — Q 3   Kt — B 3
13. Q R — Q 1   P — Q 4

Black has succeeded in eliminating his backward Pawn, but his
Q side Pawns still prove to be
weak and in need of protection.
White's next strong move forces
an additional weakness on the K
side.

14. Kt — K Kt 5! P — Q 5

This advance is forced; for
14. ....Castles; 15. P — K 5

wins a piece, and if 14. ....P ×
P; 15. Q — K 2, Q — Kt 3; 16.
Kt × B, P × Kt; 17. Kt × P,
Q × P; 18. Kt — Q 6 ch, B ×
Kt; 19. Q × P ch, etc.

15. Kt × B   B P × Kt
16. Kt — R 4   Q — R 4

Black cannot proceed with his
development by 16. ....Castles
because of 17. Q — B 4 winning
a Pawn. He therefore has to divert his Queen to the Q wing to
protect his Pawns, thereby leaving his centre and K side without
adequate means of fending off
White's attack.

17. P — Q Kt 3   R — Q 1

Hoping for 18. Q — B 4, K —
B 2 followed by 19. ....Q —
Kt 4.

18. Kt — Kt 2!   Kt — R 4

And not 18. ....Q × P; 19. Kt
— B 4 trapping the Queen.

19. B — K 5   Castles
20. Kt — B 4   Q — Kt 5
21. Q — R 3   P — Kt 3

Black must resign himself to
the loss of a Pawn; the text creates a fresh weakness, but Black
is preparing a desperate counter-
attack which would have succeeded against anything but the
most accurate handling on White's
part.

22. Q × P ch   R — B 2
23. P — Kt 4   B — R 5

Or 23. ....Kt — Kt 2; 24.
B × Kt, K × B; 25. Kt — K 5.

24. P × Kt   B × P ch
25. K — R 1   Q — B 6

If 25. ....B × R; 26. P × P,
P × P; 27. Q × P ch, K — B 1;
28. Kt—Q 6, R (B 2) — Q 2;
29. Q — B 6 ch, K — Kt 1; 30.
Q — R 8 mate. Now, however,
Black seems to have acquired a
most menacing position with an
immediate mating threat.

Position after 25. ....Q — B 6

26. R — K 3 !

A beautiful and complete answer to all Black's threats.

26. ......   Q × B P
26. ....B × R; 27. P × P,
P × P; 28. Q × P ch leads into
a similar variation to that noted
after Black's 25th move.

27. K R — Q 3   Q — K 7
28. Kt — Q 6   R × Kt
29. B × R   B — K 8

Dangerous to the last — the
threat of mate, however, can be
parried by a winning series of
checks.

30. Q — K 8 ch   K — Kt 2
31. P — R 6 ch   Resigns

6
TWENTY–THIRD AND LAST MATCH GAME, NEW YORK, 1909

Queen's Gambit Declined, Tarrasch Defence

White	Black
F. J. MARSHALL	CAPABLANCA

1. P — Q 4   P — Q 4
2. P — Q B 4   P — K 3
3. Kt — Q B 3 P — Q B 4

The Tarrasch Defence, with
which Black takes on the onus of
an isolated Pawn in order to obtain free play for the minor pieces.
At the time this game was played
it enjoyed a great reputation, Tarrasch himself claiming that it was
the only correct defence to the
Queen's and going so far as to give
Black's third move an exclama-
tion mark of approval in his book
Die Moderne Schachpartie.

Capablanca explains that he
had been shown a game between
Rubinstein and Mieses in which
the latter had employed the Tarrasch Defence and, impressed by
Mieses' play, he decided to use it
against Marshall.

Nowadays, however, this defence is considered inferior to the
other main normal defence lines.

4. B P × P   K P × P
5. Kt — B 3   Kt — Q B 3
6. P — K Kt 3

This is the manœuvre which has brought the Tarrasch Defence into such disfavour — the Bishop is placed so as to put the utmost pressure on Black's isolated Pawn.

6. ......   B — K 3

Mieses' move; it is not a particularly good one, as the Bishop plays a purely defensive role on K 3. Better is the usual 6. .... Kt — B 3; 7. B — Kt 2, B — K 2.

7. B — Kt 2   B — K 2
8. Castles   Kt — B 3
9. B — Kt 5

With this White only helps Black's game. Correct is 9. P × P, B × P and now either 10. Kt — K Kt 5 as recommended by Bogoljuboff, or, better still, to proceed along lines similar to those advocated by Réti and play 10. Kt — Q R 4, B — K 2; 11. B — K 3, Castles; 12. Kt — Q 4 and White has much the better game.

9. ......   Kt — K 5 !

This immediate freeing manœuvre gives Black an excellent game.

10. B × B

If 10. B — K 3, P — B 5; 11. Kt — Q 2, P — B 4 to Black's advantage.

10. ......   Q × B
11. Kt — K 5

And not 11. P × P, Kt × Kt breaking up White's Q side. Here Rubinstein continued against Mieses in the game mentioned above 11. R — B 1, Kt × Kt; 12. R ×

Kt, P — B 5; 13. Kt — K 5, Castles K and now instead of 14. P — Kt 3, Q — Kt 5 he should have played 14. P — B 4 threatening both P — B 5 and P — K 4.

Marshall's move is ingenious and good enough for equality.

11. ......   Kt × Q P

Best; the endeavour to split up White's Pawns by 11. .... K Kt × Kt; 12. P × Kt, Kt × Kt : 13. P × Kt gives Black an extremely bad game after 13. .... Castles K (if 13. .... Q — Q 2; 14. P — K B 4, P — K Kt 3; 15. P — K 4!); 14. B × P, Q R — Q 1; 15. P — K 4, B — R 6 (or 15. .... B × B; 16. P × B, Q × P: 17. P — Q B 4, P — Q Kt 4; 18. R — K 1!); 16. R — K 1, Q × P; 17. Q — Kt 3, P — Q Kt 3; 18. P — K B 4, Q — K 2; 19. P — Q R 4 followed by P — Q R 5 with command of all the open lines.

12. Kt × Kt   P × Kt
13. P — K 3

White loses a piece after 13. B × P, B — R 6.

13. ......   Kt — B 6 ch
14. Kt × Kt ?

Marshall captures the wrong way. He should have simplified the game by 14. B × Kt, P × B; 15. Q — R 4 ch, B — Q 2; 16. Kt — B, Q × Kt; 17. Q — K 4 ch, Q — K 2; 18. Q × K P and Black could hardly escape the draw.

It is true that Capablanca states that at the time it was his inten-

tion to avoid simplification by 15.
.... K — B 1, but this would lead
to rather the better game for
White after 16. K R — Q 1, P —
B 3; 17. Kt × P, K — B 2; 18.
Q — K B 4 and now if 18. ....
K R — Q 1; 19. Kt — Kt 5 ch, K
— Kt 1; 20. Kt × B, Q × Kt; 21.
Q — B 7 ch, etc.

Position after 14. Kt × Kt ?

14. ......   P × Kt
15. Q × P   Castles K !

Played with a nonchalant dis-
regard for White's threatened Q
× Kt P. Black now has the advantage of the Q side pawn majority and he utilizes this with the
utmost finesse.

16. K R — B 1 ?

Marshall, discouraged by his
poor showing in the match hitherto, plays in a purely negative
way in a vain attempt to stem
Black's Q side advance.

It is true that after 16. Q × P,
Q × Q; 17. B × Q, Q R — Kt 1
followed by 18. .... R × P White

has a lost endgame, but he should
have tried to obtain a compensating counterattack by 16. P — K 4
followed by Q — K 3, P — B 4
and P — B 5.

From now on Black's positional
advantage increases with every
move.

16. ......   Q R — Kt 1
17. Q — K 4

Threatening 18. B — R 3, but
here again P — K 4 with an advance on the K side was the indicated line.

17. ......   Q — B 2
18. R — B 3   P — Q Kt 4
19. P — Q R 3   P — B 5
20. B — B 3

If 20. P — Kt 3, Q — R 4
forces White to play 21. P —
Q Kt 4 leaving Black with the extremely powerful passed Pawn on
B 5. A better resistance, however,
would have come from the reor-
ganization of his Rook position,
e.g. 20. R — Q 1, K R — Q 1; 21.
R (B 3) — B 1.

20. ......   K R — Q 1
21. R — Q 1   R × R ch
22. B × R   R — Q 1

As a result of the last few
moves, Black has attained command of the only open file and this,
in conjunction with his Q side
pawn majority, is sufficient to ensure the win.

23. B — B 3   P — Kt 3

A simple but very powerful
move. It immediately threatens

the win of a piece by 24. .... B —
Q 4 ; 25. Q — Kt 4, P — K R 4 ; it
also frees the Rook from the back
rank by giving the King an outlet
and holds out the possibility of
B — B 4 followed by R — Q 7.

24. Q — B 6   Q — K 4 !

So as not to waste a tempo in
defending the Kt Pawn after 24.
.... Q × Q ; 25. B × Q.

25. Q — K 4

Otherwise Black plays R —
Q 7 with devastating effect.

25. ......   Q × Q
26. B × Q   R — Q 8 ch

Played to prevent the White
King from reaching the centre by
K — B 1 and K — K 2.

27. K — Kt 2   P — Q R 4

Now White is powerless against
the advance of the Queen side
Pawns ; Black will very soon force
a winning passed Pawn.

28. R — B 2   P — Kt 5
29. P × P   P × P
30. B — B 3   R — Kt 8
31. B — K 2   P — Kt 6
32. R — Q 2

If 32. R — B 3, R × P ; 33. B
× P, R — B 7 winning a piece.

32. ......   R — Q B 8

With the terrible threat of R —
B 7 ; in order to prevent this
White must lose a piece.

Position after 32. .... R — Q B 8

33. B — Q 1   P — B 6
34. P × P   P — Kt 7
35. R × P

And not 35. B — B 2, R × B !

35. ......   R × B
36. R — B 2

Resignation was in order here.

36. ......   B — B 4
37. R — Kt 2   R — Q B 8
38. R — Kt 3   B — K 5 ch
39. K — R 3   R — B 7
40. P — K B 4   P — R 4

Threatening mate by B —
B 4 ch, R × P ch, K — Kt 2 and
P — B 3.

41. P — Kt 4   P × P ch
42. K × P   R × R P
43. R — Kt 4   P — B 4 ch
44. K — Kt 3

44. K — Kt 5 moves into a mating net after 44. .... K — Kt 2.

44. ......   R — K 7
45. R — B 4   R × P ch
46. K — R 4   K — Kt 2
47. R — B 7 ch   K — B 3

48. R — Q 7   B — Kt 7
49. R — Q 6 ch   K — Kt 2
Resigns.

7
NEW YORK, 1910

Queen's Gambit Declined,
Slav Defence

White	Black
CAPABLANCA	C. JAFFE
1. P — Q 4	P — Q 4
2. Kt — K B 3	Kt — K B 3
3. P — K 3	P — B 3
4. P — B 4	P — K 3
5. Kt — B 3	Q Kt — Q 2
6. B — Q 3	B — Q 3
7. Castles	Castles
8. P — K 4	P × K P
9. Kt × P	Kt × Kt
10. B × Kt	Kt — B 3

The position is now exactly the
same as Game No. 25 against
Scott at Hastings, 1919. As noted
there, 10. . . . . P — B 4 is best.

11. B — B 2   P — K R 3

Otherwise White can play B —
Kt 5 followed by Q — Q 3.

12. P — Q Kt 3   P — Q Kt 3
13. B — Kt 2   B — Kt 2

Scott adopted the formation
Q — K 2 and K R — Q 1, but obtained a lifeless game.

14. Q — Q 3   P — Kt 3

Black is afraid of P — Q 5 followed by B × Kt with a mating
attack, but the text creates a fatal
weakness of which White takes
prompt advantage. His game is,
however, so inferior that it is dif-

ficult to suggest a plausible con-
tinuation. 14. . . . .Q — B 2 loses
after 15. P — B 5 and 16. P —
Q 5. Perhaps the best is 14. . . . .
R — K 1; 15. Q R — K 1, B —
K 2, though White has no difficulty
in maintaining the attack by 16.
Kt — K 5.

15. Q R — K 1   Kt —↗ R 4 ?

Hoping to play Kt — Kt 2 so
as to fend off any eventual R × P,
but he is not allowed time for this
and the text merely precipitates
disaster. Best, since there must be
bests even in such miserable positions, is 15. . . . .Q — K 2 with
some sort of playable defence.

16. B — B 1   K — Kt 2

The other way of protecting the
R Pawn by 16. . . . .B — B 5 also
fails against 17. R × P. Now, in
the brief space of four moves
White demolishes Black's entire
K side Pawn structure.

Position after 16. . . . .K — Kt 2

17. R × P !   Kt — B 3

If 17. . . . .P × R White mates
in two moves.

18. Kt — K 5 !

There is a nice carefree touch about this move, leaving the Rook permanently *en prise*.

18. ......   P — B 4

Black's belated discovery that he has not completed his Q side development only makes matters worse. His only way to prolong the game is 18. ....B × Kt, though after 19. R × B White's win is merely a matter of technique.

Black cannot take the Rook because of 19. Q × P ch, K — R 1: 20. Q × P ch, K — Kt 1; 21. Q — Kt 6 ch, K — R 1; 22. R — K 1. Q — K 1; 23. Q — R 6 ch, K — Kt 1; 24. R — K 3 followed by mate.

19. B × P ch !   K × B
20. Kt × P ch ! Resigns

A beautiful example of how to take advantage of the weakness that results from injudicious Pawn moves in front of the Castled King.

CHAPTER TWO

Rapid Development—The Visit to Europe

THE tournament at San Sebastian in 1911 shows Capablanca employing the grand style, commencing straight away with the famous game against Bernstein in the first round which is full of beautiful and complicated combinations. The little-known game that follows, against Burn, is an excellent variation on a Steinitzian theme against a particularly dour opponent.

His next visit to Europe, in 1913, was also productive of many fine games. This period contains the first example of his Q Kt — Q 2 manœuvre against P — Q B 3 in the Queen's with which he convincingly defeated Alekhine at St. Petersburg, 1913. His partiality for this move runs throughout his career and is to be observed as late as Carlsbad, 1929 (see Game No. 63 against Treybal). Here too Bernstein again provided the foil for some of Capablanca's finest achievements, notably in the magnificent Game No. 16, which contains an entrancing series of great combinations. Admirable too is his Morphy-like win with the black pieces against Alekhine in St. Petersburg, 1914, and his succinct punishment of eccentricity against Blackburne at the same tournament. The methodical way in which this is accomplished is especially deserving of note; first an attack is repelled, next mastery over the centre is achieved, and, finally, Black's K side is demolished.

The results of the four tournaments are given overleaf.

SAN SEBASTIAN, 1911

	Capablanca	Rubinstein	Vidmar	Marshall	Nimzovitch	Schlechter	Tarrasch	Bernstein	Spielmann	Teichmann	Janowski	Maroczy	Burn	Duras	Leonhardt	
1 Capablanca	–	0	½	½	1	½	½	1	1	½	1	½	1	½	1	9½
2 Rubinstein	1	–	½	½	½	½	½	½	½	½	1	½	½	1	1	9
3 Vidmar	½	½	–	0	½	½	½	1	½	½	1	½	1	1	1	9
4 Marshall	½	½	1	–	½	½	½	½	½	1	1	½	½	0	1	8½
5 Nimzovitch	0	½	½	½	–	½	0	½	1	1	½	½	½	½	1	7½
6 Schlechter	½	½	½	½	½	–	½	0	½	½	1	½	½	1	½	7½
7 Tarrasch	½	½	½	½	1	½	–	1	½	0	½	½	1	0	½	7½
8 Bernstein	0	½	0	½	½	1	0	–	1	1	½	1	0	1	0	7
9 Spielmann	0	½	½	½	0	½	½	0	–	½	½	1	½	1	1	7
10 Teichmann	½	½	½	0	0	½	1	0	½	–	0	½	½	1	1	6½
11 Janowski	0	0	0	0	½	0	½	½	½	1	–	0	1	1	1	6
12 Maroczy	½	½	½	½	½	½	½	0	0	½	1	–	½	½	0	6
13 Burn	0	½	0	½	½	½	0	1	½	½	0	½	–	0	½	5
14 Duras	½	0	0	1	½	0	1	0	0	0	0	½	1	–	½	5
15 Leonhardt	0	0	0	0	0	½	½	1	0	0	0	1	½	½	–	4
	4½	5	5	5½	6½	6½	6½	7	7	7½	8	8	9	9	10	

NEW YORK, 1913

	Capablanca	Marshall	Jaffe	Janowski	Chajes	Stapfer	Kupchik	Tenenwurzel	Whitaker	Kline	Rubinstein	Morrison	Liebenstein	Zapoléon	
1 Capablanca	–	½	0	1	½	1	1	1	1	1	1	1	1	1	11
2 Marshall	½	–	½	½	1	½	1	1	1	1	1	1	1	½	10½
3 Jaffe	1	½	–	1	1	1	1	½	1	1	0	½	1	0	9½
4 Janowski	0	½	0	–	½	½	1	1	1	1	1	½	1	1	9
5 Chajes	½	0	0	½	–	1	½	1	0	1	1	½	1	1	8
6 Stapfer	0	½	0	½	0	–	½	½	1	1	1	1	1	1	8
7 Kupchik	0	0	0	0	½	½	–	½	1	0	1	1	1	1	6½
8 Tenenwurzel	0	0	½	0	0	½	½	–	0	½	1	1	½	1	5½
9 Whitaker	0	0	0	0	1	0	0	1	–	½	0	1	1	1	5½
10 Kline	0	0	0	0	0	0	1	½	½	–	1	½	0	1	4½
11 Rubinstein	0	0	1	0	0	0	0	0	1	0	–	1	1	½	4½
12 Morrison	0	0	½	½	½	0	0	0	0	½	0	–	1	1	4
13 Liebenstein	0	0	0	0	0	0	0	½	0	1	0	0	–	1	2½
14 Zapoléon	0	½	1	0	0	0	0	0	0	0	½	0	0	–	2

HAVANA, 1913

	Marshall	Capablanca	Janowski	Chajes	Kupchik	Jaffe	Blanco	Corzo	
1 Marshall	—	½ 1	1 0	½ 1	½ 1	½ 1	1 1	1 ½	10½
2 Capablanca	½ 0	—	0 1	½ 1	1 ½	1 ½	1 1	1 1	10
3 Janowski	0 1	1 0	—	1 0	½ 1	½ ½	1 1	½ 1	9
4 Chajes	½ 0	½ 0	0 1	—	0 1	0 1	½ 0	1 1	6½
5 Kupchik	½ 0	0 ½	½ 0	1 0	—	1 0	0 1	1 1	6½
6 Jaffe	½ 0	0 ½	½ ½	1 0	0 1	—	1 0	0 ½	5½
7 Blanco	0 0	0 0	0 0	½ 1	1 0	0 1	—	½ 1	5
8 Corzo	0 ½	0 0	½ 0	0 0	0 0	1 ½	½ 0	—	3

ST. PETERSBURG, 1914

	Capablanca	Lasker	Tarrasch	Alekhine	Marshall	Bernstein	Rubinstein	Nimzovitch	Blackburne	Janowski	Gunsberg	
1 Capablanca	—	½	½	1	½	1	½	1	1	1	1	8
2 Lasker	½	—	½	½	½	0	1	½	1	1	1	6½
3 Tarrasch	½	½	—	½	½	1	½	1	1	0	1	6½
4 Alekhine	0	½	½	—	1	½	1	½	½	½	1	6
5 Marshall	½	½	½	0	—	1	½	½	1	1	½	6
6 Bernstein	0	1	0	½	0	—	½	½	½	1	1	5
7 Rubinstein	½	0	½	0	½	½	—	½	½	1	1	5
8 Nimzovitch	0	½	0	½	½	½	½	—	0	½	1	4
9 Blackburne	0	0	0	½	0	0	½	1	—	0	1	3½
10 Janowski	0	0	1	½	0	0	0	½	1	—	½	3½
11 Gunsberg	0	0	0	0	½	½	0	0	0	½	—	1

FINAL

		Lasker	Capablanca	Alekhine	Tarrasch	Marshall	
1 Lasker	6½	—	½ 1	1 1	1 ½	1 1	13½
2 Capablanca	8	½ 0	—	½ 1	1 0	1 1	13
3 Alekhine	6	0 0	½ 0	—	1 1	1 ½	10
4 Tarrasch	6½	0 ½	0 1	0 0	—	0 ½	8½
5 Marshall	6	0 0	0 0	0 ½	1 ½	—	8

8
FIRST ROUND,
SAN SEBASTIAN, 1911

Ruy Lopez, Steinitz Defence

White	Black
CAPABLANCA	O. BERNSTEIN
1. P — K 4	P — K 4
2. Kt — K B 3	Kt — Q B 3
3. B — Kt 5	Kt — B 3
4. Castles	B — K 2
5. Kt — B 3	

A solid continuation, but not so energetic as 5. P — Q 4.

5. ......   P — Q 3

Transposing into the Steinitz Defence; again White's best reply is 6. P — Q 4. His exchange of Bishop for Knight merely relieves Black of one of his development problems.

6. B × Kt ch   P × B
7. P — Q 4   P × P

This gives away considerable ground in the centre and White's pieces can utilize this to form a K side attack. The great Russian master, Tchigorin, always played in such positions the centre supporting move, Kt — Q 2. Then after 8. P × P, P × P, Black's broken Pawn formation is fully compensated by his freedom of movement and two Bishops; the importance of possessing a Pawn on K 4 is that it limits the action of White's minor pieces, e.g. the K Kt cannot reach K B 5 via Q 4 as it does in the actual game.

8. Kt × P   B — Q 2
9. B — Kt 5

A move practised and popularized by Dr. Lasker, but, despite his numerous successes, it cannot be held to give White such lasting pressure as is to be obtained by the Tarrasch manœuvre 9. P — Q Kt 3 and 10. B — Kt 2 when the Bishop exerts a powerful latent attack on the long diagonal.

In direct contrast to this, the more immediately aggressive 9. B — Kt 5 soon loses its effect and in fact its eventual exchange cannot be avoided.

9. ......   Castles
10. R — K 1

In order to prevent the threatened 10. ....Kt × P; 11. B × B, Kt × Kt. However, a stronger method of creating an attack was 10. Q — Q 3 followed by Q R — K 1 and P — K B 4, by which means both Rooks would be used in the K side attack.

10. ......   P — K R 3
11. B — R 4   Kt — R 2

The best method of obtaining equality was shown in the 3rd Match game between Capablanca and Lasker in 1921 where the latter played 11. ....R — K 1; 12. Q — Q 3, Kt — R 2; 13. B × B, R × B; 14. R — K 3, Q — Kt 1; 15. P — Q Kt 3, Q — Kt 3.

12. B × B   Q × B
13. Q — Q 3

White could have prevented the Black Kt from re-entering the game via K Kt 4 by 13. P — B 4, but such a move would be out of harmony with the presence of the K Rook on K 1 (instead of K B 1, cf. the note to White's 10th move).

13. ...... Q R — Kt 1

Black is carefully preparing a plan for counterattack on the Q side; but carefully as he plans he does not see far enough and his policy is a mistaken one. The text move is, of course, not bad in itself, since it develops a piece with the gain of a tempo — it is the manœuvre that it prepares which is false.

Best is the centralizing move 13. ....K R — K 1 as in an exhibition game, Bernstein–Lasker, Moscow, 1914, which continued 14. R — K 3, Kt — B 1; 15. Q — B 4 (a weak move, correct was Q R — K 1); 15. ....P — B 4; 16. Kt — Q 5, Q — K 4!; 17. Kt — Kt 3, B — K 3 with advantage to Black.

14. P — Q Kt 3 Kt — Kt 4

This and his next three moves are part of his plan. The prudent course was the defensive but safe 14. ....K R — K 1 followed by 15. ....Kt — B 1.

15. Q R — Q 1

In order to play Q — R 6 without having to take into account the variation (after 15. Q — R 6), 15. ....Q — K 4; 16. Kt × P, Q × Kt; 17. Kt × R, R × Kt; 18. Q × R P, R — K 1 with the better game for Black.

More convincing, however, is the line given by Tarrasch, 15. P — B 4! Kt — K 3; 16. Kt — B 5, Q — B 3; 17. P — K 5, P × P; 18. P × P, Q — Q 1; 19. Q R — Q 1 with a very fine game.

15. ...... Q — K 4

Partly so as to be able to meet 16. Q — R 6 by Q — B 4, but also with a more evil purpose in mind.

16. Q — K 3 Kt — K 3
17. Q Kt — K 2 Q — R 4 ?

This diversion of Black's main piece from the K side in order to threaten a Pawn is positionally unjustified and can only be explained psychologically; Black obviously underestimates his youthful and comparatively unknown opponent.

Best was the simple 17. ....Kt × Kt at once exchanging off one of the menacing Kts and opening up the Bishop's diagonal so as to control K B 4.

18. Kt — B 5! Kt — B 4

And so another piece is diverted from the K side. Black dare not capture the Q R Pawn because of 18. ....Q × P; 19. Q — B 3 (with the threat 20. R — R 1); 19. ....Q — R 3; 20. Kt — B 4! whereupon Capablanca gives the following winning variation: 20. ....P — B 3; 21. Q — Kt 3, P — Kt 4; 22. Kt — Kt 6, R — B 2; 23. Kt × P ch, K — Kt 2; 24. Kt × R, K × Kt (Kt 3) (or 24. ....K × Kt (B 2); 25. P — K B 4!); 25. Kt × Q P, P × Kt; 26. R × P, R — Kt 2; 27. P — K 5.

19. Q Kt — Q 4   K — R 2

White was threatening 20. Kt
× B P, B × Kt; 21. Kt — K 7 ch
followed by Kt × B, etc.

20. P — K Kt 4

A very interesting way of continuing the attack; White first se-
cures his outpost on K B 5 in order to bring the other Kt round to
K R 5 via K 2 and Kt 3. The direct assault by 20. Q — Kt 3, P
— Kt 3; 21. Kt — K 7 fails to
give more than equality after 21.
....Q R — K 1! (not 21. ....Q
— Kt 3; 22. P — K 5, P — Q 4;
23. P — K 6!); 22. K Kt × B P,
Q — Kt 3; 23. Q — Q B 3, Kt ×
P; 24. Q — R 5, etc.

20. ......   Q R — K 1

Black would lose his Queen
after 20. ....Q × P; 21. R —
R 1, Q — Kt 7; 22. K R — Kt 1.

21. P — K B 3   Kt — K 3
22. Kt — K 2

A brilliant offer of two Pawns
for a profoundly conceived attack
on the King.

22. ......   Q × P ?

Pardonably failing to grasp the
true purport of White's plans and
possibly still not realising the calibre of his opponent. Correct was
22. ....Q — Kt 3, and though
his game is inferior to White's
after 23. K — Kt 2, Q × Q; 24.
Kt × Q followed by 25. P —
Q B 4, he has good chances of saving the draw.

23. Kt(K 2)—Kt 3   Q×BP ?

Too greedy; a much better defence was 23. ....P —⌐B 3 and if
24. Kt — R 5, R — B 2.

24. R — Q B 1   Q — Kt 7
25. Kt — R 5   R — K R 1

And not 25. ....P — Kt 3; 26.
Q × P ch, K — Kt 1; 27. P —
K 5, P × Kt; 28. Kt P × P, Q ×
P; 29. R — K 2 followed by R —
Kt 2 ch.

But Capablanca points out that
an adequate defence was provided
by 25. ....P — Kt 4. If then 26.
P — K 5, Kt — B 5! gives Black
the better game, so White does
best to go for the perpetual check
resulting after 26. R — B 3, Kt —
B 5; 27. Kt × Kt, P × Kt; 28.
Q × B P, Q × R; 29. Q × P ch.

26. R — K 2   Q — K 4
27. P — B 4   Q — Kt 4

At length the Queen has been
driven away from the vital point
at K Kt 2 and the storm breaks
loose.

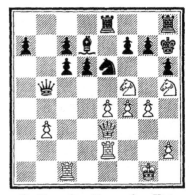

Position after 27. ....Q — Kt 4

28. Kt(B 5)×Kt P   Kt—B 4

Abandoning the Rook is equivalent to resignation. However, other continuations, though offering more resistance, lead also to an eventual loss, e.g. 28. .... Kt × Kt; 29. Kt — B 6 ch, K — Kt 3; 30. Kt × B, P — B 3 (or 30. .... P — K R 4; 31. P — B 5 ch and if K — R 2, 32. Kt — B 6 mate); 31. P — K 5, K — B 2; 32. Kt × P, R — K 2; 33. Kt — K 4, P × P; 34. P × P, Q × K P; 35. R — B 5, Q — K 3; 36. Q — B 3 ch, K — Kt 3; 37. Q — Q 3 and wins. Or Black can play 28. .... R — Q 1; 29. P — B 5, Kt — B 1 (if 29. .... Kt × Kt; 30. Kt — B 6, mate, or 29. .... Kt — Kt 4; 30. P — R 4); 30. P — Kt 5, Q — Kt 3; 31. P × P, Q × Q ch; 32. R × Q, Kt P; 33. K — B 2, R — K Kt 1; 34. R — K Kt 1, Kt — R 2; 35. Kt — B 6! and White wins.

29.	Kt × R	B × Kt
30.	Q — Q B 3	P — B 3
31.	Kt × P ch	K — Kt 3
32.	Kt — R 5	R — Kt 1
33.	P — B 5 ch	K — Kt 4
34.	Q — Kt 3 ch	K — R 5
35.	Q — Kt 3 ch	K — Kt 4
36.	P — R 4 mate	

For this complicated game, by no means flawless, but containing some very intriguing and deep combinations, White was awarded the first brilliancy prize.

9
THIRD ROUND, SAN SEBASTIAN, 1911
Ruy Lopez

White	Black
CAPABLANCA	A. BURN
1. P — K 4	P — K 4
2. Kt — K B 3	Kt — Q B 3
3. B — Kt 5	P — Q R 3
4. B — R 4	Kt — B 3
5. P — Q 3	

White intends to build up the same slow, solid formation à la Steinitz that he employed in his match with Marshall (cf. Game No. 4).

| 5. ...... | P — Q 3 |
| 6. P — B 3 | B — K 2 |

The best way for Black to take advantage of the slow nature of Steinitzian development is to fianchetto his K Bishop, e.g. 6. .... P — K Kt 3; 7. Q Kt — Q 2, B — Kt 2; 8. Kt — B 1, Castles; 9. Kt — Kt 3, P — Q Kt 4; 10. B — B 2, P — Q 4; 11. Q — K 2, R — K 1; 12. Castles, B — Kt 2; 13. B — Kt 5, P — Q 5; 14. Q R — Q 1, Q — Q 3 and Black stands well (Treybal–Grünfeld, Teplitz-Schönau, 1922).

The move actually played, though sound enough, condemns the Bishop to a more passive rôle than it would serve if fianchettoed — very important too is the fact that the fianchetto Pawn formation prevents White from gaining control of K B 5; for the Steinitz plan is largely concerned

with the placing of a Kt on that
square.

	7. Q Kt — Q 2	Castles
	8. Kt — B 1	P — Q Kt 4
	9. B — B 2	P — Q 4 !

An excellent move; Black
strives to open up the position in
the centre and so divert White
from his projected K side attack.

10. Q — K 2

Or 10. B — Q 2, R — K 1; 11.
Kt — Kt 3, B — B 1; 12. Castles,
P × P; 13. P × P, B — K 3; 14.
P — Kt 3, B — K Kt 5 with a lev-
el game (Tartakower–Réti, New
York, 1924).

10. ...... P × P

It was unnecessary to release
the tension so soon in the centre.
Best is 10. . . . R — K 1; 11. P —
K R 3, P — Kt 5 and now if 12.
P — B 4 ? (better is 12. B —
Kt 5); 12. . . . Kt — Q 5; 13. Kt
× Kt, P × Kt; 14. B P × P, Kt
× Q P; 15. B — Kt 3, Kt — Kt 3;
16. Q — R 5, R — B 1 with much
the better game for Black (Vajda–
Lundin, Folkestone, 1933).

11. P × P B — Q B 4

This underlines the note to
Black's 6th move; now the Bishop
seeks a more active diagonal.

	12. B — Kt 5	B — K 3
	13. Kt — K 3	R — K 1
	14. Castles K	Q — K 2

Position after 14. . . . .Q — K 2

14. . . . . B × Kt was correct
here, after which White would still
have a somewhat superior game
owing to the possession of two
Bishops. After Black's 14th move
the full force of White's attack is
unleashed and Black loses at least
a Pawn.

15. Kt — Q 5 ! B × Kt

If 15. . . . .Q — Q 1; 16. Q R
— Q 1, B — Q 3; 17. B × Kt, P
× B; 18. Kt — R 4, K — R 1; 19.
Q — R 5 and wins.

16. P × B Kt — Kt 1
17. P — Q R 4 !

A strong move which takes advantage of the fact that the two
Black Rooks are momentarily cut
off from each other.

17. ...... P — Kt 5

17. . . . .P × P would save the
Pawn, but would lead to a devas-
tating attack after 18. B × P,
R — Q 1; 19. Q R — Q 1, B —
Q 3; 20. Kt — R 4, Q Kt — Q 2;

21. Kt — B 5, Q — B 1; 22. B ×
Q Kt, R × B; 23. B × Kt, P ×
B; 24. R — Q 3, K — R 1; 25. R
— Kt 3 followed by Q — R 5 and
R — Kt 7.

18. P × P   B × P
19. B × Kt   Q × B
20. Q — K 4   B — Q 3

If 20. ....Q — K Kt 3; 21. Q
× B, Q × B; 22. Q R — B 1, Q
— Q 6; 23. K R — Q 1 and wins.
But now White wins a Pawn and
still retains an attack.

21. Q × P ch   K — B 1
22. Kt — R 4   Q — R 3

And not 22. ....P — Kt 3; 23.
B × P!

23. Q × Q   P × Q
24. Kt — B 5   P — K R 4
25. B — Q 1

Not merely winning a second
Pawn but creating a formidable
passed Pawn on the K R file.

25. ......   Kt — Q 2
26. B × P   Kt — B 3
27. B — K 2!

White rightly does not attempt
to retain the second Pawn by B —
B 3 because of 28. ....P — K 5.
In any case, his passed K R Pawn
is sufficient to ensure the win.

27. ......   Kt × P
28. K R — Q 1   Kt — B 5
29. B — B 4

The fact that the Bishops are
of opposite colours is here a help
to White; contrast the passive position of Black's piece with the active attacking nature of White's.

29. ......   K R — Q 1

The Bishop cannot move because of 30. R — Q 7.

30. P — K R 4   P — Q R 4
31. P — K Kt 3   Kt — K 3 ?

A weak move which allows
White to obtain two united passed
Pawns; in addition it doubles
Black's own Pawns on the K file
and is thereby equivalent to losing
another Pawn. A better resistance
would have been offered by 31.
....Kt — Kt 3 followed by 32.
....Kt — K 2.

32. B × Kt   P × B
33. Kt — K 3   K R — Kt 1
34. Kt — B 4   K — K 2
35. Q R — B 1

Threatening 36. Kt × B, P ×
Kt; 37. R — B 7 ch.

35. ......   R — R 2
36. R — K 1   K — B 3
37. R — K 4   R — Kt 5
38. P — Kt 4!

Showing sublime unconcern for
Black's threat of R × R P which
would be met by 39. Kt × B winning a piece.

38. ......   R — R 3
39. R — B 3   B — B 4
40. R — B 3 ch   K — Kt 2
41. P — Kt 3   B — Q 5
42. K — Kt 2   R — R 1
43. P — Kt 5   R — R 3
44. P — R 5   R × Kt

Played with the exasperation
induced by the helpless nature of
his game for the last twenty moves.

45. P × R   R — B 3
46. P — Kt 6   Resigns

10

BUENOS AIRES, 1911

Queen's Gambit Declined

White	Black
CAPABLANCA	L. MOLINA
1. P — Q 4	P — Q 4
2. P — Q B 4	P — K 3
3. Kt — Q B 3	Kt — K B 3
4. B — Kt 5	Q Kt — Q 2
5. P — K 3	P — B 3

As though about to play the Cambridge Springs Defence; if so, he changes his mind next move.

6. Kt — B 3	B — K 2
7. P × P	

To either 7. R — B 1 or Q — B 2 Black has the satisfactory reply of 7. ....Kt — K 5. But the best move here is simply 7. B — Q 3.

7.	Kt × P

7. ....K P × P was a good alternative.

8. B × B	Kt × B

And now 8. ....Q × B was to be preferred.

9. B — Q 3	P — Q B 4

As will soon become evident Black cannot avoid this early opening up of the position.

10. Castles	Castles
11. P × P	Kt × P ?

If Black wishes to regain the Pawn he must play 11. ....Q — R 4, though after 12. R — B 1, Q × B P; 13. Kt — K 4 his position is not to be envied. After the text there follows the familiar sacrifice on R 7 with, however, some fresh points of further play.

Position after 11. ....Kt × P ?

12. B × P ch !

The prime requisite of this combination is that a Black Kt should not be within easy reach of K B 3. For example, had Black's Q Kt been still at Q 2 the sacrifice would have been unsound.

12.	K × B
13. Kt — Kt 5 ch	K — Kt 3

Other moves lose more quickly, e.g. 13. ....K — Kt 1; 14. Q — R 5, R — K 1; 15. Q × P ch, K — R 1; 16. Q R — Q 1, etc., or 13. ....K — R 3; 14. Kt × P ch winning the Queen.

14. Q — Kt 4	P — B 4

If 14. ....P — K 4 Capablanca gives the following fine variation: 15. Kt — K 6 dis. ch, K — B 3; 16. P — B 4, P — K 5; 17. Q — Kt 5 ch, K × Kt; 18. Q

— K 5 ch, K — Q 2; 19. K R —
Q 1 ch, Kt — Q 6; 20. Kt × P,
K — B 3; 21. R × Kt, Q × R;
22. R — B 1 ch, K — Kt 3; 23.
Q — B 7 ch followed by mate in
five moves.

15. Q — Kt 3   K — R 3
16. Q — R 4 ch K — Kt 3
17. Q — R 7 ch K — B 3

If 17. ....K × Kt; 18. Q ×
Kt P ch, K — R 4 (or 18. ....
Kt — K 3; 19. P — B 4 ch); 19.
Kt — K 2, P — K 4; 20. Kt —
Kt 3 ch, K — R 5; 21. Q —
R 6 ch, K — Kt 5; 22. P — B 3
mate.

18. P — K 4   Kt — Kt 3

Best; the threat is 19. ....R
— R 1. If at once 18. ....R —
R 1; 19. P — K 5 ch, K × Kt; 20.
P — B 4 ch, K — Kt 5; 21. P —
R 3 ch, K — Kt 6; 22. R — B 3
mate.

19. P × P

Capablanca points out that 19.
P — B 4 would have been more
immediately conclusive; for then
if 19. ....P × P; 20. Q R — Q 1,
Q — Kt 3; 21. R — Q 6 and wins.

19. ....   P × P
20. Q R — Q 1 Kt — Q 6

If 20. ....Q — K 1 or Q —
R 4; 21. Kt — Q 5 ch wins. Black
now threatens R — R 1 winning
the Queen. It is extraordinary,
nevertheless, how White's attack
continues with unabated vigour.

Position after 20. ....Kt — Q 6

21. Q — R 3   Kt (Q 6) — B 5

If 21. ....K × Kt; 22. R ×
Kt, Q — R 4; 23. R — Kt 3 ch, K
— B 3; 24. Q — R 7, Kt — B 5;
25. Q × Kt P ch, K — K 3; 26.
R — K 1 ch, etc.

22. Q — Kt 3   Q — B 2
23. K R — K 1 Kt — K 7 ch

This loses at once, but Black
cannot save the game; if, for ex-
ample, 23. ....P — Q R 3 (to
prevent Kt — Kt 5) then 24. R —
Q B 1, Q — Kt 1; 25. Kt —
R 7 ch, K — B 2; 26. Kt × R, K
× Kt; 27. Q — K 3, B — Q 2; 28.
P — K Kt 3, Kt — K 3; 29. Kt —
Q 5 followed by 30. Kt — Kt 6.
Nor can Black develop the Bish-
op, since 23. ....B — K 3; 24. R
× B ch, Kt × R allows White to
mate by 25. Kt — Q 5 and if 23.
....B — Q 2; 24. Kt — Q 5 ch,
Kt × Kt; 25. Kt — R 7 ch, K —
B 2; 26. Q × Q, Kt × Q; 27. R
× B ch, K — Kt 1; 28. Kt × R,
etc.

24. R × Kt   Q × Q
25. Kt — R 7 ch   K — B 2
26. R P × Q   R — R 1
27. Kt — Kt 5 ch K — B 3
28. P — B 4   Resigns

For there is no way of meeting the two threats of Kt — Q 5 and R — Q 6 ch.

11
HAVANA, 1913

Queen's Pawn

White	Black
J. Corzo	Capablanca
1. P — Q 4	Kt — K B 3
2. P — Q B 4	P — Q 3

This irregular defence gives White too much ground in the centre; its solitary advantage lies in the rareness with which one encounters it, with a resultant proneness to error by over-bookish players.

3. Kt — Q B 3   Q Kt — Q 2
4. P — K 4   P — K 4
5. P — B 4 ?

This over-energetic move leaves White very insecurely placed in the centre. A good solid continuation is 5. K Kt — K 2 followed by P — K Kt 3 and B — Kt 2.

Also good is 5. P — Q 5, as Capabanca himself played against Riumin at Moscow in 1936, with the continuation 5. .... Kt — B 4; 6. P — B 3, B — K 2; 7. B — K 3, Castles; 8. P — Q Kt 4, Q Kt — Q 2; 9. B — Q 3, Kt — K 1; 10. K Kt — K 2, P — K Kt 3; 11. Castles, P — Q R 4; 12. P —

Q R 3, Kt — Kt 2; 13. B — R 6, with marked advantage to White.

5. ......   P × Q P

Now Black by continually attacking the K Pawn will interfere with White's normal development; the text move has the additional advantage of bringing White's Queen prematurely into the open, where it is liable to attack by Black's minor pieces.

6. Q × P   Kt — B 4
7. B — K 3   Q — K 2 !

Strongly played; the K Bishop is to be developed by a K fianchetto whilst the attack is intensified on White's centre.

8. Kt — Q 5

A loss of time, but there is no better move. If 8. P — K 5 then 8. .... Kt — Kt 5 whilst 8. B — Q 3 gives Black the advantage of two Bishops.

8. ......   Kt × Kt
9. K P × Kt   B — B 4
10. Kt — B 3

Allowing Black to gain a strong attack by his next fine move. Correct was 10. Castles, and although Black could still play 10. .... P — K Kt 3 after 11. B — B 2 White would be threatening R — K 1.

10. ......   P — K Kt 3 !
11. K — B 2

If 11. Q × R, Q × B ch; 12. B — K 2 (or 12. K — Q 1, Kt — K 5); 12. .... B — Q 6; 13. Kt — Kt 1, Kt — K 5, etc.

Somewhat better than the text, however, is 11. Castles, B — Kt 2 ; 12. Q — Q 2, Kt — K 5 ; 13. Q — K 1, though Black would still have the attack.

11.	......	R — K Kt 1
12.	R — K 1	B — Kt 2
13.	Q — Q 1	Kt — K 5 ch
14.	K — Kt 1	K — B 1

Here the King is much safer than on the Q side; e.g. 14. .... Castles Q; 15. B × R P! P — Kt 3; 16. Q — R 4, K — Kt 2; 17. P — B 5! and White wins.

15.   B — Q 4   P — K Kt 4!

A move of great vigour which opens up more lines of attack.

Position after 15. .... P — K Kt 4 !

16. B × B ch

In this interesting position White is continually hampered by the hidden threat to his King. For if 16. Kt × P, B × B ch; 17. Q × B, Kt × Kt; 18. R × Q, Kt — R 6 mate. Or if 16. P × P, Kt × P; 17. B × B ch (worse still are both 17. Kt × Kt, B × B ch; 18. Q × B, Q × R or 17. R × Q, Kt

— R 6 ch; 18. P × Kt, B × B mate); 17. .... R × B; 18. Kt × Kt, Q × Kt; 19. Q — B 1, Q — Kt 3; 20. Q — K 3, P — K B 3; 21. P — B 5, R — Q 1; 22. P — B 6 (otherwise Black plays Q R — Q 2 followed by Q R — K 2); 22. .... P × P and Black has a won game.

16.	......	R × B
17.	Kt — Q 4	B — Q 2
18.	P — K B 5	

White has a clearly lost ending after 18. B — Q 3, P — K B 4; 19. B × Kt, P × B; 20. P — K B 5, Q — K 4; 21. Kt — K 6 ch, B × Kt; 22. B P × B, P — Q B 3; 23. Q — K 2, P × P; 24. P × P, Q × Q P; 25. Q × P, Q × P; 26. R × Q, R — B 1; 27. K — B 2, R — B 7 ch; 28. R — K 2, R × R ch; 29. K × R, K — K 2, etc.

| 18. | ...... | Q — K 4 |
| 19. | Q — Q 3 | R — K 1 |

This is the best move and is played with the intention of an eventual sacrifice of the exchange. Not so effective would be 19. Kt — B 4; 20. Q — Q 2, Q — B 3; 21. P — Q Kt 4 and White has freed his position.

20. Kt — K 6 ch

White has no option but to go in for this complication, since Black threatens to take off his K B Pawn and if 20. P — K Kt 4, Q — B 5 is decisive.

| 20. | ...... | P × Kt |
| 21. | B P × P | |

Position after 21. B P × P

21. ......   R × P !

A fine positional sacrifice based
on two main considerations: (1)
Black's Kt is the key to his attack
and must be preserved. (2)
White's K Rook is, and will remain for most of the game, completely out of play.

Other continuations lead to
White's advantage, e.g. 21. ....
B — B 1; 22. R × Kt, Q × Kt P;
23. P — K R 4!

22. P × R   B — B 3
23. Q — B 3 ch

Otherwise Black plays P —
Kt 5 with the threat of Q — B 5
or B 4 ch.

23. ......   Q — B 5
24. Q — K 3

Capablanca gives the following
attractive variation showing that
White dare not exchange Queens:
24. Q × Q, P × Q; 25. P —
K R 4, P — B 6; 26. R — Q 1, P
— B 7 ch; 27. K — R 2, Kt —
Kt 6; 28. R — Q 2, Kt × R; 29.
K × Kt, R × P!

24. ......   K — K 2
25. P — Q Kt 4

And not 25. P — K R 4, Kt —
Q 7; 26. Q × Q, P × Q; 27. R —
K 2, Kt × B; 28. K × Kt, P —
B 6!

25. ......   P — Kt 3
26. P — Kt 5   B — Kt 2
27. P — Kt 3   Kt — Q 7 !
28. Q — Q B 3 ?

This superficially powerful
move overlooks Black's 29th move
in reply and shortens White's resistance. Correct was 28. B —
Kt 2, Q × Q ch; 29. R × Q, Kt
× P; 30. R — Q B 3, B × B; 31.
K × B, P — Q 4, though Black
would still win the end game after
32. R — K 1, K — Q 3; 33. R —
B 2, R — K 2; 34. R (B 2) —
K 2, P — Q 5, etc.

28. ......   Kt — B 6 ch
29. K — B 2   Q — B 1
30. P — B 5

Desperation in an utterly lost
position; Black can now pick and
choose amongst a variety of winning methods.

30. ......   Kt — K 4 dis.ch
31. K — Kt 1   Kt — B 6 ch
32. K — B 2   Kt P × P
33. Q — R 5   Kt — K 4 dis.ch
34. K — Kt 1   Q — B 6
35. Q × P ch   K — B 3
36. Q × Q P   Q × R ch
37. K — B 2   Q × P ch

Resigns, the Queen being lost
after 38. K — K 3, Q × P Q. This
game was awarded the brilliancy
prize.

12

ST. PETERSBURG, 1913

Ruy Lopez, Morphy Defence

White	Black
CAPABLANCA	F. DUS-CHOTIMIRSKI
1. P — K 4	P — K 4
2. Kt — K B 3	Kt — Q B 3
3. B — Kt 5	P — Q R 3
4. B — R 4	Kt — B 3
5. Castles	B — K 2
6. R — K 1	P — Q Kt 4
7. B — Kt 3	P — Q 3
8. P — B 3	Kt — Q R 4
9. B — B 2	P — B 4
10. P — Q 4	Q — B 2
11. Q Kt — Q 2	

So far the normal line in this variation; more usual nowadays is 11. P — R 3 to prevent the development of Black's Bishop to K Kt 5, but there is nothing wrong with the text move.

| 11. ...... | Kt — B 3 |

After 11. ....Castles White may proceed as in the game Alekhine–Fine, Hastings, 1936, 12. Kt — B 1, B — Kt 5; 13. Kt — K 3, B × Kt; 14. Q × B, B P × P; 15. Kt — B 5, P × P; 16. Q × P, K R — Q B 1; 17. Q — K Kt 3, B — B 1; 18. B — Q 3, Kt — B 3; 19. B — Kt 5 with an attack well worth the Pawn.

12. Kt — B 1

Stronger is 12. P — Q R 4, R — Q Kt 1; 13. R P × P, R P × P; 14. P × K P, P × P; 15. Kt — B 1, B — K 3; 16. Kt — K 3, Cas-

tles; 17. Kt — Kt 5, K R — Q 1; 18. Q — B 3, R — Q 3; 19. Kt — B 5 and White gains the advantage of two Bishops (Rauser–Riumin, Leningrad, 1934).

| 12. ...... | B P × P |

With the idea of starting a vigorous attack on the Q side.

13. P × P	B — Kt 5
14. P — Q 5	Kt — Q 5
15. B — Q 3	Castles K

An analysis in that fine Swedish book on the openings, *Lärobok,* shows that Black can get an excellent game here by 15. .... Kt — R 4; 16. B — K 3, B × Kt; 17. P × B, Kt — B 5; 18. R — B 1, Q — Q 1. If now 19. B × Kt (B 4), P × B; 20. B — Kt 1, Q — Kt 3! (and not 20. .... B — B 3; 21. P — K 5! and wins).

| 16. B — K 3 | Q R — B 1 ? |

There is no reason why Black should not adopt a line similar to that given in the last note and play 16. .... B × Kt followed by 17. .... Kt — R 4, etc. After the text move his Pawns are badly split up and in need of protection. Finally, if his heart was set on this line, he should have played 16. .... K R — B 1 as the other Rook should remain on the Q R file to protect the Q R Pawn, the weakness of which, as so often in the Ruy Lopez, soon becomes apparent.

| 17. B × Kt | P × B |
| 18. P — Q R 4! | Q — Kt 3 |

Were the Q Rook on R 1 now Black could have played P — Kt 5 followed by Kt — Q 2 — B 4, with a good counter on the Q wing.

19. P × P   P × P

White now prepares a K side attack which will be facilitated by incidental attack on Black's isolated Pawns.

Black in turn intends to counter with attack along the Q B file and the Kt manœuvre via Q 2 — B 4 to R 5.

20. P — R 3   B × Kt

If 20. ....B — R 4; 21. P — Kt 4, B — Kt 3; 22. Kt — Kt 3 followed by an eventual Kt — B 5.

21. Q × B   Kt — Q 2
22. K R — B 1

It is important to contest control of the Q B file as otherwise Black would play 22. ....Kt — B 4 followed by Kt × B, Q — B 4, Q — B 5, etc.

22. ......   Kt — B 4

Not without its drawbacks is the alternative line 22. ....Kt — K 4; 23. Q — K 2, Kt × B; 24. Q × Kt, B — Kt 4; 25. Kt — Q 2, P — Kt 3; 26. P — K Kt 3, P — B 4; 27. P — B 4 and the weakness of Black's isolated Pawns really becomes manifest.

23. P — Q Kt 4!   Kt — R 5

Wrongly continuing with his original plan, which is proved faulty by White's 25th and 26th moves. He could have still obtained a tenable game by 23. .... Kt × B; 24. Q × Kt, B — B 3.

24. R × R   R × R
25. P — K 5!   P — Kt 3

And not 25. ....P × P; 26. Q — B 5!

Position after 25. ....P — Kt 3

26. P — K 6!

A fine move which breaks up the basis of Black's defence on the K side. Now if 26. ....P × P; 27. Q — Kt 4 and wins.

26. ......   R — K B 1
27. Kt — Kt 3

The Kt comes into play with decisive effect; again if 27. .... P × P; 28. Q — Kt 4 wins.

27. ......   Q — Kt 2

If 27. ....P — B 4; 28. B × B P, P × B; 29. Kt × P, R × Kt; 30. Q × R, Q — B 2; 31. Q — B 7 ch, K — R 1; 32. P — B 4, P — Q 6; 33. P — B 5, P — Q 7; 34. P — B 6 and wins.

28. Kt — B 5!   P × P

Black is lost, however he plays; if 28. ....P × Kt; 29. Q × P, K

— Kt 2 ; 30. Q × R P ch, K —
B 3 ; 31. P — B 4 followed by
mate ; whilst if 28. . . . . K — R 1 ;
29. Q — K 4, B — B 3 ; 30. Kt ×
P (Q 6), etc.

29. P × P   Q — B 2

Allowing White to bring off an-
other surprise coup ; but if 29.
. . . . Q — R 2 ; 30. Q — Kt 4 and
Black's Pawns will fall.

30. Q — B 6 !

This forcing move wins the
Q Kt Pawn and means that after
the inevitable exchange of Queens
White's advanced passed Pawn
will cost Black the exchange.

30.	Q — Q 1
31. Kt × B ch	Q × Kt
32. B × Q Kt P	Kt — B 6
33. Q — Q 7	Q × Q

Otherwise the Pawn advances
to Queen.

34. B × Q   R — Q Kt 1

Black loses more Pawns after
34. . . . . Kt — Q 4 ; 35. R — Q 1,
R — B 5 ; 36. P — Kt 3, R —
K 5 ; 37. B — B 6, R — K 4 ; 38.
R × P, Kt — K 2 ; 39. R × P.

35. P — K 7   K — B 2

Black could have now resigned,
but he appears still to be hoping
for some sort of swindle with his
Q Pawn.

36. R — K 1	R — K 1
37. B × R ch	K × B
38. R — K 6	P — Q 4
39. K — B 1	Kt — Kt 4
40. K — K 2	Kt — B 2
41. R — K 5	Kt — R 3
42. P — Kt 5	Kt — Kt 5
43. P — Kt 6	P — Q 6 ch
44. K — Q 2	K — Q 2
45. P — K 8=Q ch	K — Q 3
46. Q — K 7 ch	K — B 3
47. Q × Kt	Resigns

13
ST. PETERSBURG, 1913

*Queen's Gambit Declined,
Slav Defence*

White	Black
CAPABLANCA	A. ALEKHINE
1. P — Q 4	P — Q 4
2. P — Q B 4	P — Q B 3
3. P — K 3	Kt — B 3
4. Kt — K B 3	P — K 3
5. Q Kt — Q 2	

A move largely based on psychological grounds ; Black, having
already played P — Q B 3, will
be reluctant to play P — Q B 4
as this would appear to be the
waste of a tempo. So the Kt will be
better placed on Q 2 in order to
retake the Bishops Pawn should
Black be so unwise as to exchange
Pawns — or alternatively to support the manœuvre Kt — K B 3
— K 5 by going in turn to K B 3.

5. . . . . . .   Q Kt — Q 2

Nevertheless, 5. . . . . P — B 4
was the right way to take advantage of the fact that the Kt being
on Q 2 rather than Q B 3 fails to
bring pressure to bear on Black's
Q 4.

The game Alekhine–Vidmar,
Semmering, 1926, continued here,

5. ....P — B 4; 6. B — K 2, Kt
— B 3; 7. Castles, B — Q 3; 8. P
— Q R 3, P × Q P; 9. K P × P,
P — Q R 4; 10. B — Q 3, Cas-
tles; 11. R — K 1, P — Q Kt 3;
12. P — Q Kt 3, B — Kt 2; 13. B
— Kt 2, Kt — K 2 with full equal-
ity.

6. B — Q 3   B — K 2
7. Castles   Castles
8. Q — B 2

This is not so strong as 8. P —
Q Kt 3 by which White can complete his development along offen-
sive lines and at the same time re-
serves his Queen for K 2, a more
effective square for the piece in
this position. If then 8. .... P —
Q Kt 3; 9. B — Kt 2, B — Kt 2;
10. Q — K 2, P — Q R 4; 11. P
— Q R 4, B — Kt 5; 12. P —
K 4, P × K P; 13. Kt × P with
the better game for White (Alekhine–Bogoljuboff, 6th match
game, 1934).

. 8. ......   P × P ?

This move plays into White's
hands and gives him control of
K 5. Correct was 8. .... P — B 4.

9. Kt × P   P — B 4
10. Q Kt — K 5

Threatening to win a Pawn by
Kt × Kt, etc.

10. ......   P × P
11. P × P   Kt — Kt 3

Black has difficulty in developing his K side; his plan of bringing the Kt to Q 4, though con-
suming time, seems the best avail-

able. However, White by a series
of subtle manœuvres is able to re-
duce Black's resistance on both
flanks.

12. Kt — Kt 5

Forcing Black to weaken his K
side by P — Kt 3.

12. ......   P — K Kt 3
13. Kt (Kt 5) — B 3

In order to complete his development by bringing the Q Bishop
out, followed by R — B 1 with
control of the Q B file.

Capablanca points out that he
could also have played 13. Q —
K 2 and if then 13. .... Q × P;
14. Kt (Kt 5) — B 3, followed by
B — K R 6 and Kt — Kt 5 with a
winning attack. However, Black
need not take the proffered Pawn
and would do best to reply 13.
.... Q Kt — Q 4.

13. ......   K — Kt 2

Preventing 14. B — K R 6.

14. B — K Kt 5   Q Kt — Q 4
15. R — B 1   B — Q 2
16. Q — Q 2   Kt — K 1
17. B × B   Q × B
18. B — K 4 !

The Kt on Q 4 is the centre of
Black's defence and White hastens
to exchange for it a Bishop which
is merely biting on granite.

18. ......   B — Kt 4 ?

A weak move. After which
White's attack proceeds on oiled
wheels; better was 18. .... K Kt
— B 3; 19. B × Kt, Kt × B and
if 20. Kt — Kt 4, P — B 3; 21.

Q — R 6 ch, K — R 1 with a fair defensive position.

19. K R — K 1

Threatening B × Kt followed by Kt × Kt P.

19. ......   Q — Q 3
20. B × Kt   P × B

And not 20. ....Q × B; 21. R — B 5.

Position after 20. ....P × B

21. Q — R 5 !

This strong move gains command of the 7th rank.

21. ....   P — Q R 3

If he wishes to prevent an eventual R — B 7, Black must submit to a weakened Pawn position after 21. ....B — B 3; 22. Kt × B, P × Kt and White by concentrating his major pieces on the backward Q P Pawn and the isolated Q R Pawn should win the end game.

22. Q — B 7   Q × Q
23. R × Q   P — R 3

Otherwise White plays Kt — Kt 5 threatening both Kt × B P and Kt — K 6 ch. It is therefore impossible to save the Kt Pawn.

24. R × P   Q R — B 1

Hoping to obtain a counterattack by playing R — B 7 in his turn, but his remaining pieces are too pinned down on the K side.

25. P — Q Kt 3   R — B 7
26. P — Q R 4   B — K 7
27. Kt — R 4 !

After this powerful move Black's entire K side collapses.

27. ......   P — K R 4
28. Kt (R 4) × P   R — K 1
29. R × P ch   K — R 3
30. P — B 4   P — R 4
31. Kt — R 4

After which Black cannot avert mate and only staves it off for a few moves by sacrificing the exchange.

31. ......   R × Kt
32. B P × R   K — Kt 4
33. P — Kt 3   Kt — Kt 5
34. R — Kt 7 ch   K — R 6
35. Kt — Kt 2   Resigns

This was Capablanca's first encounter with Alekhine. Who could have imagined, after seeing this stunning defeat, that the victim, fourteen years later, would score a decisive victory over his opponent in a world championship match?

14
MOSCOW, 1914

Queen's Gambit Declined

White	Black
O. Bernstein	Capablanca
1. P — Q 4	P — Q 4
2. P — Q B 4	P — K 3
3. Kt — Q B 3	Kt — K B 3
4. Kt — B 3	B — K 2
5. B — Kt 5	Castles
6. P — K 3	Q Kt — Q 2
7. R — B 1	P — Q Kt 3

This move was regarded with much favour at the time this game was played, but it has long since become obsolete, largely owing to the innovations of Capablanca himself. The normal move now is 7. ....P — B 3, since it is regarded necessary to block the Q B file.

| 8. P × P | P × P |
| 9. Q — R 4 |

This move of Duras is not so strong as either (*a*) 9. B — Q 3, B — Kt 2; 10. Castles, P — B 4; 11. Q — K 2, P — B 5; 12. B — Kt 1, P — Q R 3; 13. Kt — K 5, P — Kt 4; 14. P — B 4, Kt — K 5; 15. B × Kt, P × B; 16. Kt × Kt, Q × Kt; 17. B × B, Q × B; 18. P — B 5, P — B 3; 19. R — B 4 with marked advantage to White (Vidmar–Yates, London, 1922) or (*b*) Capablanca's own move, 9. B — Kt 5, B — Kt 2; 10. Castles, P — B 4; 11. Q — R 4, P — Q R 3; 12. B × Q Kt, Kt × B; 13. B × B, Q × B; 14. P × P, P × P; 15. Q — K B 4, Q R —

B 1; 16. K R — Q 1 and White has a strong attack on Black's weakened Pawns.

| 9. ...... | B — Kt 2 |

Here, however, Black does best to sacrifice a Pawn by 9. ....P — B 4; 10. Q — B 6, R — Kt 1; 11. Kt × P, Kt × Kt; 12. Q × K Kt, B — Kt 2; 13. B × B, Q × B; 14. Q — Kt 5, Q × Q; 15. Kt × Q, P × P; 16. P × P, Kt — B 3 and White, being greatly behind in development, will be unable to retain the Pawn, e.g. 17. P — B 3, K R — Q 1; 18. R — Q 1, P — K R 3; 19. Kt — R 3, Kt — Q 4; 20. K — B 2, Q R — B 1; 21. B — Q 3, Kt — Kt 5; 22. B — Kt 1, Kt — B 7, etc.

| 10. B — Q R 6 | B × B |
| 11. Q × B | P — B 4 |

The play now centres round the familiar "hanging Pawns" question. The two Pawns on Black's Q 4 and Q B 4 are a potential source of both strength and weakness — weakness because they may have to be defended by the minor pieces and strength because their continuous threat of advancing and counterattacking in the centre may give Black more than adequate counter chances.

12. B × Kt

A simplification which has been criticised by some annotators; but the recommended alternative of 12. Castles gets White nowhere after 12. ....Q — B 1; 13. Q — K 2, Q — Kt 2.

12.	......	Kt × B
13.	P × P	P × P
14.	Castles	Q — Kt 3
15.	Q — K 2	

15. Q × Q would obviously prove to Black's advantage, since it both strengthens his Pawn chain and opens up the Rook file.

| 15. | ...... | P — B 5 |

This is a most intriguing move from the positional point of view. Normally, one would condemn it unhesitatingly, since it gives White's Kt an excellent post on Q 4 and weakens Black's Q 4 by making it irrevocably backward.

But the move is really based on a profound appreciation of the position; primarily it fixes White's Q Kt Pawn for attack; next it opens up a diagonal for Black's Bishop and, finally, if a Kt does settle on Q 4 it will temporarily impede White's attack by major pieces on Black's backward Pawn.

16. K R — Q 1 ?

White, convinced that Black's last move is positionally weak, hastens to take advantage of it by direct attack. Had he realised its true implications, however, he would have played 16. P — K 4! P × P; 17. Kt × P, Q R — Kt 1; 18. Kt × Kt ch, B × Kt; 19. Q × P, Q × P and the position is clearly drawn.

| 16. | ...... | K R — Q 1 |
| 17. | Kt — Q 4 | |

Still peacefully unconscious of approaching disaster; the manœu-vre given in the last note was still open to White.

| 17. | ...... | B — Kt 5! |

This, in conjunction with White's next obliging move, converts a defensive piece into a most dangerous attacking weapon.

18. P — Q Kt 3 ?

It is true that White has now the inferior game, since he has been positionally outplayed. But this move gives Black a passed Pawn which, though isolated, can be easily supported and continually threatens a decisive advance.

White does best to keep on the defensive by 18. Q — B 2, though Black would still retain the initiative by 18. ....Q R — Kt 1.

| 18. | ...... | Q R — B 1 |
| 19. | P × P | |

19. Kt — R 4, Q — R 4! only puts the Kt out of play and gives Black the additional threat of P — B 6.

19.	......	P × P
20.	R — B 2	B × Kt
21.	R × B	Kt — Q 4!
22.	R — B 2	

And not 22. R × P, Kt — B 6 winning the exchange. One now realises the true strength of Black's passed Pawn.

22.	......	P — B 6
23.	K R — Q B 1	R — B 4
24.	Kt — Kt 3	R — B 3
25.	Kt — Q 4	R — B 2
26.	Kt — Kt 5	

An endeavour to exchange Kts which fails against a very neat trap.

His best defence is 26. Q — K 1, K R — Q B 1; 27. Kt — K 2, Q — R 4; 28. P — K 4, Kt — Kt 5; 29. R × P, Kt × P; 30. R × R, Q × Q ch; 31. R × Q, R × R; 32. R — R 1, R — B 7; 33. K — B 1, K — B 1 and Black will have considerable difficulty in winning, though he should do so in the long run.

26. ......   R — B 4
27. Kt × P ?

Losing at once; he had to go back with the Kt to Q 4.

27. ......   Kt × Kt
28. R × Kt   R × R
29. R × R

Position after 29. R × R

29. ......   Q — Kt 7 !

After which horrible shock White resigns, since the Rook is lost.

15
SIXTH ROUND,
ST. PETERSBURG, 1914

Ruy Lopez, Steinitz Defence

White	Black
A. ALEKHINE	CAPABLANCA
1. P — K 4	P — K 4
2. Kt — K B 3	Kt — Q B 3
3. B — Kt 5	P — Q 3
4. P — Q 4	P × P
5. Kt × P	B — Q 2
6. Kt — Q B 3	Kt — B 3
7. Castles	

A more vigorous method of play and one more calculated to retain the initiative is the immediate occupation of the central outposts by 7. B × Kt, P × B; 8. Q — B 3, P — B 4; 9. Kt — B 5, B × Kt; 10. Q × B, Q — Q 2; 11. Q — B 3, R — Q Kt 1; 12. Castles, B — K 2; 13. P — Q Kt 3, Castles; 14. B — Kt 5, Kt Q 4; 15. Kt × Kt (Löwenfisch–Oubinin, Leningrad, 1934), after which White's Kt is superior to Black's Bishop and Black's Pawn formation is faulty.

7. ......   B — K 2
8. Kt — B 5

Here again 8. B × Kt followed by Q — B 3 and Kt — B 5 was correct. The manœuvre in the text should only be employed when White is ready to recapture with a piece and not the K Pawn. For on B 5 the Pawn is really a handicap and stultifies White's attack.

The Tarrasch manœuvre of P — Q Kt 3 and B — Kt 2 will not achieve much here, as was shown in the game Lasker–Capablanca, New York, 1924, which continued 8. P — Q Kt 3, Kt × Kt; 9. Q × Kt, B × B; 10. Kt × B, Kt — Q 2; 11. B — R 3, P — Q R 3 (if 11. . . . . B — B 3; 12. Q — B 4); 12. Kt — B 3, B — B 3; 13. Q — K 3, Castles; 14. Q R — Q 1, B × Kt; 15. Q × B, R — K 1 and resulted in an early draw.

8.	B × Kt
9. P × B	Castles
10. R — K 1	

This is an illogical continuation; White must endeavour to exploit his preponderance of Pawns on the K wing by a Pawn advance. He should play 10. P — K Kt 4 and now if P — Q 4; 11. P — Kt 5, Kt — K 5; 12. Kt × Kt, P × Kt; 13. B × Kt, P × B; 14. Q — Kt 4 with advantage to White. Consequently Black does best to continue after 10. P — K Kt 4, Kt — Q 2 when White can follow up his plan with 11. P — B 4.

10.	Kt — Q 2
11. Kt — Q 5	B — B 3
12. P — Q B 3	

Otherwise White will be unable to develop his Q Bishop because of the vulnerability of his Q Kt Pawn; but the very fact that he has to resort to such cumbrous methods condemns White's system.

| 12. . . . . . . | Kt — Kt 3 |
| 13. Kt × B ch | |

Instead of inviting this attack on the K B Pawn, White should have supported it by 13. P — K Kt 4.

| 13. . . . . . . | Q × Kt |
| 14. B × Kt | |

With the plan of attacking Black's weakened Q Pawn position, but Capablanca, who plays the whole game with a wonderfully sure appreciation of its true positional aspects, foils this attack by a series of subtle tactical finesses which at the same time give him mastery of the centre.

14.	P. × B
15. Q — B 3	K R — K 1
16. B — K 3	P — B 4

Depriving White's Bishop of the square on Q 4 and so enabling Black to concentrate his Rooks in the centre. The reader will note throughout the game how poor a role White's Bishop plays, especially in contrast to the activity of the Black Kt.

| 17. R — K 2 | R — K 4 |
| 18. Q R — K 1 | Q R — K 1 ! |

Not falling into the trap of 18. . . . . R × P; 19. B — Q 4 threatening mate and winning the exchange; whilst 18. . . . . Q × P; 19. Q × Q, R × Q; 20. B × P would dissipate Black's advantage.

| 19. Q — Kt 7 | |

All part of White's plan, but it carries with it the fatal marks of a flank diversion at the expense of lost ground in the centre. 19. P — K Kt 4 is no longer playable because of 19. . . . . P — K Kt 3.

19. ......   Q × P
20. Q × B P   Q — K 3
21. Q × R P

And so White's plan has been carried out and he has won his Pawn on the Q side; but at what a terrific cost in position! There is a lasting pin on his K file and his Queen is completely cut off from the K side and must helplessly watch Black's attack burst on the solitary White King.

21. ......   Kt — Q 4
22. K — B 1

Hoping to be allowed time to play Q — R 4 and Q — B 2 and so relieve the pin on the K file, but Black has prepared a thunderstroke.

22. ......   Kt — B 5
23. R — Q 2

Position after 23. R — Q 2

23. ......   Kt × P !

A decisive blow, after which White's position rapidly crumbles to pieces.

24. K × Kt
If 24. R (K 1) — K 2, Q — R 6 wins.

24. ......   Q — Kt 5 ch
25. K — B 1

Mate follows after 25. K — R 1, Q — B 6 ch; 26. K — Kt 1, R — Kt 4 ch, etc.

25. ......   Q — R 6 ch
26. K — K 2   R × B ch !
27. P × R   Q × K P ch
28. K — Q 1   Q × R(K8)ch
29. K — B 2   Q — K 5 ch
30. K — Kt 3 ?

White's game is clearly lost, but this and the next two moves shorten the agony; more resistance would have been offered by 30. K — B 1 when Black does best to play simply 30. ....P — K R 3, for if 31. R × P, Q — B 5 ch; 32. R — Q 2, R — Q 1 and wins; whilst after 31. Q — B 7, R — K 8 ch; 32. R — Q 1, Q — B 5 ch; 33. K — B 2, Q — K 5 ch; 34. K — B 1, R × R ch; 35. K × R, Q — Kt 8 ch he loses two more Pawns.

30. ......   Q — B 3
31. P — Q R 4

Desperation; however, if he wished to continue he should have played 31. P — B 4 to prevent Black's advance of the Q Pawn.

31. ......   P — Q 4 !
32. P — R 5

Leads to a mating finish. A more prolonged fight could have been put up by 32. R — K B 2, P — B 3; 33. R — Kt 2, P — Kt 3.

32. ......   Q — Kt 4 ch
33. K — R 3

Or 33. K — B 2, Q — R 5 ch; 34. P — Kt 3, Q — R 7 ch; 35. K — Q 3, Q — Kt 8 ch; 36. R — B 2, Q — B 8 ch; 37. K — Q 2, R — K 7 ch; 38. K — Q 3, Q — B 6 mate.

33. ......   R — Kt 1
34. K — R 2   P — R 3

This move is necessary, for in order to give mate Black must be able to move his Rook off the back rank without being troubled by snap mates from the White Queen.

35. P — R 6   Q — Kt 6 ch

Resigns, as he is mated after 36. K — Kt 1, R — K 1; 37. R — Q B 2, R — K 8 ch; 38. R — B 1, R — K 7; 39. Q — Kt 7, R × P ch, etc.

16
SEVENTH ROUND,
ST. PETERSBURG, 1914

Queen's Gambit Declined

White	Black
CAPABLANCA	O. BERNSTEIN
1. P — Q 4	P — Q 4
2. Kt — K B 3	Kt — K B 3
3. P — B 4	P — K 3
4. Kt — B 3	Q Kt — Q 2
5. B — Kt 5	B — K 2
6. P — K 3	P — B 3

Dr. Bernstein had worked out a method of defence commencing with this move that is very much akin to what was later known as the Meran Defence. It consists of an early and violent counterattack on the Q wing and also resembles the Meran in being equally unreliable and positionally unsound.

Best is the normal 6. ....Castles.

7. B — Q 3

White rightly refuses to allow Black's departure from the normal to interfere with his natural plan of development. More self-conscious attempts to defeat Black's system only recoil on White's head; e.g. 7. Q — B 2, Kt — K 5; 8. B × B, Q × B; 9. Kt × Kt, P × Kt; 10. Q × P, Q — Kt 5 ch; 11. Kt — Q 2, Q × Kt P; 12. Q — Kt 1, Q — B 6; 13. Q — B 1, Q — R 4; 14. P — B 5 ? (White should have contented himself with equality by 14. B — Q 3); 14. ....P — K 4 and Black has the better game (Reshevsky–Tylor, Nottingham, 1936).

7. ......   P × P
8. B × B P   P — Kt 4

Not altogether satisfactory for Black is the freeing manœuvre 8. ....Kt — Q 4; 9. B × B, Q × B; 10. Q — B 2, Kt × Kt; 11. Q × Kt, Castles; 12. Castles K, P — Q Kt 3; 13. Q — Q 3, R — Q 1; 14. Q — K 2, P — Q B 4; 15. Q R — Q 1, B — Kt 2; 16. B — R 6 and after the inevitable exchange of Bishops Black will suffer from a weakness on the white squares (Samisch–Selesnieff, Pistyan, 1922).

| 9. B — Q 3 | P — Q R 3 |
| 10. P — K 4 | P — K 4 ? |

This temporary sacrifice of a Pawn is strategically wrong. It dangerously loosens Black's position and also means loss of time for White calmly proceeds with his development, whilst Black has to devote many moves to regain the Pawn. The chief penalty Black pays is the unhappy position of his uncastled King as contrasted with the White King safely tucked away on the flank.

Instead of running such deadly risks, Black should play 10. . . . . P — B 4.

11. P × P	Kt — Kt 5
12. B — K B 4	B — B 4
13. Castles	Q — B 2

And not 17. . . . . Q — K 2; 18. P — K 6, P × P (18. . . . . Q × P ?; 19. Kt — Kt 5 wins a piece); 19. P — K 5 ! with a positionally won game for White.

14. R — B 1

At first glance, merely a routine move placing the Rook opposite the opposing Queen, but in reality White is already preparing a magnificent combination of which this move is a vital part.

| 14. . . . . . . | P — B 3 |

If 14. . . . . K Kt × P; 15. Kt × Kt, Kt × Kt; 16. Kt — Q 5, P × Kt; 17. P — Q Kt 4 and wins, for if 17. . . . . B × P ch; 18. R × B, Q — Q 3; 19. Q — R 5 wins a piece.

| 15. B — Kt 3 | P × P |

Black has now regained his Pawn, but at great cost in development.

Position after Black's 15th move

16. P — Kt 4 !

The fact that this Pawn offer cannot be accepted means that the Black Bishop will have to retreat and abandon one diagonal or the other. We shall meet this diversionary Pawn sacrifice again and again in Capablanca's games; cf. Game No. 78 from his match against Euwe.

| 16. . . . . . . | B — R 2 |

For if 16. . . . . B × P; 17. Kt — Q 5, Q — Q 3; 18. Kt × B, Q × Kt; 19. R × P Castles; 20. B — B 2 and White threatens either B —Kt 3 ch followed by Kt — Kt 5 or Q — Q 5 ch winning material.

The Bishop has to retreat along the R 2 diagonal since 16. . . . . B —Q 3; 17. B × Kt P, R P × B; 18. Kt Kt P wins two Pawns and

16. . . . . B — K 2 fails against 17.
Kt — Q 5.

Now, however, with the Bishop
forced away from the K side
White lets loose the full blast of
his attack.

17. B × Kt P !   R P × B
18. Kt × Kt P   Q — Q 1
19. Kt — Q 6 ch   K — B 1
20. R × P

Threatening Kt × B followed
by Q — Q 6 ch and Q — K 6 ch.

20. . . . . . .   Kt — Kt 3

Not 20. . . . . Q Kt — B 3 ; 21.
Kt × B winning a piece.

21. B — R 4 !

Very subtly played; White is
about to force Black to accept the
exchange in order to drive his
King into the open.

The simple 21. Kt × P would
give White more than enough material for his sacrificed piece and
should prove sufficient to win but
would be neither so conclusive or
elegant.

21. . . . . . .   Q — Q 2
22. Kt × B   Q × R

Forced; if 22. . . . . Q × Q; 23.
R × Q, R × Kt; 24. R × R ch,
Kt × R; 25. R — Q 8 ch, etc.

23. Q — Q 8 ch   Q — K 1

If 23. . . . . K — B 2; 24. Kt —
Q 6 ch followed by mate.

24. B — K 7 ch   K — B 2
25. Kt — Q 6 ch   K   Kt 0
26. Kt — R 4 ch   K — R 4

Black is mated after 26. . . . . K
— R 3; 27. Kt (Q 6) — B 5 ch,

K — R 4; 28. Kt × P ch, K —
R 3; 29. Kt (R 4) — B 5 ch, K —
Kt 3; 30. Q — Q 6 ch. etc.

27. Kt × Q   R × Q
28. Kt × P ch   K — R 3
29. Kt (Kt 7)—B 5ch   K — R 4

Position after 29. . . . . K — R 4

30. P — K R 3 !

A beautifully quiet but deadly
move which forms a fitting climax
to the combination initiated on
White's 16th move. The threat of
31. P × Kt ch, K × P; 32. P —
B 3 ch, K — R 4; 33. P — Kt 4
mate compels Black to return the
Rook after which White is three
Pawns to the good in addition to
his attack.

30. . . . . . .   Kt — B 1

The only way of averting mate.

31. P × Kt ch   K × P
32. B × R   R × B
33. P — Kt 3

This move shows that White has
another mating net in mind. The
two knights working in combination with each other and the Pawns

will wear a ring around the King until the White Rook can be worked to the 7th rank to administer the *coup de grâce.*

Meanwhile Black's pieces must be employed in staving off the advance of the passed Q side Pawns.

33.	R — Q 7
34. K — Kt 2	R — K 7
35. P — R 4	Kt — Kt 3
36. Kt — K 3 ch	K — R 4
37. P — R 5	Kt — Q 2
38. Kt(R 4)—B 5	Kt — B 3
39. P — Kt 5	B — Q 5
40. K — B 3	R — R 7
41. P — R 6	B — R 2
42. R — B 1	R — Kt 7
43. P — Kt 4 ch	K — Kt 4
44. R — B 7	R × P ch
45. K × R	Kt×Kt Pch
46. K — B 3	Resigns

With this game, Capablanca won a well deserved 1st brilliancy prize. Bernstein seems to have been able to provide the exactly right type of opposition in order to bring out the most artistic elements of Capablanca's style.

17

ELEVENTH ROUND, ST. PETERSBURG, 1914

Ruy Lopez, Bird's Defence

White	Black
CAPABLANCA	J. H. BLACKBURNE
1. P — K 4	P — K 4
2. Kt — K B 3	Kt — Q B 3
3. B — Kt 5	Kt — Q 5

This defence cannot be recommended; it loses a move without any compensation in position. Blackburne employed it three times in this tournament, losing twice and drawing once.

4. Kt × Kt	P × Kt
5. Castles	P — K Kt 3

The logical method to get the most out of the Pawn at Q 5 by using it as a spearhead for the attack by the Bishop on the long diagonal.

6. P — Q 3	B — Kt 2
7. Kt — Q 2	

In the 4th round Tarrasch against the same player continued (after a transposition of moves) 7. P — Q B 3, Kt — K 2; 8. P × P, B × P; 9. Kt — B 3, P — Q B 3; 10. B — Q B 4, P — Q 3; 11. B — K 3, B — Kt 2; 12. Q — B 3, Castles; 13. B — Kt 3, K — R 1; 14. Q — Kt 3, B — Kt 3; 15. B × B, P × B; 16. Q — R 3 with the better game for White.

With the text move Capablanca plans a different type of game consisting of the advance of the K side Pawns supported by the Kt on B 3 to attack Black's K side.

7.	Kt — K 2
8. P — K B 4	P — Q B 3

With this Black inaugurates a spirited attempt at counter-attack on the Q wing.

9. B — B 4	P — Q 4
10. B — Kt 3	Castles
11. Kt — B 3	P — Q B 4

11. ....P × P; 12. P × P, B — Kt 5, though less ambitious,

would have given him a safer game.

12. P — K 5   P — Q Kt 4
13. P — B 3   P — B 5
14. B — B 2

Now White cannot be prevented from establishing a Pawn on Q 4; this in turn will secure his position in the centre, thereby permitting him to devote his attention to a K side advance.

14. ......   P × Q B P
15. Kt. P × P   Q — R 4

An abortive attack which wastes a move. Black may have feared 16. B — R 3 and played the Q to R 4 to prevent this, but he should have stuck to his original plan and played 15. ....P — Q R 4; if then 16. B — R 3, R — K 1; 17. P — Q 4, Kt — B 3 with the threat of P — Kt 5 at least gives Black counterplay. The negative policy of passive defence he now pursues can only lead to disaster.

16. B — Q 2   B — Kt 5
17. P — Q 4   Q — Kt 3

Threatening 18. ....P — Kt 5 and if 19. P × P, B × Kt followed by Q × P ch.

18. R — Kt 1

Providing against the above threat and by menacing in turn P — Q R 4 forcing Black to take further defensive measures.

18. ......   P — Q R 3
19. P — K R 3   B — B 4

Best; 19. ....B × Kt; 20. Q × B would give White a still more crushing game because of his two Bishops and also on account of his attack on Black's weak Q Pawn.

20. P — Kt 4   B × B
21. Q × B   P — B 4

Black cannot permit P — B 5.

22. K — R 2

White prepares for the final assault on the K side; the major pieces are to be brought into action.

22. ......   Kt — B 3

Hoping to be able to play Kt — Q 1 — K 3, but there is no time for this and White can now destroy Black's K side.

In any case it must be remarked that Black is positionally lost; after the best defensive move 22. ....K — R 1 White will proceed with 23. R — Kt 1 followed by B — K 3, Q — K B 2, Q — K R 4 and Kt — Kt 5, and against this attack there appears no adequate defence.

23. R — Kt 1   Kt — Q 1
24. P × P   R × P
25. Kt — R 4   R — R 4

Position after 25. ....R — R 4

26. Kt × P !   P × Kt

Unfortunately, he cannot play 26. ....Q — K 3 because of 27. P — B 5 and if 27. ....R × P ; 28. Q × R.

27. R × K Kt P   Q — Kt 1

After this White removes the last piece on the K side that serves a true defensive purpose. The best defence was 27. ....Q — B 2, though Black is still lost after 28. Q R — Kt 1, R — R 2; 29. P — B 5, Q — Q 2; 30. B — Kt 5, and

now if 30. ....K — R 1; 31. R × B wins, whilst if 30. ....K — B 1; 31. R — Q 6, Q — Q B 2; 32. B × Kt, R × B; 33. R × R ch, Q × R; 34. P — B 6, etc.

28. R × B ch !   K × R
29. R — Kt 1 ch   K — B 1
30. Q — Kt 6   R × P ch
31. K × R   Resigns

Black's King cannot be defended; e.g. 31. ....Q — B 1 ch; 32. P — B 5, Kt — B 2; 33. P — K 6, etc.

CHAPTER THREE

On the Way to the World Championship— The Match with Lasker

THE first part of Capablanca's play in this period was concentrated in New York against not quite so formidable opposition as that encountered in Europe. The natural progress towards the world's championship was temporarily barred by the war, and Capablanca's chief rivals were Janowski and Marshall. Victories over other American players were facile and over easy to achieve, but these two provided sturdy opposition, productive of excellent games. The student is recommended to study carefully the scientific exploitation of positional advantage that is to be seen in his game against Janowski at the Rice Memorial Tournament and there is an especially neat and elegant game against the Polish master at New York, 1918. Marshall was extremely formidable to Capablanca round about this period and, in fact, beat him in our tournament in New York — an extremely rare event. But the *pièce de résistance* of this phase of Capablanca's career is his wonderful victory over the American master in the first round of the 1918 New York tournament. Marshall had prepared an intensely complicated variation of the Ruy Lopez yielding a most venomous and lasting attack. Capablanca, realising all this, accepted the challenge and won a great dramatic victory by a reliance on the first pure principles of the art of chess. The reader will forgive this rather ecstatic description of the game when he plays it through himself, for it is indeed a masterpiece.

His match against Kostich was disappointingly dull; after the first particularly tough and hard-fought struggle, the Serbian master lost heart and the quality of the games suffered as a result. Almost equal disappointment must be felt about the world championship match against Lasker. The latter was obviously out of form during most of the encounter and consequently, apart from the two games given here, the match was sadly lacking in the great achievements that one would expect from the contest between two of the greatest players of all time.

NEW YORK, 1914

	Capablanca	Duras	Black	Chajes	Kupchik	Marder	Tenenwurzel	Adair	Bernstein	Beynon	Phillips	Grommer	
1 Capablanca	—	1	1	1	1	1	1	1	1	1	1	1	11
2 Duras	0	—	1	1	1	½	1	½	1	1	½	1	8½
3 Black	0	0	—	1	½	½	1	1	1	1	1	1	8
4 Chajes	0	0	0	—	1	1	1	0	1	1	1	1	7
5 Kupchik	0	0	½	0	—	1	1	1	1	1	½	1	7
6 Marder	0	½	½	0	0	—	1	1	½	1	1	1	6½
7 Tenenwurzel	0	0	0	0	0	0	—	1	1	1	1	½	4½
8 Adair	0	½	0	1	0	0	0	—	½	½	½	1	4
9 Bernstein, J.	0	0	0	0	0	½	0	½	—	1	1	1	4
10 Beynon	0	0	0	0	0	0	0	½	0	—	½	1	2
11 Phillips	0	½	0	0	½	0	0	½	0	½	—	0	2
12 Grommer	0	0	0	0	0	0	½	0	0	0	1	—	1½

NEW YORK, 1915

	Capablanca	Marshall	Chajes	Kupchik	Bernstein	Lasker	Hodges	Michelsen	
1 Capablanca	—	½ ½	1 1	1 1	1 1	1 1	1 1	1 1	13
2 Marshall	½ ½	—	1 ½	1 1	1 1	½ 1	1 1	1 1	12
3 Chajes	0 0	0 ½	—	0 1	1 0	½ 0	1 1	1 1	7
4 Kupchik	0 0	0 0	1 0	—	1 0	0 1	1 1	1 1	7
5 Bernstein, J.	0 0	0 0	0 1	0 1	—	½ ½	1 1	1 ½	6½
6 Lasker, Ed.	0 0	½ 0	½ 1	1 0	½ ½	—	½ ½	½ 1	6½
7 Hodges	0 0	0 0	0 0	0 0	0 0	½ ½	—	0 1	2
8 Michelsen	0 0	0 0	0 0	0 0	0 ½	½ 0	1 0	—	2

NEW YORK, 1916
Preliminary Tournament

		Capablanca	Janowski	Kostich	Kupchik	Chajes	Rosenthal	Bernstein	Fox	Schroeder	Black	Hodges	Tenenwurzel	Perkins	Banks	
1	Capablanca	–	1	½	1	1	½	1	1	1	1	1	1	1	1	12
2	Janowski	0	–	1	0	½	1	½	½	1	1	1	1	½	½	8½
3	Kostich	½	0	–	1	½	1	0	0	1	½	1	1	1	1	8½
4	Kupchik	0	1	0	–	0	1	1	0	1	½	1	1	1	1	8½
5	Chajes	0	½	½	1	–	½	½	1	0	1	0	1	1	1	8
6	Rosenthal	½	0	0	0	½	–	½	1	1	1	1	½	½	1	7½
7	Bernstein, J.	0	½	1	0	½	½	–	0	½	½	1	1	1	½	7
8	Fox	0	½	1	1	0	0	1	–	0	1	½	1	0	1	7
9	Schroeder	0	0	0	0	1	0	½	1	–	1	0	½	1	½	5½
10	Black	0	0	½	½	0	0	½	0	0	–	½	1	1	1	5
11	Hodges	0	0	0	0	1	0	0	½	1	½	–	0	1	1	5
12	Tenenwurzel	0	0	0	0	0	½	0	0	½	0	1	–	½	1	3½
13	Perkins	0	½	0	0	0	½	0	1	0	0	0	½	–	½	3
14	Banks	0	½	0	0	0	0	½	0	½	0	0	0	½	–	2

NEW YORK, 1916
Final Tournament

		Capablanca	Janowski	Chajes	Kostich	Kupchik		Final Total
1	Capablanca	–	1	0	½	½	12	14
2	Janowski	0	–	1	½	1	8½	11
3	Chajes	1	0	–	1	½	8	10½
4	Kostich	½	½	0	–	½	8½	10
5	Kupchik	½	0	½	½	–	8½	10

NEW YORK, 1918

		Capablanca	Kostich	Marshall	Chajes	Janowski	Black	Morrison	
1	Capablanca	–	½ ½	1 1	1 1	1 1	½ 1	1 1	10½
2	Kostich	½ ½	–	½ 1	½ 1	½ 1	½ 1	1 1	9
3	Marshall	0 0	½ 0	–	0 1	1 ½	1 1	1 1	7
4	Chajes	0 0	½ 0	1 0	–	0 1	1 1	1 ½	6
5	Janowski	0 0	½ 0	0 ½	1 0	–	1 0	0 1	4
6	Black	½ 0	½ 0	0 0	0 0	0 1	–	½ 1	3½
7	Morrison	0 0	0 0	0 0	0 ½	1 0	½ 0	–	2

HASTINGS, 1919

	Capablanca	Kostich	Thomas	Yates	Michell	Wahltuch	Olland	Scott	Marchand	Conde	Winter	Cole	
1 Capablanca ..	-	½	1	1	1	1	1	1	1	1	1	1	10½
2 Kostich	½	-	½	1	1	½	1	1	1	1	1	1	9½
3 Sir G. Thomas ..	0	½	-	½	½	½	½	1	1	½	1	1	7
4 Yates	0	0	½	-	1	½	1	1	1	1	0	1	7
5 Michell	0	0	½	0	-	0	1	0	1	1	1	1	5½
6 Wahltuch	0	½	½	½	1	-	0	1	0	0	1	1	5½
7 Olland	0	0	½	0	0	1	-	0	0	1	1	1	4½
8 Scott	0	0	0	0	1	0	1	-	1	1	0	½	4½
9 Marchand	0	0	0	0	0	1	1	0	-	0	1	1	4
10 Conde	0	0	½	0	0	1	0	0	1	-	0	1	3½
11 Winter	0	0	0	1	0	0	0	1	0	1	-	0	3
12 Cole	0	0	0	0	0	0	0	½	0	0	1	-	1½

18
NEW YORK, 1915
Ruy Lopez, Morphy Defence

White	Black
CAPABLANCA	A. KUPCHIK

1.	P — K 4	P — K 4
2.	K — K B 3	Kt — Q B 3
3.	B — Kt 5	P — Q R 3
4.	B — R 4	Kt — B 3
5.	Castles	B — K 2
6.	R — K 1	P — Q Kt 4
7.	B — Kt 3	P — Q 3
8.	P — B 3	Kt — Q R 4
9.	B — B 2	P — B 4
10.	P — Q 4	Q — B 2
11.	P — K R 3	

So far both players have proceeded along the well-known and well-worn paths of the orthodox defence to the Ruy Lopez. The normal line for Black now is 11. ....Castles; 12. Q Kt — Q 2, Kt — B 3; 13. P — Q 5, Kt — Q 1; with a solid position on the K side

and hopes for counterplay on the other wing.

11.	......	Kt — B 3
12.	B — K 3	Castles

The drawback to Black's line is that it is not a true transposition of moves, since in the interim White has been able to develop his Q Bishop. For after 11. ....Castles 12. B — K 3 would not be good on account of 12. ....Kt — B 5.

13.	Q Kt — Q 2	R — Q 1

Not a happy manœuvre; Black hopes to maintain the *status quo* in the centre whilst proceeding with a Q side counter-attack under the impression that his K side can be adequately guarded by the two minor pieces. White's subsequent fine play shows that this is all ill founded. The K Rook is needed for the King's defence and on Q 1 it prevents the Kt from retreating to its best square when attacked by White's Q Pawn.

Black's best plan appears to be immediate counter-attack by 13. .... P — Kt 5, for that the normal developing move of 13. .... B — Q 2 is not good enough was demonstrated in the game L. Steiner–Asgtalos, Maribor, 1934, which continued 14. R — Q B 1, K R — B 1; 15. Kt — B 1, Kt — Q R 4; 16. K Kt — Q 2, B — K 1; 17. Kt — K Kt 3, Kt — Q 2; 18. Kt — B 5, B — B 1; 19. Q — Kt 4 with marked advantage to White.

14. R — B 1	B — Q 2
15. Kt — B 1	P — Kt 5
16. P — Q 5	Kt — R 2

This is the weak point in Black's game; the Kt, now, and for the whole length of the game, not only serves no useful purpose, but is actually an encumbrance to the other Black pieces.

17. P — B 4	Kt — B 1
18. P — Kt 4	Kt — Kt 3
19. P — Kt 3	P — Q R 4

Both sides are proceeding along thematic lines. White will develop a massive K side attack whilst Black will hope for counterattack on the Q R file.

20. Kt — Kt 3	P — Kt 3
21. K — R 2	P — R 5
22. R — K Kt 1	P × P
23. P × P	B — K B 1

Necessary, since White was threatening 24. B — R 6 followed by 25. Kt — B 5.

24. Q — Q 2	R — R 7
25. B — Kt 5	B — Kt 2
26. Q — K 3	

White must unpin his K Bishop as otherwise Black can play 26. .... Kt — R 5 and if 27. P × Kt, P — Kt 6; when the resulting opening up of the Q side would be to Black's advantage!

26.	K R — R 1
27. B — Kt 1	R (R 7) — R 6
28. Kt — K 1	

This Kt is destined for Q B 2 where it will completely nullify Black's hard-earned mastery of the Q R file.

28.	K — R 1

28. .... Kt R 5 would lose the exchange after 29. Kt — B 2 and 28. .... B R 5; 29. B — B 2 merely loses a tempo, since the Bishop will eventually have to retreat because of the unsoundness of 29. .... Kt × B P; 30. Q — K 2 and Black loses a piece.

Black therefore determines to dig himself in on the K side and defy White's assault.

Immediate disaster would result after 28. .... P — R 3; 29. B × P, B × B; 30. Q × B, R × P; 31. Kt — B 5, Kt — K 1; 32. Kt — K 7 mate.

29. Q — Q 3	Kt — Kt 1
30. Kt — B 2	R (R 6 — R2
31. Q R — B1	B — K 1
32. B — K 3	Kt — Q 2
33. Kt — K 1	Q — Q 1
34. P — Kt 5 !	

A powerful move which is the prelude to the final assault. Black can do nothing much to better his position, but must wait to see what form this assault will take.

34.	. . . . . .	Q — R 4
35.	P — R 4	Q — Q 1
36.	P — R 5	Q — K 2
37.	Kt — B 3	Kt — Kt 3
38.	R — R 1	Q — Q 2
39.	K — Kt 2	Kt — K 2
40.	P × P	P × P
41.	R — R 3	B — B 2
42.	Q R — R 1	B — Kt 1

Position after 42. . . . . B — Kt 1

43. Kt — B 5 !   R — K B 1

If 43. . . . . P × Kt; 44. P × P, B — B 1; 45. P — Kt 6 winning easily.

44. Kt × B   K × Kt
45. Q — K 2   Resigns

Black is quite helpless against the many threats on his King, the chief of which is the manœuvre Kt — R 2 — Kt 4 — B 6.

19
NEW YORK, 1915

Ruy Lopez, Morphy Defence

White	Black
CAPABLANCA	O. CHAJES
1. P — K 4	P — K 4
2. Kt — K B 3	Kt — Q B 3

3.	B — Kt 5	P — Q R 3
4.	B — R 4	Kt — B 3
5.	Castles	Kt × P

The open variation of this defence which lacks the solidity that belongs to the close line that results after 5. . . . . B — K 2, but which has as compensation more active play for the Black minor pieces.

The chief strategical problem arising in this open line is the question of the control of Black's Q B 4; if White can seize this he has a strategically won game, as is demonstrated by the course of the present encounter.

6.	P — Q 4	P — Q Kt 4
7.	B — Kt 3	P — Q 4
8.	P × P	B — K 3
9.	P — B 3	B — K 2
10.	Q Kt — Q 2	Kt — B 4

The defect of this move is that when Black endeavors to obtain a counter-attack by P — Q 5 the King will be left dangerously exposed in the centre; so 10. . . . . Castles is much to be preferred.

11. B — B 2   P — Q 5

Black's position becomes too loose and weak on the White squares after 11. . . . . B — Kt 5; 12. R — K 1, Castles; 13. Kt — Kt 3, Kt — K 5; 14. B — B 4, P — B 4; 15. P × P e.p., Kt × P (B 3); 16. Q — Q 3 (Alekhine-Nimzovitch, St. Petersburg, 1914).

12. Kt — K 4 !

This strong move eventually allows White to place his Bishop on K 4 whence it exerts a crippling effect on Black's Q wing.

12. ......   P × P,

This exchange is forced, since White threatens to win the Q Pawn by Kt × Kt followed by B — K 4. An interesting analysis by Tarrasch shows that Black cannot preserve the *status quo* by 12. .... Q — Q 4; 13. Kt × Kt, B × Kt; 14. B × Kt 3, Q — Q 2; 15. B × B, P × B; 16. P × P, Kt × Q P; 17. B — K 3, R — Q 1; 18. R — B 1, Kt × Kt ch; 19. Q × Kt, B × B; 20. P × B and the position is hopeless for the second player.

13. Kt × Kt   B × Kt

The apparent win of a Pawn by 13. .... Q × Q; 14. R × Q, P × P leads to the loss of a piece after 15. B × Kt P, B × Kt; 16. B — K 4, B — Q 2; 17. Q R — B 1.

14. B — K 4   Q — Q 2

And not 14. .... B — Q 2; 15. Q — Q 5, B — K 2; 16. P — K 6, P × P; 17. Q — R 5 ch, K — B 1; 18. Kt — K 5 winning the exchange.

15. P × P

So far the game has gone exactly according to an analysis Capablanca had made and published a few months previously. Chajes had studied this and decided that the position was, contrary to Capablanca's opinion, better for Black. His decision, however, was completely erroneous, as is shown by the present game.

15. ......   R — Q 1
16. Q × Q ch   B × Q
17. R — Q 1   Kt — K 2

Position after 17. .... Kt — K 2

It is interesting to observe that Black still cannot Castle his King into safety, for if 17. .... Castles; 18. B — K 3, B × B; 19. R × B, R × R; 20. B × Kt and White wins two pieces for the Rook.

No better is the retreat with the Kt — Kt 1 as in a game Capablanca–Hodges from the same tournament, which continued 17. .... Kt — Kt 1; 18. Kt — Q 4, B — K 2; 19. B — K 3 and White controls the centre.

18. Kt — Q 4   P — R 3 ?

Losing a vital move owing to a shallow appreciation of the position. Black thinks it imperative to prevent the pinning of the Kt by White's B — K Kt 5, but does not realise White's Bishop will be more effective still when placed on the other wing. 18. .... Castles is still disastrous for Black after 19. Kt — Kt 3, B — Kt 3 (if 19. .... B — B 4; 20. R × R, R × R;

21. B — Kt 5 and wins) ; 20. B — R 3, K R — K 1 ; 21. B × Kt, R × B ; 22. B — B 6, K — B 1 ; 23. R — Q 3, K — Q 1 ; 24. Q R — Q 1 and White wins by playing his Kt to K Kt 3 via B 1 and K 2. This forces an eventual P — K Kt 3, whereupon the Kt goes to K 4 and K B 6.

Capablanca suggests 18. .... B — K Kt 5 as the best resource, but after 19. R — Q 3 Black is again without a resonably good continuation. If, for example, 19. ....Castles then 20. B — Kt 5, K R — K 1; 21. R — Kt 3, B — Q 2 (not 21. ....B — R 4; 22. Kt — B 6!); 22. B — K B 6, P — Kt 3; 23. R — Q 1 followed by 24. P — K R 3 and 25. K R — Q 3.

   19. Kt — Kt 3   B — Kt 3
   20. B — R 3.

Obtaining lasting control of the square Q B 5; it is instructive to note how this cripples Black's game.

   20. ......   P — K R 4

Since he cannot Castle, he must try and develop his K R via K R 3.

21. R — Q 3	B — Kt 5
22. R × R ch	K × R
23. Kt — B 5	R — R 3
24. P — K R 3	B — B 1
25. R — Q 1 ch	K — K 1
26. K — B 1	P — Kt 4

To prevent White from gaining further ground in the centre by P — K B 4, but this advance radically weakens the K side Pawn structure.

27. Kt — Q 3   P — K B 4

White was threatening to win a Pawn by B — B 1; Black can now only try to delay the end; his position crumbles to pieces.

28. P × P e.p.	R × P
29. R — K 1	B — K 3

The marked attack on the K file must be staved off; if 29. .... R — K 3; 30. B — Kt 6 ch, R × B; 31. R × Kt ch, K — Q 1; 32. Kt — K 5, etc.

   30. B — B 3   R — R 3

A Pawn is lost however Black plays; if 30. ....P — R 5; 31. B — B 1; or 30. ....P — K Kt 5; 31. P × P, P × P; 32. B × P, B × B; 33. R × Kt ch, K — Q 1; 34. R — Kt 7 winning a piece.

31. B × P ch	K — Q 2
32. B — K Kt 4	Kt — B 3
33. R × B	R × R
34. B — B 1	

Winning the last Pawn on the K side, after which Black could resign with an easy conscience. The rest of the game needs no comment.

34.	K — Q 3
35. B × R	K × B
36. B × P	B — R 4
37. B — Q 2	K — Q 4
38. P — K R 4	Kt — K 4
39. Kt × Kt	K × Kt
40. P — R 5	P — B 4
41. P — Kt 4	K — B 3
42. K — K 2	P — B 5
43. P — B 4	K — B 2
44. K — B 3	B — Q 1
45. K — K 4	P — R 4
46. K — Q 5	B — K 2

| 47. P — Kt 5 | K — Kt 1 |
| 48. P — B 5 | Resigns |

20

RICE MEMORIAL TOURNA–
MENT, NEW YORK, 1916

Queen's Gambit Declined
Orthodox Defence

White	Black
CAPABLANCA	A. SCHROEDER
1. P — Q 4	P — Q 4
2. Kt — K B 3	P — K 3
3. P — B 4	Kt — K B 3
4. Kt — B 3	Q Kt — Q 2
5. B — Kt 5	B — K 2
6. P — K 3	Castles
7. R — B 1	P — Q R 3

Not so good as the normal move in the Orthodox defence, 7. ....
P — B 3. It attempts to solve the problem of the development of the Q Bishop by an eventual P — Q Kt 4 and B — Kt 2. But it creates a ragged Pawn structure on the Q side which is easily assailable by White.

| 8. Q — B 2 | |

Good enough, and better than the over-aggressive 8. P — B 5 or the too tame 8. P — Q R 3 which Capablanca used so often without much success in the world championship match against Alekhine. But best of all is 8. P × P as he played in Game No. 51 against Mieses at Bad Kissingen.

8.	R — K 1
9. B — Q 3	P × P
10. B × P	P — Kt 4
11. B — Q 3	B — Kt 2
12. P — Q R 4	

Forcing Black to advance the Q Kt Pawn and so preventing him from playing P — Q B 4 — Q B 5, as Schroeder did in a previous round against Perkins. For the next few moves White concentrates on trying to avert P — Q B 4 by Black. Schroeder eventually achieves this, but only at the cost of creating weaknesses elsewhere.

| 12. ...... | P — Kt 5 |
| 13. B × Kt | |

A clever finesse, as a result of which Black is unable to post a Kt on K B 1 and so render his K side safe.

| 13. ...... | Kt × B |
| 14. Kt — K 4 | Kt × Kt |

Forced, otherwise White plays Kt — B 5 with a strategically won game.

| 15. B × Kt | B × B |

After which White's Queen has a dominating position in the centre; but if 15. ....P — Kt 6; 16. B × P ch, K — R 1; 17. Q — Q 3, P — Kt 3; 18. B × P, P × B; 19. Q × Kt P with a crushing attack.

| 16. Q × B | P — Q B 4 |

Best, since White threatens 17. Q — B 6 with great pressure on the Q side.

17. P × P	Q — R 4
18. P — Q Kt 3	B × P
19. Kt — Kt 5	P — R 3

Permitting the ensuing winning combination; yet Black is curiously helpless. If he plays 19. ....P — Kt 3, then 20. Q — B 3 wins. For 20. ....R — R 2 and 20. ....P — K B 4 fail against 21. Q — B 6 and 21. Kt × K P respectively; whilst if 20. ....R — K B 1; 21. Q — R 3, P — R 4; 22. Kt × K P, P × Kt; 23. Q × P ch, K — R 2 (if 23. ....K — Kt 2; 24. Q — K 5 ch or 23. ....R — B 2; 24. Q × P ch, R — Kt 2; 25. Q — Q B 6); 24. Q — Q 7 ch, K — R 1; 25. Q — B 6, Q R — B 1; 26. Q × Kt P, B — Kt 3; 27. R × R, R × R; 28. Q — R 6 ch, K — Kt 1; 29. Q — K 6 ch, etc. Three are many subvariations in this line, but all lead to a loss for Black.

Position after 19. ....P — R 3

20. Q — R 7 ch   K — B 1
21. Q — R 8 ch

A far-sighted sacrifice of the Kt for two Pawns and the initiative. Not so decisive is 21. Kt — K 4, B — Kt 3; 22. Q — R 8 ch, K — K 2; 23. Q × Kt P, Q — K B 4; 24. Kt — Kt 3, Q — Q 6 when although White has won a Pawn he

is forced on the defensive with 25. Q — Kt 2.

Capablanca points out that the beauty of the combination resides in the prevision that Black will be unable to stem the advance of White's passed K R Pawn owing to the necessity for tying up his pieces in the defence of his King.

21.	K — K 2
22. Q × Kt P	P × Kt
23. Q × Kt P ch	K — Q 3
24. K — K 2	Q R — B 1
25. R — B 4	K — B 3

Black decides to play his King over to the Q side, where it is in comparative safety and will also act as support to the Queen. Other moves are still more disastrous, e.g. 25. ....B — Kt 3; 26. R — Q 1 ch.

26. K R — Q B 1   K — Kt 3
27 P — R 4

Now that all Black's pieces are occupied with defence, White advances this Pawn with decisive effect.

Position after 27. P — R 4

27. ......   P — B 4

This move leads to a disappointingly rapid finish. Capablanca had expected 27. ....R — B 2 when he had prepared the following intriguing variations: 28. P — R 5, K R — Q B 1; 29. P — R 6, B — Q 3; 30. Q × Q ch, K × Q; 31. R × R, R × R (if 31. ....B × R; 32. R — B 6 wins); 32. R × R, B × R; 33. P — B 4, B — Q 1; 34. P — Kt 4, B — B 3; 35. P — Kt 5, B — R 1; 36. P — K 4, K — Kt 3; 37. P — B 5, P × P; 38. P × P, K — B 4; 39. P — Kt 6, P × P; 40. P × P, etc.

28. Q — Kt 7   R — K 2
29. Q — K 5

Now Black is helpless against the advance of the K R Pawn.

29. ......   R — B 3

This loses offhand, but he has no good continuation.

30. R × B   Resigns

21
RICE MEMORIAL TOURNAMENT, NEW YORK, 1916

Queen's Gambit Declined, Slav Defence

White	Black
CAPABLANCA	D. JANOWSKI
1. P — Q 4	Kt — K B 3
2. Kt — K B 3	P — Q 4
3. P — B 4	P — B 3
4. Kt — B 3	B — B 4

This early development of the Bishop should lead to a bad game for Black; better is 4. ....P × P.

5. Q — Kt 3

Not the best way of profiting from Black's premature Bishop move. The correct procedure was demonstrated in the game Torre-Gotthilf, Moscow, 1925, which continued 5. P × P, P × P (or 5. ....Kt × P; 6. Q — Kt 3, Q — Kt 3; 7. Kt × Kt, Q × Q; 8. Kt — B 7 ch, K — Q 2; 9. P × Q, Kt × Kt; 10. B — B 4 ch, etc.); 6. Q — Kt 3, Q — Kt 3; 7. Kt × P, Kt × Kt; 8. Q × Kt, P — K 3; 9. Q — Kt 3, Q × Q; 10. P × Q, B — B 7; 11. B — Q 2, B × P; 12. P — K 4, P — B 3; 13. B — B 3, B — B 7; 14. Kt — Q 2 and now Black's unfortunate Q Bishop is worse off than ever.

5. ......   Q — Kt 3
6. Q × Q

Hoping to gain advantage from doubling and isolating Black's Q side Pawns; but Black gains more than adequate compensation in the extra open lines for his Rooks. White could still play 6. P × P with variations similar to those given in the last note.

6.	P × Q
7. P × P	Kt × P
8. Kt × Kt	P × Kt
9. P — K 3	Kt — B 3
10. B — Q 2	B — Q 2 !

This retreat is really an attacking move; Black intends to play P — Q Kt 4, Kt — R 4 and Kt — B 5. The text move is necessary to

force the advance of the Q Kt
Pawn.

11. B — K 2

Janowski obviously does not
realise the true potentialities in
Black's position, but is under the
impression that the game is drift-
ing down to a tame draw. Had he
fathomed Black's intentions, he
would have prevented the manœuvre mentioned in the last note
by 11. B — Kt 5.

11. ......   P — K 3
12. Castles K

Another evil entailed in White's
11th move is that the King is deprived of its natural developing
square on K 2. In this type of
middle-end game the King is much
better placed in the centre than on
the wing.

12. ......   B — Q 3
13. K R — B 1   K — K 2
14. B — B 3   K R — Q B 1
15. P — Q R 3 ?

In his desire to free the Rook
from defence of the Q R Pawn,
White creates a hole on the Q side
and thereby intensifies the force
of Black's coming manœuvre.
Best was 15. Kt — Q 2 at once.

15. ......   Kt — R 4
16. Kt — Q 2   P — B 4 !

This game is a fine example of
positional strategy. White's only
counter to Black's activity on the
Q wing is an advance in the centre.
Black's last move at once delays

and modifies the strength of this
counter.

17. P — K Kt 3   P — Q Kt 4
18. P — B 3   Kt — B 5
19. B × Kt

He takes off with the Bishop in
order to play P — K 4 as soon as
possible.

19. ......   Kt P × B
20. P — K 4   K — B 2

In view of the threatened P —
K 5, Black's King vacates the
K B 1 diagonal for his Bishop so
as to avoid impeding the action of
his Rooks on the open file.

21. P — K 5   B — K 2
22. P — B 4   P — Q Kt 4

Black now develops the second
phase of his strategy, which consists of attack on both wings by
P — Q Kt 4 and P — K Kt 4. By
continually increasing pressure
along these two lines and improv-
ing the position of his pieces, he
aims at reaching a culminating
moment when White's game falls
like a ripe apple.

23. K — B 2   R — R 5
24. K — K 3   K R — Q R 1
Threatening P — Kt 5.

25. Q R — Kt1   P — R 3
26. Kt — B 3   P — Kt 4
27. Kt — K 1   R — K Kt 1
28. K — B 3   P × P
29. P × P   R (R S)—R1
30. Kt — Kt 2   R — Kt 5
31. R — Kt 1   Q R — K Kt 1
32. B — K 1

Position after 32. B — K 1

32. ......   P — Kt 5

A powerful temporary Pawn sacrifice which brings the Q Bishop into play.

33. P × P

Or 33. B × P, B × B; 34. P × B, P — R 4 and White is helpless against the further advance of this Pawn, 35. P — R 3 or R 4 failing against R — Kt 6 ch.

33. ......   B — R 5
34. R — Q R 1

This loses rapidly, since it allows the Bishop to reach K 5 via Q B 7. Necessary therefore was 34. R — Q B 1, when Black would have to proceed more gradually with 34. ....B — Kt 6 followed by the regrouping of his Rooks on to Q R 1 and Q Kt 1 with eventual invasion of the seventh rank via Q R 7.

34. ......   B — B 7
35. B — Kt 3

Forced, otherwise the Kt is lost.

35. ......   B — K 5 ch
36. K — B 2   P — R 4
37. R — R 7

Loses the exchange, but White is helpless against the threat of P — R 5.

37. ......   B × Kt
38. R × B   P — R 5
39. B × P   R × R ch
40. K — B 3   R × R P
41. B × B

If 41. R × B ch, K — B 1; 42. B — B 6, R (Kt 1) — R 1.

41. ......   R—R 6ch
42. K — B 2   R—Q Kt6
43. B — Kt5dis.ch K — Kt 3
44. R — K 7   R × P ch
45. K — B 3   R — Q R 1
46. R × P ch   K — R 2

Resigns, since R — R 6 ch cannot be parried.

22

FIRST ROUND, NEW YORK, 1918

Ruy Lopez, Morphy Defence

White	Black
CAPABLANCA	F. J. MARSHALL
1. P — K 4	P — K 4
2. Kt — K B 3	Kt — Q B 3
3. B — Kt 5	P — Q R 3
4. B — R 4	Kt — B 3
5. Castles	B — K 2
6. R— K 1	P — Q Kt 5
7. B — Kt 3	Castles

A variation from the normal 7. ....P — Q 3 followed by Kt —

Q R 4 and P — Q B 4; it soon appears that Marshall has something new up his sleeve.

8. P — B 3

Although suspecting that his opponent has a prepared variation in store, Capablanca refuses to depart from the normal line. 8. B — Q 5 in order to take advantage of Black's omission of P — Q 3 gets White nowhere after 8. ....Kt × B; 9. P × Kt, Kt — Kt 5; 10. Kt — B 3, B — Kt 2.

8. ......   P — Q 4

The Marshall variation, which sacrifices a Pawn in return for a very violent attack.

9. P × P   Kt × P

The position already contains exciting possibilities. Intriguing but not quite sound is 9. ....P — K 5; 10. P × Kt, P × Kt; 11. Q × P, B — K Kt 5; 12. Q — Kt 3, R — K 1; 13. P — K B 4 (13. P — B 3 fails against 13. ....Q — Q 6; 14. P × B, B — B 4 ch); 13. ....B — Q 3; 14. R — K 5! P — K R 4 (if 14. ....B × R; 15. P × B, Q — K 2; 16. P — Q 4! B — R 4; 17. B — Kt 5 and White wins); 15. P — Q 4, B × R; 16. B P × B, Kt — R 2; 17. P — K R 3, B — B 4; 18. B — R 6, P — Kt 3; 19. P — K 6 with a winning attack.

10. Kt × P

Accepting the Pawn and the complex consequences that ensue. If White declines the Pawn in order to complete his development by 10. P — Q 4, then after 10. ....P × P; 11. Kt × P, Kt × Kt; 12. Q × Kt, Kt — B 3; 13. Q × Q, B × Q the first player is left with nothing more than a draw.

10. ......   Kt × Kt
11. R × Kt   Kt — B 3

With the powerful threat of B — Q 3, followed by Kt — Kt 5. Now the purpose of the Pawn sacrifice becomes clear; Black, profiting from the temporary misplacement of White's Rook and the fact that White has had to expend moves in order to capture the Pawn, is able to complete his own development quickly and institute a violent K side attack.

12. R — K 1

It later becomes apparent that this Rook is better placed to defend the K side on K 2. Therefore White should have played first of all 12. P — Q 4 and then if 12. ....B — Q 3; 13. R — K 2.

12. ......   B — Q 3
13. P — K R 3   Kt — Kt 5

This offer cannot be accepted; for if 14. P × Kt, Q — R 5; 15. P — Kt 3, B × P (Kt 6); 16. P × B, Q × P ch; 17. K — B 1, B × P winning the Queen.

Now, however, White has to play very accurately indeed to avoid disaster. Tartakower suggests that a more lasting form of attack was to be obtained by 13. ....B — Kt 2; 14. P — Q 4, Q — Q 2, but White still has ade-

quate defensive resources, e.g. 15.
B — K 3, Q — B 3; 16. P — B 3,
K R — K 1; 17. Kt — Q 2, B —
Kt 6; 18. R — K 2, Kt — Q 4;
19. B × Kt, Q × B; 20. Kt —
K 4, B — R 5; 21. B — B 2 and
Black is left with no compensation
for the Pawn sacrifice.

14. Q B 3!

White rightly prefers to parry
the attack by counter-attack, both
on the Q R and, in certain variations, on the K B Pawn.

14. ......   Q — R 5
15. P — Q 4!

It adds a piquant flavour to the
game to find that the only way for
White to save it is by calmly ignor-
ing the violent demonstration on
his K side in order to continue his
Q side development.

Of course 15. Q × R leads to
mate in two after 15. ....Q × P
ch. If White tries to finish off the
game by 15. R — K 8 then' after
15. .... B — Kt 2!; 16. R × R ch,
R × R; 17. Q × Kt, R — K 1!;
18. K — B 1, Q — K 2; 19. Q —
Q 1 (or 19. B — K 6, B — Q 4!);
19. .... Q — K 5; 20. P — B 3, Q
— K 4; 21. P — Q 4, Q — B 7; 22.
Kt — Q 2, B — Kt 6; 23. Kt —
K 4, B × Kt; 24. P × B, R × P
Black will deliver mate (if 25. B
× P ch, K — R 1!).

Interesting, too, is the variation
15. R — K 4, P — K R 4; 16. P —
Q 4, B — Kt 2; 17. R × Kt, P ×
R; 18. Q × B, Q R — K 1; 19.
B — K 3, R × B winning.

Position after 15. P — Q 4 !

15. ......   Kt × P

The only way, but a most fero-
cious one, of continuing the attack.
15. .... P — K R 4 would allow
White to get in a valuable defensive move by 16. B — K 3.

16. R — K 2!

And not 16. Q × Kt, B — B 7
ch (if 16. .... B — Kt 6; 17. Q
× P ch, etc.); 17. K — B 1, B —
Kt 6; 18. Q — K 2, B × P; 19. P
× B, Q R — K 1; 20. B — K 3,
B × R; 21. Q × R, Q × P ch; 22.
K — B 2, Q — R 5 ch; 23. K —
B 1, Q × Q ch; 24. K × Q, R ×
B ch with a won end game for
Black.

16. ......   B — Kt 5

Other moves are not so effective,
e.g. 16. .... Kt — Kt 5; 17. Kt —
Q 2 followed by Kt — B 1 and
Black's attack disappears; or 16.
.... Kt × P ch; 17. P × Kt, B ×
P; 18. R — K 4 or, finally, 16.
.... B × P; 17. P × B, Kt ×
P ch; 18. K — B 1 and Black has
no means of continuing the attack.

17. P × B

Better than 17. Q × Kt, B — Kt 6, and now if 18. Q — B 1, B × R; 19. Q × B, Q R — K 1 and Black wins.

17. ......   B — R 7 ch

If 17. ....Kt × P; 18. B — K B 4.

18. K — B 1   B — Kt 6

In answer to 18. .... Kt — R 8, White can reply 19. B — K 3, Kt — Kt 6 ch; 20. K — K 1, Kt × R dis. ch; 21. K × Kt, Q R — K 1; 22. Kt — Q 2, Q — K 2; 23. R — R 1 with a won game.

19. R × Kt

The alternative is 19. K — K 1, when Black cannot play Q R — K 1 because of 20. Q × P ch; however, Black would first play 19. .... P — R 3, after which Q R — K 1 is a real menace.

19. ......   Q — R 8 ch
20. K — K 2   B × R

Position after 20. .... B × R

No better than the text is 20. .... Q × B, when White plays 21. Q × B, Q × P ch; 22. K — Q 3 (and not 22. Kt — Q 2, Q R — K 1 ch; 23. K — Q 1, Q × R ch; 24. K — B 2, R — K 8; 25. Q × P, P — Kt 5; 20. R × P, as occurred in a match game, Moritz–Emmrich, when, although White won, Black could have at once forced a draw by 26. .... Q — Q 8 ch); 22. .... Q × R; 23. K — B 2, P — Kt 5; 24. P — Kt 5, P × P; 25. Q × P (B 3) with a won end game.

21. B — Q 2   B — R 5
22. Q — R 3

White takes advantage of the position of the Bishop on R 5 to offer exchange of Queens, and Black must keep up a series of checks to avoid this; meanwhile White's King reaches security on Q B 2.

22. ......   Q R — K 1 ch
23. K — Q 3   Q — B 8 ch
24. K — B 2

After this White's material superiority must eventually tell; the game is a triumph for calm defence and counter-attack by White.

24. ......   B — B 7

24. .... B — Q 1 was rather better, since it would have avoided White's next pinning manœuvre.

25. Q — B 3   Q — Kt 8

In reply to 25. .... R — K 7, Capablanca gives the following

variation as winning for White:
26. Kt — R 3, R × B ch; 27. K
× R, Q × R; 28. Q × B, Q ×
P ch; 29. Kt — B 2, P — B 4; 30.
B — Q 5.

26. B — Q 5	P — B 4
27. P × P	B × P
28. P — Q Kt 4	B — Q 3

Or 28. .... B — K 6; 29. B ×
B, R × B; 30. Kt — Q 2, Q × R;
31. Q × R, Q — Kt 7 ch; 32. K
— Q 3 and again White's advantage in material must decide the
game in his favour.

But now, at length, White is
able to open up the game so as to
give favourable action to all his
pieces, after which the end comes
quickly.

29. P — R 4!	P — R 4
30. P × Kt P	P × P
31. R — R 6	P × P
32. Kt × P	B — Kt 5
33. P — Kt 6	B × Kt
34. B × B	P — R 3
35. P — Kt 7	R — K 6

Desperation; but there is no
parrying the threat of R — R 8.
Now White forces checkmate in six
moves, commencing with 36. B ×
P ch.

23
SIXTH ROUND,
NEW YORK, 1918

Queen's Gambit Declined

White	Black
CAPABLANCA	D. JANOWSKI
1. P — Q 4	P — Q 4
2. Kt — K B 3	Kt — K B 3

3. P — B 4	P — K 3
4. B — Kt 5	Q Kt — Q 2
5. P — K 3	P — B 3
6. Q Kt — Q 2	

With this move White avoids
the Cambridge Springs Defence
and brings the opening on to lines
similar to those of Game No. 13
against Alekhine. In that game, as
in this, White was able to control
K 5 after recapturing on Q B 4
with the Kt.

6.	B — K 2
7. B — Q 3	P × P

This exchange is just what
White was playing for, and should
have been avoided at all costs.
Black's best continuation is 7.
.... Castles, and if 8. Castles, P
— Q Kt 3; 9. P — K 4, P × K P;
10. Kt × P, B — Kt 2; 11. Q —
B 2, P — K R 3; 13. B × Kt, Kt
— B 3; 14. B — Q 3, P — B 4
with a solid position.

8. Kt × P	Castles
9. Castles	P — B 4
10. R — B 1	

Positional and strong, but still
more vigorous was 10. Q Kt —
K 5, preventing Black from developing the Q Bishop by P — Q Kt 3
because of Kt — Q B 6.

10.	P — Q Kt 3
11. Q — K 2	B — Kt 2
12. K R — Q 1	Kt — Q 4

This, owing to White's powerful
reply, is only an illusory freeing
move.

13. Kt — Q 6 !

A subtle move, as a result of which Black's Bishop has to go to Q B 3, where it is open to attack by White's Rook.

B — Q B 3   13. ......

13. .... B × B; 14, Kt × B results in the loss of either the K R Pawn or the Q B Pawn for Black.

14. Kt — K 4   P — B 4

Black's position was already inferior, but this rash move creates ruinous holes in his Pawn structure. The best defence was 14. .... R — B 1, since after 15. B × B, Q × B; 16. P × P, Kt × P; 17. Kt × Kt, P × Kt Black has some compensation for his isolated Pawns in open lines and freedom of movement for his pieces.

15. B × B   Q × B
16. Q Kt — Q 2

Intending to travel to K 5 via Q B 4.

16. ......   P — K 4

In order to avoid the last-mentioned manœuvre, after which slow suffocation would result, Black plays to get rid of his backward Pawn. But a new defect becomes apparent in his position — the weakness on the long diagonal K Kt 1 — Q R 7.

17. P × K P   Q Kt × P
18. Kt × Kt   Q × Kt
19. Kt — B 3   Q — K 2

After other Queen moves, White would play B — B 4 with a lasting

pin on the Kt, e.g. 19. .... Q — B 3; 20. B — B 4, Q R — Q 1; 21. P — K 4, P × P; 24. R — Q 2, K — B 1; 25. Q R — Q 1, P — Q Kt 4; 26. B — Q 3, R — R 4; 27. B — K 4.

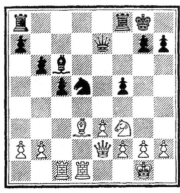

Position after 19. .... Q — K 2

20. Kt — Q 4 !

It is remarkable how effective this Kt has proved; it has moved seven times and on each occasion an increasing deterioration has been observed in Black's position.

20. ......   P × Kt

Forced; if 20. .... B — Q 2; 21. B — B 4 winning offhand.

21. R × B   Kt — Kt 5

21. .... P × P; 22. B — B 4 loses the Kt; the weakness on this diagonal becomes more and more apparent.

22. B — B 4 ch   K — B 1
23. R — K 6 !   P — Q 6

An ingenious attempt to disturb the harmony of White's game, but

Capablanca refuses to be drawn from his thematic line.

24. R — P!   Q — B 4

Planning a counter-demonstration on the Q side; if 24. . . . . . Q — Kt 4; 25. R — Kt 3, P — Q R 4; 26. P — Q R 3, etc.

25. R — Q 4   P — Q Kt 4
26. B × P   Kt × P
27. B — B 4   Kt — Kt 5
28. Q — R 5

The *coup de grâce;* White now threatens R — R4.

28. . . . . . .   P — Kt 3

Position after 28. . . . . P — Kt 3

29. R × P!   Q R — Q 1
30. R — Kt 7   Resigns

For after 30. . . . . K × R; 31. Q — Kt 5 ch, K — R 1; 32. R × R Black has no adequate reply to the threatened Q — B 6 ch. For this beautifully neat game White was awarded the second brilliancy prize.

24

FIRST MATCH GAME, HAVANA, 1919

Petroff Defence

White	Black
CAPABLANCA	B. KOSTICH
1. P — K 4	P — K 4
2. Kt — K B 3	Kt — K B 3
3. Kt × P	P — Q 3

The immediate recapture is a positional trap resulting in a marked advantage for White, e.g. 3. . . . . Kt × P; 4. Q — K 2, Q — K 2; 5. Q × Kt, P — Q 3; 6. P — Q 4, P — K B 3; 7. Kt — Q B 3.

4. Kt — K B 3   Kt × P
5. Q — K 2

The most solid of the three alternatives for White here; it results in a slight positional advantage which needs the utmost care on White's part to preserve. But this whole game is a grand example of the elaborate accumulation of minute advantages in order to achieve a winning game. Kostich puts up a sturdy and obstinate resistance, which nevertheless proves unavailing against Capablanca's subtle and scientific play.

The other lines, 5. P — Q 4, P — Q 4; 6. B — Q 3, B — Q 3 or 5. Kt — B 3, Kt × Kt; 6. Q P × Kt, B — K 2; 7. B — Q 3, Castles; 8. Castles, B — Kt 5, give equality only.

5. . . . . . .   Q — K 2
6. P — Q 3   Kt — K B 3
7. B — Kt 5   Q × Q ch

Somewhat increasing White's advantage in development, but other methods of defence also lead to the inferior game for Black, e.g. 7. ....Kt — B 3; 8. Kt — B 3, B — K 3; 9. Castles, Castles; 10. P — Q 4, P — Q 4; 11. Kt — K 5, Q — K 1; 12. Q — B 3 and now if 12. ....Kt × Kt; 13. P × Kt, B — Kt 5; 14. Q — B 4, B × R; 15. P × Kt, B — R 4; 16. B — Kt 5, P — B 3; 17. P × P, B × P; 18. B × R, Q × B; 19. Q — B 5 ch, K — Kt 1; 20. Q × B, B × Kt; 21. P × B, P × B; 22. Q — K 5 ch, K — R 1; 23. R — Q 1 and wins.

Or, as in the game Lasker–Marshall, St. Petersburg, 1914, 7. ....B — K 3; 8. Kt — B 3, Q Kt — Q 2; 9. Castles, P — Kt R 3; 10. B — R 4, P — K Kt 4; 11. B — Kt 3, Kt — R 4; 12. P — Q 4, Kt × B; 13. R P × Kt, P — Kt 5; 14. Kt — K R 4, P — Q 4; 15. Q — Kt 5, etc.

8. B × Q   B — K 2
9. Kt — B 3   B — Q 2

A defensive move to prevent Kt — Q Kt 5. If 9. ....Kt — B 3; 10. Kt — Kt 5, K — Q 1; 11. Castles K, P — Q R 3; 12. Q Kt — Q 4, Kt × Kt; 13. Kt × Kt, P — B 4; 14. Kt — B 3, B — K 3; 15. B — Q 2, P — R 3; 16. P — Q Kt 3 with advantage to White (Kashdan–Mikenas, Folkestone, 1933).

10. Castles K

Not so strong is 10. Castles Q, P — K R 3: 11. B — R 4, Kt —

B 3; 12. P — Q 4, Castles Q; 13. K R — K 1, Q R — K 1; 14. B — B 4, Kt — Q 1 with equality as in the game Fine–Kashdan, New York, 1934.

10. ......   Castles
11. K R — K 1   Kt — B 3
12. P — Q 4

Threatening B — Kt 5 followed by P — Q 5.

12. ......   K R — K 1
13. B — Kt 5   P — Q R 3

Black, reasonably enough, is not content with passive defence, but embarks on a counter-attack on the Q side; the advance, however, is of dubious value, since it weakens the Q side Pawn structure. It is true White was threatening 14. P — Q 5 followed by 15. B × K Kt, etc., but this was best parried by 13. ....K — B 1.

14. B — Q R 4   P — Q Kt 4
15. B — Kt 3   Kt — Q R 4
16. R — K 3   P — B 3
17. Q R — K 1

White's pressure on the K file has now become uncomfortably strong for Black; if now 17. .... B — Q 1. then 18. B × Kt, B × B; 19. Kt — K 4, B — K 2; 20. Kt — B 5, P × Kt; 21. R × B winning at least a Pawn.

17. ......   K — B 1
18. B — K B 4

Threatening R × B followed by B × Q P — the Q side weakness begins to tell.

18. ......   Kt — Kt 2
19. P — K R 3

This quiet little routine move is
none the less powerful since it
serves the threefold purpose of
preventing Black from freeing his
position by 19. ....B — Kt 5, allowing White's King a flight
square in case of eventual Rook
checks on the back rank, and
eliminating the possibility of
Black's exchanging off White's
valuable Q Bishop by Kt — K
R 4.

19. ......   P — R 3
20. B — R 2   B — Q 1
21. R × R ch   B × R
22. P — Q R 4

White must now endeavour to
break open the position as far as
possible in order to profit from the
superior placing of his pieces on
the open lines.

22. ......   P — Q B 4

Black in turn strives to increase
the range of his Bishops, but has
obviously failed to take into account White's 24th move. Somewhat better would have been 22.
....B — R 4

23. Kt — K 4   Kt × Kt

Black can neither play 23. ....
P — B 5; 24. Kt × Q P nor 23.
....B —K 2; 24. Q P × P, P ×
B P; 25. Kt × Kt followed by 26.
B — Q 5, etc. Now, however, he
hopes to emerge with a good game
after 24. R × Kt, R — B 5, but
White maintains the initiative by a
subtle finesse.

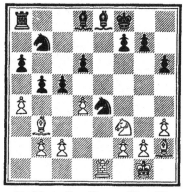

Position after 23. ....Kt × Kt

24. B — Q 5 !   R — R 2
25. B × Kt (K 4) B — K 2
26. R P × P   R P × P
27. P × P   P × P

White's advantage lies in the
superior attacking position of his
two Bishops contrasted with the
defensive nature of the Black
pieces. He now forces a repetition
of moves in order to gain time on
the clock.

28. B — Kt 8   R — R 1
29. B — Kt 3   R — R 2
30. B — Kt 8   R — R 1
31. B — Kt 3   R — R 2
32. Kt — K 5

Threatening to secure the ad-
vantage of two Bishops against
Bishop and Knight by 33. Kt —
B 6.

32. ......   Kt — Q 1
33. P — Kt 3

A necessary precaution against
the threatened 33. ....B — K
B 3 followed by P — B 5 and R
K 2; but also with the intention of
fixing Black's Q side Pawns.

| 33. . . . . . . | Kt — K 3 |
| 34. B — Q 5 | |

Now 34. Kt — B 6 would lead
to the loss of a Pawn by 34. . . . .
B × Kt; 35. B × B, Kt — Q 5;
36. B — K 4, R — R 7.

34.	Kt — Q 5
35. P — Q B 3	Kt — B 4
36. B — R 2	P — Kt 5

Black must play with the utmost
vigour here. In reply to any passive defensive move, White will
play 37. B — B 6 followed by B
× B, P — K Kt 4, Kt — B 6 and
B — Q 6 winning a piece.

37. P — Kt 4	Kt — Q 3
38. P — Q B 4	R — R 6
39. R — K 3	Kt — B 1

Kostich defends himself skil-
fully and now regroups his pieces
to parry the threatened 40. B —
B 6 followed by 41. B × B, and
if 41. . . . .Kt × B; 42. Kt — Q 7
ch. etc.

40. B — Kt 7	Kt — R 2
41. B — Q 5	P — B 3
42. Kt — B 3	Kt — B 3
43. Kt — R 4	Kt — Q 5
44. Kt — B 5 !	

A masterly move. White has no
reason to fear the doubled Pawns
on the K B file; on the contrary,
the presence of the Pawn on K B 5
has a formidable cramping effect
on Black's game.

| 44. . . . . . . | Kt × Kt |
| 45. P × Kt | B — Q 2 |

46. B — K 4	R — R 3
47. R — Q 3	B — B 3
48. B × B	R × B
49. K — Kt 2	

The commencement of an
ominous King's march. Travelling
via the white squares, the King
will penetrate to K Kt 6 with decisive effect. The reader should
note how hampered Black is in the
defence of his position by the circumstance that his Pawns are on
the same coloured squares as his
Bishop, thereby impeding this
piece's activity and on the other
hand permitting full scope to
White's Bishop.

49.	R — R 3
50. K — B 3	R — R 7
51. B — Kt 3	K — K 1
52. B — B 4	R — R 6
53. B — K 3	R — R 8
54. K — Kt 4	R — R 2
55. K — R 5	K — B 2
56. R — Q 5	R — R 6

The defensive 56. . . . .R — B 2
loses after 57. P — R 4, B — B 1;
58. R — Q 8, B — K 2; 59. R —
Q R 8, R — Q 2 (Black is in zugzwang and must surrender either
the Q B file or the second rank);
60. R — B 8, R — Q 6; 61. B ×
B P, B × B; 62. R × B, R × P;
63. R — B 7 ch, etc.

57. R — Q 7	K — K 1
58. R — Q 3	K — B 2
59. P — R 4	R — R 2
60. R — Q 5	R — R 4
61. R — Q 7	K — K 1
62. R — Q 3	K — B 2

Once Black allows White to play K — Kt 6 his K side Pawns are doomed.

63. R — Q 5

Position after 63. R — Q 5

63. ......   R — R 6

Black was in zugzwang and had no saving move. If 63. .... B — B 1; 64. R — Q 7 ch, K — K 1; 65. R — Q B 7, B — K 2; 66. K — Kt 6, B — B 1; 67. R — B 8 ch, etc.

64.	B × B P	B × B
65.	R × B	R × P
66.	R — B 7 ch	K — B 1
67.	K — Kt 6	R — K B 6
68.	R — B 7 ch	K — K 1
69.	R × Kt P	R — B 5
70.	P — R 5	R × Q B P
71.	K × P	

Converting the K R Pawn into a decisive winning factor, since the Black King remains cut off for ever from the K R file by the Rook. White now finishes off his stubborn opponent in the most accurate style.

71. ......   K — B 1
72. R — Kt 7   R — Kt 5

And not 72. .... K — Kt 1 because of 73. P — B 3 ! followed by 74. K — Kt 6 with the threat of mate.

73. P — B 3 !

Forcing the Rook off the 5th rank since 73. .... R — B 5 would be met by 74. K — Kt 6

73. ......   R — Kt 4
74. R × P   K — B 2

If 74. .... R × B P; 75. K — Kt 6 wins.

75.	R — Kt 4 !	R × P
76.	P — B 4	R — R 4
77.	R — Kt 7 ch	K — B 1
78.	R — Kt 7	P — B 4
79.	K — Kt 6	R — R 3 ch
80.	K × P	R — R 4 ch
81.	K — Kt 4	R — R 3
82.	K — Kt 5	R — Q B 3
83.	P — B 5	K — Kt 1
84.	P — B 6	R — B 8
85.	R — Kt 7 ch	K — B 1
86.	P — R 6	Resigns

Black cannot prevent the K R Pawn from queening; a very fine game indeed by Capablanca and one which manifestly weakened Kostich's will to resist in the remaining games of the match, since in none of the other games did the Jugoslav master put up such a sturdy opposition.

25
SIXTH ROUND, HASTINGS, 1919

Queen's Gambit Declined, Slav Defence

White	Black
CAPABLANCA	R. H. SCOTT
1. P — Q 4	P — Q 4
2. P — Q B 4	P — Q B 3
3. Kt — K B 3	Kt — B 3
4. P — K 3	P — K 3
5. Q Kt — Q 2	Q Kt — Q 2
6. B — Q 3	

So far the same as in his game *v*. Alekhine at St. Petersburg, 1913 (Game No. 13).

| 6. ...... | B — Q 3 |

Alekhine's B — K 2 is better than the text, since on Q 3 the Bishop is exposed to attack by White's Kt and Pawns whilst it is badly needed for defence on K 2.

| 7. Castles | Castles |
| 8. P — K 4 | |

As mentioned in game No. 13, 8. P — Q Kt 3 leads to a more lasting initiative for White.

8.	P × K P
9. Kt × P	Kt × Kt
10. B × Kt	Kt — B 3 ?

This natural move is completely wrong. It drives the Bishop where it wants to go and leaves Black with no future possible plan to develop. The right move is 10. ....P — Q B 4, as was played in the game Grünfeld–Bogoljuboff, Berlin, 1926, with the continuation: 11. B — B 2, Q — B 2; 12. Q — Q 3, P — B 4; 13. R — Q 1, P × P; 14. Q × P, B — B 4; 15. Q — R 4, Kt — B 3 with a fair game for Black.

| 11. B — B 2 | P — Q Kt 3 |
| 12. Q — Q 3 | P — K R 3 |
| 13. B — Kt 5 was threatened. |

| 13. P — Q Kt 3 | Q — K 2 |

Since White can place a Rook on the half-open K file with latent threats on the Queen, Black would have done far better to play this piece to B 2.

| 14. B — Kt 2 | R — Q 1 |

Black cannot afford to take his Queen away from the centre by 14. ....B — R 6; 15. B × B, Q × B; 16. Kt — K 5 and White has the terrible threat of Kt — Kt 4.

| 15. Q R — Q 1 | B — Kt 2 |
| 16. K R — K 1 | |

White has now massed his pieces in their ideal attacking position and next move the onslaught commences.

| 16. ...... | Q R — B 1 |
| 17. Kt — R 4 | B — Kt 1 |

It has already become irrelevant, from the point of view of saving the game, what Black does. If he plays 17. ....Q — B 1 then 18. P — Q 5 followed by B × Kt gives White a mating attack.

| 18. P — Kt 3 |

A typical Capablanca consolidating move which makes all safe before the final attack.

18. ...... K — B 1

It now dawns upon Black that he has no good continuation, and in this bankrupt state of mind he moves his King up and down whilst White gets on with the job of demolishing him.

19. Q — K B 3 K — Kt 1

If 19. ....P — B 4; 20. P — Q 5.

20. Kt — B 5

Forcing the Black Queen off the Kt, after which Black's game falls to pieces.

20. ...... Q — B 2

Capablanca here points out, with quiet glee, how all Black's pieces are now apparently massed for an attack that never even existed.

Position after 20. ....Q — B 2

21. Kt × P ch K — B 1
22. P — Q 5

A long-expected move which comes with all the more crushing

force for being delayed until White's attack is at its maximum.

22. ...... B P × P
23. B × Kt P × B

If 23. ....P × Kt, White would not take the Rook, but would start a mating attack by 24. Q — R 5.

24. Q × B P K — K 1
25. R × P ch P × R
26. Q × P ch K — B 1
27. Q — B 6 ch

Resigns as mate follows in a couple of moves. This game was awarded the *Daily Mail* prize for the best game played by a foreign master in the tournament.

26
TENTH MATCH GAME, HAVANA, 1921

Queen's Gambit Declined, Orthodox Defence

White	Black
E. LASKER	CAPABLANCA
1. P — Q 4	P — Q 4
2. P — Q B 4	P — K 3
3. Kt — Q B 3	Kt — K B 3
4. B — Kt 5	B — K 2
5. P — K 3	Castles
6. Kt — B 3	Q Kt — Q 2
7. Q — B 2	

An interesting alternative to the more usual 7. R — B 1 and one which leads to a tense struggle in the centre owing to the isolated Q Pawn that may result for either side.

7. ......   P — B 4!

The most vigorous reply by which Black frees his game. 7. ....P — B 3 as Capablanca played in the 4th game of this match leads to a bad game for Black after 8. P — Q R 3, R — K 1; 9. R — Q 1, P — Q R 3; 10. B — Q 3, P × P; 11. B × P, Kt — Q 4; 12. B × B, Q × B; 13. Kt — K 4! K Kt — B 3; 14. B — Q 3, Kt × Kt; 15. B × Kt, P — R 3; 16. Castles, P — Q B 4; 17. Kt — K 5 (Eliskases–Landau, Noordwijk, 1938).

Too passive is 7. ....P — Q Kt 3; 8. P × P, P × P; 9. B — Q 3, B — Kt 2; 10. Castles K, P — K R 3; 11. B — K B 4, P — R 3; 12. K R — Q 1, Kt — K 1; 13. Q R — B 1 and White has a powerful attack along the Q B file (Keres–Smyslov, Moscow, 1939).

8. R — Q 1

8. Castles Q, which was at one time very popular in this position, is too risky and gives Black an attack on White's King, as was shown in the game Notileur–Teichmann, Carlsbad, 1911: 8. ....Q — R 4; 9. B P × P, K P × P; 10. P × P, Kt × P; 11. Kt — Q 4, B — K 3; 12. K — Kt 1, Q R — B 1; 13. B — Q 3, P — K R 3; 14. B × Kt, B × B; 15. B — B 5, K R — Q 1; 16. B × B, P × B; 17. Q — Kt 6; R — Q 3.

Exchange of Pawns in the centre also leads to nothing for White, e.g. 8. B P × P, K P × P; 9. B — Q 3, P — B 5; 10. B — B 5, P — K Kt 3; 11. B — R 3, P — Q R 3; 12. Castles K, P — Kt 4; 13. K R — K 1, B — Kt 2; 14. B × Q Kt, Kt × B; 15. B × B, Q × B; 16. P — K 4, P × P; 17. Kt × K P, B × Kt; 18. R × B, Q — Q 3; or, as in the game Kostich–Teichmann, Carlsbad, 1911, 8. Q P × P, Kt × P; 9. R — Q 1, Q — R 4; 10. P × P, P × P; 11. B — Q 3, Q Kt — K 5 with a fine game for Black.

8. ......   Q — R 4

The thematic freeing manœuvre in this variation which in conjunction with the opening up of the Q B file by 7. ....P — Q B 4 gives Black his counter-attack on the Q side.

9. B — Q 3

Threatening B × P ch; in the 7th game of the match, Capablanca played here 9. B P × P, Kt × P; 10. B × B, Kt × B; 11. B — Q 3, Kt — K B 3; 12. Castles, P × P; 13. Kt × P, B — Q 2; 14. Kt — K 4, Kt (K 2) — Q 4; 15. Kt — Q Kt 3, Q — Q 1; 16. Kt × Kt ch, Kt × Kt; 17. Q — B 5, Q — Kt 3 and a draw was agreed after another five moves.

9. ......   P — K R 3
10. B — R 4   B P × P

Deciding to release the tension in the centre and isolate White's Q Pawn. An alternative and satisfactory continuation is 10. .... Q P × P; 11. B × P, Kt — Kt 3; 12. B — K 2 (otherwise Kt — Q 4 is still more dangerous); 12. ....

B — Q 2; 13. Castles, Q R —
B 1.

Too artificial, however, is 10.
....Kt — Kt 3; 11. P × Q P,
B P × P; 12. P — Q 6, B × P;
13. B × Kt, P × B; 14. Kt × P
and Black's K side is fatally dis-
rupted (Alekhine–Foltys, Pode-
brady, 1936).

11. K P × P

And not 11. Kt × P, Kt — K 4 !

11.	P × P
12. B × P	Kt — Kt 3
13. B — Q Kt 3	B — Q 2
14. Castles	Q R — B 1

At Moscow in 1935 Capablanca
varied here against Stahlberg with
14. ....B — B 3, but got a bad
game after 15. Kt — K 5, B —
Q 4; 16. Kt × B, Q Kt × Kt; 17.
Q — K 2, Q R — Q 1; 18. P —
B 4.

15. Kt — K 5

A strong attacking move — but
not the strongest. The logical continuation was 15. Q — K 2 at once
unpinning the Kt and threatening
an eventual P — Q 5; if then 15.
....Q Kt — Q 4; 16. Kt — K 5,
B — B 3; 17. P — B 4 with the
better game, since Black cannot
play 17. ....Kt × Kt; 18. P ×
Kt, Q × B P because of 19. B —
K 1 winning the Queen.

15. ......   B — Kt 4 !

A strong move preventing White
from playing Q — K 2 with variations similar to that given in the
last note.

16. K R — K 1   Q Kt — Q 4

White was threatening Kt —
Kt 6; if Black tries to parry this
by 16. ....B — B 5, then 17. B
× B, Kt × B; 18. B × Kt, B ×
B ; 19. Kt — Q 7, K R — Q 1; 20.
Kt × B ch, P × Kt; 21. R —
Q 3 gives White a winning at-
tack (Euwe–Landau, Noordwijk,
1938).

Position after 16. ....Q Kt — Q 4

17. B × Kt (Q 5) ?

After this Black gets the upper
hand. An analysis by G. Breyer
has shown that White can obtain
a clear-cut draw by 17. B × Kt
(B 6). Black cannot reply 17. ....
Kt × B because of 18. Kt — Kt 6,
K R — K 1 (or 18. ....P × Kt;
19. R × P, B — B 5; 20. R × B,
etc.); 19. R × P, P × R; 20. B ×
P ch, K — R 2; 21. Kt — B 8 db
ch, K — R 1; 22. Q — R 7 ch,
Kt × Q; 23. Kt — Kt 6 mate.

So he must play 17. ....B ×
B; 18. B × Kt, P × B; 19. Q —
B 5, B — B 3; 20. Kt — Kt 4 (or
20. Kt — Q 7, B × Kt; 21. Q × B

(Q 7), K R — Q 1; 22. Q — B 5, R — B 5; 23. Kt × P, Q × Kt; 24. R — K 8 ch, R × R; 25. Q × Q, R × P; 26. Q — B 3, R — Q 7; 27. P — K Kt 3, R × Kt P and Black will have no difficulty in drawing); 20. ....B — K Kt 4; 21. P — B 4, P — K Kt 3; 22. Q — K 5, Q R — K 1 with a level game.

In the last variation, instead of playing 19. Q — B 5, White can introduce interesting complexities by 19. Kt — Kt 4, B — Kt 4; 20. P — B 4, B × P (or 20. ....B — K R 5; 21. P — K Kt 3, B — Q 1; 22. Q — B 5, R × Kt 1; 23. P × R, Q × B P; 24. Q × P, B — Q B 3; 25. Q — Kt 3, Q × Q; 26. P × Q, B — B 6 with an easy draw); 21. Q — B 5, B — Kt 4; 22. Q × P, P — R 3; 23. P — Q R 4, R (Q B 1) — Q 1; 24. Q × P, B × P; 25. P — Kt 4, Q — K B 4; 26. Kt × P ch, B × Kt; 27. Kt × B, Q — B 7; 28. Kt — B 5, B — K 6 ch; 29. K — R 1, B × P; 30. Q × P, B × Kt and draws.

Apart from its intrinsic interest, this analysis is of considerable importance in sustaining the claim that at no stage in his match with Lasker did Capablanca ever obtain a really inferior position.

17.	Kt × B
18. B × B	Kt × B
19. Q — Kt 3	B — B 3

After 19. ....B — R 3; 20. Kt — Q 7, K R — Q 1; 21. Kt — B 5, P — Q Kt 3; 22. Kt × B, Q × Kt; 23. P — Q 5 the position would simplify down to an obvious draw.

| 20. Kt × B | P × Kt |
| 21. R — K 5 | |

If 21. Kt — R 4, K R — Q 1; 22. R — K 5, R — Q 4; 23. P — B 4, Kt — B 4 and White's Q Pawn is very weak indeed.

| 21. ...... | Q — Kt 3 |
| 22. Q — B 2 | |

Exchange of Queens would be wrong here, since it would unite Black's Q side Pawns.

| 22. ...... | K R — Q 1 |
| 23. Kt — K 2 | |

Too defensively played. It is true that an immediate 23. R — Q B 5 would lose a Pawn after 23. ....R × P !, but White could have obtained some play by 23. Kt — R 4 when Black does best to retire the Queen by 23. ....Q — Kt 1 : 24. R — Q B 5, R — Q 3 followed by Q R — Q 1, Q — Kt 2 and Q — Q 2.

| 23. ...... | R — Q 2 |
| 24. R × R | |

After which Black loses his one remaining weakness on the Q B file, but no better is Lasker's suggestion of 24. R — K 3 because of 24. ....Kt — B 4; 25. R — Q Kt 3, Q — Q 1; 26. R — Kt 4, Q — Q 2; 27. R — B 4, P — K 4 winning the Q Pawn, since 28. Q — B 3 fails against 28. ....P × P; 29. Kt — P ? R — Q 1.

24.	B P × R
25. Q — Q 2	Kt — B 4
26. P — Q Kt 3	

Not a very impressive move; less weakening is the alternative given by Lasker: 26. P — K Kt 3. If instead 26. Kt — Kt 3, then 26. .... Kt — Q 3; 27. P — Q Kt 3, R — B 3; 28. P — K R 3, Q — B 2 followed by R — B 7.

| 26. ...... | P — K R 4 |

This natural-looking move played to preserve the Kt on B 4 from attack by P — K Kt 4 should have provided White with the opportunity of a favourable exchange and must therefore be deemed premature. Best is 26. .... P — Kt 3 and if 27. P — K Kt 4, Kt — Q 3; 28. R — Q B 1, R × R ch; 29. Kt × R, Kt — K 5 and Black retains the initiative.

Position after 26. .... P — K R 4

27. P — K R 3 ?

A weak move which falls in with Black's plans much too meekly. Correct was 27. Kt — Kt 3, after which Bogoljuboff has shown White should draw, e.g. 27. .... Kt × Kt; 28. R P × Kt, R — B 3; 29. Q — B 4, R — B 7. 30. R — Q 2, R — B 8 ch; 31. K — R 2, Q — B 3; 32. P — K Kt 4, P × P (if 32. .... P — R 5; 33. P — Kt 5, Q — B 6; 34. P — Kt 6 and draws); 33. Q × P, Q — B 6; 34. Q — Kt 5, P — B 3; 35. Q — B 4, K — B 2; 36. R — K 2 and White's threats of Q — K 3 and an eventual perpetual are adequate to hold the position.

| 27. ...... | P — R 5 ! |

A strong move preventing both Kt — Kt 3 and also P — K Kt 4, since after 28. P — K Kt 4, P × P e.p. White's K side would be terribly weakened.

| 28. Q — Q 3 | R — B 3 |

Preventing White from playing Q — R 6 after Black's Queen leaves this rank for its more attacking position on Kt 5.

| 29. K — B 1 | P — Kt 3 |
| 30. Q — Kt 1 | |

Very defensively played and allowing Black to proceed with his plan of penetration into the Q side. However, 30. Q — Q 2 as recommended by Tartakower can be easily met by 30. .... Q — B 2 with the potent threat of R — B 7.

| 30. ...... | Q — Kt 5 ! |
| 31. K — Kt 1 | P — Q R 4 ! |

Capablanca's handling of this phase of the game is very instructive. The advance of the Q R Pawn at once eliminates the remaining weakness in his Pawn position and gives White an additional isolated Pawn.

| 32. Q — Kt 2 | P — R 5 |
| 33. Q — Q 2 | |

Lasker hopes to obtain relief by the exchange of Queens; any attempt to maintain the *status quo* leads to rapid disaster, e.g. 33. R — Kt 1, P — R 6; 34. Q — R 1, R — B 7 and White is quite lost.

33.	Q × Q
34. R × Q	P × P
35. P × P	R — Kt 3
36. R — Q 3	

And not 36. R — Kt 2, R — Kt 5 winning a Pawn.

| 36. ...... | R — R 3 |
| 37. P — K Kt 4 | |

This now necessary and not so dangerous now that the Queens have been exchanged. The Black Rook cannot be prevented from reaching the 7th rank. For if 37. R — Q 2, R — Kt 8 ch; 38. K — R 2, R — Q Kt 8 wins a Pawn as also occurs after 37. Kt — B 3, R — R 8 ch; 38. K — Kt 1, R — Q B 8; 39. P — Q Kt 4, R — B 7; 40. K — Kt 1, R — Kt 7; 41. P — Kt 5, R — Kt 5.

| 37. ...... | P × P e.p. |
| 38. P × P | |

Or 38. Kt × P, R — R 8 ch; 39. K — Kt 2, Kt — Q 3; 40. K — B 3, R — Q Kt 8; 41. K — K 3, R — Kt 7 and since Black's Rook cannot be moved from its dominating position, White must help-lessly watch him bring up his King into action, followed by exchanging off Knights at the appropriate moment.

| 38. ...... | R — R 7 |
| 39. Kt — B 3 | R — Q B 7 |

Threatening Kt × Q P.

| 40. Kt — Q 1 | Kt — K 2 |

Black's Kt has fulfilled its purpose on B 4 in laming White's game and now it is manœuvred to the other wing in order to attack and win one of the weak Q side Pawns.

41. Kt — K 3	R — B 8 ch
42. K — B 2	Kt — B 3
43. Kt — Q 1	R — Kt 8 !

Position after 43. ....R — Kt 8 !

Lasker has set an artful trap into which Capablanca declines to fall. For the plausible 43. ....Kt — Kt 5; 44. R — Q 2, R — K 8; 45. Kt — Kt 2, R × Kt; 46. R × R, Kt — Q 6 ch; 47. K — K 2, Kt × R; 48. K — Q 2 leads to a draw, since Black's Kt is trapped.

44. K — K 2

The Q Kt Pawn is now lost in any event, but in view of the powerful stranglehold which the Black Rook possesses on the position, White would have done better to have played 44. K — K 1, Kt — R 4; 45. K — Q 2, R × P (not 45. ....Kt × P; 46. K — B 2); 46. R × R, Kt × R ch; 47. K — B 3 when the ending would be not without considerable technical difficulties for Black.

44. ......   R × P
45. K — K 3   R — Kt 5

With White's Rook in a passive position Black rightly prefers to avoid exchanging and finishes off the ending in irreproachable style.

46. Kt — B 3   Kt — K 2

Threatening to win the Q Pawn by Kt — B 4 ch.

47. Kt — K 2   Kt — B 4 ch
48. K — B 2   P — Kt 4
49. P — Kt 4   Kt — Q 3
50. Kt — Kt 1   Kt — K 5 ch
51. K — B 1   R — Kt 8 ch
52. K — Kt 2   R — Kt 7 ch
53. K — B 1   R — B 7 ch
54. K — K 1   R — Q R 7

The two pieces having attained a position of maximum efficiency, Black now proceeds to bring his King into the game. White can do nothing but watch Black's merciless dissection of his position.

55. K — B 1   K — Kt 2
56. R — K 3   K — Kt 3
57. R — Q 3   P — B 3

58. R — K 3   K — B 2
59. R — Q 3   K — K 2
60. R — K 3   K — Q 3
61. R — Q 3   R — B 7 ch
62. K — K 1   R — K Kt 7
63. K — B 1   R — Q R 7
64. R — K 3   P — K 4

Forcing a passed Pawn.

65. R — Q 3

Or 65. Kt — K 2, Kt — Q 7 ch; 66. K — B 2, P — K 5; 67. R — Q B 3, Kt — B 6; 68. K — K 3, Kt — K 8; 69. K — B 2, Kt — Kt 7; 70. K × Kt, R × Kt ch; 71. K — B 1, R — Q 7, etc.

65. ......   P × P
66. R × P

If 66. Kt — K 2, K — B 4; 67. Kt × P, K — B 5; 68. R — Q 1, Kt — B 6 winning the Kt.

66. ......   K — B 4
67. R — Q 1   P — Q 5
68. R — B 1 ch   K — Q 4

Resigns since the Kt is lost after 69. R — Q 1, Kt — Kt 6 ch; 70. K — K 1, R — K Kt 7.

27
ELEVENTH MATCH GAME, HAVANA, 1921

Queen's Gambit Declined, Orthodox Defence

White	Black
CAPABLANCA	E. LASKER
1. P — Q 4	P — Q 4
2. Kt — K B 3	P — K 3
3. P — B 4	Kt — K B 3
4. B — Kt 5	Q Kt — Q 2

5. P — K 3   B — K 2
6. Kt — B 3   Castles
7. R — B 1   R — K 1

This move has rightly been superseded by 7. ....P — B 3 since it leads to a too constricted game for Black.

8. Q — B 2   P — B 3
9. B — Q 3

Strongest of all here is 9. P — Q R 3 with the idea of eventually retiring the K Bishop to Q R 3 (after Black has played Q P × B P).

9. ......   P × P
10. B × P   Kt — Q 4
11. B × B   R × B

Incorrect, though obviously the intention behind his 7th move. He should have transposed into the normal orthodox line by 11. .... Q × B; 12. Castles, Kt × Kt; 13. Q × Kt, P — K 4.

12. Castles   Kt — B 1
13. K R — Q 1   B — Q 2

This Bishop is to be brought to K 1 where it will have considerable defensive value. Black is intent on building up as solid a position as possible. Its one drawback is that he is confined to the two back rows and will eventually have to make some sort of weakening move in order to obtain freedom of manœuvre for his pieces.

It should be pointed out that to develop the Bishop on Q Kt 2 will lead to a still worse game for Black after 13. ....P — Q Kt 3; 14. P — Q R 3, B — Kt 2; 15. P —

Q Kt 4, R — B 1; 16. Q — K 2 followed by 17. B — R 6.

14. P — K 4   Kt — (Q 4) Kt 3

14. ....Kt × Kt on the principle of simplification of a crowded position by exchange would have been preferable, but Lasker has chosen from the outset to pursue a more complicated course.

15. B — B 1 !

This and the next six moves form an object lesson in the art of constricting one's opponent.

15. ......   R — B 1
16. P — Q Kt 4 !

Once and for all preventing Black from playing P — Q B 4; at the same time, there looms up the prospect of manœuvring White's Kts to the weak black squares on Q B 5 and Q 6.

16. ......   B — K 1
17. Q — Kt 3   R (K 2) — B 2

An interesting move which is aimed at preventing either P — Kt 5 or P — Q 5 on White's part.

18. P — Q R 4

A typical advance in such positions; Black's Kt is to be driven back to impede the action of the other pieces whilst there will also be eventual threats on Black's Q side Pawn structure.

18. ......   Kt — Kt 3
19. P — R 5   Kt — Q 2
20. P — K 5

A critical moment. White now makes the decision to allow Black the by no means inconsiderable advantage of a square for his Kt on Q 4 in order to place his own Kt on Q 6. The course of the game will demonstrate that White's positional judgment is absolutely right in thus committing itself.

Position after 20. P — K 5

20. ......   P — Kt + 3

Black prepares for an eventual breakthrough by P — Q B 4.

21. Kt — K 4   R — Kt 1
22. Q — B 3

A move lacking in precision, as a result of which Black gains a tempo on his 23rd move. 22. Q — R 3 at once was correct. Capablanca's own suggestion of P — R 6 followed by Kt — Q 6 would be inferior, since it would relieve the tension on the Q side.

22. ......   Kt — B 5
23. Kt — Q 6   Kt — Q 4
24. Q — R 3   P — B 3

Black's haste to get rid of the Kt on Q 6 is easily comprehensible; nevertheless, he should have

prepared the text move by 24. ..... Q — K 2, thereby creating a latent pin on the Kt and Q and threatening the Q Kt Pawn after 25. Kt × B, R × Kt.

25. Kt × B

Forced, since Black was threatening 25. ....B — R 4.

25. ......   Q × Kt
26. P × P !

Very strong; now Black's K side Pawns are much weakened.

26. ......   P × B P

It is clear that 26. ....Kt × P would leave the K Pawn very weak indeed.

27. P — Kt 5

White proceeds to the attack with admirably logical calm. First the position on the Q side is to be cleared up and then he will start the final attack on the weakened K side position.

27. ......   R (Kt 1) — B 1

Best; White was threatening Kt P × P followed by B — Kt 5 and Q — Q 6 and if 27. ....P — Q B 4; 28. Q P × P, Kt × P; 29. B — B 4 when Black is most precariously placed.

28. P × B P   R × P
29. R × R   R × R
30. P × P   P × P
31. R — K 1

Played with rather too much subtle discretion. Most effective here is the blunt 31. B — Kt 5.

31. ......   Q — Q B 1
32. Kt — Q 2   Kt — B 1

If 32. ....R — B 6; 33. Q — Q 6, R — B 3 (33. ....Kt — B 1; 34. Kt — K 4, R — B 3; 35. Q — R 3 would result in a similar position to the actual game); 34. Q — Kt 3 ch, K — R 1; 35. Kt — K 4, Q — B 2; 36. Q — R 3, Kt — B 5; 37. Q — R 6 would leave White with a won game (27. ....R — B 8 ? 28. Kt × P !).

33. Kt — K 4   Q — Q 1
34. P — R 4

Position after 34. P — R 4

Black had been threatening 34. ....P — B 4; 35. Kt — Q 2, R — B 6; 36. Q — R 1, Q — Kt 4. But now if 34. ....P — B 4; 35. B — Kt 5, R — B 2; 36. Kt — Kt 5, R — K 2; 37. B — B 4, R — K 1; 38. Q — Q Kt 3 and White wins.

34. ......   R — B 2

After this Black is irretrievably lost. Better was 34. ....P — R 3

threatening P — B 4, when White would have no clear-cut way to victory.

35. Q — Kt 3

Threatening B — B 4 followed by B × Kt and Q × P ch.

35. ......   R — K Kt 2
36. P — Kt 3   R — R 2
37. B — B 4   R — R 4
38. Kt — B 3

Threatening 39. R × P, Kt × R ; 40. B × Kt, etc.

38. ......   Kt × Kt
39. Q × Kt   K — B 2
40. Q — K 3   Q — Q 3
41. Q — K 4   R — R 5

Hastening the end; a more prolonged resistance could have been put up by 41. ....R — R 2. After the text, the Rook remains fatally far from the scene of action.

42. Q — Kt 7 ch   K — Kt 3

Or 42. ....Q — K 2; 43. Q — B 6, R — R 2; 44. P — Q 5.

43. Q — B 8   Q — Kt 5
44. R — Q B 1   Q — K 2

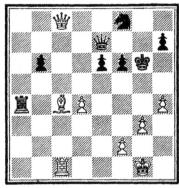

Position after 44. ....Q — K 2

Now Capablanca finishes the game off neatly. If 44. ....Q — R 6 he gives the following variation: 45. B — Q 3 ch, P — B 4 (neither 45. ....Q × B; 46. Q — K 8 ch nor 45. ....K — R 3; 46. R — B 7 are of any avail for Black); 46. Q — K 8 ch, K — R 3; 47. R — K 1, R — R 1; 48. R × P ch, Kt × R; 49. Q × Kt ch, K — Kt 2; 50. Q — K 5 ch followed by mate.

45. B — Q 3 ch   K — R 3

If 45. ....P — B 4; 46. B × P ch, K — B 3 (or 46. ....P × B; 47. Q — B 6 ch, etc.); 47. R — B 7, Q — Q 3; 48. R — B 6 and wins.

46. R — B 7   R — R 8 ch
47. K — Kt 2   Q — Q 3
48. Q × Kt ch   Resigns

Mate being inevitable — a game marked by original strategy.

CHAPTER FOUR

World Champion

WE now come to a time when Capablanca was at the height of his powers. The style in which the games are won is impeccably clear and convincing. There is too a pervading sense of easy natural power that makes them exceptionally attractive. This is well in evidence in the London Tournament of 1922, where Capa's play abounds in positional ideas of the highest order. Consider, for example, the brilliant fashion in which Bogoljuboff is persuaded to allow his Q Bishop to be perpetually cut off from play in Game No. 28; charming too is the lucid victory against Vidmar in the next game.

Though outdistanced by the great Lasker and defeated by Réti in the New York tournament of 1924, Capablanca produced a host of remarkable games here, and the chief difficulty has been to limit the number selected. Both the games against Tartakower (it was a double-round tourney) are well worthy of inclusion, the Polish master's lively and original style giving rise to many intriguing situations. A remarkable Rook and Pawn endgame is to be seen in the first, and the second game is played with admirable energy. The game against Yates is a study in the exploitation of minute advantages, and the English master puts up a characteristically dogged resistance. Another instructive positional triumph is the win against Bogoljuboff, where the ex-Russian player is once more outmanœuvred strategically. Abounding in interesting points is the great struggle against Lasker, where the play, though by no means flawless, is of almost breathless excitement from start to finish.

LONDON, 1922

	Capablanca	Alekhine	Vidmar	Rubinstein	Bogoljuboff	Réti	Tartakower	Maroczy	Yates	Atkins	Euwe	Znosko-Borowski	Wahltuch	Morrison	Watson	Marotti	
1 Capablanca	–	½	1	½	1	1	½	½	1	1	1	1	1	1	1	1	13
2 Alekhine	½	–	½	1	½	½	½	½	1	1	1	1	½	1	1	1	11½
3 Vidmar	0	½	–	0	1	½	1	½	1	½	1	1	1	1	1	1	11
4 Rubinstein	½	0	1	–	½	½	1	1	½	0	1	½	1	1	1	1	10½
5 Bogoljuboff	0	½	0	½	–	½	1	1	0	1	½	0	1	1	1	1	9
6 Réti	0	½	½	½	½	–	½	½	1	1	½	1	0	1	0	1	8½
7 Tartakower	½	½	0	0	0	½	–	½	1	0	1	1	1	½	1	1	8½
8 Maroczy	½	½	½	0	0	½	½	–	1	½	½	1	½	0	1	1	8
9 Yates	0	0	0	½	1	0	0	0	–	1	1	1	1	1	½	1	8
10 Atkins	0	0	½	1	0	0	1	½	0	–	0	1	½	½	0	1	6
11 Euwe	0	0	0	0	½	½	0	½	0	1	–	0	1	0	1	1	5½
12 Znosko-Borowski	0	0	0	½	1	0	0	0	0	0	1	–	1	½	1	0	5
13 Wahltuch	0	½	0	0	0	1	0	½	0	½	0	0	–	1	1	½	5
14 Morrison	0	0	0	0	0	0	½	1	0	½	1	½	0	–	0	1	4½
15 Watson	0	0	0	0	0	1	0	0	½	1	0	0	0	1	–	1	4½
16 Marotti	0	0	0	0	0	0	0	0	0	0	0	1	½	0	0	0	1½

NEW YORK, 1924

	Lasker	Capablanca	Alekhine	Marshall	Réti	Maroczy	Bogoljuboff	Tartakower	Yates	Lasker	Janowski	
1 Lasker	—	½ 0	1 ½	½ 1	1 1	1 1	1 1	½ 1	½ 1	½ 1	1 1	16
2 Capablanca	½ 1	—	½ ½	½ ½	0 1	½ 1	1 1	1 1	1 ½	½ 1	½ 1	14½
3 Alekhine	0 ½	½ ½	—	½ ½	1 0	1 ½	½ ½	½ ½	1 1	½ ½	1 1	12
4 Marshall	½ 0	½ ½	½ ½	—	½ 1	0 ½	0 1	½ 0	½ 1	1 ½	1 1	11
5 Réti	0 0	1 0	1 0	½ 0	—	½ ½	0 1	1 1	1 0	1 0	1 1	10½
6 Maroczy	0 0	½ 0	0 ½	1 ½	½ ½	—	0 1	½ ½	1 1	½ 1	1 0	10
7 Bogoljuboff	0 0	0 0	½ ½	1 0	1 0	1 0	—	0 1	1 1	½ 1	0 1	9½
8 Tartakower	½ 0	0 0	½ ½	½ 1	0 0	½ ½	1 0	—	1 0	½ 0	½ 1	8
9 Yates	½ 0	0 ½	0 0	½ 0	0 1	0 0	0 0	0 1	—	1 1	½ 1	7
10 Lasker	½ 0	½ 0	½ ½	0 ½	0 1	½ 0	½ 0	½ 1	0 0	—	0 ½	6½
11 Janowski	0 0	½ 0	0 0	0 0	0 0	0 1	1 0	½ 0	½ 0	1 ½	—	5

28
SIXTH ROUND,
LONDON, 1922

Ruy Lopez, Morphy Defence

White	Black
CAPABLANCA	E. D. BOGOLJUBOFF

1. P — K 4   P — K 4
2. Kt — K B 3   Kt — Q B 3
3. B — Kt 5   P — Q R 3
4. B — R 4   Kt — B 3
5. Castles   B — K 2
6. R — K 1   P — Q Kt 4
7. B — Kt 3   P — Q 3
8. P — B 3   Castles

The normal continuation for Black is 8. .... Kt — Q R 4 followed by Q — Q B 4 and Q — B 2. Instead, Bogoljuboff develops an original idea of his own, the purpose of which is to exert stress on White's centre, and, taking advantage of this pressure, to force the exchange of a Kt for the attacking Bishop on the white squares.

9. P — Q 4

Accepting the implicit challenge, White occupies the centre. He has two other main courses open to him. Firstly, he can transpose back to the normal line by 9. P — K R 3, Kt — Q R 4; 10. B — B 2, P — B 4, etc., or he can play the more restrained 9. P — Q 3, Kt — Q R 4; 10. B — B 2, P — B 4; which of the three lines he chooses depends on the temperament of the player, since none can be positively claimed as superior.

9. ......   P × P

This is premature, since it allows White to develop his Q Kt on B 3 if so inclined. In subsequent games Bogoljuboff played 9. .... B — Kt 5 after which White's best line is to close the centre by 10. P — Q 5, Kt — Q R 4; 11. B — B 2, P — B 3; 12. P × P.

10. P × P   B — Kt 5
11. B — K 3

Best here is Kt — B 3; in a game at Mährisch-Ostrau, 1923, Lasker gained a clear-cut endgame advantage against Bogoljuboff by 11. Kt — B 3, Kt — Q R 4; 12. B — B 2, P — B 4; 13. P × P, P × P; 14. P — K 5, Q × Q; 15. R × Q, Kt — Q 2; 16. P — K R 3, B — K 3; 17. Kt — Q 5, B × Kt; 18. R × B.

11. ......   Kt — Q R 4

In an earlier round of this tournament Bogoljuboff played the more violent 11. .... P — Q 4 against Yates, but after 12. P — K 5, Kt — K 5; 13. Kt — B 3, B — Kt 5; 14. R — Q B 1, Kt — K 2; 15. P — K R 3, B — K R 4; 16. B — B 2, B × Q Kt; 17. P × B, P — K B 4; 18. P × P e.p., R × P; 19. P — Kt 4, B — Kt 3; 20. Kt — K 5, Kt × Q B P; 21. Q — Q 2, Kt — K 5; 22. B × Kt, P × B; 23. B — Kt 5 White had a positionally won game.

12. B — B 2   Kt — B 5
13. B — B 1

This retrogressive manœuvre is curiously strong; now that Black has committed himself on the Q side (the Kt on Q B 5 inevitably implies a Q side advance by P — Q B 4) White will find a better development for his Q Bishop on Q Kt 2.

13.	......	P — B 4
14.	P — Q Kt 3	Kt — Q R 4
15.	B — Kt 2	

This allows Black to carry out his plan of exchanging Kt for Bishop. If White wishes to avoid this, he must develop his Q Kt at once in order to give his K Bishop a flight square on Kt 1; e.g. 15. Q Kt — Q 2, Kt — B 3; 16. P — K R 3, B — R 4; 17. P — K Kt 4, B — Kt 3; 18. P — Q 5, Kt — Kt 5; 19. B — Kt 1, P — Q R 4; 20. P — Q R 3, Kt — R 3; 21. B — Kt 2 with the better game.

15.	......	Kt — B 3
16.	P — Q 5	Kt — Kt 5
17.	Q Kt — Q 2	Kt × B
18.	Q × Kt	R — K 1

This, and his 21st move, show that Black is suffering from over-ambition, no doubt due to a very optimistic appraisal of the position — always a failing with Bogoljuboff. Instead, he should strive to gain equality by 18. .... Kt — Q 2 followed by B — B 3.

19. Q — Q 3

Capablanca was afterwards of the opinion that 19. P — Q R 4 was stronger, but the text move has much to be said for it. The Q Kt is free to go to Kt 3 or K 3 via K B 1 and the potential threat of P — Q R 4 is made more powerful.

| 19. | ...... | P — K R 3 |

Position after 19. ....P — K R 3

19. ....Kt — Q 2 was still to be preferred, since 20. P — Q R 4 can be met by 20. ....Q — Kt 3 and the variation advised by Tartakower 19. ....Kt — Q 2; 20. P — K 5, B × Kt; 21. Kt × B, P × P; 22. Kt × P, Kt × Kt; 23. B × Kt, B — Q 3; 24. B × B, Q × B; 25. Q R — Q 1 does not seem to lead to more than equality.

| 20. | Kt — B 1 | Kt— Q 2 |
| 21. | P — K R 3 | B — R 4 ? |

A strategical error, as a result of which Black has a Bishop permanently out of play. He should have played 21. ....B × Kt; 22. Q × B, B — B 3 and the game is quite level. The theoretical power of two Bishops has obviously caused Black to overlook the possible impotence of one of them.

22. K Kt — Q 2 !

This regrouping of Kts is an original conception by which White nullifies Black's counter-attack on the Q side.

22. ......   B — B 3
23. B × B   Q × B
24. P — Q R 4   P — B 5!

Black does his best to make the situation as critical as possible; with this move he at once obtains a fine post for his Kt and forces a passed Pawn on the Q side.

25. Kt P × P   Kt — B 4
26. Q — K 3

Superficially it appears wrong to place the Queen on the same file as the enemy Rook, but it is imperative to retain control of the square K B 4, as will be seen in the next few moves.

26. ......   P × R P
26. ....P × B P was also playable, since on Q B 5 the Pawn is not immediately vulnerable. If then 27. K R — B 1, P — B 6!; 28. R × P, Kt × K P; 29. Kt × Kt, R × Kt; 30. Q × R, Q × R with equality. However, White would proceed very much as in the actual game with 27. P — B 4 followed by P — Kt 4 and P — B 5, and when this manœuvre was accomplished he would concentrate his forces on the Q B Pawn.

27. P — B 4   Q — K 2

The Queen has to retire to permit the advance of Black's B Pawn, since White was threatening both P — B 5 and P — K 5.

28. P — Kt 4   B — Kt 3
29. P — B 5   B — R 2

White's Pawn structure leaves a great deal to be desired, there being two bad holes on K 5 and Q B 5, but Black is effectively a piece down.

30. Kt — Kt 3   Q — K 4
31. K — Kt 2   Q R — Kt 1
32. Q R — Kt 1   P — B 3

Black prepares to bring the Bishop back into play via K Kt 1 and in addition White's K Pawn is now permanently backward; the one disadvantage to this move — a great one, however — is that it permits White to establish a piece on K 6.

Tartakower recommends instead 32. ....R — Kt 7; 33. R × R, Q × R, since 34. R — Q Kt 1, Q — B 7; 35. K — B 3, Kt — Kt 6; 36. Kt (Kt 3) — B 1, P — B 3 gives Black the better game. However, White can play 34. R — K 2 with variations similar to the actual game.

Position after 32. ....P — B 3

33. Kt — B 3   R — Kt 7 ch
34. R × R   Q × R ch
35. R — K 2   Q — Kt 6
36. Kt — Q 4   Q × Q

Black cannot afford even the one tempo necessary to capture the Q B P, for after 36. . . . . Q × P; 37. Kt — K 6! R — Kt 1 (37. . . . . Kt × Kt; 36. Q P × Kt leaves Black hopelessly placed); 38. Kt × Kt, P × Kt; 39. R — Q 2, R — Kt 6; 40. Q — B 2, P — R 6; 41. P — Q 6 White has a clearly won game.

37. R × Q   R — Kt 1
38. R — Q B 3   K — B 2

Better than 38. . . . . R — Kt 7 ch; 39. K — B 3, Kt — Kt 6; 40. Kt (Kt 3) — K 2 followed by Kt — K 6 and Black has merely pushed White on the path he wants to go.

39. K — B 3   R — Kt 7
40. Kt(Kt 3)—K 2   B — Kt 1
41. Kt — K 6!

Very neatly timed; Black is obviously lost after 41. . . . . Kt × Kt; 42. B P × Kt ch, K — Kt 2; 43. Kt — Q 4, B — R 2; 44. P — B 5, etc. Nor can Black play 41. . . . . Kt × P; 42. K × Kt, R × Kt ch; 43. K — Q 4 and White will follow up with P — B 5 with a winning passed Q Pawn.

41. . . . . . .   Kt — Kt 6
42. P — B 5 !   P × P
43. Kt × B P   Kt — Q 7 ch
44. K — B 2   K — K 2

After this natural-looking move, Black loses quickly; a stouter resistance would have been put up by 44. . . . . Kt — Kt 8; 45. Kt × P (R 4), Kt × R; 46. Kt × R, Kt — P ch; 47. K — K 3, Kt — Q 3 though Black would still lose eventually after 48. K — Q 4, K — K 2; 49. Kt — K B 4 followed by Kt — K 6.

45. K — K 1   Kt — Kt 8
46. R — Q 3   P — R 6
47. P — Q 6 ch   K — Q 1
48. Kt — Q 4!

Forcing the Black Rook to retreat because of the threat of mate in 2.

48. . . . . . .   R — Kt 3
49. Kt(Q 4)—K 6ch B × Kt
50. P × B   R — Kt 1
51. P — K 7 ch   K — K 1
52. Kt × P   Resigns

For if 52. . . . . P — R 7; 53. Kt × R, P — R 8 = Q; 54. P — Q 7 ch and Black is soon mated.

29

THIRTEENTH ROUND, LONDON, 1922

Queen's Gambit Declined, Orthodox Defence

White	Black
CAPABLANCA	M. VIDMAR

1. P — Q 4   P — Q 4
2. Kt — K B 3   Kt — K B 3
3. P — B 4   P — K 3
4. Kt — B 3   B — K 2
5. B — Kt 5   Q Kt — Q 2

6. P — K 3   Castles
7. R — B 1   P — B 3
8. Q — B 2

After this move Black should have no difficulty in securing equality; best is the normal move 8. B — Q 3.

8. ......   P × P

This manœuvre should be adequate if correctly followed up. Also good for Black is 8. ....Kt — K 5; 9. B × B, Q × B; 10. Kt × Kt, P × Kt; 11. Q × P, Q — Kt 5 ch; 12. Kt — Q 2, Q × Kt P with a level game.

9. B × P   Kt — Q 4
10. B × B

And not 10. Kt — K 4, Q — R 4 ch; 11. K — K 2, P — B 3; 12. B — R 4, Q Kt — Kt 3 which is good for Black.

10. ......   Q × B
11. Castles   P — Q Kt 3 ?

A disastrous mistiming of moves, as a result of which White gains complete control of the Q B file. Correct was first 11. ....Kt × Kt and then P — Q Kt 3.

12. Kt × Kt   B P × Kt

This is the point; Black cannot recapture by 12. ....K P × Kt because of 13. B — Q 3 and white wins a Pawn. Now the White Queen will occupy the weak square on Q B 7.

13. B — Q 3   P — K R 3

13. ....Kt — K B 3 would likewise be met by White's next

move after which Black cannot free himself.

14. Q — B 7   Q — Kt 5

Position after 14. ....Q — Kt 5

Black's last move is a desperate freeing attempt which fails against White's fine combination. He hopes to induce White to play P — Q Kt 3, whereupon Kt — B 3, Q — R 6 and B — R 3 would give him complete emancipation, but the logic of positions of this nature is such that the more forceful the endeavour to break loose the greater the collapse.

It must be observed that quieter moves would also prove unavailing, e.g. 14. ....R — K 1; 15. B — Kt 5 or 14. ....R — Q 1; 15. Kt — K 5;

15. P — Q R 3 !   Q — R 5

Against 15. ....Q × Kt P Capablanca gives the following variation: 16. R — Kt 1, Q × R P; 17. B — Kt 5, Q — K 2 (or 17. ....Kt — B 3; 18. R — R 1, Q — Kt 5; 19. K R — Kt 1 and the

Queen is lost); 18. B — B 6, R
— Kt 1; 19. Kt — K 5, Q — Q 1;
20. Q × R P, Kt × Kt; 21. P ×
Kt and Black will lose a piece.

16. P — R 3	Kt — B 3
17. Kt — K 5	B — Q 2

Any attempt to develop the Q
side results in loss of material.
If 17. ....B — R 3; 18. P — Q
Kt 3, Q — R 4; 19. Kt — B 6, Q
× P; 20. R — R 1 and the Bishop
is lost.

18. B — B 2	Q — Kt 4
19. P — Q R 4	Q × Kt P
20. Kt × B	

Hastily played; White overlooks Black's next move by which
he escapes with the loss of the
exchange for a Pawn. Instead, 20.
R — Kt 1, Q — R 7; 21. B —
Kt 3 would have won a clear
piece. This is an unfortunate
blemish on White's otherwise impeccable play; nevertheless, the
technique involved in winning the
final part of the game is instructive and by no means easy.

20.	Q R — B 1
21. Q — Kt 7	

Owing to the pin that eventually arises on the Bishop and
Rook, White cannot win a piece
by 21. Kt × Kt ch, P × Kt; 22.
Q — Kt 3 ch, K — R 1, etc.

21.	Kt × Kt
22. B — R 7 ch	K × B
23. R × R	R × R
24. Q × R	Kt — B 3
25. R — B 1	Q — Kt 5

If 25. ....Kt — K 5; 26. Q
— B 2 and exchange of Queens
is forced.

26. Q — B 2 ch	K — Kt 1
27. Q — B 6	Q — R 6
28. Q — R 5 ch	K — R 2
29. R — B 7	Q × R P

Black has no defence now that
the White Queen and Rook are
working in unison. The passive
29. ....K — Kt 3 loses even
quicker after 30. Q × R P, Q —
B 1; 31. Q × P, etc.

30. R × B P	Q — Q 8 ch
31. K — R 2	Q — R 4

Necessary; for if 31. ....P —
Q R 4; 32. Q — K B 8, Kt —
R 4; 33. P — Kt 4.

32. Q × R P	Q — Kt 3
33. R — B 8	Q — B 4

This and the next few moves
represent the last flicker of resistance; Black threatens to
regain the exchange by Kt —
Kt 5 ch.

34. R — B 7	Q — Kt 3
35. R — Kt 7	Kt — K 5
36. Q — R 2	P — K 4
37. Q × P	P × P
38. R — Kt 8	Kt — B 3
39. Q × P	Q — B 4
40. R × P	Q × P
41. Q — Q 3 ch	K — Kt 1
42. R — Kt 8 ch	Resigns

Further resistance is useless
after 42. ....K — B 2; 43. R —
Kt 7 ch, K — K 3; 44. R × P.

30
SIXTH ROUND,
NEW YORK, 1924

Queen's Pawn, Dutch Defence

White   Black
CAPABLANCA   S. TARTAKOWER

1. P — Q 4   P — K B 5
2. Kt — K B 3

The usual move nowadays is 2. P — K Kt 3; for the Dutch Defence generally resolves into a struggle for the possession of K 4, and the fianchettoed Bishop is useful both for this purpose and also to hamper the development of Black's Q side. It soon becomes clear that Capablanca, in order to avoid a prepared line by his opponent (a well-known expert on the Dutch Defence), intends to steer clear of all normal channels into completely uncharted seas.

2. ......   P — K 3
3. P — B 4   Kt — K B 3

Here, or on the next move, Black should play the more aggressive B — Kt 5 ch, e.g. 3. .... B —Kt 5 ch; 4. B — Q 2, Q — K 2; 5. Kt — B 3, Kt — K B 3 followed by 6. ——— P — Q Kt 3 and 7. .... B — Kt 2 with command of K 5.

4. B — Kt 5   B — K 2
5. Kt — B 3   Castles
6. P — K 3   P — Q Kt 3
7. B — Q 3   B — Kt 2
8. Castles   Q — K 1

In the second round, against Marshall, Tartakower tried the premature 8. .... Kt — K 5; 9. B × B, Q × B; 10. B × Kt, P × B; 11. Kt — Q 2, Q — R 5; 12. Q Kt × P and a Pawn is lost, since, if 12. .... B × Kt; 13. P — K Kt 3, R — B 3; 14. P — B 4, etc.

The text threatens Q — R 4 followed by Kt — Kt 5 and B × Kt.

9. Q — K 2 !   Kt — K 5

For now if 9. .... Q — R 4; 10. P — K 4, P — K R 3 ?; 11. B — B 4, P — Q 3; 12. P × P winning a Pawn. Black therefore tries to exchange off as many pieces as possible.

10. B × B   Kt × Kt
11. P × Kt   Q × B
12. P — Q R 4   B × Kt ?

This move is antipositional; after having gone to such trouble to fianchetto the Bishop and so obtain some measure of control over K 5, it is a foolish waste of time to exchange it for the much less active Kt.

Instead, Black should complete his development — not by 12. .... Kt — B 3; 13. K R — Q 1, Kt — R 4; 14. P — B 5, P × P; 15. R — Kt 5, B × Kt; 16. Q × B, P — B 5; 17. B — B 2, Kt — Kt 6; 18. B × Kt, P × B; 19. R × P and White's control both of the open file and the long diagonal assure him great positional advantage — but by playing 12. .... P — Q 3 followed by 13. .... Kt — Q 2.

13. Q × B   Kt — B 3
14. K R — Kt 1   Q R — K 1

Intending 15. ....P — K 4,
which White's next move immediately prevents.

15. Q — R 3   R — B 3

An abortive attempt at a K
side attack; more to the point
would have been the move recommended by Alekhine in the tournament book: 15. ....P — K
Kt 4. There could then be some interesting play with Black countering on the wing and White concentrating on the centre as follows: 16. P — B 4, P — Kt 5;
17. Q — Kt 3, P — K R 4; 18.
P — K 4, P — R 5; 19. Q — K 3.
However, the positional advantage would still be with White.

16. P — B 4!   Kt — R 4
17. Q — B 3   P — Q 3

17. ....P — B 4 would be met
by 18. R — Kt 5! P × P; 19.
B P × P, R — Q B 1; 20. P —
B 5!

18. R — K 1   Q — Q 2

Position after 18. ....Q — Q 2

A most interesting position;
Black moves the Queen off the K
file in order to avoid the discovery
of an attack upon it by the White
Rook. For if 18. ....P — K 4;
19. P — K 4, P × B P; 20. P ×
P, Q × R ch; 21. R × Q, R
× R ch; 22. K — B 2, R — K 6;
23. Q — Q 5 ch, K — B 1 and
here the Queen will prove supe-
rior to the two Rooks owing to
the exposed nature of Black's
King, e.g. 24. B — K 4, R ×
Q B P; 25. Q — R 8 ch, K —
K 2; 26. Q — K Kt 8, R × Q
B P; 27. Q × P ch, R — B 2; 28.
P — B 6 ch, K — K 3; 29. B —
Q 5 ch and wins.

19. P — K 4   P × P

Black cannot permit 20. P —
K 5.

20. Q × P   P — Kt 3
21. P — Kt 3   K — B 1

White menaces an eventual P
— R 4 — R 5 and Black therefore
moves his King out of mating
range.

22. K — Kt 2   R — B 2

Better for Black would have
been the exchange of Queens,
since after 22. ....Q — B 3; 23.
Q × Q, Kt × Q the superficially
attractive 24. P — B 5 is not
really good for White. It is true
that it threatens 25. B — Kt 5,
but this is easily met by 24. ....
Kt — R 4 and now White is considerably embarrassed as to what
to do with his Q side Pawns. If
he plays 25. P × Q P, P × P;

26. R — K 3, R — B 1 and it is Black who is attacking, not White.

So White would do best to play 24. P — R 4 followed by P — K R 5, as in the actual game.

23. P — R 4   P — Q 4

This leads to a lost Rook and Pawn ending, conducted with great skill and accuracy by Capablanca.

For the reasons given in the last note, 23. ....Q — B 3 was to be preferred. There is not much hope offered of saving the game by exchanging Knight for Bishop as in 23. ....Kt × P; 24. B × Kt, P — Q 4; 25. B × P, Q × B (or 25. ....P × B; 26. Q × R ch, Q × Q; 27. R × Q ch, K × R; 28. P — Q R 5); 26. P — Q R 5 and Black's Pawn position is extremely weak.

24. P × P   P × P
25. Q × R ch   Q × Q
26. R × Q ch   K × R
27. P — R 5 !

Very strong; now White's Rook must reach the 7th rank.

27. ......   R — B 3

With the double idea of defending the K Kt Pawn, and preparing a counter-attack on White's Q B Pawn. If 27. ....P × P; 28. R — R 1, K B 1; 29. R × P winning either the K R or Q Pawn.

28. P × P   P × P
29. R — R 1   K — B 1

In order to play R — B 3 without being pinned by the B on Kt 5.

30. R — R 7   R — B 3
31. P — Kt 4   Kt — B 5
32. P — Kt 5

Here the game was adjourned. White was threatening 33. R — R 6 followed by P — B 5.

32. ......   Kt — K 6 ch

No better is 32. ....Kt — Q 7; 33. R — R 6, Kt — K 5; 34. P — B 4, etc.

33. K — B 3   Kt — B 4

Position after 33. ....Kt — B 4

Tartakower gives the following interesting variation as his reason for not playing 33. ....Kt — Q 8; 34. R — R 6, K — Kt 2; 35. P — B 5, Kt × P; 36. K — B 4, Kt — K 5; 37. B × Kt, P × B; 38. P — B 6 ch! R × P ch; 39. P × R ch, K × R; 40. K × P, K — R 2; 41. K — Q 5, K — Kt 1; 42. K — B 6, P — K Kt 4; 43. K × P, P — Kt 5; 44. P — Q 5, P —

Kt 6; 45. P — Q 6, P — Kt 7; 46.
P — Q 7, P — Kt 8 = Q; 47. P
— Q 8 = Q ch and wins.

34.	B × Kt	P × B
35.	K — Kt 3 !	

Planning a mating net by
working the King round to K B 6
and advancing the Pawn to Kt 6,
after which Black is quite helpless.

35.	......	R × P ch
36.	K — R 4	R — B 6

If 36. ....R — B 8; 37. K —
R 5 (and not 37. P — Kt 6, R —
R 8 ch; 38. K — Kt 5, R × R; 39.
P × R, K — Kt 2; 40. K × P, P
— B 4 and Black draws); 37.
....K — Kt 1; 38. R — Q 7 win-
ning; or 36. ....P — R 4; 37. P
— Kt 6, P — Kt 4; 38. P × P, P
— R 5; 39. K — Kt 5, P — R 6;
40. K — B 6 and Black is in a
mating net.

37.	P — Kt 6	R × P ch
38.	K — Kt 5	R — K 5

Or 38. ....R × P; 39. K —
B 6, K — Kt 1; 40. R — Q 7 and
White mates.

39.	K — B 6	K — Kt 1
40.	R — Kt 7 ch	K — R 1
41.	R × P	R — K 1
42.	K × P	R — K 5

After 42. ....P — R 3; 43. R
— R 7, P — Kt 4; 44. P — R 5
White wins the Q R Pawn and
eventually plays P — Q R 7 and
R — Q Kt 8, the Black Rook being tied to the back rank owing
to the threat of mate.

43.	K — B 6	R — B 5 ch
44.	K — K 5	R — Kt 5
45.	P — Kt 7 ch	K — Kt 1

Black might well have resigned
here, since 45. ....R × P; 46. R
× R, K × R; 47. K × P is obviously lost for him. The Rook and
Pawn endgame from the 27th
move to this point was most instructive.

46.	R × P	R — K Kt 8
47.	K × P	R — Q B 8
48.	K — Q 6	R — B 7
49.	P — Q 5	R — B 8
50.	R — Q B 7	R — Q R 8
51.	K — B 6	R × P
52.	P — Q 6	Resigns

31

SEVENTH ROUND,
NEW YORK, 1924

Queen's Pawn,
King's Indian Defence

White	Black
CAPABLANCA	F. D. YATES
1. P — Q 4	P — K Kt 3
2. Kt — K B 3	Kt — K B 3
3. Kt — B 3	

An unusual but very solid method of dealing with the King's Indian Defence. It foreshadows
play with the minor pieces rather
than the gradual construction of
a centre by Pawn moves.

3.	......	P — Q 4

Necessary to prevent P — K 4;
the consequences of allowing this
are shown by the game Tarrasch-
Davidson, Semmering, 1926,
which continued 3. ....B — Kt 2;

4. ....P — K 4, Castles; 5. B — K Kt 5, P — K R 3; 6. B — K B 4, P — Q 3; 7. Q — Q 2, K — R 2; 8. Castles, P — Q R 4; 9. B — Q 3, Kt — R 3; 10. P — K 5, Kt — Kt 1; 11. P — K R 4, Kt — Kt 5; 12. P — R 5 with an overwhelming attack.

4. B — B 4 B — Kt 2
5. P — K 3 Castles
6. P — K R 3

A move unjustly criticised by Alekhine in the tournament book. It provides a means of maintaining the Bishop on the long diagonal in the event of 6. .... Kt — R 4 and, more important still, it prevents the development of Black's Q Bishop by 6. ....B — K Kt 5.

Colle, against Euwe at Amsterdam, 1928, omitted this move and played instead 6. B — Q 3, P — B 4; 7. P × P, Q Kt — Q 2; 8. Castles, Kt × P; 9. B — K 5, B — Kt 5; 10. P — K R 3, Kt × B; 11. P × Kt, B × Kt; 12. Q × B, P — K 3 leaving Black with a most satisfactory game.

6. ...... P — B 4
7. P × P Q — R 4

With the idea of opening up an attack by Kt — K 5. This attack proves to be illusory, and consequently the Q move is a mere waste of time. Better would have been 7. ....Q Kt — Q 2.

8. Kt — Q 2 !

An excellent preventative move, disposing once and for all of Black's threatened Kt — K 5.

8. ...... Q × B P

If now 8. ....Q Kt — Q 2; 9. Kt — Kt 3; or 8. ....Kt — K 5; 9. Q Kt × Kt, P × Kt; 10. P — Q B 3.

9. Kt — Kt 3 Q — Kt 3
10. B — K 5

From now on Capablanca utilises the fact that he has three minor pieces in play very cleverly indeed. His object is to force the exchange of Black's fianchettoed Bishop and so weaken him on the black squares. He therefore first induces Black to play P — K 3 by the threat of B × Kt followed by Kt × P.

10. ...... P — K 3

If 10. ....B — K 3; 11. B — Q 4, Q — Q 1; 12. Kt — B 5, and White gains the advantage of two Bishops.

11. Kt — Kt 5 Kt — K 1

Forced, since 11. ....Kt — R 3; 12. B — Q 4 would lose the Q R Pawn.

12. B × B Kt × B
13. P — K R 4 !

Introducing a fresh menace to the Black position; after suitable preparation, White will play P — K R 5 with attack on the weakened Black K wing.

13. ...... P — Q R 3
14. Kt — B 3 Kt — B 3
15. B — Q 3 P — B 4 ?

This worsens Black's Pawn structure to no purpose. Black must try to complete his development and institute a counter-attack by 15. ....Q — B 2 followed by P — Q Kt 4 and B — Kt 2.

16. Q — Q 2

Preparing to Castle Q side and also threatening Kt — R 4 — B 5.

16. ......   Kt — K 4
17. B — K 2   Kt — B 5

As a result of this move, White can force the exchange of Queens and is left with the superior Rook and minor piece endgame, since Black's Pawn position is bad and White will control the Q file. But if 17. ....B — Q 2; 18. Q — Q 4.

18. B × Kt   P × B
19. Q — Q 4   Q — B 2

19. ....Q × Q; 20. Kt × Q, P — K 4; 21. Kt — B 3, R — K 1; 22. Castles Q leaves White in full control of the Q file. Nevertheless, White is not to be prevented from exchanging Queens.

20. Q — B 5   Q × Q
21. Kt × Q

Black's weakness on the black squares will tell heavily on him in the ensuing endgame. In addition, his Pawns being on the same colour squares as his Bishop, the development and action of this piece are considerably circumscribed. In contrast, the activity of the White Knights is very marked.

It is instructive to observe how

Capablanca weaves a win out of these intangible advantages.

Position after 21. Kt × Q

21. ......   P — Kt 3

If 21. ....R — Q 1; 22. K — K 2 followed by Q R — Q 1 and Black will be unable to contest possession of the Q file.

22. Kt (B 5) — R 4   R — Kt 1
23. Castles Q

Threatening R — Q 6, hence Black's next two moves.

23. ......   P — Q Kt 4
24. Kt — B 5   R — Kt 3
25. P — Q R 4

This, and White's next move, destroy Black's advanced Pawn chain on the Q side, and with it disappears the only favourable aspect of Black's position.

25. ......   Kt — R 4

If 25. ....R — Q B 3; 26. Kt — Q 7, B × Kt (forced, any Rook move loses the exchange); 27. R × B, P — Kt 5; 28. Kt — K 2, R — K B 2; 29. K R — Q 1, R —

B 2; 30. R × R (Q B 7), R × R;
31. R — Q 6 and White will win
one of the Q side Pawns.

26. P — Q Kt 3   B P × P
27. B P × P   P × P
28. Kt (B 3) × P   R — Q B 3
29. K — Kt 2   Kt — B 3

Attempts at a counter-attack
only lead Black into further diffi-
culties, e.g. 29. . . . . P — K 4; 30.
R — Q 5, P — K 5; 31. K R —
Q 1 or 29. . . . . P — B 5; 30. P
— K 4.

30. R — Q 2   P — Q R 4

This Pawn, the melancholy
remnant of a once impressive
Pawn chain, eventually proves indefensible on Q R 4. But it is
equally lost on Q R 3, for if 30.
. . . . P — K 4;   31.   K R — Q 1
followed by R — Q 6.

31. K R — Q 1   Kt — Q 4
32. P — Kt 3

Played with merciless precision; Black is not allowed a
counter-attack by P — B 5.

32. . . . . . .   K R — B 2
33. Kt — Q 3

This Kt is eventually bound for
Q B 4 in order to attack the Q R
Pawn. Contrast the free and
powerful action of this piece with
the miserable, passive rôle of the
Q Bishop.

33. . . . . . .   R — Q Kt 2
34. Kt — K 5   R (B 3) — B 2
35. R — Q 4   K — Kt 2
36. P — K 4 !

Nicely timed; Black is forced
to accept a further weakness on
K 3 and exchange Pawns, as
otherwise he loses the only
strength in his position — the
powerful post of the Kt on Q 4.

36. . . . . . .   P × P
37. R × P   R — Kt 4
38. R — Q B 4   R × R
39. Kt × R   B — Q 2

Containing a veiled threat of
exchange of this useless piece for
the Kt on R 4. But White is now
ready for the final manœuvre to
win the Q R Pawn, which he does
by a series of neatly calculated Kt
moves.

Position after 39. . . . . B — Q 2

40. Kt — B 3   R — B 4
41. Kt — K 4   R — Kt 4
42. Kt (K 4) — Q 6 R — B 4
43. Kt — Kt 7   R — B 2
44. Kt (Kt 7) × P

Now White is a passed Pawn
up, and the winning of the game
is a matter of technique. Black,
however, puts up a dogged resistance (Yates was not the sort of

player to give in without a prolonged struggle), and White has
to play both accurately and in-
cisively.

44.	. . . . . .	B — Kt 4
45.	Kt — Q 6	B — Q 2
46.	Kt (R 5) — B 4	R — R 2
47.	Kt — K 4	P — R 3
48.	P — B 4	B — K 1
49.	Kt — K 5	R — R 1
50.	R — Q B 1	B — B 2
51.	R — B 6	B — Kt 1
52.	Kt — B 5	R — K 1

Not 52. ....K — B 3; 53. Kt
— Kt 4 ch winning a Pawn.

53.	R — R 6	R — K 2
54.	K —R 3	B — B 2
55.	P — Q Kt 4	Kt — B 2
56.	R — B 6	Kt — Kt 4 ch
57.	K — Kt 2	Kt — Q 5
58.	R — R 6	B — K 1

Or 58. ....Kt — B 4; 59. Kt
— K 4, R — Kt 2; 60. K — B 3,
R — B 2 ch; 61. R — B 6 and
exchange of Rooks would only ac-
celerate Black's loss; whilst the
Black Rook dare not leave the
second rank owing to the unfortunately helpless position of the
Bishop.

59.	P — Kt 4	K — B 3
60.	Kt — K 4 ch	K — Kt 2
61.	Kt — Q 6	B — Kt 4
62.	R — R 5	B — B 8

Or 62. ....B — K 1; 63. Kt ×
B ch, R × Kt; 64. R — R 7 ch,
etc. Now, the Bishop being diverted from the scene of action,
White is able to weave a mating
net with his beautifully posted
Kts.

| 63. | R — R 8 | P — Kt 4 |

Black must give up a Pawn to
avert, temporarily at any rate, the
threat of mate by 64. Kt —
K 8 ch, K — R 2; 65. Kt — B 6 ch,
K — Kt 2; 66. P — Kt 5.

64.	B P × P	P × P
65.	P × P	B — Kt 7
66.	R — K 8	R — Q B 2

Exchange of Rooks obviously
leads to a completely lost minor
piece endgame.

67.	R — Q 8	Kt — B3
68.	Kt — K 8 ch	K — B 1
69.	Kt × R	Kt × R
70.	K — B 3	B — Kt 2
71.	K — Q 4	B — B 1
72.	P — Kt 6	Kt — Kt 2
73.	Kt — K 8 !	Kt — Q 1

Not 73. ....K × Kt; 74. P —
Kt 7.

74.	P — Q Kt 5	K — Kt 1
75.	P — Kt 5	K — B 1
76.	P — Kt 7 ch	K — Kt 1
77.	P — K Kt 6	Resigns

For White will deliver mate by
78. K — K 3; 79. Kt — Kt 4; 80.
Kt — R 6.

32
NINTH ROUND,
NEW YORK, 1924

Queen's Pawn Opening

White	Black
E. D. Bogoljuboff	Capablanca
1. P — Q 4	Kt — K B 3
2. Kt — K B 3	P — Q 4
3. P — K 3	

This voluntary imprisonment of White's Q Bishop usually indicates White's determination to guide the game on one of two fixed lines; the first, favoured by Colle, consists of complete development of all pieces, followed by P — K 4 in the hope that this delayed advance will be all the more effective in combination with the stored-up energy of White's pieces; the second lies in Rubinstein's variation, where, after due preparation, White launches an attack both on the Q B file and the centre.

It soon becomes apparent that Bogoljuboff has not made up his mind which course to pursue and his half-hearted opening tactics are in direct contrast to Black's simple but vigorous counter measures.

3. ......   P — K 3

Or Black can play 3. .... P — B 4 at once, and there is also the possibility of developing his Q Bishop by 3. .... B — B 4. If then 4. B — Q 3, P — K 3; 5. B × B, P × B; 6. Q — Q 3 (Black gets a very good game after 6. Castles, Q Kt — Q 2; 7. P — B 4, P × P; 8. Q — R 4, B — Q 3; 9. Q Kt — Q 2, Castles; 10. Kt × P, Kt — Kt 3; Colle–Alekhine, San Remo, 1930, White should now have played 11. Q — B 2, but committed the positional error of opening the Q R file by 11. Kt × Kt); 6. .... Q — B 1; 7. Castles, B — Q 3 with an excellent game.

4. B — Q 3

First signs of indecision — the normal developing move in the Colle system is 4. Q Kt — Q 2.

4. ......   P — B 4
5. P — Q Kt 3

Now 5. Q Kt — Q 2 would be met by P — B 5. If White wishes to continue with the Colle variation, he should play 5. P — B 3.

5. ......   Kt — B 3
6. Castles

And now, playing along Rubinstein lines, 6. P — Q R 3 followed by B — Kt 2, Castles, Q Kt — Q 2 and P — Q B 4 would have given White a settled and secure plan of development.

6. ......   B — Q 3
7. B — Kt 2   Castles
8. Q Kt — Q 2

Here 8. P — Q R 3 is an imperative necessity; strangely enough, the obvious developing of the Q Kt is a decisive strategic blunder.

8. ......   Q — K 2 !

With a double threat of 9. .... P — K 4 or, as in the actual game, 9. .... P × P followed by a weakening of White's Q wing by B — R 6.

9. Kt — K 5

Parrying one of the threats, but it would have been better to allow P — K 4 and proceed 9. P — Q R 3, P — K 4; 10. P × B P,

B × P; 11. P — K 4, R — Q 1;
12. Q — K 2 with an equal game.

9. ......   P × P
10. P × P   B — R 6
11. B × B   Q × B
12. Q Kt — B 3

After the exchange of Bishops, White has a marked weakness on the Q side, and the remainder of the game centres round Black's scheme to exploit this.

12. ......   B — Q 2
13. Kt × Kt

Anticipating Black's attack on the Q B file by Q R — B 1 and Kt — Q Kt 5.

13. ......   B × Kt
14. Q — Q 2

Bogoljuboff attempts to regain control of some of the black squares and also frees the back line for his Rooks; rather more effective, however, would have been 14. Q — B 1, Q — Q 3; 15. Kt — K 5, Q R — B 1; 16. Q — K 3.

14. ......   Q R — B 1
15. P — B 3 ?

Exchanging the weakness of the square on Q B 3 for a much more serious weakness of Pawn position. White should leave his Q side Pawns severely alone and play instead 15. Kt — K 5 followed by P — K B 4.

15. ......   P — Q R 3 !

A very fine move by which Black forces the exchange of his inactive Bishop for White's best placed piece, the Bishop on Q 3.

16. Kt — K 5   B — Kt 4
17. P — B 3

17. B × B would only open up another line for Black's Rooks.

17. ......   B × B
18. Kt × B   R — B 2
19. Q R — B 1   K R — B 1
20. R — Q B 2   Kt — K 1

Threatening to bring another piece to bear on the unfortunate Q B Pawn by Kt — Q 3 — Kt 4.

21. K R — B 1   Kt — Q 3
22. Kt — K 5 ?

This mechanical preference for K 5 leads to early disaster. A better defence would have been afforded by 22. Kt — B 5, though Black would still be able to maintain the pressure by 22. .... P — K 4; 23. Kt — R 4, P — K 5.

22. ......   Q — R 4

Threatening 23. .... Kt — Kt 4.

23. P — Q R 4

Preventing the above-mentioned threat but at the cost of a further fatal weakening.

If 23. Kt — Q 3 then not 23. .... Kt — Kt 4 because of 24. Kt — B 5, P — Q Kt 3; 25. Kt — R 4 and White has managed to secure his position. Instead, Black should play 23. .... P — Q Kt 3 at once.

23. ......   Q — Kt 3

Position after 23. ....Q — Kt 3

24. Kt — Q 3

The combined effect of the pins on the Q Pawn and the Q B file force White to abandon the Pawn. For if 24. R — Kt 1, Kt — B 4; 25. R (B 2) — B 1, P — B 3; 26. Kt — Kt 4 (or 26. Kt — Q 3, Kt × P; 27. P × Kt, Q × P ch; 28. K — R 1, Q × Kt!); 26. .... P — K 4 and White loses the Q Pawn; whilst if 24. P — Q Kt 4 then P — Q R 4; 25. P — Kt 5, Kt — B 5; 26. Kt × Kt, R × Kt; 27. R — R 1, P — K 4 and again the Q Pawn is lost.

24.	......	Q × P
25.	Kt — B 5	Q — Kt 3
26.	R — Kt 2	Q — R 2
27.	Q — K 1	P — Q Kt 3
28.	Kt — Q 3	R — B 5
29.	P — R 5	

Another Pawn must be given up, since after 29. R — R 2, Q — B 2; 30. R — R 3, P — Q Kt 4; 31. P × P, Kt × P; 32. R × P, Kt × B P White is quite lost.

29.	......	P × P
30.	Kt — B 5	Kt — Kt 4
31.	R — K 2	

Now comes a sudden decisive stroke.

31.	......	Kt × Q P !
32.	P × Kt	R (B 1) × Kt

Resigns, as White has nothing better than to descend to an end-game three Pawns down after 33. R — Kt 8 ch, Q × R; 34. P × R, Q — Kt 4, etc. A drastic example of the weaknesses liable to ensue after a purposeless Queen's fian-chetto.

33

THIRTEENTH ROUND, NEW YORK, 1924

Ruy Lopez, Morphy Defence

White	Black
G. Maroczy	Capablanca
1. P — K 4	P — K 4
2. Kt — K B 3	Kt — Q B 3
3. B — Kt 5	P — Q R 3
4. B — R 4	Kt — B 3
5. Castles	B — K 2
6. R — K 1	P — Q Kt 4
7. B — Kt 3	Castles

The usual, and better, move is 7. ....P — Q 3 so as to be able to proceed with Kt — Q R 4 and P — Q B 4.

8. P — B 3

For here White could have played with considerable effect 8. P — Q R 4.

8. ......   P — Q 3

Game No. 22, Capablanca-Marshall, New York, 1918, dem-

onstrates the perils of 8. .... P
— Q 4 — for both sides! The sacrifice of the Pawn is, however,
unsound for Black.

9. P — K R 3

The alternative is 9. P — Q 4
allowing the pin of the Kt by 9.
....B — Kt 5. White then has to
determine how to defend his Q
Pawn. He can either play 10. P
— Q 5, Kt — Q R 4; 11. B —
B 2, Kt — Q 2 and Black will
play P — K Kt 3 and eventually
P — K B 4; or he can develop
a piece by 10. B — K 3, P × P;
11. P × P, Kt — Q R 4; 12. B —
B 2, P — B 4; 13. Q Kt — Q 2,
Kt — B 3; 14. P — K R 3, B ×
Kt; 15. Kt × B with an approxi-
mately level game. White's possession of two Bishops is a strong,
potential advantage in this open
position, but Black has a solid,
compact game.

9.	Kt — Q R 4
10. B — B 2	P — B 4
11. P — Q 3	

Tame and a contradiction of his
9th move, the sole purpose of
which is to prevent B — K Kt 5
after White has played P — Q 4;
this last move is, of course, the
normal and right method of play.
After the text the initiative falls
to Black.

11.	Kt — B 3
12. Q Kt — Q 2	P — Q 4
13. Kt — B 1	P × P

But here Black over-simplifies
and allows White the chance of
obtaining equality. The right

move to maintain pressure is 13.
.... P — Q 5.

14. P × P	B — K 3
15. B — Q 2	

This cumbrous move is inferior
to 15. Q × Q, K R × Q; 16. P —
Q Kt 3 followed by B — K 3 and
Q R — Q 1 with an easy draw.

15.	R — R 2!

A strong move which prepares
to obtain control of the Q file by R
— Q 2.

16. Kt — Kt 5

An interesting counter; White
forces the Bishop to move in order
to establish at Kt on K B 5.

16.	B — B 5
17. Kt — K 3	B — Q 6
18. B × B	Q × B
19. Kt — B 5	P — R 3
20. R — K 3	Q — Q 1
21. Kt — B 3	R — Q 2
22. Q — B 2	

More aggressive would have
been 22. Q — B 1 followed by R
— K 1 with the threat of B × P.

22.	P — B 5

Position after 22. .... P — B 5

23. Kt × B ch ?

Having gone to such pains to establish the Kt on B 5, it was foolish to exchange it for the less important Bishop; with correct play here, a draw is the natural result, e.g. 23. P — Q R 4, B — B 4; 24. R — K 2, R — Q 6; 25. P × P (if 25. B × P, P × B; 26. Q — B 1, Kt — K 2 and Black can fend off White's attack); 25. ....P × P; 26. R — R 6, Kt — Kt 1; 27. R — R 1, Kt — B 3 and Black must submit to a draw by repetition of moves.

23. ......   Q × Kt
24. P — Q R 4

If White tries to bring the other Kt to K B 5 by 24. Kt — R 4 then ....Q — Q 1; 25. R — K 2, Kt — K 2 and Black will play R — Q 6 with the threat of Kt × P.

24. ......   K R — Q 1
25. P × P   P × P
26. K R — K 1   Q — K 3

This allows White to form a solid defensive position from which it will prove difficult if not impossible to dislodge him.

Best was 26. ....R — Q 6; 27. R — R 6, Q — Q 2 and Black will play Kt — K 2 — Kt 3 followed by Kt — R 4 — B 5 with a strong attack both in the centre and on the K side.

27. B — K 3   R — Q 6
28. Kt — Q 2   Kt — K 2

And here 28. ....Q — Q 2 was stronger, since White could not then play 29. P — B 3 because of 29. ....R × Kt.

29. P — B 3

By this and his next four moves White consolidates his game into a position proof against any attack.

29. ......   Kt — R 4
30. Kt — B 1   P — B 4

This is the best chance of maintaining the attack; on other moves White would play R — R 5 and double the Rooks on the Rook file.

31. B — B 2   Q — K Kt 3
32. K — R 2

Now 32. ....Kt — B 5 is met by 33. B — Kt 3.

32. ......   Q — Kt 4

Preparing to bring the Kt on K 2 into action on Kt 3.

33. B — K 3   Kt — B 5

Here the game was adjourned in a position in which White could count on a safe draw.

Position after 33. ....Kt — B 5

34. Kt — Kt 3 ?

Falling into a neat trap and losing the game. He should have

played the obvious 34. B × Kt
and after 34. ....Q × B ch; 35.
K — R 1 (and not 35. K — Kt 1,
R — Q 7; 36. Kt × R, R × Kt;
37. Q — B 1, Q — Kt 4; 38. P
— K Kt 4, Q — B 5 with a mating attack); 35. ....Q — Kt 4
(if now 35. ....R — Q 7; 36. Kt
× R, R × Kt; 37. Q — B 1, Q —
Kt 4; 38. R — K Kt 1, etc.); 36.
Q — B 2, P — B 5; 37. R — R 5
and Black is forced on the defensive.

34. ......   R × B

A decisive sacrifice, the point of
which is seen on Black's next
move.

35. R × R   Kt × Kt P !

Maroczy had overlooked this
move, only taking into calculation
35. ....Kt × R P, to which he
had the adequate reply, 36. Kt —
B 1. Now White's King side is
completely shattered.

36. R — K 2   Kt — B 5
37. R — Q 2

If the Rook moves elsewhere
then 37. ....Q — R 5 wins at
once.

37. ......   R — K B 1

Not the quickest way of finishing the game. Strongest was the
simple 37. ....R × R ch; 38. Q
× R, Q — R 5 and White is helpless against the threat of Q ×
P ch, e.g. 39. Kt × P, Q × P ch;
40. K — Kt 1, Kt × Kt; 41. P ×
Kt, Q — Kt 6 ch; 42. K — R 1,
Q × P ch and Black will remove

the Pawn on K B 4, after which
White's game will be resignable.

Or White may play 39. Q —
K B 2, Kt × P; 40. Q — K 1, Kt
— B 5 dis ch; 41. K — Kt 1, Kt
— Q 6 and Black wins the Kt on
Kt 3.

38. Kt — R 1

White, in turn, his morale de-
stroyed by Black's surprise 35th
move, fails to find the best move
for further resistance. He should
have played 38. Q — Q 1 and
then if 38. ....Q — R 5; 39. Q
— K B 1, P × P; 40. P × P, Kt
— Q 6; 41. Kt — B 5, Kt × Kt;
42. P × Kt, P — K 5; 43. R —
R 7, P — K 6; 44. R — Kt 2, R
— B 2; 45. R × R, K × R; 46.
Q — B 3, Q — B 5 ch; 47. Q ×
Q, Kt × Q; 48. R — Kt 1 and
Black must content himself with
a draw by 48. ....Kt — Q 6; 49.
R — Kt 2, Kt — B 5 etc.

The best method of continuing
Black's attack is Alekhine's sug-
gestion of 38. ....P — K R 4
threatening P — R 5; if then 39.
R — Q 8, P — R 5; 40. R ×
R ch, K × R and White is lost.

38. ......   Q — R 4
39. Kt — B 2   Kt(K 2) — Kt 3

Preferring to bring the other
Kt into play rather than allow a
slackening of the attack by 39.
....Q × P; 40. R — K Kt 1, Kt
(K 2) — Kt 3; 41. Q — Q 1, Q
— K 6; 42. R   Kt 3.

40. Q — Q 1   Kt — R 5
41. R — Q 8   Kt × P ch
42. K — R 1

Or 42. K — Kt 1, Q — Kt 4 ch, etc.

42. ......   Kt — Q 6
43. R × Kt

Forced; if 43. R × R ch, K × R; 44. K — Kt 2, Q — Kt 4 ch; 45. K × Kt, Q — B 5 ch; 46. K — Kt 2, Q × Kt ch; 47. K — R 1, Q — Kt 6 followed by Kt — B 7 ch.

43. ......   P × R
44. Q × P   P — B 5
45. Q — Q 1

If 45. Q × P, R — Q 1; 46. Q — B 1, R — Q 7 and the threat of R × Kt followed by Q × P mate cannot be met.

45. ......   R — B 3
46. R — R 8 ch   K — R 2
47. Q — Q 8   Kt — Kt 4
48. Q — Kt 8 ch   K — Kt 3
49. Q — K 8 ch   Kt — B 2
50. Q — Q B 8   Q — B 6 ch
51. K — Kt 1   Q — Kt 6 ch

More immediately decisive was 51. ....Q — K 6; 52. R — R 1 (Black threatened Q — K 8 ch followed by P — B 6 ch); 52. ....K — R 2; 53. K — B 1, Kt — Q 3; 54. Q — R 8, Kt — B 5 and there is no reply to the threatened Kt — Q 7 ch.

52. K — B 1   P — B 6
53. Q — Kt 4 ch   Q × Q
54. P × Q

Or 54. Kt × Q, R — B 5; 55. R — R 5, R × P; 56. R × P, P — R 4; 57. Kt — B 2, R — K 7; 58. P — B 4, P — K 5; 59. P —

B 5, P — K 6; 60. Kt — Q 1, Kt — K 4; 61. P — B 6, Kt — Q 6; 62. Kt × P, R — K 8 ch mate.

54. ......   K — Kt 4
55. R — R 5   Kt — Q 3
56. Kt — Q 3   K × P
57. Kt × P ch   K — Kt 6

Resigns; the relative position of the Kings makes further resistance impossible, e.g. 58. Kt — Q 7, R — B 2; 59. Kt — B 5, Kt — B 5 followed by Kt — K 6 ch and P — B 7 ch.

34

FOURTEENTH ROUND, NEW YORK, 1924

Queen's Gambit Declined, Slav Defence

White	Black
CAPABLANCA	EM. LASKER
1. P — Q 4	Kt — K B 3
2. P — Q B 4	P — B 3
3. Kt — Q B 3	P — Q 4
4. P × P	

This Exchange variation is not so simple and clear-cut as it seems, but contains many subtle points at which either side may easily go astray.

4. ......   P × P
5. Kt — B 3   Kt — B 3
6. B — B 4   P — K 3

Out of the many alternatives at his disposal, Black selects the safest line. It is remarkable how complicated the position really is — for Black can play:

(a) 6. ....B — B 4 and now if 7. Q — Kt 3, Kt — Q R 4; 8. Q — R 4 ch, B — Q 2; 9. Q —

B 2, R — B 1; 10. P — K 3, P — Q Kt 4 with the better game for Black (Kan–Lasker, Moscow, 1935). So White does better to play 7. P — K 3, P — Q R 3 (an analysis by the Australian master, Purdy, shows the inferiority of 7. ....Q — Kt 3; 8. Q — Kt 3, Q × Q; 9. P × Q, R — B 1; 10. Kt — K 5, P — Q R 3; 11. Kt × Kt, R × Kt; 12. P — Q Kt 4, P — Q Kt 4; 13. R × P !); 8. Kt — K 5, R — B 1; 9. P — K Kt 4, B — Q 2; 10. B — Kt 2, P — K 3; 11. Castles, P — R 3; 12. B — Kt 3, P — K R 4; 13. Kt × B, Kt × Kt; 14. P × P with advantage to White (Alekhine–Euwe, Avro, 1938).

(b) As in the match game, Euwe–Keres, 1939, 6. ....Q — R 4; 7. P — K 3, Kt — K 5; 8. Q — Kt 3, P — K 3; 9. B — Q 3, B — Kt 5; 10. B × Kt, P × B; 11. Kt — Q 2, Castles; 12. Castles K, Q — K B 4; 13. Kt (Q 2) × P, B × Kt; 14. Kt — K 3, Q — Q 4; 15. P × B with much the superior position for White.

(c) 6. ....Kt — K 5; 7. P — K 3, Kt × Kt; 8. P × Kt, P — K 3; 9. B — Q 3, B — Q 3; 10. B × B, Q × B; 11. Castles, Castles and now either 12. P — B 4 or, as in the game Alekhine–Tartakower, Pistyan, 1922, 12. P — K 4, P × P; 13. B × P, B — Q 2 with the freer position for White.

(d) 6. ....Q — Kt 3; 7. Kt — Q R 4, Q — R 4 ch; 8. B — Q 2, Q — Q 1; 9. P — K 3, P — K 3; 10. B — K 2 (too tame; cor-

rect is the more aggressive 10. B — Q 3, since 10. ....Kt — Q Kt 5 merely loses time after 11. B — Kt 1 followed by P — Q R 3); 10. ....B — Q 3; 11. Castles, Kt — K 5; 12. B — K 1, Castles; 13. Kt — Q 2, Kt × Kt with equality (Eliskases–Bogoljuboff, Bad Nauheim, 1935).

7. P — K 3   B — K 2

Black gets into difficulties after 7. ....B — Q 3; 8. B — Kt 3! (and not 8. B × B, Q × B; 9. B — K 2, Castles; 10. Castles, P — Q R 3; 11. Q — Kt 3, P — Q Kt 4; 12. K R — B 1, B — Q 2; 13. Q — Q 1, K R — B 1; 14. P — K R 3, Kt — Q R 4; 15. Kt — K 5, Kt — B 5 with an excellent game for Black); 8. ....Castles; 9. B — Q 3, R — K 1; 10. R — Q B 1, P — Q R 3; 11. Castles, Q — K 2; 12. B — R 4, B — Q 2; 13. B — Kt 1, P — K R 3; 14. Q — Q 3, Q — Q 1; 15. P — Q R 3, K — B 1; 16. P — K 4, P × P; 17. Kt × P, B — K 2; 18. B × Kt, P × B; 19. Kt — Kt 3 with a strong attack (Mattison–Havasi, Paris, 1924).

8. B — Q 3   Castles

In the 9th Round Lasker played 8. ....Kt — K R 4 and obtained a good game after 9. B — Kt 3, but much stronger for White is 9. B — K 5!

9. Castles

Simplest and best; equality only is to be obtained by 9. R — Q B 1, Kt — K R 4; 10. B — K 5, P — B 3; 11. B — Kt 3, Kt × B;

12. R P × Kt, P — K Kt 3; 13. P — Q R 3, B — Q 2; 14. Kt — Q 2, R — B 2 (Pirc–Fine, Stockholm, 1937); nor can White achieve much by 9. B — Kt 3, Q — Kt 3; 10. Q — K 2, B — Q 2; 11. Castles K, Kt — Q Kt 5; 12. B — Kt 1, K R — Q B 1 (Selesnieff–Rubinstein, Mährisch-Ostrau, 1923).

9. ......   Kt — K R 4

A manœuvre of dubious value which places Black in considerable practical difficulties. Black's best line of play is 9. ....B — Q 2 followed by the development of a counter-attack on the Q side by R — Q B 1, P — Q R 3, P — Q Kt 4, etc.

10. B — K 5

Stronger than 10. B — Kt 3, which merely loses the Bishop for the Kt without recompense; but an excellent alternative is 10. R — B 1, since after 10. ....Kt × B; 11. P × Kt White has a strong hold on K 5. The text move leads to very interesting complications.

Position after 10. B — K 5

10. ......   P — B 4

This delayed formation of a stonewall position is the best manœuvre at Black's disposal. Exchange of the Kt for Bishop leads to a very bad game for Black, e.g. 10. ....Kt × B; 11. Kt × Kt, Kt — B 3; 12. P — B 4, P — K Kt 3; 13. Q — B 3 as in the 7th match game, Marshall–Janowski, 1905.

10. ....P — B 3 also fails against 11. B — B 4 since if 11. ....Kt × B; 12. P × Kt Black's backward Pawn on K 3 will be a very serious handicap in view of the half-open K file.

Not good for White is the tempting sacrificial variation 10. .... P — B 3; 11. Kt — Kt 5, Q — K 1; 12. B × P ch, K — R 1; 13. Q — Kt 1, P — B 4 and White loses a piece without compensation.

11. R — B 1   Kt — B 3
12. B × Kt

Preventing Kt establishing itself on K 5.

12. ......   P × B

At first glance this way of recapturing seems odd, but in reality it provides Black with the best counter-chances. For if 12. .... B × B; 13. Kt — Q R 4 followed by Kt — B 5 giving White strong pressure on the Q B file.

In addition, by the text move Black prevents enemy pieces from placing themselves on K 5; whilst there is also the possibility of a

K side attack on the open K Kt file.

13. Kt — K R 4

In order to bring his K Rook into play by P — B 4 and R — B 3 and also with the immediate threat of P — K Kt 4. This last menace is met at once by Black.

```
13. ......      K — R 1
14. P — B 4     R — K Kt 1
15. R — B 3     B — Q 2
16. R — R 3
```

Threatening Q — R 5 followed by Kt — Kt 6, but as Black can meet this easily enough it would have been better to have played simply 16. R — Kt 3.

```
16. ......      B — K 1
```

If Black plays 16. ....Q — K B 1 in order to bring the Queen over to the K side and so avoid its being cut off from this wing by the Bishop on K 1, then, as Alekhine shows in the tournament book, White has a winning sacrifice by 17. Kt × Q P, P × Kt; 18. Kt × P, B × Kt; 19. B × B, R — Kt 2; 20. Q — Kt 3 with three Pawns for the piece plus a strong attack.

17. P — R 3.
With Q — B 2 in mind.

```
17. ......      R — Kt 2
```

A strong move which makes secure Black's second rank and projects an attack on the K Kt file by B — B 2 and Q — K Kt 1.

18. R — Kt 3

With the object of attacking on the K R file after exchange of Rooks. If instead 18. Q — B 2, B — B 2; 19. B × P ?, P × B; 20. Kt × P, B — Kt 3 !

```
18. ......      R × R
```

Black gets the inferior endgame after 18. ....Q — Q 2; 19. R × R, K × R; 20. P — K Kt 4, P × P; 21. Q × P ch, K — R 1; 22. P — B 5, B — B 2; 23. P × P, Q × P (not 23. ....B × K P; 24. Q — R 5); 24. Q × Q, B × Q; 25. B — B 5, R — Kt 1 ch; 26. K — B 2, B — B 2; 27. Kt — R 4. In this variation, Black's Pawns impede the action of his pieces.

The exchange is therefore forced, as otherwise White can play R × R followed by K — R 1 and P — K Kt 4.

```
19. P × R       R — B 1
20. K — B 2
```

Preparing an attack on the K R file.

```
20. ......      Kt — R 4
21. Q — B 3
```

This inexact move wastes a tempo, as it leaves the Q Kt Pawn unguarded. Capablanca, absorbed in the many possible variations of the preceding moves, had got into time trouble, a most unusual thing for him. As he himself pointed out at the end of the game, the correct move here was 21. Q — K 2.
Unsound is the tempting Kt

sacrifice 21. P — K Kt 4, P × P;
22. Q × P, P — B 4; 23. Kt ×
B P, P × Kt; 24. B × P, R — B 2
(and not 24. ....R — B 3 as
given by Tartakower, since
White then wins by 25. R —
K R 1 and if 25. ....P — K R 3
or R 4; 26. B — K 6!); 25. R —
K R 1, B — K B 3; 26. B — K 6,
B — B 3.

21. ......   Kt — B 5
22. Q — K 2

Recognising his error and plac-
ing the Queen on its right square.
Bad would be 22. Kt — Q 1, Kt
× Kt P!

22. ......   Kt — Q 3

This excellent Kt manœuvre
makes Black's position safe
against threatened Kt sacrifices
by White. If instead 22. ....B
— B 2; 23. Kt × B P, P × Kt;
24. B × P, R — B 2; 25. R —
K R 1, B — Kt 1; 26. Kt — Kt 5,
R — B 3; 27. Q — R 5 winning.

23. R — K R 1

Position after 23. R — K R 1

23. ......   Kt — K 5 ch ?

This is premature and gives
White the eventual chance of sacrificing a piece for three Pawns
and an attack. The lapse is all
the more surprising in view of
Black's admirable play hitherto.
Correct was 23. ....B — B 2
and if 24. P — K Kt 4 then and
then only Kt — K 5 ch; 25. B ×
Kt, B P × B and White's Queen
being unable to reach K Kt 4.
Black's position is perfectly secure.

24. B × Kt   B P × B

If 24. ....Q P × B; 25. P —
K Kt 4, P × P; 26. P — B 5, P
— K 4; 27. Q × P, P × P; 28.
Kt — Kt 6 ch, B × Kt; 29. P ×
B, P × Kt; 30. R × P ch, K —
Kt 1; 31. Q — K 6 ch followed by
mate.

If on move 25 Black plays 25.
....B × P then 26. P × P, Q —
Kt 3; 27. Kt — Kt 6 ch, K —
Kt 1; 28. P × B, R × Kt; 29. R
× P, winning according to an
analysis by Tartakower.

25. Q — Kt 4   P — B 4

Forced; if either 25. ....R —
B 3 or B — B 2 then 26.
P — B 5!

26. Kt × B P

This correct sacrifice gives
White three Pawns for the piece
and an enduring attack. Retiring
the Queen would lose the initiative, e.g. 26. Q — K 2, B × P or
26. Q — R 3 (threatening Kt ×

B P followed by Q × P ch), then simply B × Kt.

26.	P × Kt
27. Q × P	P — K R 4
28. P — K Kt 4	

White must not greedily snatch the Q Pawn at once by 28. Kt × P because of 28. . . . . R — B 7 ch; 29. K — Kt 1, Q — Q 3 (otherwise White plays Q — K 5 ch); 30. Q × P, R — B 8 ch; 31. K — R 2, R × R ch; 32. K × R, B — Q B 3; 33. Q × B, Q × Kt; 34. Q — K 5 ch, Q × Q; 35. Q P × Q, B — K 5 and it is Black who wins, not White!

| 28. . . . . . . | R — B 3 |
| 29. P — Kt 5 | |

White in his turn falters and fails to find the winning move, which was 29. Kt × Q P! The variation given in the previous note no longer holds good, since White has a flight square for his King. After 29. Kt × Q P, R — B 7 ch; 30. K — Kt 3, P — R 5 ch; 31. K — R 3, Q — Q 3; 32. Q — K 5 ch, Q × Q; 33. Q P × Q, B — Q 1; 34. R — Q 1, R × Q Kt P; 35. P — K 6 Black is helpless against the Pawn advance.

Or, according to the fine analysis by Alekhine in the tournament book, 29. Kt × Q P, B — R 5 ch; 30. P — Kt 3, R — B 7 ch; 31. K — Kt 1, R — B 8 ch; 32. K — Kt 2, R — B 7 ch; 33. K — R 3, P × P ch; 34. K × P, B — Q 2; 35. R × B ch, Q × R ch; 36. P × Q, B × Q ch; 37. K × B, R

× P; 38. K — K 6, K — Kt 2; 39. P — B 5, K — B 1; 40. P — R 5, R — Q R 7 (not 40. . . . . R — K R 7; 41. Kt — B 4 followed by P — B 6 and Kt — Kt 6 ch, etc.); 41. P — B 6, R × P; 42. P — R 6, R — R 3 ch; 43. K — B 5; K — Kt 1; 44. Kt — K 7 ch forcing the Queening of a Pawn.

After the move actually played, White should have no more than a draw.

Position after 29. P — Kt 5

29. . . . . . .   K — Kt 1

This should draw, too, but simplest, and therefore preferable as giving less chance of error, was Alekhine's suggestion 29. . . . . R — Q 3; 30. P — K Kt 4, K — Kt 1; 31. P × P, Q — Q 2; 32. Q × Q, B × Q and the power of two Bishops would be sufficient to stem the advance of White's passed Pawns.

From the fact that Lasker avoids the simpler drawing lines for the next few moves one may deduce that he was suffering from

the illusion that his position held
out winning chances.

30. Kt × Q P

If 30. P — K Kt 4, R — Q 3 as
in the last note. And bad for
White would be the exchange of
Queens by 30. Q × P ch, Q × Q;
31. Kt × Q, B — Q 1; 32. Kt —
B 3, B — Kt 3, etc.

30. ......   B — B 2
31. Kt × B ch   Q × Kt
32. P — K Kt 4   P × P

The game was adjourned here
with Black still disdaining the
forced draw that could have been
obtained by 32. ....R — B 7 ch;
33. K — Kt 3 (and not 33. K —
B 1 or K — Kt 3 because of 33.
....Q — B 2 with a mating at-
tack by R — B 8 ch and Q —
B 7 ch); 33. ....R — K 7; 34.
P — Kt 6, P — R 5 ch!; 35. R
× P, R × P ch; 36. K — Kt 2
(not 36. K — B 2, Q × R ch, 37.
K × R, Q — K 8 mate); 36.
....R — K 7 ch; 37. K — B 1, R
— K 8 ch!, etc.

33. Q — R 7 ch   K — B 1
34. R — R 6   B — Kt 1

Again a simpler method of
drawing was by 34. ....R × R;
35. Q × R ch (if 35. P × R, Q —
R 5 ch); 35. ....K — Kt 1 and
now either (a) 36. P — Kt 6, B
— Kt 6; 37. P — B 5, Q —
Q B 2; 38. P — B 6, Q —
B 7 ch; 39. K — Kt 3, Q —
B 2 ch with perpetual check, for
if 40. K × P, B — Q 2 ch followed by mate, or (b) 36. P —

B 5, B — B 5; 37. Q — R 4, Q —
K B 2; 38. Q × P, B — K 3; 39.
Q × P, Q × P ch and Black has
an easy draw, since the three
Pawns are not united.

35. Q — B 5 ch   K — Kt 2

Not 35. ....K — K 1; 36. R
× R, P × R; 37. Q — B 8 ch followed by Q × B P and 35.
....B — B 2 loses the piece after
36. P — Kt 6.

36. R × R   P × R
37. K — Kt 3

Or 37. Q × Kt P, P — B 4; 38.
P × P, Q × B P; 39. P — B 5,
Q — B 7 ch; 40. K — Kt 3, Q —
Kt 8 again drawing easily.

Position after 37. K — Kt 3

37. ......   Q — K 3 ?

A decisive error leading to a
lost ending. After the game Lasker was of the opinion that 37.
....B — Q 4 would have drawn,
since in reply to 38. Q × P Black
can break up the position by 38.
....P — B 4; but Réti's analysis

shows that White has winning chances after 38. Q — B 8, Q — K 3; 39. Q — B 7 ch followed by 40. Q × R P.

The right move to hold the draw is 37. ....B — B 2!, the point being that if now 38. P — Kt 4, Q — K 3; 39. K × P is impossible because of B — R 4 ch winning the Queen. Or if 38. Q — B 8, Q — K 3; 39. Q — Kt 7, Q — B 5; 40. P — B 5, Q — K 7 with perpetual check.

The move played allows White to bring his King into play with powerful effect, in contrast to the variations above, where the King is a positive handicap.

38. K × Kt P   Q × Q ch

Exchange of Queens cannot be avoided; for if 38. ....Q — B 5; 39. Q — B 6 ch and Q — R 6 mate, whilst if either 38. ....Q — K 2 or Q — Q 3; 39. Q — K 5 ch.

39. K × Q   B — Q 4
40. P — Kt 4   P — R 3
41. K — Kt 4

Preparing the final Pawn advance.

41. ......   B — B 5
42. P — B 5   B — Kt 6
43. K — B 4   B — B 7

If 43. ....B — Q 4; 44. K — K 5 followed by P — Q R 4 and P — Kt 5.

44. K — K 5   K — B 2
45. P — R 4   K — Kt 2

Or 45. ....B × P; 46. K × P and the three united passed Pawns win easily.

46. P — Q 5 !

Neatly forcing another passed Pawn.

46. ......   B × P

If 46. ....P × P; 47. K × P, B × P; 48. K × P, etc.

47. P — Q 6   P — B 4
48. P × P   B — B 3
49. K — K 6   P — R 4
50. P — B 6 ch Resigns

For this extremely complicated game Capablanca was awarded the third brilliancy prize; its many vicissitudes are to be explained by the tense psychological nature of the contest between World and ex-World Champion, between tournament leader and his nearest rival.

35

FIFTEENTH ROUND,
NEW YORK, 1924

Réti's Opening

White   Black
CAPABLANCA   D. JANOWSKI

1. Kt — K B 3

Impressed by Réti's handling of the opening in this tournament, Capablanca chooses the Czechoslovakian master's system. No doubt he also thought it advisable to use hypermodern strategy against such a cut-and-thrust player of the old school as Janowski. If so, he must have been disappointed in the results, since

Black's conduct of the opening is impeccable. It is only in the middle game that he goes astray.

| 1. ...... | P — Q 4 |
| 2. P — K Kt 3 | |

This is a slower and not very formidable form of the Réti opening. The true and incisive Réti system arises after 2. P — B 4.

| 2. ...... | P — Q B 4 |
| 3. B — Kt 2 | |

Immediate attack on the centre by 3. P — Q 4 would be to Black's advantage after 3. ....P × P; 4. Kt × P, P — K 4.

3.	Kt — Q B 3
4. Castles	P — K 4
5. P — B 4	

In order to increase the scope of White's King Bishop, Capablanca encourages Black's advance in the centre. But the move is too early and clear-cut to fit in with the Réti system — a system which is characterised by the use of ambiguous latent threats to mystify the opponent; and as a result Black gets a strong hold on the centre.

Better would have been 5. P — Q 3 and if 5. ....B — Q 3; 6. Q Kt — Q 2, K Kt — K 2; 7. P — B 4, P — Q 5; 8. Kt — K 4 and White will obtain the positional advantage of two Bishops.

5.	P — Q 5
6. P — Q 3	B — Q 3
7. P — K 3	K Kt — K 2
8. P × P	

A premature release of tension in the centre. Correct was 8. Q Kt — Q 2 with the threat of 9. Kt — K 4. Black's best reply would then be 8. ....B — B 2 followed by Castles and P — K B 3.

8.	B P × P
9. P — Q R 3	P — Q R 4
10. Q Kt — Q 2	Kt — Kt 3
11. R — K 1	Castles
12. Q — B 2	R — K 1
13. P — Kt 3	

White wishes to play an eventual P — Q Kt 4 and so hastens to anticipate Black's P — Q R 5.

| 13. ...... | P — R 3 |

First signs of faltering by Black; having obtained an excellent opening, he shows by this and the next few moves that he does not know what to do with it. He wishes to play B — K 3 without being bothered by Kt — K 4 — Kt 5, but the right method of guarding against this was 13. ....P — B 3. It is instructive to observe how, later on, White profits from the resultant weakening of Black's K side (cf. move 36 onwards).

| 14. R — Kt 1 | B — K 3 |
| 15. P — K R 4 | Q R — B 1 |

And this move, prompted by the automatic motive of placing the Rook opposite the Queen, is definitely bad, since it allows White's attack to get under way. Correct was the line given by Alekhine in the tournament book, 15. ....Q — K 2; 16. P — R 5,

Kt — B 1; 17. P — B 5, B ×
B P; 18. Kt × K P, Kt × Kt; 19.
R × Kt, B — Q 3; very promis-
ing for Black, then, is the Pawn
sacrifice; 20. R — Q Kt 5, Q R —
B 1, etc.

| 16. P — B 5 | B — Kt 1 |

And not 16. ....B × B P; 17.
Q × B, Kt — Q Kt 5; 18. P ×
Kt and White gains too much ma-
terial for the Queen.

17. Kt — B 4	P — B 3
18. B — Q 2	K — R 1
19. P — Q Kt 4	P × P
20. P × P	Kt — R 2
21. Q — B 1	

Threatening B × P.

| 21. ...... | Kt — Kt 4 |

Black has cleverly parried the
above threat, for if 22. B × P,
Kt — B 6; 23. R — R 1, P —
K 5!

22. Kt — R 2	Q — K 2
23. R — R 1	R — B 2
24. R — R 5	B — Q 2

If 24. ....Kt — R 2; 25. Kt
— Q 6, R — Q 1; 26. Q — R 3
and White controls most of the
board.

25. Kt — Kt 6	B — B 3
26. Q — B 4	Kt — R 2
27. Kt — Q 5	

Forcing Black to exchange his
one well-posted minor piece; the
power of the Bishop on the white
squares is very marked for the
rest of the game.

| 27. ...... | B × Kt |
| 28. Q × B | P — B 4 |

White was threatening 29. Q
— K 4, Kt — B 1; 30. P — B 4,
R — Q 2; 31. Kt — B 3, etc.
However, the text only provides
further targets for White's at-
tack.

29. Q — B 3	Q — B 3
30. P — R 5	Kt — K 2
31. P — Kt 4!	

A powerful move that forces
more open lines for White.

| 31. ...... | P — B 5 |

Or 31. ....P × P; 32. Q ×
Q, P × Q; 33. Kt × P and White
wins a Pawn whilst Black's position breaks to pieces.

| 32. Q — K 4 | K Kt — B 3 |
| 33. Q R — R 1 | Q R — K 2 |

White was threatening B × P.

| 34. Q — Kt 6 | Q — B 1 |

Exchange of Queens equally
leads to a loss, e.g. 34. ....Q ×
Q; 35. P × Q, Kt — Kt 4 (35.
....R — K 3 is also met by B —
Q 5); 36. B — Q 5, Kt — B 2;
37. B — B 7, R — Q 1; 38. Kt —
B 3 and Black is left without a
good move.

| 35. Kt — B 3 | |

Threatening 36. Kt — R 4.
White refuses to fall into the trap
of 35. B — K 4, Q — Kt 1; 36.
Kt — B 3, R — K 3; 37. Q —
B 5, R — K B 1.

35. ......   R — K 3
36. Kt — R 4

After this, however Black plays, he must lose the exchange.

36. ......   R — B 3
37. B — K 4   Q — Kt 1

Position after 37. ....Q — Kt 1

38. B — Q 5!   Kt — K 2

If 38. ....Q — B 1; 39. Q — K 4.

39. Q × R (B 6)   P × Q
40. B × Q   R × B
41. P — B 3   P — B 4

Losing quickly, but the game is obviously not to be saved.

42. B × P   K Kt — B 3
43. Kt — Kt 6 ch   K — R 2

If 43. ....R × Kt; 44. P × R, P × B; 45. R — K 8 ch, K — Kt 2; 46. R × B, etc.

44. B × K P   Kt × B
45. R × Kt   B × R
46. R × Kt   Resigns

36
NINETEENTH ROUND, NEW YORK, 1924
King's Gambit Accepted

White	Black
S. TARTAKOWER	CAPABLANCA
1. P — K 4	P — K 4
2. P — K B 4	P × P
3. B — K 2	

This limited Bishop's Gambit is an old variation much favoured by that eccentric but gifted British master, Bird. Reintroduced and played four times by Tartakower, in the New York Tournament, it is not without point since (*a*) the Bishop can eventually be effectively developed to K B 3, whilst the K Kt is brought to K 2; (*b*) it is not so exposed as on Q B 4, where it might facilitate counter-attack by Black's P Q 4; (*c*) it preserves White from checks on an eventually open K file.

But these virtues are mainly negative, and with correct vigorous play by Black the initiative should pass into the latter's hands.

3. ......   P — Q 4!

The strongest and clearest method of arresting the initiative from White.

In the 3rd round Yates played 3. ....Kt — Q B 3; 4. P — Q 4, P — Q 4; 5. P × P, Q × P; 6. Kt — K B 3, B — Kt 5; 7. Kt — B 3, B — Kt 5; 8. Castles, B × Q Kt; 9. P × B, K Kt — K 2; 10. B × P and White. with two Bishops and the open lines, has much the superior game.

Somewhat artificial, but good enough for equality, is 3. ....Kt — K 2, as played by Alekhine in the 9th round, with the continuation 4. P — Q 4, P — Q 4; 5. P × P, Kt × P; 6. Kt — K B 3, B — Kt 5 ch; 7. P — B 3, B — K 2; 8. Castles, Castles; 9. P — B 4, Kt — K 6; 10. B × Kt, P × B; 11. Q — Q 3, B — B 3; 12. Kt — B 3, Kt — B 3; 13. Kt — Q 5 and now Black should have played 13. ....R — K 1.

Interesting, too, is 3. ....P — K B 4, since the continuation recommended by Tartakower, 4. P — K 5, gives Black the better game after 4. ....P — Q 3; 5. P — Q 4, P × P; 6. P × P, Q × Q ch; 7. B × Q, Kt — B 3; 8. B × P, B — B 4.

4. P × P	Kt — K B 3
5. P — B 4	P — B 3
6. P — Q 4	B — Kt 5 ch !

Much better than 6. ....P × P; 7. B × P, P × P; 8. B × P, B — Kt 5 ch; 9. Kt — B 3, Castles; 10. Kt — K 2, B — Kt 5; 11. Castles, Q Kt — Q 2; 12. Q — Kt 3, B × Q Kt; 13. P × B, as played in the 1st round between Tartakower and Bogoljuboff, when White again enjoys two Bishops with open lines.

7. K — B 1

For if 7. B — Q 2 not B × B ch; 8. Q × B with a good game, but 7. ....Kt — K 5 !; 8. Kt — K B 3 (if 8. B × B, Q —

R 5 ch wins); 8. ....Kt × B; 9. Q Kt × Kt, P × P with an excellent game for Black.

| 7. ...... | P × P |
| 8. B × P | |

If 8. P — B 5 Black should refrain from compromising his K side position by 8. ....P — K Kt 4, but should play simply 8. ....Castles.

| 8. ...... | P × P |
| 9. B × Kt | |

Totally overlooking Black's fine reply; best was 9. B × P.

Position after 9. B × Kt

| 9. ...... | Kt — Q 4 ! |

There is a good deal of poetic justice about this move; White was threatening Q — R 4 ch winning the Bishop, but Black not only parries this, but in addition wishes to win the Queen by Kt — K 6 ch.

10. K — B 2

If 10. B — B 4, Q — B 3 ! again threatening Kt — K 6 ch.

10.	R × B
11. B × P	Castles
12. Kt — K B 3 ?	

Possibly White does not realise how inferior his position has become; in any case, he underestimates the strength of Black's next move. He should play 12. B × Kt, Q × B; 13. Kt — Q B 3, though even then Black's two Bishops assure him much the preferable game.

| 12. ...... | Kt — B 3 |
| 13. Kt — B 3 | P — Q Kt 4 ! |

Black is conducting the whole game with great energy; he could have accepted the Pawn offered, but would have lost some of his initiative after 13. ....B × Kt; 14. P × B, Kt — K 5 ch; 15. K — Kt 1, Kt × P; 16. Q — Kt 3, Kt — K 5; 17. R — K 1, Kt — Q 3; 18. B — Q 5.

| 14. B — Q 3 | |

If 14. Kt × P, Kt — K 5 ch (stronger than 14. ....P — Q R 3; 15. Kt — B 3, B × Kt; 16. P × B, Kt — Kt 5 ch; 17. K — Kt 1, R — Kt 7; 18. Q — B 1 ! Q — Kt 3; 19. B — Kt 3 and White has consolidated his position); 15. K — Kt 1, P — Q R 3; 16. Kt — B 3, Kt × Kt; 17. P × Kt, B × P; 18. R — B 1, B — Kt 7; 19. R — B 2, B — Kt 5 and White will be unable to parry Black's many threats.

| 14. ...... | Kt — Kt 5 ch |
| 15. K — Kt 1 | B — Kt 2 |

| 16. B — B 5 | B × K Kt |
| 17. P × B | Kt — K 6 ! |

This sacrifice of a Pawn, which White is forced to accept, gives Black time to regroup his pieces in a final attack on White's weakened K side.

18. B × P ch	K — R 1
19. Q — Q 3	B × Kt
20. P × B	Kt — Q 4
21. B — K 4	Kt — B 5
22. Q — Q 2	Q — R 5
23. K — B 1	

In order to avoid the threatened manœuvre of R — Kt 3, P — B 4 and R — Kt 3 ch followed by R — Kt 7, and also hoping to be able to offer exchange of Queens by Q — K B 2; but Black does not allow him time for this.

| 23. ...... | P — B 4 |
| 24. B — B 6 | R — B 3 |

Forcing White to shut off his Bishop from the defence of the K side.

| 25. P — Q 5 | R — Q 1 |

Now White is helpless; the immediate threat is 26. ....R × B, and if the Queen moves anywhere there comes immediate disaster, e.g. 26. Q — K B 2, Q — R 6 ch; 27. K — K 1, Kt — Q 6 ch or 26. Q — Q B 2, Q — R 6 ch; 27. K — K 1, R × B; 28. P × R, Kt — Q 6 ch followed by Kt — Kt 5 dis ch, since 29. K — K 2 would be met by Q — Kt 7 ch, etc.

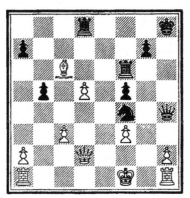

Position after 25. ....R — Q 1

26. R — Q 1   R × B
27. P × R   R × Q
28. R × R   Kt — Q 3
29. R — Q 6   Q — B 5 ch
30. K — Kt 2   Q — K 7 ch

Resigns; for if 31. K — Kt 1, Kt — B 5 or 31. K — Kt 3, Q — K 4 ch; another triumph for Capablanca's natural, easy elegance.

CHAPTER FIVE

Victory and Disaster

THE Moscow Tournament of 1925 was a comparative setback for the World Champion. Both Bogoljuboff and Lasker were ahead of him in the prize list, and he was twice defeated by Russian lesser lights. However, his play improved rapidly towards the end; starting with a beautiful little victory over his old rival, Marshall, he swept on to a magnificent combinational masterpiece against Subarew that deservedly won the first brilliancy prize. Then comes the brilliantly exciting win against the Tournament leader, Bogoljuboff, in which we first observe a type of sacrifice that Capablanca was to make peculiarly his own. And, finally, in the penultimate round, Gotthilf is utterly routed in a very brief number of moves.

Sliding quickly over the tournament at Lake Hopatcong in 1926, from which we give a pleasing example of a victory over Lasker the loser, we now come to what was probably Capablanca's greatest triumph in his tournament career, New York, 1927. Playing four games each against five of the strongest players in the world (Alekhine, Nimzovitch, Vidmar, Spielmann, Marshall), not only did he emerge undefeated, but with a final score of 14 points, 2½ ahead of his nearest rival, Alekhine. The games are correspondingly fine and of a rich variety. The two Nimzovitch games are models of positional perfection which Nimzovitch himself used to illustrate his own theories in books on the game. Alekhine is disposed of in surprisingly summary fashion in Game No. 43, and the game against Vidmar contains the typical Capablanca combination by exchange to secure a won endgame. Most impressive of all is the masterpiece against Spielmann, a game of the highest order, in which positional genius and combinational brilliance are finely blended.

But this high point in Capablanca's career was the prelude to disaster. To the astonishment of practically the whole of the chess-playing world (Réti was the only far-sighted exception), Alekhine challenged and defeated him in a match for the World Championship at Buenos Aires that very same year. Here again, as in Capablanca's previous matches against Kostich and Lasker, the play was not so good or so interesting as one would have expected from two such great masters of the game. Too many of the games end in dull draws before play has properly commenced, and, of those games that are fought out sternly to a finish, only a few are free from regrettable blunders or lapses in judgment. The openings, too, suffer from a certain monotony in treatment; after playing through all the games of the match, one tends to wish that the Cambridge Springs Defence had never been invented. We therefore give but three games from a match the historic importance of which far outweighs the intrinsic value of the games played.

MOSCOW, 1925

	Bogoljuboff	Lasker	Capablanca	Marshall	Tartakower	Torres	Réti	Romanowsky	Grünfeld	Iljin-Zhenevsky	Bogatyrchuk	Rubinstein	Spielmann	Verlinsky	Löwenfisch	Rabinovitch	Yates	Gotthilf	Sämisch	Dus-Chotimirsky	Subarew	
1 Bogoljuboff	—	½	0	½	1	1	0	½	1	1	½	½	1	1	1	1	1	1	1	1	1	15½
2 Lasker	½	—	½	1	½	0	½	1	½	1	1	1	1	1	0	½	1	½	½	1	1	14
3 Capablanca	1	½	—	1	1	½	½	½	½	0	1	½	½	0	½	½	1	1	1	1	1	13½
4 Marshall	½	0	0	—	½	0	1	1	½	0	1	1	1	1	1	1	½	½	0	1	1	12½
5 Tartakower	0	½	0	½	—	½	1	½	½	½	½	1	1	1	½	1	1	½	½	½	½	12
6 Torres	0	1	½	1	½	—	½	0	½	½	0	½	½	1	1	½	0	1	1	1	1	12
7 Réti	1	½	½	0	0	½	—	1	0	1	1	½	0	½	½	1	1	1	½	½	½	11½
8 Romanowsky	½	0	½	0	½	1	0	—	1	0	½	0	0	1	1	1	1	½	1	1	1	11½
9 Grünfeld	0	½	½	½	½	½	1	0	—	1	½	0	½	½	½	1	1	½	½	½	½	10½
10 Iljin-Zhenevsky	0	0	1	1	½	½	0	1	0	—	½	½	1	0	0	½	1	½	½	1	1	10½
11 Bogatyrchuk	½	0	0	0	½	1	0	½	½	½	—	1	½	½	½	1	½	½	½	½	1	10
12 Rubinstein	½	0	½	0	0	½	½	1	1	½	0	—	0	1	0	0	0	1	1	1	1	9½
13 Spielmann	0	0	½	0	0	½	1	1	½	0	½	1	—	0	1	½	½	½	1	0	1	9½
14 Verlinksy	0	0	1	0	0	0	½	0	½	1	½	1	1	—	1	½	0	½	1	1	0	9½
15 Löwenfisch	0	1	½	0	½	0	½	0	½	1	½	0	0	0	—	1	1	½	½	1	½	9
16 Rabinovitch	0	½	½	0	0	½	0	0	0	½	0	1	½	½	0	—	1	1	½	1	1	8½
17 Yates	0	0	0	½	0	1	0	0	0	0	½	1	½	1	0	0	—	½	1	0	1	7
18 Gotthilf	0	½	0	½	½	0	0	0	½	½	½	0	½	½	½	0	½	—	1	0	½	6½
19 Sämisch	0	½	0	1	½	0	½	½	½	½	½	0	0	0	½	½	0	0	—	1	0	6½
20 Dus-Chotimirski	0	0	0	0	½	0	½	0	½	0	½	0	1	0	0	0	1	1	0	—	1	6
21 Subarew	0	0	0	0	½	0	½	0	½	0	0	0	0	1	½	0	0	½	1	0	—	4½

LAKE HOPATCONG, 1926

	Capablanca	Kupchik	Maroczy	Marshall	Lasker	
1 Capablanca ..	—	1 ½	1 ½	½ ½	1 1	6
2 Kupchik	0 ½	—	1 ½	½ 1	1 ½	5
3 Maroczy ..	0 ½	0 ½	—	1 ½	1 1	4½
4 Marshall ..	½ ½	½ 0	0 ½	—	1 0	3
5 Lasker	0 0	0 ½	0 0	0 1	—	1½

NEW YORK, 1927

	Capablanca	Alekhine	Nimzovitch	Vidmar	Spielmann	Marshall	
1 Capablanca ..	—	1 ½	1 ½	½ ½	½ ½	1 1	14
	—	1 ½	1 ½	1 ½	1 ½	½ 1	
2 Alekhine	0 ½	—	½ 0	½ ½	1 ½	½ 1	11½
	½ ½	—	½ 1	½ ½	½ 1	½ 1	
3 Nimzovitch ..	0 ½	½ 1	—	1 0	1 1	1 ½	10½
	0 ½	½ 0	—	0 ½	½ ½	½ 1	
4 Vidmar	½ ½	½ ½	0 1	—	½ ½	½ 0	10
	0 ½	½ ½	1 ½	—	½ ½	1 ½	
5 Spielmann	½ ½	0 ½	0 0	½ ½	—	½ ½	8
	0 ½	½ 0	½ ½	½ ½	—	1 ½	
6 Marshall	0 0	½ 0	0 ½	½ 1	½ ½	—	6
	½ 0	½ 0	½ 0	0 ½	0 ½	—	

37

THIRTEENTH ROUND, MOSCOW, 1925

Réti's Opening

White	Black
CAPABLANCA	F. J. MARSHALL

1. Kt — K B 3

Capablanca had a partiality for the English Opening (1. P — Q B 4) and very often employed it as a variant from the hackneyed Queen's or Ruy Lopez. Here he adopts a kindred form — Réti's Opening — a compliment (voluntary or involuntary) to the striking game which Réti won against him at New York, 1924.

1.	......	Kt — K B 3
2.	P — B 4	P — K 3

An excellent alternative is 2. ....P — K Kt 3; 3. Kt — B 3, P — Q 4 with possibilities of transposition into a favourable variation of the Grünfeld Defence. Not to be recommended, however, is the symmetrical defence by 2. ....P — B 4; 3. P — K Kt 3, P — K Kt 3; 4. B — Kt 2, B — Kt 2; 5. Castles, Castles; 6. Kt — B 3, Kt — B 3; 7. P — Q 4, P × P; 8. Kt × P and White has the better game (Euwe–Colle, 7th match game, 1924); White's control of the centre is demonstrated by the continuation of this game, which went 8. ....Kt × Kt, 9. Q × Kt, P — Q 3; 10. Q — R 4, R — K 1; 11. B — R 6, B — R 1; 12. P — K R 3, Q — Kt 3; 13. P — Kt 3, B — Q 2; 14. Q R — B 1, B — B 3; 15. P — K 4.

3. P — K Kt 3

Showing a determination to pursue the Réti system; 3. Kt — B 3 could transpose the game to a normal Queen's by 3. ....P — Q 4; 4. P — Q 4.

The actual text move may appear quite usual nowadays, but the opening of this game caused quite a sensation at the time when Réti's theories were still regarded as a string of somewhat bizarre and novel paradoxes. The fact that the World Champion himself was dabbling in these new-fangled notions came as a shock to the classical die-hards, but, as Nimzovitch remarked apropos of this game, to be a world champion and play classically are one and the same thing.

3. ......   P — Q 4

Fianchettoing Queen's side will eventually leave White in control of the centre, e.g. 3. ....P — Q Kt 3; 4. B — Kt 2, B — Kt 2; 5. Castles, B — K 2; 6. Kt — B 3, P — B 4 (or 6. ....Castles; 7. P — Q 3, P — B 4; 8. P — K.4, Réti–Grünfeld, Semmering, 1926); 7. P — Q 4, P × P; 8. Kt × P, B × B; 9. K × B, Kt — B 3; 10. P — K 4.

4. P — Kt 3

Réti himself preferred the more nonchalant 4. B — Kt 2, and if ....P × P then 5. Q — R 4 ch, Q Kt — Q 2 (or 5. ....B — Q 2; 6. Q × B P, B — B 3; 7. Castles, B — K 2; 8. Q — B 2, Castles; 9. Kt — B 3, Q Kt — Q 2; 10. R — Q 1, P — K 4; 11. P — Q 4 and White has the better game, Réti–Vidmar, London, 1927); 6. Castles, B — K 2; 7. Q × B P, P — B 4; 8. P — Kt 3, P — Q R 3; 9. Q — B 2, Kt — Q 4; 10. B — Kt 2, B — B 3, 11. Kt — B 3, Kt — Kt 5; 12. Q — B 1, Castles; 13. Kt — K 4, B × B; 14. Q × B, P — Q Kt 3; 15. P — Q 4 and there are several weak points on Black's Q side (Réti–Grünfeld, Vienna, 1928).

4. ......   P — B 4

The imperturbable Marshall refuses to be put off by hypermodern theories with regard to the inadvisability of an early occupation of the centre and the necessity of avoiding too immediate a clash with the enemy forces there; and, indeed, the alternative of

presenting a block against White's
K Bishop by 4. .... P — B 3 suffers from the defect of leaving
Black's Q Bishop without a future.

The text move is played with
an eye on eventual aggression by
P — Q 5.

>   5. B — K Kt 2   Kt — B 3
>   6. Castles   B — K 2

Or Black can close the centre
at once by 6. .... P — Q 5; 7. P
— Q 3, B — Q 3 (here we prefer 7. .... P — K 4); 8. P —
K 4, P — K 4; 9. Kt — K 1, Q —
K 2; 10. P — B 4 and White
stands better (Tartakower–Janowski, Ghent, 1926).

>   7. P — Q 3

Not particularly effective is the
more usual 7. P × P, Kt × P; 8.
B — Kt 2, Castles; 9. P — Q 4,
P — Q Kt 3; 10. Kt — B 3, Kt ×
Kt; 11. B × Kt, B — Kt 2; 12.
P × P, B × P with a level game
(Euwe–Flohr, 16th match game,
1932).

Capablanca prefers the text
move, since it keeps the game as
closed as possible and thereby
gives Marshall the type of game
he most dislikes; herein lay the
secret of his continued and outstanding successes against Marshall, great player though the latter was. Capablanca was always
able to guide the game along
paths most disliked by his opponent.

>   7. ......   Castles
>   8. B — Kt 2   P — Q 5

Logically enough played, since
it shuts in White's Q Bishop and
maintains a wedge in the centre;
an interesting alternative is an attempt at counterplay on the Q
side by P — Q R 4 — Q R 5.

>   9. P — K 4

Once again, psychologically
played and based on Marshall's
aversion to the close game. Otherwise, the objectively best move
was 9. P — K 3.

>   9. ......   P × P e.p.

Against the theme of his 8th
move, since now White's Bishops
have excellent play along the
open diagonals. Correct was 9.
.... P — K 4 and if 10. Kt —
Kt, Kt — K 1; 11. P — B 4, P —
B 3 with a level game.

>   10. P × P

White has now obtained an interesting example of what Nimzovitch called the " small but
elastic Pawn centre." Black tries
to neutralise White's central advantage by counter-action on the
flanks.

>   10. ......   Kt — K Kt 5

To 10. .... P — K 4 White replies 11. Kt — B 3 and Black has
become distinctly weak on the
white squares.

With the text move, Black is
planning to attack White's centre in the belief — erroneous,
however — that Q 3 is weak.

>   11. Q — K 2   B — B 3
>   12. Kt — B 3   Q — R 4

Making place for the Rook on
Q 1 and in the hope of creating
pressure on White's Q side. Here
Nimzovitch and Bogoljuboff both
advise 12. ....B — Q 2 and
claim that Black's game there-
after is quite good. But White
need not fall into the tactical
trap, 13. K — R 1, Kt — K 2;
14. P — K R 3 ? Kt — B 4 !, and
instead can play, as Tartakower
gives, 13. Kt — Q 2, K Kt —
K 4; 14. Kt — K 4, B — K 2; 15.
Q R — Q 1 with a magnificent
position.

13. Q R — B 1   R — Q 1

In pursuance of the policy initiated by his 10th move, Black
weakens his K side defences — of
which Capablanca takes incisive
advantage.

14. P — K R 3   K Kt — K 4

Position after 14. ....K Kt — K 4

15. Kt — K 4 !

This powerful move, being the
finishing touch to White's previous central play, has a crushing

effect on Black's K side. Marshall
is already quite lost.

15. ......   Q × P

Hopeless is 15. ....Kt ×
Kt ch; 16. Q × Kt, since 16.
....B × B; 17. Q × P ch leads
to mate in 2.

16. Kt × B ch   P × Kt
17. Kt × Kt   Kt × Kt

Mate follows after 17. ....P
× Kt; 18. Q — R 5, Q × B; 19.
Q × B P ch, K — R 1; 20. B —
K 4.

18. B — K 4 !

Very economically played; Q 3
is protected and R 7 is attacked.

18. ......   B — Q 2

If 18. ....P — B 4 then 19.
R — R 1, Q × Kt P; 20. B × Kt,
P × B; 21. Q — Kt 4 ch, etc.

19. R — R 1   Q × P
20. K R — Kt 1

Simply winning a piece or the
Queen, and therefore good
enough. Immediately after the
game, Capablanca demonstrated
an alternative and much prettier
method of winning, which, however, he avoided on account of its
undue complications.

After 20. B × Kt, P × B; 21.
Q — Kt 4 ch, K — B 1, White
has the following piquant continuation: 22. R × P ch !, K × R;
23. Q — Kt 5 ! (a beautifully
tranquil way of cutting off the
Black K's escape); 23. ....R —
K B 1; 24. B × R P, B — B 3
(the only way of avoiding mate,
its point appears on the 31st

move of this variation); 25. B — Kt 6 ch, K — Kt 2; 26. B — B dis ch, K — B 2; 27. Q — Kt 6 ch, K — K 2; 28. Q × P ch, K — Q 1; 29. Q — Q 6 ch, K — K 1; 30. B — Kt 6 ch, R — B 2; 31. R — K B 1, B — B 6; 32. Q — K 6 ch (and not 32. R × B ?, Q — Q 8 ch); 32. ....K — Q 1; 33. Q × R and Black can resign.

20. ......   Q — Kt 5
21. B × Kt   P × B
22. R × Q   P × R

Black might well have resigned on the 20th move, but prefers to linger on hopelessly for several more moves.

23. B × P   Q R — Kt 1
24. R × P   P — Kt 6
25. Q — Q Kt 2   B — R 5
26. Q × K P   B — B 3
27. Q — Kt 5 ch   K — B 1
28. B × B   P — Kt 7
29. Q — K 7 ch   Resigns

Only just in time to avoid mate; the game is a pleasing little example of Capablanca's neat efficiency in exploiting a central advantage.

38
SEVENTEENTH ROUND, MOSCOW, 1925
Queen's Gambit Accepted

White	Black
CAPABLANCA	L. SUBAREW
1. P — Q 4	P — Q 4
2. P — Q B 4	P — K 3
3. Kt — K B 3	P × P
4. P — K 4	

This vigorous move has as the defect of its very vigour a too early simplification in the centre. 4. P — K 3 gives White a more lasting initiative.

4. ......   P — Q B 4
5. P — Q 5

Inferior to 5. B × P, as Capablanca played against Bogoljuboff in this tournament. It is true White obtains a passed Pawn, but since this can be easily blockaded by Black it should cause no difficulty to the second player.

5. ......   P × P
6. P × P   Kt — K B 3
7. B × P   B — Q 3
8. Castles   Castles
9. B — K Kt 5   B — Kt 5
10. Kt — B 3   Q Kt — Q 2

Black has completed his development and his position is satisfactory, if a trifle cramped. Capablanca now does his utmost to obtain advantage out of this last factor.

11. Kt — K 4   Q — B 2

The doubled Pawns that result on the K side are not fully compensated by the possession of two Bishops. Best is 11. ....B — K 4; 12. Q — Kt 3, B × Kt; 13. Q × B, Q — Kt 3 with an excellent game.

12. B × Kt   Kt × B

And not 12. ....B × P ch; 13. K — R 1, Kt × B; 14. P — Q 6! when Black loses a piece.

13. Kt × Kt ch	P × Kt
14. P — K R 3	B — R 4
15. R — K 1	K R — K 1
16. Q — Kt 3	P — Q R 3
17. P — Q R 4	B — Kt 3

This retreat will be forced eventually since otherwise White will play B — Q 3 followed by Kt — R 4 — B 5.

18. B — Q 3	Q — Q 2
19. Kt — Q 2 !	

This Kt is destined for K 4, where it will exert maximum pressure on Black's weak points.

19.	R — K 2
20. B × B	B P × B

Leaving a bad hole on K 3, but 20. ....R P × B loses after 21. Kt — K 4, K — Kt 2; 22. Q — K B 3, P — B 4; 23. Kt × P, B × Kt; 24. Q — B 3 ch, K — Kt 1; 25. Q × B, R × R ch; 26. R × R, Q × R P; 27. Q — K 7, Q — R 4; 28. P — Q 6, etc.

21. Kt — K 4	K — Kt 2
22. Q — Q B 3	B — K 4
23. Q × P	B × P

In his haste to regain the Pawn, Black overlooks White's fine reply. A good resource was 23. ....Q R — K 1; 24. R — K 2, B × P; 25. R × B, R × Kt, and though White still has the advantage after 26. P — R 5 Black is far from lost.

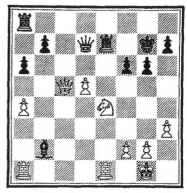

Position after 23. ....B × P

24. Kt — Kt 5 !	Q R — K 1
25. Kt — K 6 ch	K — B 2
26. Q R — Kt 1	B — K 4
27. Q — B 4	R — Q B 1
28. Q — Kt 3	B — Kt 1

Black's position has grown critical during the last few moves; if he pursues White's Queen still further by 28. ....R — B 6; 29. Q — R 2 (threatening 30. R × P); 29. ....P — Q Kt 4; 30. Q — Q 2, R — B 5 (otherwise White wins a piece by P — B 4); 31. Q — R 6 and wins.

29. P — Kt 3	Q — Q 3
30. Kt — B 4	

This regrouping of Rook and Kt very much increases the pressure on Black's game. If now 30. ....R × R; 31. R × R, R — K 1; 32. R — K 6, R × R; 33. P × R ch, K — B 1; 34. Q × P, B — B 2; 35. Kt — Q 5 winning.

30.	......	Q R — K 1
31.	R — K 6	Q — Q 2
32.	R × R ch	K × R

Black must recapture this way because of the threat of P — Q 6 dis ch.

33. Q × P

This apparently simple Pawn capture is the commencement of a very fine combination by which Capablanca forces mate or win of the Queen.

33.	......	B × Kt

Hoping for 34. P × B, Q × Q; 35. R × Q ch, K — Q 3 with distinct drawing chances. But instead there comes a beautiful surprise.

Position after 33. ....B × Kt

34. R — K 1 ch!   B — K 4

If 34. ....K — Q 1; 35. Q — R 8 ch.

35. P — Q 6 ch   K — K 3

Or 35. ....K — Q 1; 36. Q — Kt 6 ch followed by R — B 1 ch.

36.	Q — Kt 3 ch	K — B 4
37.	Q — Q 3 ch	K — Kt 4

If 37. ....K — K 3; 38. Q — B 4 ch followed by mate or win of the Queen; nevertheless, by a series of checks, Black is forced to make this sad choice.

38. Q — K 3 ch   K — B 4

Mate in two results after 38. ....K — R 4; 39. P — Kt 4 ch, K — R 5; 40. Q — R 6 mate.

39. Q — K 4 ch   K — K 3

Now White achieves the desired position given above.

40.	Q — B 4 ch	K × P
41.	R — Q 1 ch	K — K 2
42.	R × Q ch	K × R
43.	Q × P	R — Q Kt 1
44.	Q — R 7 ch	K — B 3
45.	Q × P	R — Kt 7
46.	Q × P	Resigns

This game was awarded the first brilliancy prize.

39
TWENTIETH ROUND,
MOSCOW, 1925

Queen's Pawn, Queen's Indian Defence

White	Black
GOTTHILF	CAPABLANCA
1. P — Q 4	Kt — K B 3
2. P — Q B 4	P — K 3
3. Kt — K B 3	P — Q Kt 3
4. P — K Kt 3	B — Kt 2
5. B — Kt 2	P — B 4

This move has now fallen into disfavour, since it gives White too much scope in the centre, ei-

ther 5. ....B — Kt 5 ch or 5.
....B — K 2 being preferred.

6. P × P

A tame reply which makes
Black's 5th move a good one. Correct is 6. P — Q 5, P × P; 7. Kt
— R 4, as Alekhine played
against Capablanca at New York,
1927 (see Game No. 43).

6. ......　　　B × P

Black can also recapture the
other way with good effect, e.g.
6. ....P × P; 7. Castles, Q —
B 2; 8. Kt — B 3, P — Q R 3; 9.
R — K 1, Kt — K 5; 10. Kt ×
Kt, B × Kt, as in the game
Ruben–Sultan Khan, Hamburg,
1930.

7. Kt — B 3

White should Castle at once;
by delaying to do so, he allows
Black to bring about a useful simplification that increases the power of his two Bishops.

7. ......　　　Kt — K 5
8. Kt × Kt　　 B × Kt
9. Castles　　 Kt — B 3
10. Kt — Q 2

Another exchange which weakens White's game; in view of his
timid play, it is not surprising
that Black gets a strong grip on
the position, especially in the centre. More enterprising and better
for White here is 10. P — Q R 3,
P — Q R 4; 11. B — B 4.

10. ......　　　B × B
11. K × B　　　P — Q 4
12. Q — R 4

This temporarily attacking
move has as its ultimate faulty
purpose the accomplishment of
the exchange of White's Kt for
Black's Bishop. White's position
is, however, already difficult; if
he plays 12. Kt — B 3, P × P;
13. Q — R 4, R — Q B 1; 14. Kt
— K 5, Q — B 2; 15. B — B 4,
Q — Kt 2 and Black has a
marked advantage.

12. ......　　　R — Q B 1
13. Kt — Kt 3

In pursuance of his idea,
White neglects the chance of se-
curing near equality by 13. P ×
P, Q × P ch; 14. Q — K 4.

13. ......　　　Castles
14. R — Q 1

Now 14. P × P would be bad
because of 14. ....Q × P ch; 15.
P — K 4, Q — Q 6; 16. Kt × B,
P × Kt; 17. B — K 3, Kt — Q 5
with much the better game for
Black.

14. ......　　　P — Q 5 !

This wedge in the centre gives
Black full control of the game.
The next part of the game will
consist of a gradual enveloping
of the White position by Black
Pawns, followed by an assault of
White's K side, now weakened
through lack of the fianchettoed
Bishop.

15. Kt × B

If 15. P — K 3, P — K 4 and
White will have weakened the
square K B 3 to no purpose.

15. ......   P × Kt
16. P — Q R 3

With the object of weakening Black's Pawn structure by P — Q Kt 4; Black's next two moves prevent this.

16. ......   Q — Kt 3
17. B — Q 2   P — Q R 4

17. ....Q × P; 18. Q R — Kt 1 would allow White to force a draw by repetition of moves.

18. Q — B 2   P — K 4
19. Q R — Kt 1

Intending to force P — Q Kt 4 by first playing P — Kt 3 and then doubling Rooks on the Q Kt file, but he is not allowed time for this. Should he endeavour to stem the tide of advancing Black Pawns by P — K 4, then Black will break open the position by P — K Kt 3 and P — K B 4.

19. ......   P — B 4
20. P — R 3   P — R 3
21. P — Kt 3   R — Kt 1
22. R — Kt 2   Q — Kt 2 !

An uncomfortable move to meet; apart from the tactical devastating threat of discovered check, it has the positional virtue of gaining possession of the long diagonal.

23. K — R 2

If 23. P — B 3, P — K 5; 24. P × P, Kt — K 4 with a winning attack.

23. ......   Q R — Q 1

This move has a terrible threat of which White is completely oblivious.

Position after 23. ....Q R — Q 1

24. P — Q Kt 4 ?

Fatal; necessary was 24. Q — Kt 1 if White wished to continue the game. Even then Black would have a positionally won game after 24. ....P — K 5 followed by Kt — K 4 and P — Q 6.

24. ......   P — Q 6!

Resigns; since after 25. P × P, Kt — Q 5; 26. Q — B 1, Kt — B 6 ch wins material. A drastic example of the penalty incurred by tame and colourless play.

40
NINETEENTH ROUND, MOSCOW, 1925

Queen's Gambit Accepted

White	Black
CAPABLANCA	E. BOGOLJUBOFF

1. P — Q 4   P — Q 4
2. P — Q B 4   P — K 3
3. Kt — K B 3   P × P
4. P — K 4   P — Q B 4
5. B × P

Better than 5. P — Q 5, as
Capablanca played in Game No.
38.

5. ......   P × P
6. Kt × P   Kt — K B 3
7. Kt — Q B 3   B — B 4

Black's position, suffering as it
does from lack of freedom, demands great care in defence. The
text move is not altogether satisfactory, since after White's reply
the Bishop is liable to fall victim
to a hidden attack. Nor can the
more modest 7. ....B — K 2 be
recommended, since White gets
much the better game by 8. P —
K 5, K Kt — Q 2; 9. Q — K 2,
Castles; 10. Castles, P — Q R 3;
11. R — Q 1, Q — B 2; 12. B —
B 4, P — Q Kt 4; 13. B — Q 3,
B — Kt 2; 14. Q R — B 1, and
the violent 7. ....P — K 4; 8.
Kt (Q 4) — Kt 5, Q × Q ch; 9.
K × Q, Kt — R 3; 10. B — K 3,
P — Q Kt 3; 11. P — B 3 leaves
White ahead in development. Safest is therefore 7. ....Q Kt —
Q 2, preventing the disorganising
thrust, P — K 5.

8. B — K 3   Q Kt — Q 2

Allowing White the opportu-
nity for a brilliant positional sac-
rifice. The best move is 8. ....
Castles, though White still pos-
sesses advantage in space after
9. Castles (good for Black is 9.
P — K 5, K Kt — Q 2; 10. P —
B 4, Q — Kt 3); 9. ....Q Kt —
Q 2; 10. Q — K 2 followed by
K R — Q 1.

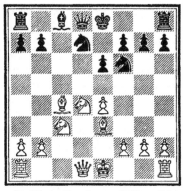

Position after 8. ....Q Kt — Q 2

9. B × P !

A sign that Capablanca had
been meditating this move for
some time is that he played B ×
P immediately after his opponent's move, without pausing to
think. It is a purely positional
sacrifice based on the superior development of White's pieces.

9. ......   P × B
10. Kt × P   Q — R 4

The only other playable move
for Black, 10. ....Q — Kt 3,
leads to an equally fierce attack
for White after 10. Kt × B, Kt
× Kt; 11. Castles, Q — B 3; 12.
R — B 1, Kt (B 4) × P; 13. Kt
× Kt, Q × Kt; 14. B — B 5, Q
— Q 4; 15. R — K 1 ch, K —
B 2; 16. R — K 7 ch, K — Kt 3;
17. B — Q 4, B — K 3 (not 17.
....R — K 1; 18. B × Kt); 18.
Q R — B 7, K R — Kt 1; 19. Q
— Q 3 ch, etc.

11. Castles

Played with admirable re-
straint; White calmly completes

his development and at the same time forces Black to open up fresh lines of attack. If White hastens to take the third Pawn, the fury of his attack noticeably diminishes, e.g. 11. Kt × P ch, K — B 2; 12. Kt — B 5, Kt — K 4; 13. Castles, B — K 3 and Black will follow up with R — Q 1 to get all his pieces in play.

11. ......   B × B

Or 11. .... K — B 2; 12. Q — Kt 3 and wins still more speedily than in the text.

12. P × B   K — B 2

If 12. .... R — K Kt 1; 13. Q — Q 6, K — B 2; 14. Kt — Q 5 and Black has no adequate defence.

13. Q — Kt 3   K — Kt 3

Mate follows after 13. .... Q — Kt 3; 14. Kt — Kt 5 dbl ch, K — Kt 3; 15. Q — B 7 ch, K × Kt; 16. Q × P ch, K — R 4; 17. R — B 5 ch, etc.

14. R — B 5   Q — Kt 3
15. Kt — B 4 ch   K — R 3

Position after 15. .... K — R 3

16. P — K Kt 4 ?

A move which should have thrown away the game; a great pity, since, as Capablanca himself showed after the game, there is a forced win by 16. Q — B 7! P — Kt 3; 17. P — K Kt 4, Q × P ch; 18. K — Kt 2, P × R (or 18. .... Kt × Kt P; 19. R — R 5 ch, P × R; 20. Q × P (R 5) ch, K — Kt 2; 21. Q × Kt ch, K — B 1; 22. Kt — K 6 ch, K — K 1; 23. Q — R 5 ch, K — K 2; 24. Kt — Q 5 ch winning the Queen); 19. P — Kt 5 ch, K × P; 20. Q — Kt 7 ch, K × Kt; 21. R — B 1 ch, K — K 4; 22. Q — K 7 ch, K — Q 5; 23. R — Q 1 ch, K — B 5; 24. Q — K 6 ch, K — B 4; 25. P — Kt 5 ch, K × P; 26. Q — Kt 3 ch followed by mate next move.

Capablanca played the text under the impression that it was simpler and better only to be rudely disillusioned by Black's reply.

16. ......   P — Kt 4
17. Q × Q

Exchange of Queens is now White's best chance; 17. Q — B 7 would fail against R — B 1, and White would lose after 17. P — K R 4, Q × P ch; 18. K — B 1, P × Kt; 19. P — Kt 5 ch, K — R 4; 20. P × Kt dis ch, K — Kt 5; 21. Q — K 6, K — B 6.

17. ......   P × Q
18. R — Q 1

Owing to White's superior development and the dangerous position of Black's King, the second player has to be extremely careful in defence before emerging on to safe ground.

Now, in his turn, Bogoljuboff makes a blunder, throwing the game back to White.

Position after 18. R — Q 1

18. ......   R — K Kt 1 ?

Correct was 18. ....P × Kt;
19. P — Kt 5 ch, K — Kt 2 (and not 19. ....K — Kt 3; 20. R — Q 6, R — B 1; 21. P × P when White gets three Pawns for the piece); 20. R — Kt 5 ch, K — B 2; 21. P × P, P — R 3; 22. R — Kt 3, Kt — R 4 and Black should win.

19. Kt(B 4)—Q 5   Kt×Kt P

Or 19. ....R — Kt 3; 20. Kt — K 7, R — Kt 2 (20. ....Kt — B 4; 21. R — Q 8!); 21. Kt (B 3) — Q 5, Kt × Kt; 22. Kt × Kt, R × P; 23. R — Q B 1, R — R 1; 24. R — Q B 7 and Black has no good continuation.

20. Kt — K 7   R — Kt 2
21. R — Q 6 ch   K — R 4
22. R — B 3 !

With this move, the game assumes a problem-like character with threats of mate continuously circling round the head of the unfortunate Black King.

22. ......   Kt (Kt 5) — B 3
If 22. ....Kt (Kt 5) — K 4
then 23. R — R 6 ch forces mate.

23. R — R 3 ch   K — Kt 5
24. R — Kt 3 ch   K — R 4
25. Kt — B 5   R — Kt 3

Position after 25. ....R — Kt 3

26. Kt — K 7

Played to gain time, but not so decisive as 26. R — R 3 ch, K — Kt 5; 27. K — Kt 2! when the Black King is in a mating net, e.g. 27. ....Kt × P; 28. R — Q 5, Kt × Kt; 29. R — R 4 ch, P × R; 30. Kt — R 6 ch, R × Kt; 31. P — R 3 mate — a charming variation pointed out by Capablanca himself.

26. ......   P — Kt 5

This sacrifice of the exchange is now Black's best chance, since 26. ....R — Kt 2; 27. Kt — B 5 allows White to restore the position as before with the above-mentioned mating attack.

27. Kt × R   K × Kt

A much stronger resistance would have been offered by 27. ....P × Kt, though White should still win in the end. After the text, the game comes to a sudden end.

28. R × P ch   K — B 2

If 28. ....K — R 4; 29. R — Kt 3 and the Black King is in a mating net.

29. R — B 4   K — Kt 2
30. P — K 5   Kt — K 1
31. R — K 6   Resigns

31. ....Kt — B 2; 32. R — K 7 ch, K — Kt 3 (if 32. ....K — Kt 1; 33. P — K 6, etc.); 33. P — K 6, Kt — B 4; 34. R × Kt, Kt × P (K 3); 35. R — Kt 4 ch, K — B 4; 36. R (B 7) — B 4 is quite hopeless for Black.

Though full of flaws, this game is one of the most interesting Capablanca ever played and contains several flashes of original genius.

41
LAKE HOPATCONG, 1926
Queen's Pawn Opening

White	Black
Em. Lasker	Capablanca
1. P — Q 4	Kt — K B 3
2. Kt — K B 3	P — K 3
3. P — K Kt 3	

An interesting anticipation of the Catalan system. It was unlucky for the player of the white pieces that Capablanca was in particularly ruthless form at the time. Had he been opposed by another and weaker player, his originality might have gained him concrete and historical rewards. As it is, it was merely instrumental in obtaining the first brilliancy prize — for his opponent.

3. ......   P — B 4
4. P — B 4

B — Kt 2 at once was to be preferred.

4. ......   P × P
5. Kt × P   P — Q 4
6. B — Kt 2

And not 6. P × P, Q × P !, whilst too dangerous is 6. Kt — Q B 3, P — K 4; 7. K Kt — Kt 5, P — Q 5; 8. Kt — Q 5, Kt × Kt; 9. Q — R 4, B — Q 2; 10. P × Kt, P — Q R 3; 11. P — K 3, Q — Kt 3 winning a piece.

6. ......   P — K 4 !

A vigorous advance which seizes the initiative.

7. Kt — K B 3   P — K 5 !

Black must now continue in the same dashing style, since 7. .... Kt — B 3; 8. P × P, Kt × P; 9. Kt × P would win a Pawn.

8. K Kt — Q 2

Unless White wishes to start undeveloping by 8. Kt — Kt 1, this is the only square for the Kt, since 8. Kt — Q 4, P × P; 9. Q

— R 4 ch, B — Q 2; 10. Q ×
B P, Kt — B 3; 11. Q Kt — B 3,
R — B 1 is manifestly to Black's
advantage, and also bad for
White is 8. Kt — K 5, B — Q 3;
9. Q — Q 4, Q — K 2; 10. P —
B 4 (if 10. B — B 4, P —
K Kt 4); 10. . . . . Kt — B 3.

8. . . . . . .   P × P
9. Q — R 4 ch

Best was 9. Castles, but White,
in his greed to win a Pawn has
overlooked Black's 10th move.

9. . . . . . .   B — Q 2
10. Q × B P   P — K 6 !

A characteristic method of exploiting an advantage in development. The extra Pawn it allows
White is really a handicap, as it
impedes the action of his pieces
and demands constant defence;
meanwhile, Black's pieces rejoice
in gloriously open lines.

Position after 10. . . . . P — K 6 !

11. P × P

Forced since 11. B × P, P ×
Kt ch; 12. B × P, B — K 3; 13.

Q — R 4 ch, Q Kt — Q 2; 14. B
× R, Q × B would leave White
quite lost.

11. . . . . . .   B — B 3
12. Castles   B × B
13. K × B   B — K 2
14. Kt — Q B 3

If 14. Q — Kt 5 ch, Black
would prefer to sacrifice another
Pawn to retain the attack by 14.
. . . . Q Kt — Q 2 rather than exchange Queens with Q — Q 2.

14. . . . . . .   Castles
15. Kt — B 3   Q Kt — Q 2
16. P — K 4   R — B 1
17. Q — Kt 5

If 17. Q — Q 3, Kt — B 4; 18.
Q × Q, K R × Q; 19. P — K 5,
K Kt — K 5; 20. Kt × Kt, Kt ×
Kt and White has no adequate
move against Black's threatened
R — B 7.

17. . . . . . .   P — Q R 3 !

The student of combinational
types may be interested to compare this with the 15th move in
Capablanca's game against Vidmar in London, 1922 (Game No.
29). From now on White's unfortunate Queen is continually harassed.

18. Q — K B 5

For 18. Q × Kt P, Kt — B 4;
19. Q — Kt 4, Q Kt × P; 20. Q
— Kt 3, Kt × Kt; 21. P × Kt,
Kt — K 5; 22. B — Kt 2, B —
B 3; 23. Q R — B 1, Q — R 4
will lead to the eventual loss of
the Q B P; whilst Black's pressure continues.

18. ......   R — B 4
19. Q — B 4

And not 19. Q — R 3 because of 19. ....R — K R 4.

19. ......   R — B 5
20. B — K 3   B — B 4 !

Black conducts the attack with great nonchalance; his Q Rook is only apparently dangerously placed and can soon be brought back to the centre.

21. Kt — Q 2

Black's advantage persists even if White decides to give the Pawn back by 21. B × B, Kt × B; 22. Q R — Q 1, Q — K 2; 23. Kt — K 5, R — Kt 5; 24. Kt — Q 3, Kt × Kt; 25. P × Kt, R × P ch.

21. ......   R — Kt 5
22. P — Kt 3   Q — K 2
23. P — Q R 3   B × B
24. Q × B   R — Kt 3
25. Q R — Q 1   R — K 3

An ideal position for the Rook; the White K P is now menaced by 26. ....Kt — B 4.

26. P — Q Kt 4   R — B 1
27. Q — Q 4 ?

White, now in great time trouble, makes a move that only worsens his plight. His best chance now is 27. R — B 5, P — K Kt 3; 28. Kt — Q 5, Kt × Kt; 29. R × Kt, Kt — B 3; 30. R — Q 4, though Black can always regain his Pawn with the better game by 30. ....R — K 1.

27. ......   R — Q 3!
28. Kt — Q 5

Fatal would be 28. Q — K 3, Kt — Kt 5; 29. Q — B 4, Kt (Q 2) — K 4; 30. P — R 3, P — K Kt 4 winning White's Queen.

28. ......   Kt × Kt
29. P × Kt   Q × P ch
30. K — Kt 1   Kt — B 3
31. Kt — Kt 3

Or 31. Q R — K 1, Q — R 4 winning the Q P, since 32. R — K 5 is met by 32. ....R × P.

31. ......   R × P
32. Q — B 2

Now Black finishes the game with a few neat strokes.

Position after 32. Q — B 2

32. ......   Q × R !
33. R × Q   R × R ch
34. K — Kt 2   Kt — Kt 5
35. Q — Kt 6

Or 35. Q — K 2, R — B 7 !

35. ......   P — K R 4

At once giving his own King an escape square and constructing a mating net for his opponent.

36. Kt — B 5   R — K 1

Resigns, as mate in a few moves cannot be prevented.

42
SECOND ROUND, NEW YORK, 1927

Queen's Gambit Declined

White	Black
A. NIMZOVITCH	CAPABLANCA
1. P — Q B 4	Kt — K B 3
2. Kt — K B 3	P — K 3
3. P — Q 4	P — Q 4
4. P — K 3	

This and the next are tame moves which surrender the initiative into Black's hands. The normal 4. B — Kt 5 is the most aggressive move. Capablanca profits by this timidity in clever and characteristic style.

4. ......   B — K 2
5. Q Kt — Q 2

White here employs an idea of Capablanca's himself — but at the wrong moment. He hopes to induce Black to play P × B P when he will retake with the Kt and so gain control of K 5. As, however, Black is able to avoid exchanging Pawns, White would have been better engaged in increasing pressure on Q 5 by 5. Kt — B 3.

5. ......   Castles
6. B — Q 3   P — B 4 !

By attacking White's Q Pawn, Black indirectly prevents him from playing P — K 4.

7. Q P × P

This exchange away from the centre is bad on basic positional grounds. Both 7. Castles and 7. P — Q Kt 3 are more in keeping with the position.

7. ......   Kt — R 3

A surprising and effective finesse; the Pawn is to be recaptured by the Kt with attack on White's Bishop. Nimzovitch had hoped for 7. ....B × P; 8. P — Q R 3 followed by P — Q Kt 4 and B — Kt 2, with command of the central squares, Q 4 and K 5.

8. Castles

Allowing Black to carry out his plan without hindrance. Instead, White should have hastened to secure a drawn game by forcing exchanges, e.g. 8. Kt — Kt 3, P × P; 9. B × P, Q × Q ch; 10. K × Q, Kt × P; 11. Kt × Kt, B × Kt; 12. K — K 2, P — Q R 3; 13. P — Q R 4, P — Q Kt 3; 14. R — Q 1, B — Kt 2; 15. P — Q Kt 3, K R — Q 1 and the game must end in a draw.

8. ......   Kt × P
9. B — K 2

If he plays 9. B — B 2 with the idea of reserving K 2 for the Queen and eventually bringing a Rook to Q 1, then Black replies 9. ....P — Q Kt 3; 10. Q — K 2, B — R 3! with the better game.

9. ...... P — Q Kt 3
10. P × P

White concentrates on simplification even to the extent of developing his opponent's game. Instead, he should have busied himself with the problem of his Q side development and played 10. P — Q R 3 followed by P — Q Kt 4 and B — Kt 2.

10. ...... Kt × P

Black's Kts are now ideally posted in the centre, and White will have to consume further time to drive them away or eliminate them by exchange.

11. Kt — Kt 3   B — Kt 2
12. Kt × Kt   B × Kt
13. Q — R 4   Q — B 3 !

A strong move serving many purposes; White's Q side development is considerably hampered, he cannot play 14. P — K 4 because of Kt — B 5, and, finally, Black's Rooks can come into action on the central files.

14. B — R 6   B × B
15. Q × B   Kt — Kt 5
16. Q — K 2   K R — Q 1
17. P — Q R 3   Kt — Q 6
18. Kt — K 1

18. R — Q 1, Kt — K 4; 19. Kt × Kt, Q × Kt still leaves the problem of White's Q side development unsolved.

18. ...... Kt × Kt
19. R × Kt   Q R — B 1
20. R — Kt 1

Preparing to play P — Q Kt 4 followed by B — Kt 2; Black's advantage seems on the point of disappearing, but Capablanca evolves a series of subtle moves confirming and increasing his command of the position.

Position after 20. R — Kt 1

20. ...... Q — K 4 !
21. P — K Kt 3

Forced, in view of Black's threatened B — Q 3. Any attempt to develop the Q side allows Black to establish a major piece on the 7th rank with a paralysing effect on White's game, e.g. 21. P — Q Kt 4, B — Q 3; 22. P — K Kt 3, Q — K 5; 23. R — Kt 2, B — K 4; 24. R — Q 2, R × R; 25. Q × R, Q — B 7 or 21. B — Q 2, B — Q 3; 22. P — K Kt 3, R — B 7, etc.

21. ...... Q — Q 4 !

A fine, centralising manœuvre which underlines White's weakness on the white squares; if now 22. P — K 4, Q — R 7; 23. B — Q 2, B × R P !

22. P — Q Kt 4   B — B 1
23. B — Kt 2   Q — R 7
24. R — R 1

In the book of the tourney,
Alekhine advises 24. Q R — Q 1,
R × R; 25. R × R, P — Q R 4;
26. P × P, P × P; 27. Q — R 6,
R — B 7; 28. R — Q 8, but this
leads to immediate disaster after
28. ....Q — Kt 8 ch; 29. K —
Kt 2, Q × B; 30. Q — Q 6, R ×
P ch followed by mate.

24. ......   Q — Kt 6
25. B — Q 4

If White plays to prevent the
Rooks from penetrating to the
7th rank by 25. Q R — B 1 then
25. ....P — Q R 4 and White
will be unable to protect his
Rook's Pawn.

25. ......   R — B 7
26. Q — R 6

White is now positionally lost;
by removing his Queen from the
centre, he allows Black to force
matters by a neat combination.
His best course is 26. Q — Q 1
(threatening R — K 2), but his
position is still very bad after 26.
....R (Q 1) — B 1; 27. R —
K 2, Q — B 5.

Position after 26. Q — R 6

26. ......   P — K 4!
27. B × K P   K R — Q 7
28. Q — Kt 7

Mate follows after 28. R —
K B 1, Q × K P; 29. B — B 4, R
× P, but a much stronger resistance could have been put up by
28. Q — B 1, Q — Q 4; 29. B —
B 4. (This is a suggestion of Dr.
Euwe's and is much better than
29. B — Q 4, Q — K R 4; 30. P
— K R 4, Q — B 6, winning easily.) Nevertheless, Black can still
win by the following manœuvre:
29. ....Q — K R 4; 30. P —
K R 4, P — K R 3!; 31. Q R —
B 1, R × P; 32. Q × R, R × Q;
33. K × R, P — K Kt 4; 34. P ×
P, P × P; 35. B — K 5, Q —
R 7 ch; 36. K — B 1, B — Kt 2;
37. B — Q 6, B — Kt 7 with a
comfortable win.

28. ......   R × P
29. P — Kt 4   Q — K 3
30. B — Kt 3

Hoping for 30. ....Q × Kt P;
31. R — K B 1 with counter-
chances, but Black has a more
conclusive continuation.

30. ......   R × P!
31. Q — B 3

If 31. B × R, Q × Kt P ch;
32. K — R 1, Q — R 6 followed
by mate.

31. ...... R (R 7) — Kt 7 ch
32. Q × R

Or 32. K — B 1, Q — B 5 ch.

32. ......   R × Q ch
33. K × R   Q × Kt P
34. Q R — Q 1   P — K R 4

35.	R — Q 4	Q — Kt 4
36.	K — R 2	P — R 4
37.	R — K 2	P × P
38.	P × P	B — K 2
39.	R — K 4	B — B 3
40.	R — B 2	Q — Q 4
41.	R — K 5 ch	K — R 2

Resigns; apart from the Pawns Black already has to the good, he can also win the Q Kt Pawn by Q — B 5, since White cannot play an eventual B — Q 6 because of Q — B 3.

43

FIFTH ROUND,
NEW YORK, 1927

Queen's Pawn, Queen's Indian Defence

White	Black
A. ALEKHINE	CAPABLANCA
1. P — Q 4	Kt — K B 3
2. P — Q B 4	P — K 3
3. Kt — K B 3	P — Q Kt 3
4. P — K Kt 3	B — Kt 2
5. B — Kt 2	P — B 4
6. P — Q 5	P × P
7. Kt — R 4	

Also good for White is Buerger's suggestion, 7. Kt — Kt 5, B — K 2; 8. Kt — Q B 3, Castles; 9. Castles, Kt — R 3; 10. Kt — R 3, Q — B 1; 11. P × P, P — Q 3; 12. P — K 4, as in the game Buerger–Colle, Tunbridge Wells, 1927.

7.	P — K Kt 3
8. Kt — Q B 3	B — Kt 2
9. Castles	Castles
10. B — B 4	

The best move here is 10. B — Kt 5, as was later demonstrated by Capablanca himself in his game against Marshall in 1929 (see Game No. 66).

| 10. ...... | P — Q 3 |
| 11. P × P | |

After 11. Kt × P, Kt × Kt; 12. B × Kt, B × B; 13. Q × B, Kt — R 3; 14. B × P, R — K 1 Black would regain the Pawn with the better game, since White cannot play 15. Q — Q 2 because of 15. ....B — K 4.

| 11. ...... | Kt — R 4 |

This provides an immediate refutation of White's 10th move; the Bishop is forced to retire with loss of time, whilst the scope of Black's K Bishop is increased.

| 12. B — Q 2 | Q Kt — Q 2 |
| 13. P — B 4 ? | |

Natural and best here is 13. P — K 4. White plans to force the Black Kt to retreat by B — B 3, but wishes to advance his K side Pawns before doing this. But too much time is taken up in the process and Black, by a series of incisive moves, obtains an overwhelming position on the Q side.

| 13. ...... | P — Q R 3 |
| 14. B — B 3 ? | |

This unhappy idea settles the positional fate of the game; Black's pieces combine more and more harmoniously whilst White's become scattered and unco-operative. Instead, White should have played 14. P — Q R 4 at once.

14.	K Kt — B 3
15. P — R 4	P — B 5 !

Very strongly played; a square is opened up for the Kt on B 4, with a possible further outpost on Kt 6. There is also the immediate threat of P — Q Kt 4, since White cannot play 17. P × P, P × P; 18. Kt × Q Kt P because of 18. .... Q — Kt 3 ch winning the piece.

16. B — K 3	Q — B 2
17. P — K Kt 4	

White tries a wild advance on the K side which merely weakens his own Pawn structure. Black, on the contrary, proceeds with the methodical exploitation of his positional advantage.

White's best course is to cut his losses and simplify by 17. K — R 1, Kt — B 4; 18. B × Kt, Q × B; 19. P — K 4.

17.	Kt — B 4
18. P — Kt 5	

Again 18. B × Kt, Q × B ch; 19. K — R 1 was preferable.

18.	K Kt — Q 2
19. P — B 5	

Giving Black another square for central operations on K 5; White's position, however, is already more than dubious. He cannot play the natural 19. B — Q 4, B × B ch; 20. Q × B, Kt — Kt 6 and the exchange is lost. He must therefore content himself with the humble 19. Kt — Kt 2.

19.	K R — K 1
20. B — B 4	B — K 4
21. B — Kt 4	

21. Kt — Kt 2 was still to be preferred; the text takes a piece off the defence of the vital Q Pawn.

21.	Kt — Kt 6
22. P × P	R P × P
23. R — Kt 1	B × Kt

Removing an important defensive piece, after which White's Q Pawn must sooner or later fall — and with this Pawn is bound up White's entire game.

24. P × B	Q — B 4 ch
25. P — K 3	Kt — K 4
26. B — B 3	

Hoping that Black will be obliging enough to capture the Q Pawn at once by 26. .... Kt × B ch; 27. Kt × Kt, B × P, when White would gain some relief by 28. Kt — Q 4; but Black has a more decisive continuation.

26.	Kt — Q 6 !

Position after 26. .... Kt — Q 6 !

Black's position is now overwhelming; White's scattered

Pawns disappear with startling rapidity.

27.	K — R 1	B × P
28.	R × Kt	Kt × B
29.	Q R — Kt 1	R × P
30.	Kt — Kt 2	R × B !

White's game is naturally lost, but Black finishes it off in the most expeditious manner.

31.	R × R	Kt × Kt
32.	K × Kt	R — K 1
33.	K — B 1	B × R
34.	Q × B	Q × P
35.	R — K 1	R × R ch
36.	K × R	Q — Kt 8 ch
37.	K — Q 2	Q × P ch
38.	K — B 1	Q — K 4
39.	K — Kt 2	K — Kt 2
40.	Q — B 2	P — Q Kt 4
41.	Q — Kt 6	P × P
42.	Q × R P	Q — K 7 ch
	Resigns.	

44

TWELFTH ROUND, NEW YORK, 1927

Ruy Lopez, Morphy Defence

White	Black
CAPABLANCA	M. VIDMAR
1. P — K 4	P — K 4
2. Kt — K B 3	Kt — Q B 3
3. B — Kt 5	P — Q R 3
4. B — R 4	Kt — B 3
5. Castles	B — K 2
6. R — K 1	P — Q Kt 4
7. B — Kt 3	P — Q 3
8. P — B 3	Kt — Q R 4
9. B — B 2	P — B 4
10. P — Q 4	Q — B 2
11. Q Kt — Q 2	Castles

Black should have taken advantage of White's omission of P — K R 3 to develop his Bishop by 11. ....B — Kt 5.

12. P — K R 3	Kt — B 3

A good alternative is 12. .... Kt — Q 2 with the idea of obtaining play on the Q side; the 5th match game between Tarrasch and Lasker in 1915 continued (after 12. ....Kt — Q 2): 13. Kt — B 1, Kt — Kt 3; 14. P — Q Kt 3, Kt — B 3; 15. P — Q 5, Kt — Q 1; 16. P — K Kt 4, P — B 3; 17. Kt — Kt 3, Kt — B 2; 18. K — R 2, P — Kt 3; 19. B — K 3, K — R 1; 20. R — K Kt 1, R — K Kt 1; 21. Q — Q 2, B — Q 2; 22. R — Kt 2, P — Q R 4; 23. R — K B 1, P — Kt 5; 24. P — B 4, P — R 5 with an excellent game for Black.

13. P — Q 5	Kt — Q 1
14. P — Q R 4	P — Kt 5 ?

Leaving White's Kt a fine square on Q B 4. Preferable is 14. ....R — Kt 1, as Vidmar later played against Keres at Nauheim in 1936, with the continuation: 15. P — B 4, P — Kt 5; 16. Kt — B 1, Kt — K 1; 17. P — Kt 4, P — Kt 3; 18. Kt — Kt 3, Kt — K Kt 2; 19. K — R 2, P — B 3; 20. R — K Kt 1, Kt — B 2 and the game is level.

15. Kt — B 4	P — Q R 4

Black fears, without much reason, that White may push his Pawn to Q R 5. He should, however, bend his energies to forcing

P — K B 4 by playing 15. ....
Kt — K 1 followed by P — B 3,
Kt — B 2, P — K Kt 3 and Kt —
K Kt 2.

Poor is 15. ....Kt — Kt 2
(not because of 16. P — R 5, R —
Kt 1; 17. B — Q 2, B — Q 2; 18.
P × P, P × P; 19. B — Q 3, B
— Kt 4, which is good for Black),
but because of 16. P × P, P ×
P; 17. P — Q Kt 3, Kt — Q R 4;
18. K Kt — Q 2.

Position after 15. ....P — Q R 4

16. K Kt × P

An interesting combination by
which White forces a large number of exchanges in order to secure a favourable endgame.

16.	B — R 3
17. B — Kt 3	P × Kt
18. P — Q 6	B × P
19. Q × B	Q × Q
20. Kt × Q	Kt — Kt 2

The alternative is 20. ....R —
Kt 1, and now if 21. B — Q B 4,
B × B; 22. Kt × B, Kt — B 3
with equality, but instead White
should play 21. Kt — Kt 5!, B ×

Kt (or 21. ....P × P; 22. P ×
P, B × Kt; 23. P × B, R × P;
24. B — Q B 4 followed by R ×
P); 22. P × B, R × P; 23. B —
Q B 4 and again R × P, when
the power of White's two Bishops
will prove overwhelming.

| 21. Kt × Kt | B × Kt |
| 22. P × P | B P × P |

Or 22. ....R P × P; 23. B —
K 3 (and not 23. P — B 3 be-
cause of B — R 3 followed by 24.
....P — B 5); 23. ....Kt × P;
24. P — B 3, Kt — B 3; 25. B ×
P, etc.

Black's difficulties now ensue
from two factors: (1) the weakness of his fixed Pawn on Q R 4;
(2) the great power of White's
two Bishops in an open position.

| 23. P — B 3 | K R — Q 1 |

If 23. ....Kt — Q 2; 24. B —
K 3, K R — B 1; 25. K R — Q 1,
R — B 2; 26. R — Q 6, Q R —
Q B 1; 27. Q R — Q 1 and White
will win the Q R Pawn.

24. B — K 3	P — K R 3
25. K R — Q 1	B — B 3
26. Q R — B 1	B — K 1
27. K — B 2	

Bringing the King nearer the
scene of action in case this proves
necessary when the major pieces
have been exchanged; but the
ending does not really get as far
as this.

27.	R × R
28. R × R	R — B 1
29. P — Kt 4	

With the threat of P — R 4, P — Kt 5 followed by R — Q 5. Premature would be 29. B — Kt 6, Kt — Q 2; 30. B × P, Kt — B 4 and Black would safely regain the Pawn.

29. ......   B — Q 2

This loses offhand, but Black has no adequate defence against the plan given in the last note. If 29. ....P — Kt 4 then 30. P — R 4 wins.

30. B — Kt 6   B — K 3

A Pawn is still lost after 30. ....R — R 1; 31. B — B 7.

31. B × B   P × B

The intervening check rather helps White, e.g. 31. ....R — B 7 ch; 32. K — K 3, P × B; 33. R — Q 2.

32. R — Q 8 ch   R × R
33. B × R   Kt — Q 2

Desperately seeking a counter on the Q side, Black's hopes are based on the apparent equal weakness of White's Q side Pawns; but the logic of the position is against him, and the White Bishop proves greatly superior to the Black Knight in such an open game.

34. B × P   Kt — B 4
35. P — Kt 3 !

Capablanca finishes off the game with his customary elegant accuracy. 35. B × P would be a bad mistake because of Kt — Q 6 ch.

35. ......   Kt × Kt P
36. B × P   Kt — Q 5
37. P — R 5   Resigns

For the Pawn can only be stopped at the expense of the Kt.

45

THIRTEENTH ROUND, NEW YORK, 1927

Queen's Gambit Declined

White	Black
CAPABLANCA	R. SPIELMANN
1. P — Q 4	P — Q 4
2. Kt — K B 3	P — K 3
3. P — B 4	Kt — Q 2

This artificial-looking move was devised by Dr. Lasker with the object of deferring (and, if possible, of hindering altogether) White's pin of the Knight by B — K Kt 5.

| 4. Kt — B 3 | K Kt — B 3 |
| 5. B — Kt 5 | B — Kt 5 |

Known as the Westphalia variation, since it was on a ship of this name that Spielmann and Dr. Vidmar analysed the move during the journey from Hamburg to New York. It is an aggressive but not altogether sound continuation.

6. P × P

A good alternative is 6. P — K 3, P — B 4; 7. B P × P; but other possibilities are inferior, e.g. (a) 6. B × Kt, Q × B (not 6. .... Kt × B ?; 7. Q — R 4 ch); 7. P — K 3, P × P; 8. B × P, P — K 4, (b) 6. Q — R 4, Q — K 2; 7. B × Kt, B × Kt ch, or

(c) 6. P — Q R 3, B × Kt ch; 7.
P × B, P — B 4; 8. P — K 3, Q
— R 4.

6. ......   P × P
7. Q — R 4

In his first round game against
Spielmann in this tournament,
Capablanca played 7. Q — Kt 3,
P — B 4; 8. P — Q R 3, B ×
Kt ch; 9. Q × B, P — B 5; 10.
Q — K 3 ch, Q — K 2; 11. Q ×
Q ch, K × Q and the game was
drawn in twenty-eight moves.

The actual text move is chosen
on positional and psychological
grounds; White is aiming at
pressure on the Queen's wing, together with the possession of two
Bishops. He counts on Spielmann's preference for clear-cut
counter-attack to further his aims.

Also good is 7. P — K 3, P —
B 4 (not 7. .... Castles; 8. B —
Q 3, P — B 4; 9. Castles, B ×
Kt; 10. P × B, P — B 5; 11. B
— B 2, Q — R 4; 12. Kt — K 5,
Q × B P; 13. Kt × Kt, Kt ×
Kt; 14. Q — Kt 1 and White re-
gains the Pawn with much the
better game owing to the threat
of B — K 7 and B — Kt 4, Ale-
khine–Vidmar, New York, 1927);
8. B — Q 3, P — B 5; 9. B —
B 2, Q — R 4; 10. Castles, B ×
Kt; 11. P × B, Q × B P; 12. Q
— Kt 1 and White's attacking
chances are well worth the Pawn
sacrificed.

7. ......   B × Kt ch ?

The expected reaction, but not
the best move, since it leaves him

painfully weak on the black
squares. Black had two better
courses open to him:

(1) The temporising 7. .... Q
— K 2; 8. P — K 3, P — B 3; 9.
B — Q 3, Castles; 10. Castles K,
P — K R 3; 11. B — R 4, R —
K 1; 12. K R — K 1, Q — B 1,
and though White retains a slight
plus, Black's position is compact
enough.

(2) The more aggressive 7.
.... P — B 4; 8. P — K 3 (the
win of a Pawn by 8. P × P would
be purely temporary and would
result in a weakening of White's
Q side Pawn position); 8. ....
Castles; 9. B — Q 3, P — Q Kt 3;
10. Castles K, B — Kt 2.

8. P × B   Castles
9. P — K 3   P — B 4

Given a question mark by Alekhine in the tournament book,
where preference is given to 9.
.... Q — K 1 so as to meet 10.
B — Q 3 with Kt — K 4!, but
after 10. Q — B 2, P — B 3; 11.
B — Q 3 Black's Queen would be
misplaced and his whole game
without life.

10. B — Q 3   P — B 5

Black's intentions are now
clear; he will round off his Q side
Pawn structure with P — Q R 3
and P — Q Kt 4 and at the same
time exert pressure on K 5 so as
to prevent any undermining by P
— K 4. White's counter-method is
most instructive.

11. B — B 2

Normally, one would class White's Queen as out of play, shut off as it is from the centre and King side; but owing to Black's weakness on the black squares, White can dedicate his Queen to concentrated pressure on the Q R file.

11. ......   Q — K 2

A logical enough continuation; Black wants to unpin his Kt by Q — K 3 and then control the centre by Kt — K 5, P — Q R 3, P — Q Kt 4 and B — Kt 2.

But all this demands time, and Alekhine has suggested an interesting and original manœuvre: 11. ....R — K 1; 12. Castles K, R — K 3, threatening pursuit of the Queen by R — R 3 and Kt 3.

White would, however, still retain an advantage by 13. B — B 5, R — R 3; 14. Q — B 2, P — K Kt 3; 15. B — R 3, Kt — B 1; 16. B × B, Q × B; 17. Kt — Q 2, and if 17. ....Q — Kt 5; 18. B — B 4 followed by P — B 3.

12. Castles K   P — Q R 3
13. K R — K 1

Threatening P — K 4, which Black hastens to prevent. It is entertaining to see how White contrives to keep this threat alive.

13. ......   Q — K 3

And not 13. ....P — Kt 4; 14. Q — R 5, B — Kt 2; 15. Q — B 7 threatening both Q × B and B × Kt.

14. Kt — Q 2   P — Kt 4
15. Q — R 5 !

Superficially considered, a simple enough move; but in reality a key move which, when viewed together with the ensuing play, demonstrates on what grandly profound lines Capablanca has planned the whole game.

Black's Q side is rotten to the core and will collapse with amazing rapidity.

15. ......   Kt — K 5

Spielmann proceeds with his plan, blissfully unaware of the mine about to detonate and destroy his whole game.

Better, though still not sufficient to save the game, was 15. ....B — Kt 2; 16. P — B 3 (not 16. Q — B 7, B — B 3) and White will still be able to force P — K 4.

16. Kt × Kt   P × Kt
17. P — Q R 4 !

This energetic move demonstrates the weakness of Black's Q side Pawn formation.

17. ......   Q — Q 4

The natural move, expecting White's retreat of the Bishop to B 4 and so gaining time to unpin the Q Rook by 18. ....B — Kt 2. However, it fails against White's coming combination, the direct outcome of his logical, purposeful strategy.

The more defensive 17. ....R — Kt 1 loses because of 18. K R — Kt 1, Q — Q 4; 19. B — B 4,

R — Kt 3; 20. P X P, R X P; 21. R X R, P X R; 22. R — Kt 1.

Position after 17. ....Q — Q 4

18. P X P!

A beautifully nonchalant sacrifice, leaving Black no good reply. Capablanca had also considered, and rejected as inconclusive, the following two variations: (1) 18. B — B 4, B — Kt 2; 19. K R — Kt 1, B — B 3 and (2) 18. B — K 7, R — K 1; 19. P X P, B — Kt 2! (not 19. ....R X B; 20. Q — K 8 ch) with equality.

18. ...... Q X B

The alternative 18. ....B — Kt 2 loses just as quickly after 19. P X P, Q X Q; 20. R X Q, R X P; 21. R X R, B X R; 22. B X P, etc.

19. B X P R — Kt 1

19. ....R — R 2 loses by the neat variation, 20. P — Kt 6, Q X Q; 21. P X R!, and if 21. .... Q X R; 22. R X Q, Kt — Kt 3; 23. R — Kt 1, or 21. ....B — Kt 2; 22. R X Q, B X B; 23. R

X P with great material advantage.

20. P X P!

One of the piquant points of this game is that White can repeatedly offer an exchange of Queens although a piece down.

20. ...... R — Kt 4

Black would be forced to give up a piece for the Q R Pawn after exchange of Queens.

21. Q — B 7 Kt — Kt 3
22. P — R 7

The advance of Q R Pawn to Q R 7 by the 22nd move in the game must be a very rare occurrence indeed.

22. ...... B — R 6

A last, dying kick; but Capablanca's crystal-clear play renders futile any attempt at creating confusion.

23. K R — Kt 1!

Simple and conclusive.

23. ...... R X R ch

Or 23. ....R — B 1; 24. Q X Kt, R X Q; 25. R X R winning easily.

24. R X R P — B 4

If 24. ....Kt — Q 4; 25. Q — Kt 8 wins.

25. B — B 3 P — B 5
26. P X P! Resigns

Since 26. ....R X P; 27. R X Kt leaves Black only 27. ....R — B 1; 28. Q X P ch, K — R 1; 29. R — Kt 8, etc., or 27. ....R

$\times$ B; 28. P — R 8 = Q ch, R —
B 1; 29. Q $\times$ B P ch.

For this splendidly conducted
game, White was awarded the
prize for the best played game in
the tournament.

46

FIFTEENTH ROUND,
NEW YORK, 1927

Caro–Kann Defence

White	Black
A. NIMZOVITCH	CAPABLANCA
1. P — K 4	P — Q B 3
2. P — Q 4	P — Q 4
3. P — K 5	

Nimzovitch favoured this move
both against the French and
Caro–Kann. Effective as it was in
his hands against the former defence, it cannot be said to have
been very successful against the
latter. Here, in contradistinction
to the French, Black is able to
develop his Q Bishop, with the
result that White is practically
forced to exchange off his valuable K Bishop.

Better are both 3. Kt — Q B 3
and 3. P $\times$ P followed by 4. P —
Q B 4.

3.	B — B 4
4. B — Q 3	B $\times$ B
5. Q $\times$ B	P — K 3
6. Kt — Q B 3	

And here more usual is 6. Kt
— K 2 when Black proceeds as
in the text 6. ....Q — Kt 3;
7. Castles, P — Q B 4; 8. P —

Q B 3, Kt — Q B 3 with pressure
on White's centre.

6.	Q — Kt 3
7. K Kt — K 2	P — Q B 4

Black is playing for a win;
otherwise he would offer exchange
of Queens by 7. ....Q — R 3,
and if White avoided this exchange by moving the Queen,
Black's piece would be left in
control of the diagonal R 3 —
B 8.

8. P $\times$ P	B $\times$ P
9. Castles	

9. Q — Kt 3 would only give
Black an attack by 9. ....Kt —
K 2; 10. Q $\times$ P, R — Kt 1; 11.
Q $\times$ P, R $\times$ P and the K B
Pawn must fall.

9.	K Kt — K 2
10. Kt — R 4	

This simple move does not noticeably advance White's game;
better and more in Nimzovitch's
normal style is 10. P — Q R 3
threatening 11. P — Q Kt 4.

10.	Q — B 3
11. Kt $\times$ B	Q $\times$ Kt
12. B — K 3	Q — B 2

Commencement of a long series of manœuvres designed to
undermine White's centre.

13. P — K B 4

Forced; but now it becomes
apparent that White is weak on
the white squares, in especial
K 4, Q B 4 and K B 5.

13.	Kt — B 4
14. P — B 3	

This move leaves the problem of the white squares untouched; better would have been 14. R — Q B 1 followed by 15. P — P B 4

14.	Kt — B 3
15. Q R — Q 1	

Nor does this move serve any useful purpose. It is reminiscent of Nimzovitch's famous " mysterious " Rook move manœuvre which constitutes part of the technique successful in so many fine games by this master. Here its object must be purely defensive and therefore innocuous to Black.

White's best course is simply 15. B — B 2 followed by 16. Kt — Q 4.

15.	P — K Kt 3

An interesting move of a semi-waiting nature. Black refrains from an immediate P — K R 4 in the hope that White will weaken his K side by the advance P — K Kt 4.

16. P — K Kt 4 ?	

Falling into the positional trap laid by his opponent. White temporarily drives away the Kt at the cost of a permanent weakening of his K side Pawns. Best was still 16. B — B 2.

16.	Kt × B
17. Q × Kt	P — K R 4
18. P — Kt 5	

Now White's Pawn structure is permanently unsound and a bad hole is left on K B 5, where the other Black Kt will eventually settle. Unfortunately he dare not play 18. P — K R 3, P × P; 19. P × P, Castles Q, since Black would obtain a formidable attack along the K R file.

18.	Castles
19. Kt — Q 4	Q — Kt 3
20. R — B 2	K R — B 1
21. P — Q R 3	R — B 2
22. R — Q 3	

White concentrates on preserving as strong a position in the centre as possible, leaving Black the onus of attempting to break through if possible.

22.	Kt — R 4

Black first tries a diversion on the Q side, realises this is ineffectual and finally develops his plan on the right wing — the King's side — from move 26 onwards.

23. R — K 2	R — K 1

A necessary precaution, as White threatened 24. P — B 5, K P × P; 25. P — K 6. This variation also plays its part if Black attempts to win a Pawn by 23. ....Kt — B 5; 24. Q — B 2, Kt × R P; 25. P — B 5 (and not 25. P × Kt, Q — Kt 8 ch); 25. .... Kt P × P; 26. P — Kt 6, P × P; 27. R — Kt 3, Kt — B 5; 28. R × P ch, R — Kt 2; 29. Q — Kt 3 winning.

Position after 23. ....R — K 1

24. K — Kt 2   Kt — B 3
25. R (K 2) — Q 2

White continues his passive
course; nevertheless, he would
have been better advised to exchange Kts at once, since he has
to do so later on under less favourable circumstances.

25. ......   R(K1)—QB1
26. R — K 2   Kt — K 2
27. R(K2)—Q2   R — B 5!

Very instructive is Capablanca's use of the Rooks along this
file; he increases the pressure on
White's Q 4 until the Rook can
pierce to K 5, where it will strike
White's weakest point — K B 4.

28. Q — R 3   K — Kt 2

A positional move bringing the
King nearer the scene of action
which proves its worth later on
(see move 32).

29. R — K B 2   P — R 4
30. R — K 2   Kt — B 4!

Forcing the exchange of
White's best placed defensive

piece, the Kt on Q 4, after which
Black can finally deal with the
problem of the attack on White's
K B Pawn.

31. Kt × Kt ch

Or 31. R (K 2) — Q 2, Kt ×
Kt; 32. R × Kt, R × R; 33. P ×
R, Q — Kt 4; 34. Q — K B 3, R
— B 8 followed by a construction
of a Zugzwang position very much
as in the actual game.

31. ......   Kt P × Kt
32. Q — B 3

White's position would crum-
ble to pieces after 32. Q × R P,
R — K R 1; 33. Q — B 3, R —
R 5.

32. ......   K — Kt 3
33. R(K2)—Q2   R — K 5
34. R — Q 4   R(B1)—B5
35. Q — B 2   Q — Kt 4
36. K — Kt 3

If 36. R × R (B 4), Q × R;
37. R — Q 4, Q — K 7! wins for
Black.

36. ......   R (B 5) × R
37. P × R

Or 37. R × R, R — K 7.

37. ......   Q — B 5

Black's winning procedure is to
work round White's two weak
points on Q 4 and K B 4 until his
two major pieces are established
on the 8th rank, when White will
be left without a good move — a
fine example of Zugzwang.

38. K — Kt 2   P — Kt 4

This apparently irrelevant advance is part of Black's plan for

eliminating White's possible innocuous Pawn moves.

39. K — Kt 1	P — Kt 5
40. P × P	P × P
41. K — Kt 2	Q — B 8
42. K — Kt 3	Q — K R 8
43. R — Q 3	R — K 8
44. R — K B 3	

Black was threatening R — K B 8 followed by Q — Kt 8 ch and White's Pawns fall.

| 44. ...... | R — Q 8 |
| 45. P — Kt 3 | R — Q B 8 ! |

Position after 45. ....R — Q B 8 !

The perfect Zugzwang position has been attained. Whatever move White now does leads to disaster.

46. R — K 3

If 46. K — R 3 or K — R 4 then 46. ....R — B 7 followed by mate. If 46. P — R 3, R — Kt 8 ch; 47. K — R 4, R — Kt 5 mate. Finally, if 46. Q — K 2, Q — Kt 8 ch; 47. Q — Kt 2, Q × Q P, etc.

| 46. ...... | R — K B 8 |

Resigns, 47. Q — K 2 being met by Q — Kt 8 ch. The winning process in this game is a model of its kind worthy of the closest study.

47

THIRD MATCH GAME, BUENOS AIRES, 1927

Queen's Pawn, Queen's Indian Defence

White	Black
CAPABLANCA	A. ALEKHINE
1. P — Q 4	Kt — K B 3
2. Kt — K B 3	P — Q Kt 3
3. P — K Kt 3	B — Kt 2
4. B — Kt 2	P — B 4
5. Castles	P × P
6. Kt × P	B × B
7. K × B	P — Q 4 ?

A risky move which allows White to open up the game to his advantage. Better is 7. ....P — Kt 3 followed by B — Kt 2 and safe enough is 7. ....Kt — B 3.

8. P — Q B 4! P — K 3

And now Black could have forced exchange of Queens by 8. ....P × P; 9. Q — R 4 ch, Q — Q 2; 10. Q × B P, Q — Q 4 ch; 11. Q × Q, Kt × Q — though after 12. P — K 4 he is considerably behind in development.

9. Q — R 4 ch   Q — Q 2

Or 9. ....Q Kt — Q 2; 10. P × P, P × P (10. ....Kt × P; 11. P — K 4!); 11. B — Kt 5, P — K R 3; 12. B × Kt, Q × B;

13. Kt — B 3 and White has already a winning advantage.

    10. Kt — Kt 5   Kt — B 3
    11. P × P   P × P

The only move; if 11. ....Kt
× P; 12. R — Q 1 and 11. ....
Q × P ch; 12. P — K 4, Q —
Q 2; 13. R — Q 1, Q — Kt 2; 14.
B — B 4, R — B 1; 15. R —
Q B 1, P — Q R 3; 16. Kt —
B 7 ch and White wins the ex-
change.

    12. B — B 4   R — B 1
    13. R — B 1

Threatening to win the game
by 14. Kt — B 7 ch, R × Kt; 15.
B × R, Q × B; 16. R × Kt, etc.

    13. ......   B — B 4

Position after 13. ....B — B 4

After the text move White wins
two minor pieces for a Rook and
Pawn when the ultimate win of
the game becomes a matter of
technique, though this is accomplished in very interesting style.
Stronger resistance is provided
by 13. ....Kt — K 5 for then if,

14. Kt — B 7 ch, R × Kt; 15. B
× R, Kt — B 4; 16. Q — K B 4,
Kt — K 3; 17. Q — Q R 4, Kt —
B 4 with a kind of perpetual
check on the Queen, since 18. Q
— Kt 5 ?, Q × B; 19. P —
Q Kt 4, P — Q R 3 would actu-
ally lose for White.

However, owing to the loose
nature of Black's position, White
is assured of gain in material by
14. P — Q Kt 4, B — Q 3; 15. B
× B, Kt × B; 16. Q Kt — B 3
and Black has three possible con-
tinuations: (a) 16. ....Castles;
17. Kt × Q P, Kt — Q 5; 18.
Kt × K Kt safely winning a
Pawn, for if 18. ....Q × Q; 19.
Kt — K 7 ch, K — R 1; 20. Kt
× P ch with mate in a few moves;
(b) 16. ....P — Q 5; 17. R —
Q 1, Kt × Kt; 18. Kt × Kt, Q —
Q 4 ch; 19. P — K 4, Q × P ch;
20. K — Kt 1, Q — Q 4; 21. R ×
P ! and Black has no defence
against the many threats; (c)
16. ....Kt × Kt; 17. Kt × Kt,
Castles; 18. Kt — Q 4, Kt —
Kt 1; 19. Q × Q, Kt × Q; 20.
Kt — B 6 winning a Pawn.

    14. P — Q Kt 4 ! B × Kt P
If 14. ....Kt × P; 15. Kt —
Q 6 ch.

    15. R × Kt   R × R
    16. Q × B   Kt — K 5
    17. Kt — Q 2   Kt × Kt
    18. Q × Kt

Unnecessarily allowing Black
to Castle; Alekhine points out
that 18. B × Kt would be stronger still, for if 18. ....Q — K 2;

19. Q — Kt 2, Q — K 5 ch; 20. P — B 3, Q × K P ch; 21. K — Kt 1 and Black cannot parry all White's threats (22. R — K 1 or 22. Kt — Q 4 or 22. Q × P).

18. ......   Castles
19. R — Q 1   R — B 4
20. Kt — Q 4   R — K 1
21. Kt — Kt 3   R (B 4) — B 1
22. P — K 3

And not 22. Q × P, Q × Q; 23. R × Q, R × P; 24. R — Q 2, R × R; 25. B × R, R — B 7, which would be to Black's advantage.

22. ......   Q — R 5
23. Q × P!

White has decided to finish off the game by direct attack on the King. He therefore allows Black to obtain two united passed Pawns on the Q side so as to concentrate his minor pieces on the other wing.

23. ......   R — B 7

Or 23. ....Q × P; 24. R — Q R 1.

24. R — Q 2   R × R P

An interesting alternative is 24. ....Q × P; 25. Q — Q 7, R — K B 1; 26. R × R, Q × R; 27. Kt — Q 4, Q — B 4; 28. Kt — B 5 (not 28. Q × P, P — K Kt 4; 29. B — B 7, R — B 1 with counter-attack); 28. ....P — Q R 4; 29. Kt — K 7 ch, K — R 1; 30. B — Q 6 followed by Kt — Kt 6 ch winning the Rook.

25. R × R   Q × R
26. Q — B 6   R — K B 1
27. Kt — Q 4   K — R 1

So as to obtain a safe haven for the Rook on K Kt 1 if White should play B — Q 6.

28. B — K 5

With immediate mating threats of 29. B × P ch, K × B; 30. Kt — B 5 ch, K — Kt 1; 31. Q — B 6.

28. ......   P — B 3
29. Kt — K 6   R — K Kt 1
30. B — Q 4   P — K R 3

Black must provide his King with an escape square; for if 30. ....P — Q R 4; 31. Kt × P, R × Kt; 32. Q × B P, Q — Kt 1; 33. P — R 4 followed by P — R 5 and P — R 6.

31. P — R 4!

An echo of the final variation in the preceding note which is the necessary prelude to the conclusive combination.

31. ......   Q — Kt 8

Position after 31. ....Q — Kt 8

32. Kt × P !   Q — Kt 3

The Rook is lost after 32. . . . .
R × Kt; 33. Q × B P, Q — R 2;
34. Q — B 8 ch, Q — Kt 1; 35
B × R ch.

33. P — R 5	Q — B 2
34. Kt — B 5	K — R 2
35. Q — K 4	R — K 1
36. Q — B 4	Q — B 1
37. Kt — Q 6	R — K 2
38. B × B P	Q — R 1 ch
39. P — K 4	R — K Kt 2
40. B × R	K × B
41. Kt — B 5 ch	K — B 2
42. Q — B 7 ch	Resigns.

Black is mated in two moves.

48
SEVENTH MATCH GAME, BUENOS AIRES, 1927

Queen's Gambit Declined, Cambridge Springs Defence

White	Black
CAPABLANCA	A. ALEKHINE
1. P — Q 4	P — Q 4
2. P — Q B 4	P — K 3
3. Kt — K B 3	Q Kt — Q 2

As though about to embark on
the Westphalia Defence; if so the
thought of the fine game Capablanca won against Spielmann
earlier on in the year (Game No.
45) must have deterred him and
Alekhine transposes into the
Cambridge Springs Defence.

4. Kt — B 3	K Kt — B 3
5. B — Kt 5	P — B 3
6. P — K 3	Q — R 4
7. Kt — Q 2	

Neither 7. B × Kt, Kt × B; 8.
B — Q 3, B — Kt 5; 9. Q —
Kt 3, P × P; 10. B × B P, Cas-
tles; 11. Castles K, B × Kt; 12. P
× B, P — Q Kt 3, nor 7. P × P,
Kt × P; 8. Q — Kt 3, B — Kt 5;
9. R — B 1, P — K 4 give White
more than equality.

7. . . . . . .   B — Kt 5

Better than 7. . . . . P × P, 8.
B × Kt, Kt × B; 9. Kt × P,
Q — B 2; 10. R — B 1 which
leaves Black somewhat constricted.

8. Q — B 2   Castles

Against Alekhine in his 10th
match game, 1934, Bogoljuboff
played 8. . . . . P × P; 9. B ×
Kt, Kt × B; 10. Kt × P, B ×
Kt ch; 11. Q × B, Q × Q ch; 12.
P × Q, K — K 2 with a tenable
though not very attractive position.

9. B — R 4

An innovation to which Ale-
khine fails to find the best reply.
The main alternatives are: (a) 9.
B — K 2, P — K 4; 10. Castles,
K P × P; 11. Kt — Kt 3, Q —
B 2; 12. K Kt × P, P × P; 13. B
× P, B × Kt; 14. P × B, Kt —
K 4 with equality, and (b) 9. B
× Kt, Kt × B; 10. B — Q 3,
R — K 1; 11. Castles, P — K 4
and again Black has succeeded in
freeing his game.

9. . . . . . .   P — B 4

Alekhine attributes his loss of
this game chiefly to the great
amount of time he took in con-

sidering the alternatives here; since he is also reported to have consumed one hour and five minutes meditating on his 12th move, it will be readily understood that his play suffered under the strain of acute time trouble.

Bad for Black would be 9. ....Kt — K 5; 10. K Kt × Kt, P × Kt; 11. B — K 2, P — K 4; 12. Castles K, P × P; 13. Kt × P, P — K B 4; 14. P — Q R 3, P × Kt; 15. P × B, Q × P; 16. P × P and White's two Bishops are very powerful in this open position.

The correct move — as occurs so often in the multifold variations of the Cambridge Springs Defence — is 9. ....P — K 4, when an analysis of Euwe's shows that Black should secure a draw by 10. Q P × P, Kt — K 5; 11. K Kt × Kt, P × Kt; 12. P — K 6, Kt — K 4; 13. P × P ch, R × P; 14. Castles Q, B × Kt; 15. Q × B, Q × Q ch; 16. P × Q, B — B 4.

Position after 9. ....P — B 4

10. Kt — Kt 3	Q — R 5
11. B × Kt	Kt × B
12. Q P × P	Kt — K 5

After this move Black's game goes rapidly downhill; the simplest and best course for Black to adopt is 12. ....B × Kt ch; 13. Q × B, Kt — K 5; 14. Q — R 5, Q × Q ch; 15. Kt × Q, Kt × Q B P with a somewhat inferior game owing to the isolated Pawn but with certain compensations as regards freedom of pieces and better development.

| 13. P × P | B × Kt ch |
| 14. P × B | Kt × P (B 4) |

As a result of the unfortunate Kt manœuvre, Black has lost a Pawn; if he plays 14. ....P × P then White can retain his extra Pawn by 15. B — Q 3.

| 15. R — Q 1 ! | P × P |
| 16. R × P | Kt × Kt |

An unprofitable exchange which rounds off White's Pawn structure and loses what compensation Black had for the lost Pawn in the shape of superior development. Black's best chance is to play 16. ....P — Q Kt 3 and now, according to an analysis by the Russo-Belgian master, Soultanbeieff, 17. R — Q 4, Q — B 3; 18. Kt × Kt, P × Kt; 19. R — K R 4, P — B 4; 20. B — B 4 ch, K — R 1; 21. Castles, B — Kt 2; 22. P — B 3, Q R — Q 1 and Black, though a Pawn down, has good counter-chances because of the misplaced White Rook.

17. P × Kt   Q — B 3
18. R — Q 4

This piece is now in an extremely powerful position from which it dominates the game.

18. ......   R — K 1

Played to restrain White from completing his development by P — B 3 and K — B 2.

19. B — Q 3

White could have preserved his Pawn by P — K 4, but rightly prefers to win by a direct attack on the King.

19. ......   Q × P
20. B × P ch   K — B 1

It is not safe to leave the King in the corner, e.g. 20. ....K — R 1; 21. B — K 4, Q — R 6; 22. R — Kt 1 and Black cannot take the Rook Pawn because of his exposed King, whilst White can quietly build up a K side attack by P — Q B 4 and Q — B 3.

21. B — K 4   Q — R 6
22. Q — Q 2   B — K 3
23. P — Q B 4   P — R 4
24. R — Kt 1

Offering up the extra Pawn in order to drive the King into the open.

24. ......   Q × P

Black precipitates disaster by accepting the Pawn and opens up fresh lines of attack for White. Instead, he should have anticipated White's attack on the K side by 24. ....Q — R 3.

25. R — R 1   Q — B 2
26. Q — Kt 2 !

A fine move threatening 27. Q — R 3 ch, K — Kt 1; 28. B — R 7 ch, K — R 1; 29. R (Q 4) — R 4 followed by mate. It also contains a hidden menace on Black's K Kt Pawn.

26. ......   Q — B 4
27. B — Q 5 !   R — R 3
28. R — K 4   R — Q 3

If Black tries direct methods of protecting his K Kt Pawn, immediate disaster results, e.g. 28. ....P — K Kt 3 ; 29. Q — B 6 and mate follows or 28. ....P — B 3; 29. R — R 8 ch winning a piece.

Position after 28. ....R — Q 3

29. R — R 7 !   K — K 2

The King must abandon the Kt Pawn for if 29. ....P — K Kt 3; 30. Q — Kt 7 ch, K — K 2; 31. Q × P ch.

30. Q × P   K — Q 1
31. B × B   P × B
32. Q × P   Q — Kt 5 ch

33. Q × Q	P × Q
34. P — B 5	R — B 3
35. R × Kt P	R × P
36. R — Q R 7	Resigns.

Black cannot avert the double exchange of Rooks for if 36. . . . . R — Q B 1 there comes the neat mate 37. R — Q 4. Capablanca conducted the final attack in his best style.

49
TWENTY–NINTH MATCH GAME, BUENOS AIRES, 1927

Queen's Gambit Declined, Cambridge Springs Defence

White	Black
CAPABLANCA	A. ALEKHINE
1. P — Q 4	P — Q 4
2. P — Q B 4	P — K 3
3. Kt — Q B 3	Kt — K B 3
4. B — Kt 5	Q Kt — Q 2
5. P — K 3	P — B 3
6. Kt — B 3	Q — R 4
7. Kt — Q 2	B — Kt 5
8. Q — B 2	P × P
9. B × Kt	Kt × B
10. Kt × P	Q — B 2

As pointed out in the notes to the previous game, 10. . . . . B × Kt ch is a good alternative line. Black loses too much time after 10. . . . . Q — Q 4; 11. Kt — Q 2, B × Kt; 12. P × B, P — K 4; 13. P — K 4, Q — K 3; 14. B — B 4, Q — K 2; 15. Castles K as in the game Grünfeld–Becker, Carlsbad, 1929.

11. P — Q R 3

Simple development gives White no advantage here. Against Alekhine at Prague in 1931, Mikenas tried 11. B — K 2; Castles; 12. Castles K, R — Q 1; 13. P — Q R 3, B — K 2; 14. P — Q Kt 4, P — Q Kt 3; 15. K R — Q 1, Kt — Q 4; 16. Kt — K 5, Kt × Kt; 17. Q × Kt, B — Kt 2 and Black can eventually free his game completely by P — Q B 4.

| 11. . . . . . . | B — K 2 |
| 12. P — K Kt 3 | |

This method of developing the Bishop gives White a more lasting initiative than 12. B — K 2, as Capablanca played in the 11th game of the match.

| 12. . . . . . . | Castles |

If 12. . . . . P — B 4; 13. B — Kt 2, P × P; 14. Kt — Kt 5 followed by 15. Kt × Q P with considerable advantage to White.

| 13. B — Kt 2 | B — Q 2 |
| 14. P — Q Kt 4! | |

A strong positional move designed to prevent Black from freeing his game by an eventual P — Q B 4.

| 14. . . . . . . | P — Q Kt 3 |

With this and his next move, Black tries to break up White's Q side, but merely succeeds in weakening his own Q wing. Instead, he should have organised a defensive position by 14. . . . . K R — Q 1 and B — K 1.

15. Castles   P — Q R 4
16. Kt — K 5!   P × P
17. P × P   R × R
18. R × R   R — B 1

White obtains an overwhelming position after 18. .... B × P; 19. Kt — Kt 5, Q — Q 1; 20. B × P.

19. Kt × B   Q × Kt
20. Kt — R 4   Q — Q 1
21. Q — Kt 3   Kt — Q 4

This is his best counter; he must block the long diagonal, for if 21. .... P — B 4; 22. Kt P × P, P × P; 23. P × P, B × P; 24. B — Kt 7, R — B 2; 25. Kt × B, R × Kt; 26. R — R 8 winning the Queen.

22. P — Kt 5   P × P
23. Q × P   R — R 1

Black could have forced the exchange of Kts, in the hope of securing a drawn ending because of the Bishops of opposite colour, but after 23. .... Kt — B 6; 24. Kt × Kt, R × Kt; 25. B — B 6, Q — Q 3; 26. R — R 8 ch, B — B 1; 27. R — B 8 he must lose a Pawn and has a very poor position indeed.

24. R — Q B 1   R — R 4
25. Q — B 6   B — R 6

Black must force the Rook off the Q B file; for if 25. .... P — Q Kt 4; 26. Q — Kt 7 threatening R — B 8.

26. R — Kt 1   B — B 1
And now if 26. .... P — Q Kt 4; 27. R × P, R × Kt.

27. B × Kt

Now White has won his Pawn, but not necessarily the game, as Black now puts up a most tenacious resistance.

27. ......   R × B
28. Kt × P   R — Q 3
29. Q — Kt 7   P — R 4
30. Kt — B 4   R — Q 2
31. Q — K 4   R — B 2
32. Kt — K 5   Q — B 1
33. K — Kt 2   B — Q 3
34. R — Q R 1   R — Kt 2
35. Kt — Q 3

An interesting alternative is 35. Kt — B 4, B — B 1; 36. R — R 6 and now if 36. .... P — Kt 3; 37. Kt — R 5, R — Kt 1; 38. R — B 6 with more pressure than in the actual game.

35. ......   P — Kt 3
36. R — R 6   B — B 1
37. R — B 6   R — B 2

Black rightly prefers the Queen ending to the Rook ending, which would indeed be quite lost after 37. .... Q — R 1; 38. R — B 7, R — R 2; 39. Q × Q, R × Q; 40. Kt — K 5.

38. R × R

Capablanca afterwards thought he would have had better chances of winning by playing an immediate 38. Kt — K 5, but Alekhine points out that Black could have forced a similar variation to that in the game by 38. .... Q — Kt 2; 39. Q — B 3, B — Kt 2.

38.	Q × R
39. Kt — K 5	B — Kt 2
40. Q — R 8 ch	K — R 2
41. Kt — B 3	

White must avoid the exchange of minor pieces which would give a clearly drawn Queen ending and must try to force a centre passed Pawn by P — K 4 and P — Q 5.

41.	B — B 3
42. Q — R 6	K — Kt 2
43. Q — Q 3	Q — Kt 2
44. P — K 4	Q — B 3
45. P — R 3	Q — B 2
46. P — Q 5	P × P
47. P × P	Q — B 6 !

Very well timed indeed; after the exchange of Queens, Black's King will reach the centre quicker than White's, and in view of the open position his Bishop is a stronger piece than the Kt. Attempts at blockade of the White Pawn whilst preserving the Queens would fail after 47. .... Q — Q 3; 48. Q — B 4, K — B 1; 49. Kt — Q 4.

48. Q × Q

Now, if 48. Q — K 4, Q — B 4; 49. P — Kt 4, P × P; 50. P × P, P — Kt 4 and White has no winning chances.

48.	B × Q
49. K — B 1	K — B 3
50. K — K 2	B — Kt 5
51. Kt — Q 4	B — B 4
52. Kt — B 6	K — B 4
53. K — B 3	K — B 3
54. P — Kt 4	P × P ch
55. P × P	

Position after 55. P × P

55. ......   K — Kt 4 ?

A mistake, after which Capablanca wins a very fine endgame. Both 55. ....B — Kt 3 and B — Q 3 would have sufficed to draw here. Capablanca gives the following variation: 55. ....B — Q 3; 56. K — K 4, K — Kt 4; 57. Kt — K 5, P — B 4 ch; 58. K — Q 4, B — Kt 1; 59. P — Q 6, B × P; 60. Kt — B 7 ch, K × P; 61. Kt × B, K — B 6 and White's last Pawn falls.

56. Kt — K 5 !   B — Q 5

However Black plays, he must lose another Pawn and with it the game. The main line is 56. ....P — B 4; 57. P — Q 6 !, P × P ch; 58. K — Kt 2 !, K — B 4; 59. P — Q 7, etc., whilst if 56. ....B — R 6; 57. P — Q 6, K — B 3; 58. P — Q 7, K — K 2; 59. Kt × B P, K × P; 60. Kt — K 5 ch winning easily.

| 57. Kt × P ch | K — B 3 |
| 58. Kt — Q 8 | B — Kt 3 |

White has a simple won Pawn ending after 58. ....K — K 4; 59. Kt — B 6 ch, K × P; 60. Kt × B, K × Kt; 61. K — B 4.

59.	Kt — B 6	B — B 4
60.	K — B 4 !	B × P

If 60. ....P — Kt 4 ch; 61. K — B 3, K — B 2; 62. K — K 2, K — K 1; 63. P — B 3, K — Q 2; 64. K — Q 3, K — Q 3; 65. K — K 4 followed by Kt — Q 4 and Kt — B 5 ch.

61.	P — Kt 5 ch	K — B 2
62.	Kt — K 5 ch	K — K 2

Or 62. ....K — Kt 2; 63. P — Q 6, B — Kt 3; 64. P — Q 7, B — B 2; 65. K — K 4, B — Q 1; 66. Kt — B 3, K — B 2; 67. K — Q 5, K — K 2; 68. K — B 6.

63.	Kt × P ch	K — Q 3
64.	K — K 4	B — Kt 6
65.	Kt — B 4	K — K 2
66.	K — K 5	B — K 8
67.	P — Q 6 ch	K — Q 2
68.	P — Kt 6	B — Kt 5
69.	K — Q 5	K — K 1
70.	P — Q 7 ch	Resigns.

A very strenuous game with an ending worthy of an endgame study.

CHAPTER SIX

Attempts at Rehabilitation

THE next few years see Capablanca engaging in tournament after tournament in an endeavour to prove to the world his right to a return match for the World Championship against Alekhine. He played in more tournaments during this period than in any before or after, and since he was in extremely fine form, a large number of great games resulted. A return match was denied him, however, and whose fault this was it is difficult, if not impossible, to say; nevertheless, the dispassionate observer can only remark what a pity it was that the chess world lost the prospect of the many fine games that another match between two such great players might have well produced.

The Bad Kissingen Tournament of 1928 shows Capablanca in scientific mood, laying clear the positional defects of his opponents with remorseless accuracy, as in his games against Tartakower, Mieses and Yates. But his best game in the tournament is that against Bogoljuboff, where the ending is managed with consummate artistry.

From the important Berlin Tournament, which Capablanca won with some ease, we have selected a remarkable pair of games against the great Polish master, Rubinstein. Capablanca, who had a great respect for the genius of this player, was justly proud of his victory over him here, and the draw is one of the most original games ever played.

Finally, there is the Budapest Siesta Tournament with Capablanca at the top of his form. The game against Havasi contains the typical Capa combination, but here with even more stunning effect, owing to Black's waste of a move. The other three games are fine illustrations of the lucid perfection of Capablanca's style.

BAD KISSINGEN, 1928

		Bogoljuboff	Capablanca	Euwe	Rubinstein	Nimzovitch	Réti	Marshall	Tartakower	Yates	Spielmann	Tarrasch	Mieses		
1	Bogoljuboff ..	–	0	½	1	½	1	1	½	1	1	1	½	8	I
2	Capablanca ..	1	–	½	½	½	½	½	1	1	0	½	1	7	II
3	Euwe	½	½	–	1	½	1	1	0	0	½	½	1	6½	III
4	Rubinstein ..	0	½	0	–	1	½	1	1	½	½	½	1	6½	IV
5	Nimzovitch ..	½	½	½	0	–	½	0	½	½	1	1	1	6	V
6	Réti	0	½	0	½	½	–	½	1	½	½	1	½	5½	
7	Marshall ..	0	½	0	0	1	½	–	0	1	1	½	½	5	
8	Tartakower ..	½	0	1	0	½	0	1	–	½	½	½	½	5	
9	Yates	0	0	1	½	½	½	0	½	–	½	½	1	5	
10	Spielmann ..	0	1	½	½	0	½	0	½	½	–	½	½	4½	
11	Tarrasch ..	0	½	½	½	0	0	½	½	½	½	–	½	4	
12	Mieses	½	0	0	0	0	½	½	½	0	½	½	–	3	

BERLIN, 1928

		Capablanca		Nimzovitch		Spielmann		Tartakower		Réti		Rubinstein		Marshall		
1	Capablanca ..	—		½	½	½	½	½	½	1	1	1	½	1	1	8½
2	Nimzovitch ..	½	½	—		½	0	½	½	1	1	0	1	1	½	7
3	Spielmann ..	½	½	½	1	—		½	0	½	0	1	1	½	½	6½
4	Tartakower ..	½	½	½	½	½	1	—		½	0	0	0	1	½	5½
{5	Réti ..	0	0	0	0	½	1	½	1	—		1	0	½	½	5
{6	Rubinstein ..	0	½	1	0	0	0	1	1	0	1	—		0	½	5
7	Marshall ..	0	0	0	½	½	½	0	½	½	½	1	½	—		4½

BUDAPEST, 1928

		Capablanca	Marshall	Kmoch	Spielmann	A. Steiner	Vajda	Havasi	H. Steiner	von Balla	Merényi	
1	Capablanca	–	½	½	½	1	½	1	1	1	1	7
2	Marshall	½	–	1	½	0	½	1	½	1	1	6
3	Kmoch	½	0	–	½	0	½	½	1	1	1	5
4	Spielmann	½	½	½	–	½	1	1	½	0	½	5
5	A. Steiner	0	1	1	½	–	0	0	1	½	½	4½
6	Vajda	½	½	½	0	1	–	½	0	½	1	4½
7	Havasi	0	0	½	0	1	½	–	½	½	1	4
8	H. Steiner	0	½	0	½	0	1	½	–	1	½	4
9	von Balla	0	0	0	1	½	½	½	0	–	½	3
10	Merényi	0	0	0	½	½	0	0	½	½	–	2

50
FIRST ROUND,
BAD KISSINGEN, 1928

Queen's Pawn, Budapest Defence

White	Black
CAPABLANCA	S. TARTAKOWER
1. P — Q 4	Kt — K B 3
2. P — Q B 4	P — K 4

Tartakower is a great exponent of the Budapest, but this is one of the defences least likely to succeed against a player of Capablanca's style. Its slightly dubious recklessness plays into the hands of one possessed of such sure positional flair.

3. P × P	Kt — Kt 5

3. ....Kt — K 5, the Fajarowicz variation, met with convincing disproof in the game, Alekhine–Tartakower, London, 1932, as follows: 3. ....Kt — K 5; 4. Kt — Q 2, Kt — B 4; 5. K Kt — B 3, Kt — B 3; 6. P — K Kt 3, Q — K 2; 7. B — Kt 2, P — K Kt 3; 8. Kt — Q Kt 1, Kt × P; 9. Castles, Kt × Kt ch; 10. P × Kt, B — Kt 2; 11. R — K 1, Kt — K 3; 12. Kt — B 3, Castles; 13. Kt — Q 5, Q — Q 1; 14. P — B 4, P — Q B 3; 15. Kt — B 3 and Black has a very bad game.

4. P — K 4	P — Q 3

Played in gambit style. Better is the more usual 4. ....Kt × K P; 5. P — B 4, K Kt — B 3; 6. B — K 3, B — Kt 5 ch; 7. Kt — B 3, though White still has rather the better game.

The early way of playing this defence was 4. ....P — K R 4; 5. Kt — Q B 3, Kt — Q B 3; 6. Kt — R 3, K Kt × K P; 7. B — K 2, P — Q 3; 8. Kt — B 4, P — K Kt 3; 9. Castles and White again has the better game (Sämisch–Spielmann, Copenhagen, 1923).

5. P × P	B × P
6. B — K 2 !	

White must play carefully here, for if 6. P — K R 3, Q — R 5; 7. Q — Q 4, B — K 4, etc., whilst 6. Kt — K B 3, B — Kt 5 ch; 7. B — Q 2, B — Q B 4 leads to a clear win for Black.

6.	P — K B 4

An interesting idea suggested by the Rumanian master, Balogh. It endeavours to obtain further attacking chances by opening up the K B file and also avoids losing time by supporting the threatened Kt. 6. ....P — K R 4; 7. Kt — K B 3, Kt — Q B 3; 8. Kt — B 3, Q — K 2; 9. B — Kt 5 ! leaves White, not only a Pawn up, but with the better position.

7. P × P	Q — K 2
8. Kt — K B 3	

Here White can win a piece by 8. P — B 5, B × B P; 9. Q — R 4 ch, Kt — B 3; 10. Q × Kt, but when this game was played, and for a considerable time after, it was thought that Black obtained in compensation too strong an attack by 10. ....Kt — Q 5. This is, however, not true, as White can continue 11. Q —

R 5 ch, K — B 1; 12. P — B 6 !.
P × P; 13. B — R 6 ch, K —
Kt 1; 14. Kt — Q B 3, Kt —
B 7 ch; 15. K — Q 1, Kt × R;
16. B — B 4 ch, B — K 3; 17. Q
× B !, R — Q 1 ch; 18. K — B 1,
Q — B 2; 19. B × B, Q × B; 20.
Kt — B 3 and wins.

    8. ......   B × B P
    9. B — Kt 5   Kt — K B 3
   10. Kt — B 3   Kt — B 3
   11. Kt — Q 5

By his last three energetic
moves, White has not only re-
tained the gambit Pawn, but pro-
cured rather the better game
without considerations of material.

   11. ......   Q — B 2
   12. Castles   Castles Q

As will be seen later on (cf.
move 18), Castling this side en-
tails certain disadvantages, but
Black's game is still inferior
after 12. ....Castles K; 13. Kt
× Kt ch, P × Kt; 14. B — R 6,
K R — K 1; 15. Kt — R 4, B —
Kt 3; 16. B — B 3 !

   13. Kt — Q 4   Kt × Kt
   14. Q × Kt   P — B 3

If 14. ....Kt × Kt, not 15. B
× R because of 15. ....Kt —
B 5, but 15. P × Kt, Q R — K 1;
16. B — Kt 4, and if 14. ....P
— B 4; 15. Q — R 4, Kt × Kt;
16. P × Kt, Q R — K 1; 17. B
— Kt 4, B × B; 18. Q × B ch, K
— Kt 1; 19. Q R — Q 1 and
White is a good passed Pawn up.
(19. ....R — K 4 ?); 20. B —
B 4 wins).

   15. B × Kt   P × B
   16. Q × B P

A momentary lapse which might
have proved costly. Correct was
16. Q × R P, P × Kt; 17. P × P,
Q × P; 18. B — B 3 with an overwhelming attack.

   16. ......   Q × Q

For here Black could have ob-
tained the better game by 16. ....
Q — Kt 3 ! 17. Q × Q, P × Q; 18.
P — K Kt 4, B × P ch; 19. K —
Kt 2, B — K 5 ch; 20. P — B 3,
P × Kt; 21. P × B, P × P.

   17. Kt × Q   B — K 4

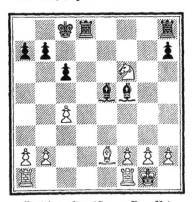

Position after 17. ....B — K 4

18. B — Kt 4 !
Neatly forcing the exchange of
one of Black's powerful Bishops.

   18. ......   B × Kt

Or 18. ....B × B; 19. Kt ×
B, B × P; 20. Q R — Q 1 and
White wins without much difficulty. The text has at least the
mechanical drawing possibilities

provided by Bishops of opposite colour.

19. B × B ch   K — B 2

Not wishing to submit to the passive position resulting after 19. ....K — Kt 1; 20. Q R — Q 1, R × R; 21, R × R, B × P; 22. R — Q 7, P — K R 3; but at any rate this variation would save the K R Pawn.

20. Q R — Q 1 !

To defend the Q Kt Pawn with the Rook would mean allowing Black to occupy the seventh rank by 20. ....R — Q 7 with a crippling effect on White's game.

20. ......   B × P
21. R × R   R × R

If 21. ....K × R; 22. R — Q 1 ch followed by 23. R — Q 7 and wins.

22. B × P   R — Q 5
23. P — Kt 3 !

It is impossible for White to defend his Q B Pawn, since after 23. B — Kt 8, R — Kt 5 the Rook pursues the Bishop wherever it goes; however, White's advance of the K side Pawns must give him the win.

23. ......   R × P
24. P — K R 4   P — Kt 4
25. K — Kt 2   P — R 4
26. P — R 5

Threatening P — R 6, B — Kt 8 and P — R 7, etc.

26. ......   B — Kt 2
27. P — B 4   B — R 3

In order to prevent P — K Kt 4.

28. R — K 1   R — R 5
29. B — Kt 8   R — Q 5
30. R — K 7 ch   R — Q 2

If 30. ....K — Q 1; 31. R — K 6 wins easily; Black is now in hopeless case.

31. R × R ch   K × R
32. K — B 3   P — B 4
33. P — Kt 4   P — B 5
34. P — Kt 5   B — B 1

Or 34. ....B — Kt 2; 35. P — R 6, B — R 1; 36. P — Kt 6.

35. P — R 6   P — R 5
36. P — B 5   K — B 3

If 36. ....P — B 6; 37. K — K 2.

37. P — R 7   B — Kt 2
38. P — B 6   P — B 6

In the vain hope that White will carelessly play 39. P × B, P — B 7; 40. P — R 8 = Q, P — B 8 = Q; 41. Q — R 6 ch, K — B 4 with drawing chances.

39. K — K 2   B — R 1
40. P — B 7   Resigns.

A very efficiently played game.

51
FIFTH ROUND,
BAD KISSINGEN, 1928

Queen's Gambit Declined,
Orthodox Defence

White	Black
CAPABLANCA	J. MIESES
1. P — Q 4	Kt — K B 3
2. P — Q B 4	P — K 3
3. Kt — Q B 3	P — Q 4
4. B — Kt 5	B — K 2
5. P — K 3	Q Kt — Q 2
6. Kt — B 3	Castles
7. R — B 1	P — Q R 3

A move of doubtful validity, indicative of a policy little likely to succeed against a Capablanca. Its intention is to play an eventual P × P, P — Q Kt 4, B — Kt 2 and P — Q B 4, but Black can be prevented from doing this quite simply and the normal move 7. ....P — B 3 is to be preferred.

8. P × P

Simplest and best, as it gives Black little chance of counter-play and opens up the prospect of obtaining pressure on the Q side. Not so good is 8. P — B 5, P — B 3; 9. B — Q 3, P — K 4; 10. P × P, Kt — Kt 5 and Black regains his Pawn with an excellent game.

8.	P × P
9. Q — Kt 3	

A new and strong move by Capablanca which brings more pressure to bear on the Q side Pawns. The normal method of play is 9. B — Q 3, P — B 3; 10. Q — B 2, R — K 1; 11. Castles, Kt — B 1 and White will proceed with operations on the Q side by P — Q R 3, P — Q Kt 4, Kt — Q R 4 and Kt — B 5 whilst Black will endeavour to counter on the K side.

9.	P — B 3
10. B — Q 3	Kt — R 4 ?

This manœuvre is always suspect in the defence to the Queen's Gambit. In order to exchange pieces it wastes two moves (for the Kt cannot remain on R 4), and Black cannot well afford this loss of time.

Instead, Black should continue on lines described in the note to the 9th move and play 10. .... R — K 1 followed by 11. .... Kt — B 1.

11. B × B	Q × B
12. Castles	K Kt — B 3

More logical is 12. ....P — K Kt 3 followed by Kt — Kt 2 and Kt — K 3 with control of the important square Q B 4.

13. Kt — Q R 4

Attacking the weaknesses on Q Kt 6 and Q B 5; this move was frequently employed by Capablanca in analogous positions in the World Championship match against Alekhine.

13.	Kt — K 5 ?

This Kt is overworked, having been moved three times in the last four moves. White benefits by his gain of tempo in accelera-

tion of his Q side attack, and
Black can now hardly recover
from his great waste of time.

15. B × Kt   Q × B

It may be that Black originally
intended 14. ....P × B; if so,
he now realises that after 15. Kt
— Q 2, Kt — B 3; 16. Kt — B 5,
R — K 1; 17. Kt — B 4 the
White Kts will prove altogether
too menacing on the Q side.

15. Q — Kt 4!

A very strong move which
dominates the weakened black
squares in his opponent's position. Black now suffers badly
from the lack of the K Bishop,
which he has been at such great
pains to exchange.

Position after 15. Q — Kt 4 !

15. ......   Q — Kt 3

Played with fatalistic resignation; a better defence was 15.
....P — B 3, though White
would still retain his winning advantage by 16. Kt — Q 2, Q —
K 3; 17. Kt — Kt 3, R — K 1;

18. Kt (Kt 3) — B 5, Kt × Kt;
19. Kt × Kt, Q — K 2; 20. R —
B 3 followed by R — Kt 3.

16. Q — K 7   P — B 3
17. R — B 3   Q — K 1
18. Q — Q 6   R — B 2
19. K R — B 1   Q — B 1
20. Q × Q ch   K × Q

If 20. ....Kt × Q; 21. Kt —
Kt 6, R — Kt 1; 22. Kt × P, etc.,
whilst taking with the Rook
would simply mean removing this
piece from its right rank.

21. Kt — K 1!

The transference of this Kt to
the Q side (either Q B 5 or
Q Kt 4, according to circumstances) represents the final kill-
ing blow in White's strategy; owing to his weakness on the black
squares, Mieses cannot adequately parry this.

21. ......   K — K 1

The tempting 21. ....P —
Q Kt fails against 22. R × P, B
— Kt 2; 23. R — B 7, etc.

22. Kt — Q 3   R — Kt 1
23. P — B 3   R — K 2
24. K — B 2   Kt — B 1
25. R — Kt 3

Forcing the return of the Kt
to Q 2 because of the threat of
Kt (R 4) — B 5 followed by Kt
× R P.

25. ......   Kt — Q 2
26. P — Kt 4   P — Q Kt 4

After which Black's position
collapses like an overweighted
pack of cards. In the long run,

however, Black must succumb to the many weaknesses in his position. Should he mark time by K — Q 1, then White will prepare a break-through on the K side by P — K R 4 — R 5, etc.

27. Kt(R 4)— B 5   Kt — Kt 3

Or 27 ....Kt × Kt; 28. R × Kt, B — Kt 2; 29. R — R 3, R — R 1; 30. R — R 5, R — Q B 2; 31. Kt — Kt 4, K — Q 2; 32. R — B 3 followed by R (B 3) — R 3, etc.

28. Kt — Kt 4   B — Kt 2

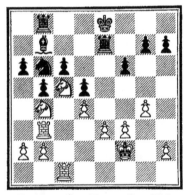

Position after 28. ....B — Kt 2

White now wins two clear Pawns, after which Black can resign with a clear conscience; Capablanca's play has been characterised by its usual crystal clarity.

29. Kt × B   R (Kt 8) × Kt
30. R × P   P — Q R 4
31. R × Kt   P × Kt
32. R × R   R × R
33. R × P   Resigns.

52
EIGHTH ROUND, BAD KISSINGEN, 1928

Sicilian Defence

White	Black
CAPABLANCA	F. D. YATES

1. P — K 4   P — Q B 4
2. Kt — K 2

A novelty, but one which, owing to Black's failure to deal properly with it, merely transposes into a normal variation.

2. ......   P — Q 3

Now White can transpose into the Dragon variation; most vigorous and correct here is 2. .... P — K 4 !

3. P — Q 4   P × P
4. Kt × P   P — K Kt 3 ?

Allowing White to obtain the Maroczy bind; necessary is 4. ....Kt — K B 3 in order to force White to shut in his Q B Pawn by 5. Kt — Q B 3.

5. P — Q B 4 !

This strong move gives White control of the centre and Black must grovel about to find a counter-attack.

5. ......   B — Kt 2
6. Kt — Q B 3   Kt — K B 3
7. B — K 2   Castles
8. Castles   Q Kt — Q 2

Played with the idea of going to B 4 and so attacking the K Pawn, but this attack is very easily met and simply loses time. Better was the usual 8. ....Kt — B 3.

9. B — K 3   Kt — B 4
10. P — B 3   B — Q 2
11. Q — Q 2

White is proceeding systematically; he first concentrates his major pieces in the centre and then, when all his forces are ready, proceeds with the final advance.

11. ......   R — B 1
12. K R — Q 1   P — Q R 3

This move results in a weakness on Q Kt 3, but Black must try to prepare some counter on the Q wing, and he also may have had in mind the idea of playing Q — B 2 without being open to attack by the Kts on Kt 5.

13. Q R — B 1   Kt — K 3

Intending Kt — R 4 and Kt — B 5.

14. P — Q Kt 3

White's Pawn structure is very impressive; Black is hard put to it to discover a reasonably good continuation.

14. ......   Kt — R 4

Consequent, but bad. He should have sought relief by exchanges by 14. ....Kt × Kt; 15. B × Kt, B — Q B 3. Even then his position is unenviable, since White can play 16. Q — K 3 threatening 17. P — B 5, P — Q 4; 18. P × P, Kt × P; 19. Kt × Kt, B × Kt; 20. B × B, K × B; 21. Q — Q 4 ch winning a piece.

15. Kt × Kt   Q B × Kt
16. Kt — R 4

Causing Black bitterly to regret his 12th move. White now threatens 17. B — Kt 6 and 18. P — B 5.

16. ......   R — B 3

Directly countering the above threat, but now White cunningly tackles the problem from the other side.

17. P — B 4   Kt — B 3
18. B — B 3

Threatening to win the exchange by P — K 5.

18. ......   Kt — Kt 5

If 18. ....B — Kt 5; 19. P — K 5, B × B; 20. P × Kt, B × R; 21. P × B winning two pieces for the Rook and Pawn.

19. P — K 5!   Kt × B
20. Q × Kt   R — B 2
21. P — Q B 5

Winning the Q Pawn; the combined pressure of White's centralised pieces is too powerful for Black to resist.

21. ......   Q — Kt 1
22. K P × P   P × P
23. R × P   R — K 1
24. Q — Q 2   P — Q Kt 4
25. Kt — Kt 6

Avoiding Black's traps of (a) 25. Kt — Kt 2, B × Kt; 26. Q × B, R × P; 27. R × R, Q × R regaining the Pawn, or (b) 25. P × P. e.p., R × R ch; 26. Q × R, Q × R winning the Rook.

25. ......   B — K B 1

Position after 25. ....B — K B 1

26. Kt — Q 5 !

The only move — but sufficient. Bad would be 26. R — B 6, R × R; 27. B × R, B × P ch!; 28. R × B, Q × Kt and Black has regained his lost Pawn.

26. ......   R × P

An ingenious move which is still more ingeniously met. If 26. ....B × R; 27. Kt — B 6 ch, K — B 1; 28. Q × B ch, R (K 1) — K 2; 29. Kt × P ch, K — Kt 2; 30. Kt — B 6, K — B 1; 31. Q — Q 4 and wins. Whilst though, after 26. ....B × Kt; 27. R × B, Black has obtained a position with Bishops of opposite colour, there is no possible chance of a draw, White's passed Pawn and strong central position being too much of a handicap for Black.

27. Kt — B 6 ch   K — R 1
28. Kt × R   R × R ch
29. Q × R   Q × Kt

29. ....B × R loses at once after 30. Kt — B 6 ch. Black must therefore descend to an end-game with the exchange and a Pawn down, and, of course, is utterly lost, despite his few last remaining kicks.

30. R × P   Q — K 2
31. Q — B 3 ch   K — Kt 1

And not 31. ....P — B 3; 32. Q — K 3 forcing exchange of Queens.

32. Q — K 5   P — Kt 5
33. B — K 4   Q — Q 1
34. P — K R 3   B × R P
35. B — Q 5 !

Acceptance of the Bishop would give Black a perpetual check by 35. P × B, Q — Q 8 ch; 36. K — B 2, Q — Q 7 ch; 37. K — B 3, Q — Q 8 ch and the King must return to B 2 since 38. K — Kt 3 would mean loss of the Rook and 38. K — K 3 would actually lose the Queen after 38. ....B — B 4 ch.

35. ......   Q — R 5
36. Q — B 6

Again 36. P × B would lead to perpetual check after B — B 4 ch; 37. K — R 2, Q — B 7 ch; 38. B — Kt 2, Q — Kt 8 ch; 39. K — Kt 3, Q — B 7 ch, etc.

36. ......   B — B 4 ch
37. K — R 2   Resigns.

53
NINTH ROUND, BAD KISSINGEN, 1928

Queen's Pawn, Queen's Indian Defence

White	Black
E. Bogoljuboff	Capablanca
1. P — Q 4	Kt — K B 3
2. P — Q B 4	P — K 3
3. Kt — K B 3	P — Q Kt 3
4. Kt — B 3	B — Kt 2
5. B — Kt 5	B — K 2
6. P — K 3	Kt — K 5
7. B × B	Q × B
8. Kt × Kt	B × Kt
9. Kt — Q 2	

For remarks about the opening, the reader is directed to Game No. 73, Ribera v. Capablanca. This game is mainly included for its remarkable ending and later middle game play. At this stage in the tournament Bogoljuboff was 1½ points ahead and would have been well content with a draw, and this explains his policy of exchanges. Best here is, however, 9. B — K 2.

| 9. ...... | B — Kt 2 |
| 10. B — K 2 | Q — Kt 4 |

An instructive move; Capablanca refuses to worsen his position by deliberately avoiding exchanges. Such a false policy would lead to anti-positional play.

It is true that as a result of the text White is able to exchange Queens, but there is no reason to avoid this if one's position is consequently bettered.

10. ....B × P ?; 11. R — K Kt 1, B — Kt 2; 12. B — B 3 followed by R × P, would be bad for Black.

| 11. B — B 3 | B × B |
| 12. Q × B | |

Played with a view to exchanging Queens. If 12. Kt × B then not Q × P; 13. R — K Kt 1 followed by R × P and the open K Kt file is in White's favour; so Black does best (after 12. Kt × B) to play 12. ....Q — B 3, where the Q is very well placed.

| 12. ...... | Kt — B 3 |

Apart from the necessity of defending the Q R, this move has latent threats of either an eventual Kt — Kt 5 or P — K 4.

13. Q — Kt 3

A policy dictated by the tournament score; Bogoljuboff hopes to obtain an easy draw once the Queens are exchanged. Curiously enough, better prospects of an easy draw are offered by White avoiding the exchange of Queens, e.g. 13. Castles K, Castles K; 14. Kt — K 4, Q — Kt 3; 15. K R — Q 1, P — B 4; 16. Kt — B 3, P — Q R 3 (to prevent Kt — Kt 5); 17. P — Q R 3 and the position is absolutely equal.

| 13. ...... | Q × Q |
| 14. R P × Q | K — K 2 |

Naturally, White should still have no difficulty in reaching a draw, but his next few moves

evince a startling lack of understanding of the position, whilst
Black's every move is subtly to
the point.

15. P — K Kt 4

With some vague idea of commencing a belated K side attack.
He should pay his opponent the
compliment of imitation and develop his King by 15. K — K 2.

15. ......   P — K R 3 !

At once putting an end to any
aggression by White on this flank.

16. P — Q R 3

A passive defensive move which
merely creates a hole in White's
Pawn structure; again 16. K —
K 2 was best.

16. ......   P — Q R 3 !

This move, on the other hand,
foreshadows a break-through by
P — Q Kt 4.

17. K — K 2   K R — Q Kt 1 !

Now, at least, White should
have realised his dangerous position and safeguarded himself ac-
cordingly; Black's concentration
of strength on the extreme Q
wing is alarmingly obvious.

18. Kt — K 4 ?

This Kt move only worsens the
position. Safest was 18. K R —
Q Kt 1, P — Q Kt 4; 19. K —
Q 3 and if P × P ch; 20. Kt ×
P, R — Kt 6 ch; 21. K — B 2,
Q R — Q Kt 1; 22. Kt — Q 2,
R (Kt 6) — Kt 4; 23. P — Q Kt 4
and White is out of danger.

Not so good is 18. P — Q R 4,
since after 18. ....P — Q Kt 4
Black will open up the Q Kt file
with attack on White's Kt Pawn,
and very bad strategically would
be 18. P — Kt 4, P — Q Kt 4 ; 19.
P — B 5, P — Q R 4; 20. P —
B 4, P × P; 21. P × P, R — R 5
with a won position for Black.

Position after 18. Kt — K 4 ?

18. ......   P — Q Kt 4
19. P — B 5

Or 19. P × P, R × P; 20.
K R — Q Kt 1,   Q R — Q Kt 1
and Black has very strong pressure on the Q side.

19. ......   P — Q 4 !
20. P × P ch e.p.

That this exchange is now inevitable is another evil consequence of White's faulty 18th
move. For if now 20. Kt — B 3
then P — Kt 5 again breaking
through on the Q Kt file; whilst
if 20. Kt — Q 2, P — K 4; 21. K
— Q 3, K — B 3 and Black will
now have threats on both wings.

20. ......   P × P

Two fresh dangers now arise for White, control of the Q B file and the square Q B 4, the latter providing the Black Kt with a fine outpost.

21. P — B 4 ?

White is still deluded by the lure of a counter-demonstration on the K side. But it soon becomes evident that he can achieve nothing on this wing; instead, he should bend all his efforts to countering Black's threats on the Q side and play 21. K R — Q B 1. Even then an analysis by Tartakower shows that Black retains the advantage: 21. ....K — Q 2; 22. R — B 2, R — R 2; 23. Q R — Q B 1, Kt — R 4; 24. Kt — Q 2, P — Kt 5!

21. ......   R — Q B 1
22. P — B 5 ?

Keeping blindly to his K side attack idea, but giving Black far too much scope of the Q wing. Another unfortunate result of the text move is that Black's King is given opportunities of eventually penetrating the K side via the holes on White's K B 4 and K Kt 5.

It was imperative to oppose Rooks on the Q B file by 22. K R — Q B 1.

22. ......   Kt — R 4
23. K — Q 3   Kt — B 5
24. Q R — Q Kt 1

Of the three passive moves at his disposal, White, his optimism now suddenly transmuted into pessimism, chooses the most passive. But if 24. R — R 2, R — B 3; 25. P — Q Kt 3, Kt — R 4; 26. R — Q B 2, Q R — Q B 1, etc.; and after 24. P — Q Kt 3, Kt — R 4; 25. Kt — Q 2, R — B 2; 26. Q R — Q B 1, Q R — Q B 1; 27. R × R, R × R; 28. P — K 4, K — B 3 Black cannot be prevented from playing K — Kt 4, since 29. R — R 5 would be met by 29. ....R — B 8.

24. ......   P — Q 4 !

Capablanca's play here and to the end of the game is perfect in its economic and beautiful exploitation of a strategically won position.

25. Kt — B 3

After 25. Kt — B 5 Black can either play with effect 25. .... P — K 4 or continue neatly with 25. ....Kt — K 4 ch; 26. P × Kt, R × Kt; 27. Q R — Q B 1, Q R — Q R 1; 28. R × R, R × R threatening both R — B 5 and P — B 3.

25. ......   R — B 3
26. P × P   P × P
27. P — Kt 5

This Pawn sacrifice is intended to prevent K — B 3 — Kt 4 and also has vague hopes of getting profit from the open K R file.

There is now, however, no sufficient means of dealing with Black's threats of penetrating with his King and also of doubling Rooks on the Q B file.

27. ......   P × P
28. R — R 5   K — B 3
29. R — R 3   Q R — Q B 1

Threatening to win two Pawns
by 30. ....Kt × P ch.

30. Kt — R 2   P — R 4 !

Not only shutting out the
White Kt, but foreshadowing an
eventual P — Q Kt 5.

31. R — B 3 ch   K — Kt 3
32. P — K Kt 4   Kt — Q 3 !

Black has envisaged a mating
net by bringing the Kt to K 5 and
the Rook to the 7th rank.

33. Kt — B 3   P — Kt 5
34. P × P   P × P
35. Kt — Q 1

If 35. Kt — R 2, Kt — K 5;
36. Kt × P, R — B 5; 37. Kt —
R 2, R — B 7; 38. R — Q 1, R
× P, etc.

35. ......   R — B 7
36. R — B 2   P — Kt 6 !

A beautifully harmonious and
thematic move; the finish is extremely pleasing.

37. R — R 1   Kt — K 5
38. R — K 2   R (B 1 — B 3
39. R — Kt 1

Black is limited to movement
of this Rook, since playing the
other pieces results in immediate
mate. If 39. Kt — B 3, R ×
Kt ch; 40. P × R, R × P mate;
or 39. R × R, R × R and 40.
....R — Q 7 mate follows.

39. ......   P — K 4 !

The final touch; mate now
looms up in quite another direction.

40. R — R 1   R (B 3) — B 5
41. R — R 5   Kt — B 4 ch !

Resigns, for he is mated by 42.
....P — K 5. The finish, as in
so many of Capablanca's best
games, presents a handsome geo-
metric picture.

Final Position

54
FIFTH ROUND,
BERLIN, 1928

Queen's Pawn Opening

White	Black
Capablanca	A. Rubinstein

1. P — Q 4   P — Q 4
2. Kt — K B 3   P — Q B 4
3. P × P

Capablanca forms a scheme for
isolating Black's Q Pawn, but
this should not prove a serious
handicap to the second player,
who is able to complete his development quite easily. The move
likely to give Black the most

trouble is 3. P — B 4 and if then B P × P; 4. Q × P, Kt — K B 3; 5. P × P, Kt × P; 6. P — K 4 or 4. ....P — K 3; 5. P × P followed by 6. B — K Kt 5.

After 3. ....P — K 3 or 3. ....Q P × P; 4. P — K 3 leading respectively to the Tarrasch Defence and the Queen's Gambit Accepted, Black has embarked on variations that are recognised as inferior by modern theory.

3. ......   P — K 3

Should Black wish to avoid the isolated Pawn he can quite well play 3. ....Q — R 4 ch followed by Q × B P.

4. P — K 4   B × P

4. ....P × P; 5. Q × Q ch, K × Q; 6. Kt — Kt 5 gives White a Pawn and the better game.

5. P × P   P × P
6. B — Kt 5 ch

A move of dubious value, the Bishop not being very effectively placed on Kt 5. Better is 6. B — K 2.

6. ......   Kt — B 3
7. Castles   Kt — K 2
8. Q Kt — Q 2

This Kt is to be developed on Q Kt 3 in order to control Q 4 and so prevent the further advance of Black's Q Pawn.

8. ......   Castles
9. Kt — Kt 3   B — Kt 3

9. ....B — Q 3 also came into consideration, leading to quite a

different type of game, with Black's counter-attack consisting of pressure on the K R rather than the K B Pawn.

10. R — K 1

Preparing for B — K 3, but this manœuvre cannot be carried out for some time, and meanwhile can get a good game by concentrating on the weak square on K B 2. Better would be 10. B — K B 4 followed by 11. P — B 3.

10. ......   B — Kt 5

Threatening B × P ch followed by Q — Kt 3 ch.

11. B — Q 3

This unhappy Bishop is still incorrectly placed; on Q 3 it is open to eventual attack and exchange by Black's Kt. Better would have been 11. P — K R 3, B — K R 4; 12. P — B 3.

11. ......   Kt — Kt 3
12. P — K R 3   B × Kt
13. Q × B   Q Kt — K 4
14. Q — B 5   Kt × B
15. Q × Kt (Q 3)

Position after 15. Q × Kt (Q 3)

15. ......   P — Q 5 ?

A strategical blunder which converts the Q Pawn into a real liability and deprives Black of any counter-attack.

Black must maintain an attack on the K side by 15. ....Q — B 3, after which White has nothing better than 16. R — B 1 (16. B — K 3, Q × P is rather to Black's advantage); 16. .... Q R — Q 1; 17. P — B 3, Kt — K 4; 18. Q — Q 1 (not 18. Q — K 2, K R — K 1); 18. .... Kt — B 5 and Black has an excellent game.

16. B — Q 2   Q — B 3
17. R — K 4

Underlining Black's error on the 15th move; White now continually improves his game by attack on Black's Q 5.

17. ......   Q R — Q 1
18. Q R — K 1   Q — B 3
19. P — Kt 3

A positional move to limit the action of Black's Kt.

19. ......   K R — K 1
20. B — R 5

A strong move threatening to win the Q Pawn by 21. B × B, P × B; 22. R × R ch, R × R; 23. R × R ch, Q × R; 24. Q × P.

20. ......   R × R
21. Q × R

Threatening 21. B × B, Q × B (or 21. ....P × B; 22. Q × Q, P × Q; 23. Kt × P); 22. R — Q 1 winning the Q Pawn.

21. ......   Kt — B 1

Allowing White to penetrate to the 7th rank with his Rook, after which, struggle as he may, Black cannot shake off White's hold on the position. It is difficult, however, to find a plausible line for Black. The text move intends a further strengthening of the Q Pawn by an eventual Kt — K 3.

Capablanca recommends as better 21. ....Q × Q; 22. R × Q, B × B; 23. Kt × B, P — B 4, but after 24. R — K 2, R — Q 2; 25. R — K 8 ch, K — B 2; 26. R — Q Kt 8, P — Kt 3; 27. Kt — B 6 Black's game is still under great pressure.

22. Q × Q   P × Q
23. R — K 7

Threatening 24. R × R P !

23. ......   R — Q 4

Parrying the above threat, but leaving Black's pieces in a passive position. More freedom would have resulted after 23. ....P — Q 6; 24. P × P, R × P, though White still maintains his grasp on the position by 25. B × B, P × B; 26. R — Kt 7, P — Q Kt 4; 27. R — B 7.

24. B × B   P × B
25. R — Kt 7   Kt — Q 2

Black has established a strong defensive position which will demand considerable efforts on White's part should he hope to pierce it. However, he suffers from the main defect of having no counter-attack, and White, by continually using the threat of mate on the back rank, is able to reach a position where Black must lose a Pawn by force.

26. R — B 7   R — Q 3

The alternative is 26. ....P — Q B 4; 27. R — B 8 ch, Kt — B 1; 28. R — Kt 8, P — B 5; 29. Kt — Q 2, P — Q Kt 4; 30. K — Kt 2, P — Kt 3; 31. K — B 3, K — Kt 2; 32. K — K 4 and the White King enters the game with decisive effect.

27. R — B 8 ch   Kt — B 1
28. Kt — Q 2   P — Q B 4

If 28. ....P — Q 6; 29. P × P, R × P; 30. Kt — Kt 3, P — Q Kt 4; 31. Kt — R 5, R — Q 7; 32. Kt × P threatening Kt — K 7 ch.

29. Kt — B 4   R — K 3
30. R — Kt 8   R — K 8 ch
31. K — Kt 2   P — K Kt 4

Black must first free his King, since 31. ....R — K 7 would be met by 32. Kt × P threatening Kt — Q 7.

32. P — Q R 4   R — Q R 8

A Pawn is lost whatever Black does; if 32. ....R — Q B 8; 33. Kt — R 3 followed by R × P and the White Q R Pawn races on to queen.

33. Kt × P   K — Kt 2
34. R — B 8   Kt — K 3
35. Kt — Q 7   R × P
36. Kt × P   R — Kt 5

If 36. ....Kt × Kt; 37. R × Kt, K — B 3; 38. K — B 3 followed by K — K 4 winning the Q Pawn shortly.

37. Kt — Q 3   R — Kt 4
38. K — B 3   P — R 3
39. P — Q Kt 4   P — R 4
40. P — Kt 4   P × P ch
41. P × P   P — B 3
42. R — B 4   K — B 2
43. Kt — B 5   Kt — Q 1
44. Kt — Kt 3   Resigns

This was the first and only time Capablanca ever defeated the great Polish master.

55
BERLIN, 1928
Queen's Pawn, Rubinstein Variation

White	Black
A. RUBINSTEIN	CAPABLANCA
1. P — Q 4	Kt — K B 3
2. Kt — K B 3	P — K 3
3. P — K 3	

Initiating a plan for restrained but powerful development that demands great care and accuracy on both sides. It differs from the Colle formation in developing the Q Bishop by a fianchetto rather than planning for an eventual P — K 4.

| 3. ...... | P — B 4 |
| 4. Q Kt — Q 2 | P — Q 4 |

In later years Capablanca would have played here 4. ....P

— Q Kt 3 followed by B — Kt 2 and Kt — B 3.

5. P — Q R 3

This modest-looking move is one of the distinctive features of Rubinstein's idea; as will be seen later on, it develops the Q B with gain of tempo — a very economical manœuvre.

5. ......   Q Kt — Q 2

If Black tries to contest control of K 4 by 5. ....Kt — B 3; 6. P × P, B × P; 7. P — Q Kt 4, B — Q 3; 8. B — Kt 2, Q — B 2 White gets the advantage by 9. P — B 4, B — Q 2; 10. R — B 1.

6. P × P   B × P

Unsatisfactory for Black is 6. ....Kt × P; 7.   P — Q Kt 4, Q Kt — K 5; 8. B — Kt 2, B — K 2; 9. Kt × Kt, P × Kt; 10. Q × Q ch, B × Q; 11. B — Kt 5 ch, B — Q 2; 12. Kt — Q 4, when White has three Pawns to two on the Q side and rather the better piece development.

7. P — Q Kt 4   B — K 2
8. B — Kt 2   Castles

Somewhat mechanically played. Now was the moment for 8. .... P — Q R 4 forcing 9. P — Kt 5, giving Black the square Q B 4 for his Kt. After the text, White obtains the initiative by a series of vigorous moves.

9. P — B 4   P × P

At Budapest, 1929, Monticelli played 9. ....P — Q Kt 3, but after 10. B — Q 3, P × P; 11. Kt × P, B — Kt 2; 12. Castles K,

R — B 1; 13. Q — K 2 he, like Capablanca in the present game, was faced with the great difficulty of finding a suitable post for his Queen, whilst White also enjoyed control of the important square, K 5.

10. Kt × P   Kt — Kt 3
11. Kt × Kt   Q × Kt
12. B — Q 3   B — Q 2
13. B — Q 4 !

Very strong; Black has now nothing better than 13. ....Q — Q 1 with loss of time. The fact that he is not content with this, but keeps his Queen in the centre, only aggravates the seriousness of his position.

13. ......   Q — B 3
14. Castles !

And not 14. R — Q B 1, Q — R 5; 15. Q × Q, B × Q; 16. R — B 7, B — Q 3 when White cannot play 17. R × Kt P because of 17. ....B — B 3.

14. ......   Q — Q 4
15. Q — K 2   K R — B 1
16. Q R — Q 1

White must now win a Pawn by force. If, for example, 16. ....Q — K R 4; 17. B × Kt, B × B; 18. B × P ch, K × B; 19. R × B and White is a Pawn to the good with a fine position. Black therefore decides to counter-attack on the Q side.

16. ......   Q — Kt 6
17. B × Kt   B × B
18. B × P ch   K × B
19. R × B   K — Kt 1

Position after 19. ....K — Kt 1

20. P — K R 4

An over refinement by which White loses the fruits of his previous fine play. In order to retain his advantage, he must simply capture the other Pawn, e.g. 20. R × Kt P, Q × R P; 21. P — Kt 4 (21. P — R 4 is met by P — R 4 very much as in the actual game); 21. ....Q R — Kt 1; 22. R × R, R × R; 23. P — Kt 5, B — K 2; 24. P — Kt 5, Q — Kt 5; 25. Kt — Q 4, B — B 4; 26. R — Q 1 and Black cannot regain his Pawn by 26. ....B × Kt because of 27. R × B, Q × P; 28. R — Q 8 ch, K — R 2; 29. Q — R 5 mate.

Now ensues some very piquant play in which Capablanca, with admirable sangfroid, permits White to rage up and down the 7th rank whilst he coolly advances the Q R P to a queening square.

20. ...... Q × R P
21. Kt — Kt 5

Threatening to win offhand by Q — R 5.

21. ...... B × Kt
22. P × B Q × Kt P
23. Q — B 3 Q — B 1
24. R × Kt P P — R 4 !

Best. Black can only prevent White from establishing his Rooks on the 7th by giving up the Q R P, and even then he would have to be content with a defensive position with an eventual loss in sight.

25. R — Q 1 P — R 5
26. R (Q 1) — Q 7

White's position now seems overwhelming, but Black puts his trust in the Q R P, and rightly so.

26. ...... P — R 6 !
27. R × P P — R 7 !
28. R × P ch

And not 28. R × Q ch, R × R and Black wins !

28. ...... Q × R
29. R × Q ch K × R
30. Q — B 6 ch K — Kt 1
31. Q — Kt 6 ch K — B 1
32. Q — B 6 ch

And draws by perpetual check — a remarkable game of a most original type.

56
FIRST ROUND, BUDAPEST SIESTA TOURNEY, 1928

Queen's Gambit Accepted

White	Black
CAPABLANCA	K. HAVASI
1. P — Q 4	P — Q 4
2. P — Q B 4	P — K 3
3. Kt — K B 3	P × P
4. P — K 4	P — Q B 4
5. B × P	P × P
6. Kt × P	Kt — K B 3
7. Kt — Q B 3	P — Q R 3 ?

Up to this move the game has been identical with that one by Capablanca against Bogoljuboff at Moscow in 1925 (Game No. 40). Bogoljuboff's 7. ....B — B 4 did not prove sufficient, but the text is even worse, since it represents the pure waste of a tempo. Best here is 7. ....Q Kt — Q 2.

8. Castles   B — B 4

Havasi is obviously ignorant of the game mentioned above and heads straight into a similar disaster. Whatever he does, he must now get the inferior game. If, for example, 8. ....P — K 4; 9. Kt — B 3, Q × Q; 10. R × Q, Kt — B 3; 11. Kt — Q 5 with a winning position.

Comparatively best is 8. .... B — K 2, though White can then maintain the pressure by 9. P — K 5.

9. B — K 3   Q Kt — Q 2

9. ....Castles was absolutely necessary; White could then continue with 10. P — K 5, K Kt — Q 2; 11. Kt — K 4, Q — B 2; 12. Q R — B 1!, and if now 12. .... Q × P; 13. Kt × B, Kt × Kt; 14. Kt — B 3, Q — R 4; 15. B × Kt, Q × B; 16. B × K P and wins.

Consequently, Black has to reply 11. ....B — K 2 when 12. P — B 4 leaves him badly placed but still alive.

10. B × K P !

The same combination as in the Bogoljuboff game, but here even more devastating, since White has had time to Castle.

10.	P × B
11. Kt × P	Q — R 4

Now 11. ....Q — Kt 3 loses at once because of 12. Kt × B, Kt × Kt; 13. Kt — R 4.

12. Kt × P ch	K — B 2
13. Kt — B 5	

Threatening Q — Kt 3 ch followed by Kt — K 2 and Kt — B 4 ch.

13.	Kt — K 4
14. Q — Kt 3 ch	K — Kt 3
15. Q R — B 1 !	

Threatening 16. B × B, Q × B; 17. Kt — K 2 with a mating attack.

15.	B — B 1

15. ....B × B; 16. P × B would only open up fresh lines of attack for White.

16. Kt — K 2 !

The attack proceeds with great energy; if now 16. ....Kt × P; 17. R × B, R × R; 18. Q — K 6 ch, etc.

16. ......   P — R 4
17. K R — Q 1!

This quiet positional move is much more conclusive than 17. B — Kt 6, Q — Kt 4; 18. Kt — B 4 ch, K — R 2; 19. R — B 7 ch, B — Q 2.

17. ......   R — K Kt 1
18. Kt — B 4 ch   K — R 2
19. B — Kt 6   Q — Kt 4
20. R — B 7 ch   K — R 1

If 20. ....B — Q 2; 21. Kt — Q 5, Kt × Kt; 22. R × Kt, Q × Q; 23. P × Q winning a piece, and if 20. ....B — Kt 2; 21. Q × R ch, K × Q; 22. R × K B ch, K — B 1; 23. R — Q 8 ch, Kt — K 1; 24. R × B, etc.

Position after 20. ....K — R 1

21. Q × Q!

This far from obvious move is the commencement of the final winning combination.

21. ......   P × Q
22. R — Q 8   R × P

Black has no saving move; if 22. ....B × Kt; 23. R × R, B × P; 24. R (B 7) — B 8, Kt — Q 2; 25. B — Q 4.

23. R (Q 8) × Q B   Kt — B 5

By utilising the threat of mate on the back rank, Black seems to have regained his lost material, but the next few moves cruelly undeceive him.

24. P — R 3   Kt × B
25. R × B!   Kt (B 3) — Q 2
26. R — B 7   R × P
27. Kt — Q 5   Resigns

A piece is lost, e.g. 27. ....R — Q 1; 28. Kt × Kt and Black cannot recapture because of mate in three.

57
FOURTH ROUND, BUDAPEST SIESTA TOURNEY, 1928

Sicilian Defence

White	Black
L. Merényi	Capablanca
1. P — K 4	P — Q B 4

Capablanca very rarely used this defence, preferring either the Caro-Kann or 1. ....P — K 4. He uses it here as an aggressive variation against an opponent who is obviously playing for a draw.

2. Kt — K B 3   P — K Kt 3

This move is the first and only inaccuracy that Capablanca com-

mits in the whole game. Either
2. ....Kt — Q B 3 or, better
still, 2. ....P — Q 3 should be
played here; after the text, White
can transpose into a very favourable variation — the Maroczy —
by 3. P — B 4, B — Kt 2; 4. P
— Q 4 with a strong bind on the
position.

    3. P — B 3 ?

This slow move allows Black
to take the initiative in the centre.

    3. ......   P — Q 4!

By taking advantage of White's
inability to attack the Queen by
Kt — Q B 3, Black obtains a fine
game.

    4. B — Kt 5 ch   B — Q 2
    5. B × B ch

Or 5. Q — K 2, P × P; 6. B
× B ch, Q × B; 7. Q × P, Kt —
K B 3; 8. Q — K 2, Kt — B 3
and Black is considerably ahead
in development.

    5. ......   Q × B
    6. P × P

Having in mind a further simplification involving the exchange
of Queens, after which he hopes
the draw will become apparent
because of the diminution of material on the board. Capablanca,
however, is not content with the
half point and extracts all that is
possible from the position to secure a win.

Had White less pacific intentions, he would have played 6. P
— K 5 followed by 7. P — Q 4.

It is true that Black would have
still enjoyed an excellent game,
but at least this way of playing
would provide him with counter-
chances and a plan of action other than the purely defensive.

    6. ......   Q × P
    7. P — Q 4   P × P
    8. Q × P   Q × Q
    9. Kt × Q   P — K 4!
    10. Kt — Kt 5 ?

A plausible move which would
be effective enough if Black were
forced to reply 10. ....Kt —
R 3. Since this is not the case,
White should have contented himself with the more modest 10. Kt
— B 2, Kt — Q B 3; 11. B —
K 3, Castles, and though Black
has the superior game, his advantage is not so marked as that he
obtains after the text move.

Position after 10. Kt — Kt 5 ?

    10. ......   K — Q 2!

With this and the next move
Black's King becomes a fighting
piece in its own right — an ex-

traordinary and rare occurrence for the second player as early as the 10th move.

11. K — K 2   K — B 3 !

There is a good deal of impish humour behind this move.

12. P — Q R 4   Kt — Q 2
13. B — K 3

If at once 13. R — Q 1, Black does best to play 13. .... P — Q R 3, since 13. .... K Kt — B 3 allows White to embark on a mating combination by 14. B — R 6, B × B ? (14. .... B — K 2 is necessary) ; 15. R — Q 6 ch, K — B 4 ; 16. Q Kt — R 3, P — R 4 ; 17. R — Q Kt 1.

13. ......   P — Q R 3
14. R — Q 1   K Kt — B 3
15. Kt — Q 2

Temporarily, at any rate, White is able to develop his pieces, but they will be rapidly driven back and disorganised. White's play is characterised by a move-to-move combinational progress rather than far-sighted positional planning.

Better than the text is 15. P — Q B 4, depriving Black's Kt of the square Q 5 and providing his own Kt with a good post for development on Q B 3.

15. ......   R — Q 1
16. Kt — R 3   Kt — Q 4
17. Kt (Q 2) — B 4   P — Kt 3

An important move with a double purpose; firstly, it prevents White's threatened Kt — R 5 ch;

secondly, it foreshadows the positional idea of blockading White's Q side Pawns by an eventual P — Q R 4.

18. R — Q 2   B × Kt

This unexpected exchange further disorganises White's pieces.

19. R × B

If 19. Kt × B, Kt × B followed by 20. .... Kt — B 4 preserves Black's advantage.

19. ......   K R — K 1
20. Kt — Q 6 ?

White pursues his hand-to-mouth existence with a faulty combination, permitting Black to obtain a terrifyingly overwhelming position in the centre. 20. R — R 1 was better.

20. ......   R — K 2 !

Not 20. .... K × Kt; 21. P — Q B 4 with advantage to White.

21. P — Q B 4

If 21. Kt — Kt 7, Kt × P ch followed by 22. .... K × Kt winning a Pawn.

21. ......   Kt × B
22. P × Kt

With vague hopes of a counter on the K B file. White is in any event positionally lost, but 22. K × Kt was to be preferred.

22. ......   Kt — B 4
23. Kt — K 4

Ingeniously escaping from material loss, but Capablanca's next series of powerful moves shows up the positional insufficiency of White's plan in glaring fashion.

| 23. | ...... | R × R ch |
| 24. | Kt × R | P — Q R 4 ! |

This fixes the Q side for good. Black's two Pawns adequately hold White's three on this wing whilst he proceeds to the final attack on the other side. The rest of the game is a model of clear-cut, incisive exploitation of thematic advantages worthy of the most careful study.

25. Kt — Kt 1

White realises Black intends P — K 5 followed by Kt — Q 6, and as compensation manœuvres his Kt so as to be able to play to Q 5 or Q 4 according to the sequence of Black's moves.

25.	......	R — Q 2
26.	Kt — Q 2	P — K 5
27.	Kt — Kt 3	Kt — Q 6
28.	Kt — Q 4 ch	K — B 4
29.	P — Q Kt 3	P — B 4
30.	R — R 1	

Hoping for time to play 31. R — K B 1, but now Black crowns his fine play with a conclusive positional sacrifice.

Position after 30. R — R 1

| 30. | ...... | R × Kt ! |

Black gives up the exchange on the correct assumption that the dominating position of his King and Kt will prevent White from stemming the advance of his K side Pawns.

| 31. | P × R ch | K × P |
| 32. | P — Kt 3 | |

If 32. P — R 4, P — B 5 followed by P — R 3 and P — K Kt 4 with an ending similar to that in the actual game.

| 32. | ...... | P — K Kt 4 |
| 33. | P — Q Kt 4 | |

In the vain hope that Black will be tempted away from his thematic purpose to play 33. .... Kt × P, when White will even win by 34. R — K B 1.

33.	......	P — B 5 !
34.	P — B 5	P — B 6 ch
35.	K — B 1	P — K 6
36.	R — K 1	Kt P × P
37.	R × P	K × R
38.	P × R P	P — B 5
	Resigns.	

58

SEVENTH ROUND,
BUDAPEST SIESTA
TOURNEY, 1928

*Queen's Gambit Declined,
Orthodox Defence*

White	Black
Capablanca	H. Steiner
1. P — Q 4	Kt — K B 3
2. P — Q B 4	P — K 3
3. Kt — Q B 3	P — Q 4
4. B — Kt 5	Q Kt — Q 2

5. P — K 3	B — K 2
6. Kt — B 3	Castles
7. R — B 1	P — B 3
8. B — Q 3	

For 8. Q — B 2, see Game No. 64.

8.	P × P
9. B × P	Kt — Q 4
10. B × B	Q × B
11. Castles	Kt × Kt
12. R × Kt	P — Q Kt 3

This is too slow and leads to White gaining command of the Q B file, as Capablanca demonstrates with a complete mastery of the necessary technique. The normal 12. ....P — K 4 is adequate and the only correct move here.

13. Q — B 2!

An attempt to exploit the presumed weakness on the Q side by 13. Q — K 2, B — Kt 2; 14. B — R 6, B × B; 15. Q × B leads to nothing after 15. ....P — Q B 4; 16. Q — Kt 7, K R — Kt 1.

13. ...... P — Q B 4

Black must play this at once as otherwise he never arrives at any freedom of position. If 13. ....B — Kt 2; 14. B — Q 3 and to avoid the loss of a Pawn Black must further weaken his position by 14. ....P — K B 4, for if 14. ....P — Kt 3; 15. B — K 4 or 14. .... Kt — B 3; 15. Kt — K 5.

14. P × P!

This apparently simple continuation contains, as is customary with Capablanca, a wealth of hidden positional meaning. Nothing

is to be achieved by obvious combinational means, e.g. 14. B — Kt 5, P × P; 15. R — B 7, Q — Q 1; 16. P × P (or 16. Kt × P, Kt — B 4); 16. ....Kt — B 3, and now bad for White would be 17. Q — B 6, Kt — Q 4; 18. R × B P ?, R × R; 19. Q × R, Kt — B 2; 20. Q — B 6, B — Q 2, etc.

14. ...... Kt × P

Now, however, 14. ....P × P would lose a Pawn after 15. B — Kt 5.

15. P — Q Kt 4 Kt — R 3

The Kt is reduced to this impotent position, since 15. ....Kt — Q 2; 16. B — Q 3, P — Kt 3; 17. R — B 7, Q — Q 1; 18. B — K 4 loses very quickly for Black.

16. P — Q R 3	B — Kt 2
17. B — Q 3	P — Kt 3
18. R — B 1 !	

Very strong, since Black loses material after 18. ....R — B 1; 19. R × R, R × R; 20. Q × R ch, B × Q; 21. R × B ch, K — Kt 2; 22. B × Kt.

18. ...... Q R — Q 1

Preparing to bring back the Kt into play via Kt 1.

19. Kt — K 5

Threatening 20. B × Kt followed by Kt — B 6.

19.	Q — Q 3
20. P — B 4	Kt — Kt 1

With this move Black contemplates the eventual sacrifice of a Pawn in order to gain freedom; but White's fine play nullifies

this and maintains his grasp on the position. If instead 20. ....
P — B 3; 21. Kt — B 3 and now if 21. ....B × Kt; 22. P × B, Kt — Kt 1; 23. B × P, P × B; 24. Q × P ch, K — R 1; 25. R — K Kt 1 followed by Q — R 6 mate. And if 21. ....P — K 4; 22. P × P, P × P; 23. B — B 4 ch, K — R 1; 24. Kt — Kt 5 winning the exchange.

Position after 20. ....Kt — Kt 1

21. R — B 7   B — R 1
22. R × R P   Kt — B 3

Hoping for 23. Kt × Kt, B × Kt; 24. Q × B, Q × B; 25. Q × Kt P, when he can force a draw by 25. ....Q — K 7; 26. P — K R 3, R — Q 7; 27. Q — Kt 7, Q × K P ch; 28. K — R 1, R — Q 2; 29. Q × R, Q × R ch, etc.

23. R × B !   Kt × Kt
24. R × R   R × R
25. B — K 2 !

In this open position, the Bishop is by far superior to the Kt.

25. ......   Q — Q 7

However Black plays, his Kt will run into trouble. If 25. ....
Kt — Q 2; 26. R — Q 1, Q — K 2 (or 26. ....Q — Kt 1; 27. Q — Q 2); 27. Q — B 7, K — B 1; 28. B — Kt 5.

26. Q × Q !

The exchange of Queens is more decisive than the immediate win of a piece by 26. P × Kt, Q × P ch; 27. K — R 1, R — Q 7; 28. Q — B 8 ch, K — Kt 2; 29. B — B 3, Q × R P and White's Pawns will prove difficult to defend.

26. ......   R × Q
27. R — B 8 ch   K — Kt 2
28. K — B 1

This quiet move is the point of White's combination; the Kt is compelled to go to a square on which it will be pinned by White's Rook.

28. ......   Kt — Q 2
29. R — Q 8   K — B 3
30. B — Kt 5   R — Q 4
31. P — Q R 4 !

And not 31. B × Kt, K — K 2; 32. R — Q Kt 8, R × B; 33. R × P, R — R 2 with drawing chances.

31. ......   R × B

Desperation, but Black is utterly lost. The Pawn ending after 31. ....K — K 2; 32. R × Kt ch, R × R; 33. B × R, K × B; 34. K — K 2 is equally hopeless.

32. P × R   K — K 2
33. R — Q B 8   P — K 4

34. R — B 6   P — K 5
35. K — K 2   P — B 4
36. K — Q 2   K — B 2
37. K — B 3   Resigns

White's King cannot be prevented from reaching Q 6; a game of the utmost neatness and precision.

59
EIGHTH ROUND, BUDAPEST SIESTA TOURNEY, 1928

Q Pawn, Nimzovitch Defence

White	Black
CAPABLANCA	Z. VON BALLA
1. P — Q 4	Kt — K B 3
2. P — Q B 4	P — K 3
3. Kt — Q B 3	B — Kt 5
4. Q — B 2	P — B 4

4. ....P — Q 4 has more adherents nowadays and also popular is the Zürich or Milner-Barry variation, 4. ....Kt — B 3.

5. P × P   B × P

For 5. ....Kt — B 3, see Game No. 61.

6. P — Q R 3   Kt — B 3
7. P — Q Kt 4

In a previous round of the same tourney, Capablanca played here 7. Kt — B 3, Kt — Q 5; 8. Kt × Kt, B × Kt; 9. P — K 3, B × Kt ch; 10. Q × B, Castles; 11. P — Q Kt 4, P — Q 4 with a level game. The text is more vigorous.

7. ......   B — K 2
8. Kt — B 3   Q — B 2 ?

A premature development of the Queen which costs Black time that he can ill afford. Better would have been 8. ....P — Q Kt 3 at once.

9. P — Kt 3 !

An economical manœuvre typical of Capablanca's style; he develops his K Bishop on its most effective diagonal and also prepares to attack the Queen with his other Bishop. The same process is commonly employed by White against a type of the Slav Defence (cf. Game No. 67, *v.* Brinckmann).

9. ......   P — Q Kt 3

And now 9. ....P — Q R 3 would be better in order to prevent an eventual Kt — Q Kt 5.

10. B — K Kt 2   B — Kt 2
11. B — B 4   P — Q 3

11. ....P — K 4; 12. B — Kt 5 followed by 13. Kt — Q 5 would be very bad for Black.

12. Kt — Q Kt 5   Q — Kt 1

If 13. ....Q — Q 1; 14. R — Q 1.

13. P — B 5 !

White opens up the position in order to profit from his greater mobility of pieces.

13. ......   P — K 4
14. P × Q P   B × P

Best; if 14. ....P × B; 15. Kt — B 7 ch, K — Q 1; 16. P × B ch, K × Kt; 17. Kt — K 5, Q

— K 1; 18. R — Q B 1 and wins.

15. R — Q 1 !

Position after 15. R — Q 1 !

This strong move is the only way to maintain the attack. For if 15. Kt × B ch, Q × Kt; 16. Kt × P, Kt × P and Black wins.

15. . . . . . .   Castles

If 15. . . . . P × B; 16. Kt × B ch, K — B 1; 17. Kt × B, Q × Kt; 18. Kt — R 4, R — B 1; 19. Q R — B 1 winning a piece. And if 15. . . . . B — K 2; 16. Kt × K P, Kt × P (or 16. . . . . Kt × Kt; 17. B × Kt); 17. P × Kt, B × B; 18. Kt — B 7 ch, K — B 1; 19. Q — B 4, B — Q 4; 20. Kt × B, etc.

16. Kt × B   P × B
17. Kt — R 4 !

Decisive; now Black cannot avoid the loss of a piece.

17. . . . . . .   Kt — Q 1
18. Kt × B   Kt × Kt
19. Q — B 6

This enhancement of the strength of the fianchettoed Bishop is striking both from æsthetic and thematic points of view.

19. . . . . . .   P × P
20. R P × P

It is unnecessary to take the piece at once and allow Black counter-chances by 20. . . . . P × P ch.

20. . . . . . .   Q — K 4
21. Q × Q Kt   Q — B 6 ch

The rest of the game is clearly a matter of technique, but it is still interesting to observe the clear-cut and elegant methods employed by Capablanca to despatch his opponent.

22. K — B 1   Q R — Q 1
23. R — K 1

Naturally, not 23. R × R, Q — B 8 ch followed by mate.

23. . . . . . .   Q × R P
24. Kt — B 5

White could have saved the Pawn by 24. P — Kt 5, but prefers to end the game by a K side attack.

24. . . . . . .   R — Q 2
25. Q — B 3   Q × P
26. R — R 4   Q — Kt 7
27. Q — B 4   K R — Q 1
28. B — B 6   R — Q 7
29. Q — Kt 5   P — Kt 3

If 29. . . . . Kt — K 1; 30. B × Kt, R × B; 31. Kt × P !

30. Kt — K 3	Q — B 6		35. Q — K 6 ch	K — R 1
31. R — Q B 4	Q — Kt 7		36. R — K 4	R — Q 8
32. R — B 4	Kt — R 4		37. R × R	R × R ch
			38. K— Kt 2	Resigns

If 32. ....R — Q 3; 33. Kt —
B 4 wins at once.

White threatens both B — Q 5
and P — Kt 4 and Black cannot
parry both threats.

33. Kt — B 4	P — B 3
34. Q — Kt 4	Q — R 7

CHAPTER SEVEN

1929—A Rich Year

THIS was probably Capablanca's most active year in the chess world and saw him play many fine games. After a beautifully accurate game against Winter at Ramsgate, we come to the great Carlsbad Tournament of 1929. This contains the drastic brevity against Mattison, the Latvian master, an even shorter game in which the Austrian theoretician, A. Becker, is crushed, and a lovely scientific game against Treybal which demonstrates the disadvantages of the Stonewall Defence. The remaining three games are especially important when considered in relation to the openings employed. Maroczy comes to grief in the Orthodox Defence to the Queen's Gambit Declined, Colle has demonstrated to him, in convincing style, the fundamental weakness of his own opening, and Marshall falls so conclusively a victim to a weak variation of the Queen's Indian Defence that nobody has had the courage to employ it since this game.

From the Budapest Tournament of this year we give two bright and flawless gems played with the usual Capablanca elegance; after which there is the Barcelona Tournament, another contest prolific in great Capablanca games. Colle succumbs to a beautifully combined K side attack in Game No. 69, and Yates has the ill luck to meet Capablanca at his most lucid and forceful. The game against Monticelli is a fine example of the so-called minority Pawn attack, and the next two games are crushing defeats for two unfortunate Spanish players.

RAMSGATE, 1929

	Thomas	Yates	Michell	Tylor	Winter	Sergeant	Price	
1 Capablanca	½	½	1	½	1	1	1	5½
2 Vera Menchik	1	½	1	½	½	½	1	5
3 Rubinstein	½	½	½	1	1	1	½	5
4 Koltanowski	½	½	½	½	1	½	1	4½
5 Maroczy	0	1	½	1	½	½	1	4½
6 Soultanbeieff	0	1	1	½	½	1	0	4
7 Znosko-Borowski	1	0	0	½	0	½	1	3

NOTE. In the above tournament the foreign masters played against the British, but not with each other.

BARCELONA, 1929

	Capablanca	Tartakower	Colle	Monticelli	Rey Ardid	Golmayo	Yates	Vera Menchik	Vilardebo	Marin	Soler	Ribera	Aguilera	Font	Torres	
1 Capablanca	-	½	1	1	1	1	1	1	1	1	1	1	1	1	1	13½
2 Tartakower	½	-	1	½	1	1	½	½	1	½	1	1	1	1	1	11½
3 Colle	0	0	-	½	1	1	1	½	1	1	1	1	1	1	1	11
4 Monticelli	0	½	½	-	½	½	1	1	0	1	½	0	1	1	1	8½
5 Rey Ardid	0	0	0	½	-	½	1	0	1	1	½	1	1	1	1	8½
6 Golmayo	0	0	0	½	½	-	1	0	1	½	½	1	1	1	1	8
7 Yates	0	½	0	0	0	1	-	½	½	½	1	1	1	1	½	7½
8 Vera Menchik	0	½	½	0	1	0	½	-	1	½	½	1	1	½	0	7
9 Vilardebo	0	0	0	1	0	½	½	0	-	1	½	½	1	1	1	7
10 Marin	0	½	0	0	0	0	½	½	0	-	1	1	½	½	½	5
11 Soler	0	0	0	½	½	½	0	½	½	0	-	½	½	½	1	5
12 Ribera	0	0	0	1	0	0	0	0	½	0	½	-	1	½	1	4½
13 Aguilera	0	0	0	0	0	0	0	0	0	½	½	0	-	1	1	3
14 Font	0	0	0	0	0	0	0	½	0	½	½	½	0	-	1	3
15 Torres	0	0	0	0	0	0	½	1	0	½	0	0	0	0	-	2

CARLSBAD, 1929

		Total
1	Nimzovitch	15
2	Capablanca	14½
3	Spielmann	14½
4	Rubinstein	13½
5	Becker	12
6	Euwe	12
7	Vidmar	12
8	Bogoljuboff	11½
9	Grünfeld	11
10	Canal	10½
11	Mattison	10½
12	Colle	10
13	Maroczy	10
14	Tartakower	10
15	Treybal	10
16	Sämisch	9½
17	Yates	9½
18	Johner	9
19	Marshall	9
20	Gilg	8
21	Thomas	6
22	Vera Menchik	3

BUDAPEST, 1929

		Capablanca	Rubinstein	Tartakower	Thomas	Vajda	Steiner	Colle	Havasi	Przepiorka	Canal	Monticelli	Van den Bosch	Brinckmann	Prokes	
1	Capablanca	–	½	½	½	1	1	1	1	½	1	½	1	1	1	10½
2	Rubinstein	½	–	½	1	½	1	0	1	½	½	1	1	1	1	9½
3	Tartakower	½	½	–	½	0	0	½	0	1	1	1	1	1	1	8
4	Thomas	½	0	½	–	1	1	0	0	1	1	½	0	1	1	7½
5	Vajda	0	½	1	0	–	1	1	½	½	½	½	1	½	½	7½
6	Steiner	0	0	0	0	1	–	½	1	0	1	1	1	1	½	7
7	Colle	0	1	½	1	0	½	–	½	0	½	1	0	½	1	6½
8	Havasi	0	0	1	1	½	0	½	–	0	0	1	½	1	1	6½
9	Przepiorka	½	½	0	0	½	1	1	1	–	½	0	0	0	1	6
10	Canal	0	½	0	0	½	0	½	1	½	–	½	½	1	½	5½
11	Monticelli	½	0	0	½	½	0	0	0	1	½	–	½	1	1	5½
12	Van den Bosch ..	0	0	0	1	0	0	1	½	1	½	½	–	0	0	4½
13	Brinckmann ..	0	0	0	0	½	0	½	0	1	0	0	1	–	1	4
14	Prokes	0	0	0	0	½	½	0	0	0	½	0	1	0	–	2½

60

SIXTH ROUND, RAMSGATE, 1929

Queen's Pawn, Nimzovitch Defence

White	Black
W. Winter	Capablanca
1. P — Q 4	Kt — K B 3
2. P — Q B 4	P — K 3
3. Kt — Q B 3	B — Kt 5
4. Kt — B 3	

A move recommended and practised by Bogoljuboff, not, however, with conspicuous success, as the doubled Pawns that result are eventual objects of attack for Black.

4. ...... P — Q Kt 3

Black decides to play for control of K 5. Not good is the immediate 4. ....Kt — K 5 since after 5. Q — B 2 Black cannot satisfactorily maintain his Kt on K 5.

An interesting alternative is the dogmatic 4. ....B × Kt ch, a classic example being the game Bogoljuboff–Nimzovitch, Carlsbad, 1929, which continued: 5. P × B, P — Q Kt 3; 6. P — Kt 3, B — Kt 2; 7. B — Kt 2, Castles; 8. Castles, R — K 1; 9. R — K 1, P — Q 3; 10. Q — B 2, B — K 5; 11. Q — Kt 3, Kt — B 3; 12. B — B 1, P — K 4; 13. P × P, Kt × P; 14. Kt × Kt, R × Kt with obvious advantage to Black.

5. P — K 3

Or White may first develop his Q B by 5. B — Kt 5 as Bogoljuboff played against Monticelli at

San Remo, 1930, with the continuation 5. . . . . B × Kt ch; 6. P × B, B — Kt 2; 7. P — K 3, P — Q 3; 8. B — Q 3, Q Kt — Q 2; 9. Castles, Q — K 2; 10. Kt — Q 2, P — K R 3; 11. B — R 4, P — K Kt 4; 12. B — Kt 3, Castles Q and Black eventually won in brilliant combinational fashion.

5. . . . . . .   B — Kt 2

Euwe, in his match against Bogoljuboff in 1929, tried the less elastic 5. . . . . Castles; 6. B — Q 3, P — Q 4; 7. Castles, B — Kt 2; 8. P × P, P × P; 9. P — Q R 3, B — K 2; 10. P — Q Kt 4 leaving White with some advantage in space.

6. B — Q 3   Kt — K 5
7. Q — B 2   P — K B 4

Black has now transposed into a favourable variation of the Dutch Defence.

8. Castles

Played, one suspects, on the assumption that Black will refrain from giving White two pairs of doubled Pawns, since this would involve allowing White the possession of two Bishops.

8. . . . . . .   Kt × Kt

Black is not to be deterred. The point is that White, having already Castled, will find it difficult and time wasting to make full use of the open K Kt file and meanwhile Black can concentrate on the weakened White Pawn formation.

9. P × Kt   B × Kt
10. Kt P × B

Bad for White is 10. B P × B, Q — Kt 4 !

10. . . . . . .   Q — Kt 4 ch
11. K — R 1   B — Q 3

Black wishes to encourage the advance of White's K B P, since this would both give him an easier object of attack and also render White's Pawn centre less mobile.

12. P — B 4   Q — R 3

Threatening P — K Kt 4.

13. R — K Kt 1   Kt — B 3
14. Q — K 2

White manœuvres his Queen over to the K side in order to strengthen the attack, but Black, by accurate play, fends this off easily enough, whilst maintaining the pressure on White's doubled Pawns.

The correct positional line for White to adopt is to expand and profit from the development of his two Bishops, e.g. 14. B — K 2 (threatening B — B 3); 14. . . . . Kt — K 2; 15. Q — R 4 and now if 15. . . . . P — B 3; 16. B — R 3, Kt — B 1; 17. Q — R 6 with a won game so that Black must play the complicated 15. . . . . Kt — Kt 1; 16. B — B 3, P — B 3; 17. B — R 3, B × B; 18. Q × B, Kt — B 3; 19. Q — Q 6, K — B 2 followed by K R — Q 1, though White would still have much more play than in the actual game.

14. . . . . . .   Q — B 3

Since P — K Kt 3 will become
inevitable sooner or later, Black
hastens to centralise the Queen
before this Pawn advance cuts
her off from the centre.

15. Q — B 3   Castles K

And not 15. ....Castles Q,
since this would place the King
in a most exposed and dangerous
position.

16. B — Q 2   P — Kt 3
17. R — Kt 2   R — B 2
18. Q R—K Kt1   Q R—K B1
19. Q — R 5

Threatening 20. R × P ch.

19. ......   R — Kt 2
20. Q — R 3   Kt — K 2
21. B — K 1

White plans to bring the Bishop to R 4 and thence to proceed
to R 6 via Kt 5. This last is easily
prevented by Black, and the chief
result of the manœuvre is the exchange of one of White's Bishops
together with a further weakening of his Pawn structure. White
would do better to play 21. Q —
B 3.

21. ......   Q — B 2
22. P — B 3   Kt — B 1
23. B — R 4   B — K 2
24. B × B

Or 24. B — Kt 5, B × B; 25.
P × B, P — Q 4 and now 26. Q
— Kt 3 would be met by P —
B 5!

24. ......   Q × B
25. Q — Kt 3   P — Q 4!

A strong move which throws a
clear light on the weakness in
White's position. White cannot
exchange Pawns because of his
backward K P, and meanwhile
Black threatens to increase pressure on the Q B P by Kt — Q 3.

Position after 25. ....P — Q 4 !

26. P -- K 4

We have arrived at the turning-
point of the game. With this ambitious move White hopes to eliminate the weakness of his doubled
Pawns, render his centre mobile
once again and free a diagonal
for his Bishop. But all these
hopes fail against the lasting
weakness on K B 4. Capablanca
takes advantage of this circumstance with his customary beautiful accuracy, and it is amusing to
see how all his manœuvres are
based on this point.

Circumspect defence would not
help White much now, for if 26.
Q — B 2, Kt — Q 3; 27. Q —
K 2, Q — Q 2 followed by 28.
....Q — R 5 would leave Black
in command of the game.

26. ......   B P × P
27. K B P × P   P × K P
28. B × P   Q — Q 3

It is interesting to observe that though Black has an isolated backward Pawn, this does not matter a jot, since he is in full possession of the initiative.

29. R — K B 2   Kt — K 2

Before further attacking the K B P the Kt is brought into the game to relieve the Rook of its defensive task on Kt 2. For if at once 29. ....R (Kt 2) — B 2; 30. B × P, P × B; 31. Q × P ch, K — R 1; 32. R — B 3 and Black cannot escape the mating attack.

30. R — K 1   R (Kt 2) — B 2
31. R(K 1)—K B 1   Kt — B 4
32. B × Kt

This is the only way of saving the K B P, since Black was threatening to get a fourth piece on it by Kt — Kt 2 — R 4.

32. ......   R × B
33. K — Kt 1

Since Black was now threatening Q — B 3 ch.

33. ......   Q — B 3
34. Q — Q 3   K — R 1

Now menacing the K B P by P — K Kt 4, which White must prevent by advancing his K R P, thereby creating a fresh weakness.

35. P — K R 4   R — K R 4
36. R—R 2   R(K R4)—K B4
37. R(R 2)—K B 2   Q — Q 3
38. Q — K 3   Q — Q 1
39. Q × P

An unwelcome exchange, but White cannot afford to mark time whilst Black further attacks his Pawns by 39. ....Q — B 3 followed by 40. ....P — B 4!

39. ......   Q × K R P
40. Q — K 3

Position after 40. Q — K 3

Now that the K R P has gone, Black delivers the final attack.

40. ......   R — K R 4
41. R — K Kt 2   Q — R 8 ch
42. K — B 2   Q — R 6!
43. Q — Kt 3

White has no defence; 43. Q × Q, R × Q merely leaves White's Pawns to be taken one after the other, and equally hopeless is 43. Q — B 3, R × P; 44. Q × R, R — K B 4; 45. Q × R, Q × Q ch; 46. K — Kt 1, Q — Q 6, etc.

43. ......   Q — K 3

And here Black can win by 43. ....R × P ch; 44. Q × R, R — K B 4 as in the last note, but the text move is even quicker.

44. K — Kt 1

If 44. P — Q 5, Q — K 5 and White's Q side Pawns fall.

44. ......   Q × P
45. R — K 1

With a momentary hope of counter-attack by R — K 7, but Black returns to his original theme and concentrates on the K B P with deadly effect.

45. ......   Q — B 2
46. R—K B2   R(R4)—K B4
47. R — K 4

If 47. R (K 1) — K B 1, P — K R 3 followed by P — K Kt 4 forcing exchange of all major pieces.

47. ......   P — K Kt 4

Resigns, since not only does he lose another Pawn, but his King is also in a hopelessly exposed position.

61
THIRTEENTH ROUND, CARLSBAD, 1929

Queen's Pawn, Nimzovitch Defence

White	Black
CAPABLANCA	H. MATTISON
1. P — Q 4	Kt — K B 3
2. P — Q B 4	P — K 3
3. Kt — Q B 3	B — Kt 5
4. Q — B 2	

Capablanca's favourite method of dealing with the Nimzovitch Defence and one which, indeed, gives White more lasting pressure than any other move, wheth-er it be the aggressive 4. Q — Kt 3; the solid 4. P — K 3, the impatient 4. P — Q R 3 or the timid 4. B — Q 2.

4. ......   P — B 4

Not very frequently encountered in modern tournament play; more usual is the move Capablanca himself played with great effect, 4. ....P — Q 4.

5. P × P

A level game results after 5. P — K 3, Kt — B 3; 6. Kt — B 3, Castles; 7. P — Q R 3, B × Kt ch; 8. Q × B, P × P; 9. P × P, P — Q 4; 10. B — Kt 5, P × P; 11. B × P, Kt — K 5 (Vidmar–Alekhine, Hastings, 1926).

5. ......   Kt — B 3

Quite a good alternative is the immediate recapture of the Pawn, e.g. 5. ....B × P; 6. Kt — B 3, P — Q 4; 7. P — K 3, Castles; 8. B — K 2, P × P; 9. B × P, Q Kt — Q 2; 10. Castles, P — Q R 3; 11. P — Q R 3, P — Q Kt 4; 12. B — K 2, B — Kt 2 with an equal game (Eliskases–A. Steiner, Ujpest, 1934).

Too artificial, however, is 5. ....Kt — R 3; 6. P — Q R 3, B × Kt ch; 7. Q × B, Kt × P; 8. P — B 3, P — Q 3; 9. P — K 4 and White has much the better game (Flohr–Botvinnik, 1933).

6. Kt — B 3   B × P
7. B — B 4

Not usually played, but still an excellent move which places the Bishop on a powerful diagonal.

The normal move is 7. B — Kt 5, which can be met either by (a) 7. ....P — Q Kt 3; 8. P — K 3, B — Kt 2; 9. B — K 2, B — K 2; 10. Castles K, R — Q B 1; 11. Q R — Q 1, P — Q 3 and Black has a constricted but solid position (Rubinstein–Sämisch, Berlin, 1926), or (b) 7. ....Kt — Q 5; 8. Kt × Kt, B × Kt; 9. P — K 3, Q — R 4; 10. P × B, Q × B; 11. B — Q 3, Castles; 12. Castles, P — Q 4 with equality (Najdorf–Golombek, Margate, 1939).

7. ......   P — Q 4

In a later round in this congress, Mattison, impressed with the result of this game, adopted the same opening against Sämisch, who played here 7. .... Castles; 8. P — K 3, P — Q Kt 3; 9. P — Q R 3, B — Kt 2; 10. R — Q 1, R — B 1; 11. B — K 2, B — K 2 with an equal game.

There is, however, nothing wrong with the move actually played in this game; it is on his 9th move that Black goes astray.

8. P — K 3   Q — R 4

Either simply Castles or else Tartakower's suggestion, 8. .... Q — K 2, would have been preferable.

9. B — K 2   B — Kt 5 ?

And this deliberate loss of time is indefensible.

Again 9. ....Castles was quite good, but best is 9. ....P — Q 5; 10. P × P, Kt × P; 11. Kt ×

Kt, B × Kt and Black stands well, since 12. B — Q 6 ? can be met by 12. ....Kt — K 5.

10. Castles K   B × Kt
11. P × B   Castles
12. Q R — Kt 1 !

A fine Capablanca move. By immediately occupying the open file, White brings pressure to bear on Black's Q side and also restricts the movement of Black's pieces.

12. ......   Q — R 6 ?

Black is still unhappily obsessed with the idea of profiting from his Queen excursion. Instead, he should have played 12. ....P × P; 13. B × P, P — Q R 3 with a very uncomfortable but defensible position.

After the text move, White's incisive play allows Black no opportunity of saving the game.

13. K R — Q 1   P — Q Kt 3
14. P × P   Kt × P

14. ....P × P is not playable, for after 15. P — B 4! Black cannot exchange Pawns because of B — Q 6, nor can he play 15. ....B — K 3; 16. P × P disclosing an attack on the Q Kt.

15. Kt — Kt 5 !   P — B 4

And not 15. ....Kt — B 3; 16. B — Q 6 or 15. ....P — Kt 3; 16. B — B 3 with a similar effect to that in the actual game.

16. B — B 3 !   Q — B 4

A plausible move which defends both Kts and attacks the

QB Pawn; it also counters White's threatened R × Kt. If, instead, 16. ....Kt × B; 17. B × Kt and wins. Good as Black's text move is, it cannot recover the time lost by his unfortunate opening manœuvres, and White's next move is crushing.

Position after 16. ....Q — B 4

17. P—B 4!   Kt(Q 4)—Kt 5

There is no saving move. For if (a) 17. ....Kt × B; 18. R — Kt 5, Q — K 2; 19. B × Kt, Q × Kt; 20. P — Kt winning a piece, or (b) 17. ....P — Q R 3; 18. B — Q 6, Q × B; 19. P × Kt, Kt — Kt 5; 20. Q — Kt 3, Kt × Q P; 21. R × Kt again winning a piece, (c) 17. ....Kt — B 3; 18. B — Q 6 and, finally, (d) 17. ....R — Q 1; 18. R — Kt 5 again winning a piece.

18. Q — Kt 3   P — K 4
19. P — Q R 3!   Kt — B 3

After 19. ....P × B; 20. P × Kt Black loses the Q Kt.

20. B × Kt   Resigns

For Black is mated after 20. ....Q × B; 21. P — B 5 dis ch, K — R 1; 22. Kt — B 7 ch.

62
EIGHTH ROUND, CARLSBAD, 1929

Queen's Gambit Declined

White	Black
CAPABLANCA	A. BECKER
1. P — Q 4	P — Q 4
2. P — Q B 4	P — K 3
3. Kt — K B 3	Kt — Q 2

For a consideration of this so-called Westphalia variation, see Game No. 45, in which Capablanca achieved a beautiful victory over Spielmann.

4. Kt — B 3   K Kt — B 3
5. B — B 4

Varying from the above-mentioned game, where he played 5. B — Kt 5.

5. ......   P × P

The normal reaction to White's B — B 4, viz. 5. ....P — B 4, is here incorrect because of 6. Kt — Q Kt 5, Q — R 4 ch; 7. P — Q Kt 4!

Simplest and best is 5. .... P — B 3.

6. P — K 3   Kt — Q 4

Not altogether satisfactory, since White can quietly continue his development and allow Black to exchange his Kt for the Bishop in return for the compensating open lines.

Better is 6. ....Kt — Kt 3; 7.

B × P, Kt × B; 8. Q — R 4 ch,
P — B 3; 9. Q × Kt, Kt — Q 4
(Alekhine–Spielmann, Carlsbad,
1923).

7.	K B × P	Kt × B
8.	P × Kt	B — Q 3
9.	P — K Kt 3	Kt — B 3
10.	Castles	Castles
11.	Q — K 2	P — Q Kt 3
12.	K R — Q 1	

Even stronger is 12. Kt —
K 5! as Tartakower played in a
later round against Becker. That
game continued 12. ....B —
Kt 2; 13. P — Q R 3, Q — K 2;
14. K R — K 1, P — B 4; 15. P
× P, B × P; 16. Q R — Q 1,
Q R — Q 1; 17. R × R, Q × R;
18. P — Q Kt 4, B — Q 3; 19.
Kt × B P! a sacrifice that should
have won, though White subsequently missed his way and only
drew.

12.	......	B — Kt 2
13.	Q R — B 1	P — Q R 3
14.	B — Q 3	B — Kt 5 ?

Black has conceived the false
idea of obtaining control of the
long diagonal Q R 1 — K R 8. He
therefore wastes a move in order
to attempt the exchange of his K
Bishop for the Q Kt and so place
his Q on Q 4.

This idea, as White succinctly
proves, only leads to Black's destruction. Instead, Black should
play 14. ....Q — K 2 followed
by the grouping of his Rooks in
the centre (Q 1 and K 1) and an
eventual P — Q B 4.

15.	Kt — K 4	Q — Q 4 ?

This leads to immediate disaster. He must now exchange both
pieces on K 5 and follow this
with P — K R 3. He would then
have the inferior position owing
to White's control of the white
squares, but he would still be
alive, with hopes of a draw.

Becker may have hoped for 16.
R × P, Q R — B 1; 17. R × R,
R × R with an attack well worth
the Pawn.

16. K Kt — Kt 5!

Threatening 17. Kt × Kt ch,
P × Kt; 18. B — K 4, etc.

16.	......	Kt — K 1

There is no saving move. If
16. ....K — R 1 (thus preventing Kt × Kt because of mate on
Kt 7) then 17. R × P with the
threat of 18. R × B, Q × R; 19.
Kt × Kt, P × Kt; 20. Q — R 5.

Position after 16. ....Kt — K 1

17. Kt × R P! P — K B 4

Black would lose the Queen
after 17. ....K × Kt; 18. Kt —
B 6 db ch; as he would too after

17. ....Kt — Q 3; 18. Kt — B 6 ch.

18. Kt (R 7) — Kt 5 ! Resigns.

There is no parrying the double threat of B — B 4 and Q — R 5. If 18. ....Q — Q 2; 19. Q — R 5, Kt — B 3; 20. Kt × Kt ch, P × Kt; 21. Q — Kt 6 ch, K — R 1; 22. Kt × P, Q × Kt; 23. R × P, etc.

63
TENTH ROUND, CARLSBAD, 1929

Queen's Gambit Declined, Stonewall Defence

White	Black
CAPABLANCA	K. TREYBAL
1. P — Q 4	P — Q 4
2. P — Q B 4	P — Q B 3
3. Kt — K B 3	P — K 3
4. B — Kt 5	

Instead of continuing the normal methods of treating the Slav Defence, i.e. 4. P — K 3 or 4. Kt — B 3, White prefers to offer Black the chance of transposing into older lines such as the orthodox variation of the Queen's Gambit Declined or the Cambridge Springs Defence.

4. ......   B — K 2

With this move Black has to make up his mind which defensive system he is going to employ. To the normal 4. ....Kt — K B 3 White will reply 5. P — K 3 followed by 6. Q Kt — Q 2; if 4. ....Q — Kt 3; 5. Q — Kt 3 and White will continue with Kt — B 3 threatening P — K 4.

The instinctive 4. ....P — B 3 deprives Black of the best post for his Kt (on K B 3) and would lead to a bad game, e.g. 5. B — B 4, B — Q 3; 6. B × B, Q × B; 7. Kt — B 3, Kt — K 2; 8. P — K 4, Castles; 9. B — Q 3, Kt — Q 2; 10. Castles, P — Q Kt 3; 11. R — K 1 and Black will be unable to prevent the powerful thrust, P — K 5.

5. B × B   Q × B

Better than Kt × B, as the Kt must be reserved for B 3 in order to control the centre.

6. Q Kt — Q 2

An idea introduced and practised with considerable success by Capablanca when his opponent has already played P — Q B 3. The theory is that it is necessary to have the Q Kt on B 3 in order to bring pressure to bear on Black's Q Pawn and so prevent an eventual P — Q B 4. But Black having already played P — Q B 3, P — Q B 4 would be wasting one tempo; so the Kt is played to Q 2 ready to retake on B 4 (should Black be so unwise as to exchange Pawns) and thus control K 5, and also so as to reinforce an eventual Kt — K 5 by Q Kt — K B 3.

6. ......   P — K B 4

Black decides upon the Stonewall formation, a system inherently unsound, since it shuts in the Q Bishop and leaves a hole

on K 4, but one which is dangerous in the hands of an attacking
player and against inaccurate
methods on White's part.

The normal and natural 6.
....Kt — K B 3 is much to be
preferred.

7. P — K 3   Q Kt — Q 2
8. B — Q 3   Kt — R 3

An artificial manœuvre much
favoured by players of this defence. K B 3 is reserved for the
Q Kt, whilst the K Kt will go to
K B 2, thence to bear on K 4 and
also permit of P — K Kt 4.

Again, the simple 8. ....K Kt
— B 3 was preferable.

9. Castles   Castles
10. Q — B 2   P — K Kt 3

A passive move, but one dictated by the nature of the defence. Both his logical continuations, Kt — K B 3 and Kt —
K B 2, would be met by P × P,
when Black would have to recapture with the B Pawn and not the
K Pawn as he desires. Then
White would play Q R — B 1
followed by Q — B 7, completely
laming Black's Q side.

11. Q R — Kt 1   Kt — B 3
12. Kt — K 5   Kt — B 2
13. P — B 4   B — Q 2

But this is altogether too mechanically played. Black should
have exchanged Kts on K 4 in order to have a Pawn and not a minor piece in that outpost. White's
next move prevents this possibility.

14. Kt(Q 2)—B 3   K R—Q 1
15. P—Q Kt 4

Preparing a menacing Pawn
attack on the Q side. This will be
supplemented later on by a similar K side attack, a merciless procedure under which Black dies
from suffocation.

15. ......   B — K 1
16. K R — B 1   P — Q R 3
17. Q — B 2

Threatening 18. Q — R 4 followed by 19. P — Kt 4.

17. ......   Kt × Kt
18. Kt × Kt   Kt — Q 2
19. Kt — B 3 !

It being the correct policy to
abstain from exchanges as far as
possible when one's opponent has
a constricted position.

19. ......   K R — B 1

Black can only mark time;
Brinckmann's suggestion in the
tournament book of 19. ....P ×
P followed by B — B 2 only adds
another weakness to Black's position since White can still proceed with his Q side attack by P
— Q R 4 and eventually P —
Q Kt 5.

20. P — B 5   Kt — B 3
21. P — Q R 4   Kt — Kt 5
22. Q — K 1   Kt — R 3
23. P — R 3   Kt — B 2

Threatening to gain some freedom by 24. ....P — K Kt 4.

24. P — Kt 4

Well timed; owing to the double attack on his K B Pawn,

Black cannot now play P —
K Kt 4. In addition, White is preparing his K side attack.

24.	B — Q 2
25. R — B 2	K — R 1
26. R — K Kt 2	R — K Kt 1
27. P — K Kt 5	

Once and for all preventing
Black's P — K Kt 4, which he
threatened again by his last move.

27.	Q — Q 1
28. P — R 4	K — Kt 2
29. P — K R 5	R — R 1
30. R — K R 2	Q — B 2
31. Q — B 3	Q — Q 1
32. K — B 2	Q — B 2
33. Q R—K R 1	Q R—K Kt 1
34. Q — R 1	R — Kt 1
35. Q — R 3	Q R — Kt 1
36. P — Kt 5 !	

After due preparation, White
makes a decisive break-through
on the Q side. This is done too at
a moment when the Rooks are
temporarily shut in on Black's K
side.

36.	R P × P

And not 36. ....B P × P; 37.
P — R 6 ch, K — B 1; 38. P —
B 6 dis ch. This variation ex-
plains White's Q manœuvre.

37. P — R 6 ch	K — B 1
38. P × P	K — K 2
39. P — Kt 6	Q — Kt 1

White's Pawn structure presents a most pleasing, æsthetic
picture. His winning procedure
is to concentrate his pieces in attack on the Q Kt Pawn.

Position after 39. ....Q — Kt 1

40. R — R 1	R — Q B 1

Naturally, if 40. ....Q — R 1,
White does not exchange, but
plays, as in the actual game, 41.
Q — Kt 4 and 42. R — R 7.

41. Q — Kt 4	K R—Q 1
42. R — R 7	K — B 1
43. R — K R 1	B — K 1
44. R (R 1) — R 1	K — Kt 1
45. R (R 1) — R 4	K — B 1
46. Q — R 3	

Now Black's Rook cannot
leave the back rank to defend the
Q Kt Pawn by R — Q 2 because
of R — R 8 winning the Queen.
The miserable constriction of
Black's pieces makes a striking
contrast with the open spaces
controlled by White.

46.	K — Kt 1
47. K — Kt 3	

White dallies with his King for
a few moves until he determines
that it is best placed on K Kt 2;
for since the Kt is destined for
Q R 5 to reinforce the attack on

the Q Kt Pawn he must not allow Black to play Kt × Kt P.

47.	B — Q 2
48. K — R 4	K — R 1
49. Q — R 1	K — Kt 1
50. K — Kt 3	K — B 1
51. K — Kt 2 !	

Now that the King is in its
right place, White's Kt can commence its winning tour.

51.	B — K 1
52. Kt — Q 2	B — Q 2
53. Kt — Kt 3	R — K 1

Or 53. ....B — K 1; 54. Kt
— R 5, R — Q 2; 55. Kt × Kt P,
R × Kt; 56. R — R 8 and the
Queen is lost.

54. Kt — R 5	Kt — Q 1
55. B — R 6 !	P × B
56. R × B	R — K 2

If 56. ....K — Kt 1 then simply 57. Kt — Kt 3 followed by
R × Q R P.

57. R × Kt ch !

White can win very much as he
likes, but he chooses the most elegant way.

| 57. ...... | R × B |
| 58. Kt × P | Resigns. |

An instructive game which is
especially an object lesson for
those ill-intentioned enough to
adopt the Stonewall Defence to
the Queen's.

64
TWENTY–FIRST ROUND, CARLSBAD, 1929

Queen's Gambit Declined
Orthodox Defence

| White | Black |
| CAPABLANCA | G. MAROCZY |

1. P — Q 4	Kt — K B 3
2. P — Q B 4	P — K 3
3. Kt — K B 3	P — Q 4
4. B — Kt 5	B — K 2
5. P — K 3	Castles
6. Kt — B 3	Q Kt — Q 2
7. R — B 1	P — B 3

The Orthodox Defence is so
solid that none of White's contin-
uations now suffice even to retain
the initiative. If he embarks on
the Rubinstein attack after 8. B
— Q 3, P × P; 9. B × P, Kt —
Q 4; 10. B × B, Q × B; 11. Cas-
tles, Kt × Kt; 12. R × Kt, P —
K 4; 13. P × P, Kt × P; 14. Kt
× Kt, Q × Kt; 15. P — B 4, Q
— K 5; 16. B — Kt 3, B — B 4;
17. Q — R 5, P — Kt 3 and an
analysis by Löwenfisch demon-
strates complete equality by 18.
Q — R 4, Q R — Q 1; 19. B —
B 2, Q — Q 4; 20. R — Q 1, Q
— R 4; 21. R × R, Q × R; 22.
Q × Q, R × Q.

And no more than equality is
obtained after the so-called strug-
gle for a tempo by 8. P — Q R 3,
Kt — K 5; 9. B × B, Q × B; 10.
Q — B 2, Kt × Kt; 11. Q × Kt,
R — K 1; 12. R — Q 1, P × P;
13. B × P, P — Q Kt 3; 14.
Castles, B — Kt 2; 15. P — K 4,
P — Q B 4   (Fine–Stahlberg,
Stockholm, 1937).

The move chosen by Capablanca should achieve no more than the rest against the correct defence.

8. Q — B 2   P — K R 3

A poor move; best is 8. ....
Kt — K 5; 9. B × B, Q × B; 10.
Kt × Kt, P × Kt; 11. Q × P
(11. Kt — Q 2, P — K B 4 is
also quite good for Black); 11.
....Q — Kt 5 ch; 12. Kt — Q 2,
Q × Kt P; 13. R — Q Kt 1, Q —
R 6; 14. Q — B 2, P — K 4 with
equality (Alekhine–van den
Bosch, Amsterdam, 1936).

9. B — R 4   P — R 3
10. P × P

If he tries to maintain the tension in the centre by 10. P —
Q R 3, then Black can obtain a satisfactory game by 10. ....P
— Q Kt 4; 11. P — B 5, P —
K 4; 12. P × P, Kt — K 1; 13.
B × B, Q × B; 14. Kt — K 2,
Kt × K P; 15. Kt × Kt, Q ×
Kt; 16. Kt — Q 4, B — Q 2;
17. B — Q 3, Kt — B 2 (Eliskases–Ragosin, Semmering-Baden, 1937).

10. ......   Kt × P

This unpinning manœuvre is not efficacious here as, owing to Black's 8th move, White need not exchange Bishops, but can retire his Bishop to Kt 3, where it is very well placed indeed. Black, therefore, would have done better to recapture with the K Pawn.

11. B — Kt 3   Q — R 4

Because of White's next manœuvre, this turns out to be mere waste of a tempo and Black's game goes rapidly downhill. Maroczy should now seek safety in exchanges by 11. ....Kt × Kt; 12. Q × Kt, P — Q B 4.

12. Kt — Q 2!   Kt × Kt
13. P × Kt   P — Q B 4

Already Black is at a loss for a really good move. If he plays 13. ....P — Q Kt 4 then 14. B — K 2, B — Kt 2; 15. B — B 3 gives White a dominating position in the centre.

14. Kt — B 4   Q — Q 1
15. R — Q 1!

This, and the next move, take excellent advantage of Black's weaknesses. Now White will gain control of the Q file.

15. ......   P × P

Now 15. ....P — Q Kt 4 would be met by 16. P × P, B × P; 17. Kt — Q 6; consequently Black is unable to avoid the opening of the Q file.

16. R × P!

With unerring positional insight, White accepts two isolated Pawns on the Q side in order to increase the central pressure.

16. ......   B — B 4
17. R — Q 2   Q — K 2
18. B — K 2

The handling of this Bishop is noteworthy. It is not developed on its normal square of Q 3, since it will exert more pressure on the long diagonal when placed on K B 3 via K 2.

18. ......   P — Q Kt 3
19. Kt — Q 6   Kt — B 3
20. Castles   R — R 2

Anticipating 21. B — B 3 and being unable to play 20. ....B — Kt 2 because of 21. Kt × B, Q × Kt; 22. B — B 3, Kt — Q 4; 23. P — B 4, etc. An analysis by Becker shows that Black cannot contest the Q file by 20. ....R — Q 1 for then 21. K R — Q 1 (threatening Kt — B 5), B — Q 2; 22. B — B 3, R — R 2; 23. Kt — Kt 7, R — Q B 1; 24. B — K 5, B — K 1; 25. Kt × B, P × Kt; 26. B — Q 6 and there is no good place for Black's Queen.

21. B — B 3   B — Q 2
22. K R — Q 1   P — K 4

Otherwise White occupies this square by 23. B — K 5 and Black has no chance of freeing his position. Nor can he relieve his position by trying to remove the Kt from Q 6, e.g. 22. .... Kt — K 1; 23. Kt — K 4, P — B 4; 24. Kt × B, P × Kt; 25. B — K 5 and White has a complete bind on the Black position.

23. B — R 4   P — K Kt 4

This nervous reaction to White's pin creates weaknesses on Black's K side and Capablanca takes immediate toll of these. But if he attempts to unpin by 23. ....Q — K 3 then 24. B — K 2 (threatening B — B 4); 24. ....P — Q Kt 4; 25. B × Kt and if Q × B; 26. Kt — K 4 wins a piece.

24. B — Kt 3   K — Kt 2
25. B — K 2 !

A quiet move hiding a deal of art. Firstly White threatens to bring the Bishop into a more attacking position on Q B 4; next he pins down the Rook to defence of his Q R Pawn, and, finally, an eventual P — K R 4 may provoke Black to play P — Kt 5 with attack on the Bishop had it remained on K B 3.

25. ......   P — Kt 4
26. P — K R 4 !   R — B 2

After this move Black loses at least a Pawn, but he has no good alternative. If 26. ....P — K Kt 5; 27. Kt — B 5 ch, B × Kt; 28. Q × B and again a Pawn falls. Or 26. ....Q — K 3; 27. P × P, P × P; 28. Kt — K 4, Kt × Kt; 29. Q × Kt, R — K 1; 30. Q × P ch again winning a Pawn because of the hanging nature of Black's Q Bishop.

Position after 26. ....R — B 2

27.	P × P	P × P
28.	Kt — B 5 ch	B × Kt
29.	Q × B	Resigns

At first sight, resignation may appear premature, but Black is quite lost; the variations giving the *coup de grâce* are, however, very interesting. If 29. ....R — K 1; 30. Q × P ch, K — R 1; 31. Q — R 6 ch, Kt — R 2; 32. B — Q 3, P — B 3; 33. B × Kt, Q × B; 34. Q × P ch, etc.

Or if 29. .... K — R 3; 30. B × K P, R — B 3; 31. R — Q 5 (and not 31. R — Q 7, Q — K 3 with drawing chances); 31. .... B — R 6 (the threat was 32. B × Kt followed by R × B, whilst if 31. ....Kt × R; 32. Q — R 3 ch, K — Kt 3; 33. B — R 5 ch, K — R 2; 34. B × P dis ch, R — R 3; 35. Q — B 5 ch followed by mate); 32. P — K B 4 and Black will soon be mated.

65
EIGHTEENTH ROUND, CARLSBAD, 1929

Queen's Pawn, Colle System

White	Black
E. COLLE	CAPABLANCA
1. P — Q 4	Kt — K B 3
2. Kt — K B 3	P — Q Kt 3
3. P — K 3	

The late Belgian master had evolved a system of opening play which was outstandingly successful except against the most accurate defence. He created the Pawn structure, P on Q 4, Q B 3, K 3, and massed his pieces so as

to bear on K 4. The strength of the system lay in the accumulation of retarded energy and the explosion of this by an eventual P — K 4.

Capablanca chooses an excellent method of countering this by indirect pressure on the centre from the wings.

3.	B — Kt 2
4. Q Kt — Q 2	P — K 3
5. B — Q 3	P — B 4
6. Castles	

Or White can delay Castling and play 6. P — B 3, B — K 2; 7. Q — K 2, Kt — Q 4 (in order to counter 8. P — K 4 with Kt — B 5); 8. P × P, P × P; 9. Kt — B 1, Q — B 2; 10. Kt — Kt 3, Kt — Q B 3; 11. B — Q 2, P — K Kt 4! and Black has a fine game (Ahues–Alekhine, San Remo, 1930).

6.	Kt — B 3 !

Temporarily preventing P — K 4; Black intends to hinder White's P — K 4 as much as possible — and in the process to complete his own development.

7. P — B 3

A move typifying the Colle system; the alternative method of developing the Q Bishop by a fianchetto which was practised by the great Polish master, Rubinstein, is best met as follows: 7. P — Q Kt 3, B — K 2; 8. P × P, P × P; 9. B — Kt 2, Castles; 10. P — B 4, Q — B 2; 11. P — K R 3, Kt — K 1; 12. P — R 3,

P — B 4; 13. Q — B 2, B — B 3 and Black has the better game (Rubinstein–Geiger, Rogasha-Slatina, 1929).

7. ......   B — K 2

Another, and very solid, method of play is that employed by Elikases in his 9th match game against Spielmann in 1936: 7. ....Q — B 2; 8. Q — K 2, B — K 2; 9. P — K 4, P × P; 10. Kt × P, Kt — K 4; 11. B — B 2, Q — B 1; 12. P — Q R 3, Kt — B 3; 13. Q Kt — B 3, Kt × Kt; 14. Kt × Kt, P — Q 3.

8. P — K 4

A level game resulted after 8. P × P, P × P; 9. P — K 4, Q — B 2; 10. Q — K 2, P — Q 3; 11. Kt — B 4, Castles K; 12. P — K 5, P × P; 13. Q Kt × P, Kt × Kt (Colle–Pirc, Frankfurt, 1930).

8. ......   P × P
9. Kt × P

And not 9. P × P, Kt — Q Kt 5; 10. B — Kt 1, B — R 3; 11. R — K 1, R — Q B 1; 12. P — Q R 3, Kt — Q 6, etc.

9. ......   Castles

Black prefers to complete his development rather than commence an evanescent counter-attack by 9. ....Kt — K 4; 10. B — B 2, B — R 3; 11. R — K 1, Q — B 2; 12. Q Kt — B 3, Kt — Kt 3 and White has rather the better game (Colle–L. Steiner, Niendorf, 1927).

10. Q — K 2

As, however, the above-mentioned Kt manœuvre will now prove effective, White would do better to exchange Kts before playing this move.

10. ......   Kt — K 4
11. B — B 2   Q — B 1

A thematic move in this defence by which Black hopes to achieve control of the diagonal Q R 3 — K B 8.

12. P — K B 4   B — R 3
13. Q — Q 1   Kt — B 3!

Naturally, not 13. ....B × R; 14. P × Kt and White wins two pieces for the Rook. It is possible that White had expected here 13. ....Kt — Q 6; 14. R — B 3 with the better game. Instead, Black returns his Kt to B 3 as part of a subtle plan for undermining White's control of the centre — in especial his K 4.

14. R — B 3   P — Kt 3!

Another fine move which anticipates an eventual P — K 5 by White and opposes a solid Pawn barrier to the possible attack by White's K Bishop.

15. Q Kt — Kt 3

Unsound would be 15. Kt × Kt, Q × Kt; 16. P — B 5, B — B 4 ch; 17. K — R 1, Kt — Kt 5 and Black has a winning attack.

15. ......   Kt × Kt
16. Kt × Kt   B — Kt 2
17. Q — K 2   B — B 4
18. R — R 3

Consequently, continuing with his plan for a K side attack; but it would have been better to have prevented Black's next move by 18. K — R 1.

Unfortunately, White cannot complete his development by either 18. B — Q 2, B × Kt ch; 19. P × B, Q × B or 18. B — K 3, Kt × P.

18. ......   Q — B 3 !

A very strong move which forces the advance of the White K Pawn and so obtains a central position for Black's K Kt.

19. P — K 5

Forced; if 19. R — K 3, Q — B 2; 20. P — K Kt 3, P — K 4 with a strong attack.

19. ......   Kt — Q 4
20. Q — B 2

Again consequently played; but better was 20. B — K 3, B × Kt; 21. P × B, though after 21. ....Q R — B 1; 22. R — Q B 1, Kt × B; 23. R × Kt, Q — Q B 5 Black would still have very much the upper hand.

White cannot play 20. B — K 4, Kt × Q B P !; 21. B × Q, Kt × Q ch, etc.

20. ......   B × Kt
21. P × B

Not 21. Q × B, Kt × P.

21. ......   Q R — B 1
22. B — Q 1

Other Bishop moves lose at once, e.g. 22. B — Q 3, Q × B ch; 23. R × Q, R × R ch; 24. B — B 1, B — R 3, etc.

And if 22. Q — R 4, P — K R 4; 23. B — Q 1, Kt × P winning.

22. ......   P — B 3 !

Very economically played; this move combines defence of the K side with attack on White's centre.

Position after 22. ....P — B 3 !

23. Q — R 4

If 23. B — Q 2 (threatening R — B 1) then ....Kt × P !; 24. B × Kt, P × P; 25. B — B 3 (or 25. P × P, R × B); 25. ....P — K 5; 26. B — K 2, P — K 6 !; 27. R × K P, R × B and Black wins — a beautiful illustration of the vigour contained in Black's apparently innocent 22nd move.

23. ......   R — B 2
24. B — B 3   Q — B 5

This attack on the Q Pawn cannot be satisfactorily met. White's helplessness is a great tribute to Capablanca's beautifully logical and subtle play.

25. B — K 3

Clever, but inadequate; there is, however, no resource. 25. Q — B 2 fails against Q × B ch.

25. ......   Kt × B
26. B × B   Kt — B 4 !

Decisive; not so strong is 26. .... Q × Q P; 27. B × R, Kt — Kt 5 dis ch; 28. K — B 1 and Black is unable to administer the *coup de grâce*.

27. Q — K 1

If 27. Q — B 2, Q — B 8 ch; 28. R × Q, R × R ch; 29. Q — B 1, R × Q ch; 30. K × R, Kt × P and wins.

27. ......   R — B 2
28. B — K 4   Q × P ch
29. K — R 1   P × P
30. B × Kt   K P × B
31. P × P   R — K 2
32. R — K 3   Q × Kt P
33. P — K 6   P × P
34. R × P   K — B 2 !

A fine finishing touch; the King itself is used as an attacking piece! After 35. R × R, R × R White's position is obviously hopeless, and he therefore resigns.

This game is Capablanca at his best, full of subtle touches for the full exploitation of positional weaknesses. After the game Colle is reported to have said: " It seems to me I did not make a weak move, but that my opponent played some very strong ones." This feeling was familiar to most of Capablanca's opponents.

66

FIFTEENTH ROUND, CARLSBAD, 1929

Queen's Pawn, Queen's Indian Defence

White	Black
CAPABLANCA	F. J. MARSHALL
1. P — Q 4	Kt — K B 3
2. P — Q B 4	P — K 3
3. Kt — K B 3	P — Q Kt 3
4. P — K Kt 3	B — Kt 2
5. B — Kt 2	P — B 4

This game may be regarded as the last nail in the coffin for this variation. White's next move is a powerful thrust which gives him control of the centre, and the subsequent play shows that Black cannot shake off this control.

Two better alternatives are 5. B — Kt 5 ch and 5. .... B — K 2, the latter giving Black a more solid game, e.g. 5. .... B — K 2; 6. Castles, Castles; 7. Kt — B 3, Kt — K 5; 8. Q — B 2, Kt × Kt; 9. P × Kt, Q — B 1; 10. P — K 4, Kt — B 3; 11. Kt — Q 2, P — K 4 (Pirc–Kan, Moscow, 1935).

6. P — Q 5	P × P
7. Kt — R 4	P — Kt 3
8. Kt — B 3	B — Kt 2
9. Castles	Castles
10. B — Kt 5	

The strongest move; not so aggressive is 10. B — B 4, as was demonstrated in the game Capablanca won against Alekhine at New York in 1927 (Game No. 43).

10. ...... P — K R 3 ?

This move eventually loses a Pawn without adequate compensation. Whatever he plays, Black has a poor position; best appears to be 10. ....Q — B 1; 11. B × Kt (not 11. Kt — Kt 5, Kt — K 5!); 11. ....B × B; 12. Kt × P, B × Kt; 13. P × B, B × Kt; 14. Q × B, Kt — B 3; 15. Q R — Q 1, R — Q 1; 16. P — R 5! with the powerful threat of P — R 6.

Or Black may prefer to sacrifice the Pawn by 10. ....Kt — B 3; 11. Kt × Q P, P — K R 3; 12. Kt × Kt ch, B × Kt; 13. B × B, Q × B; 14. Q × P, Q R — Kt 1 with a free game, but not sufficiently so to compensate for the lost Pawn (Sämisch–Réti, Bad Homburg, 1927).

Position after 10. ....P — K R 3 ?

11. Kt × Q P

In a game List–Sämisch, Berlin, 1927, Black fell into an amusing trap after 11. B × Kt, B × B ? (11. ....Q × B; 12. Kt × Q P, B × Kt; 13. Q × B trans-

poses into the present game); 12. Kt × Kt P !

11. ...... B × Kt
12. B × Kt Q × B

If 12. ....K B × B; 13. Q × B, Kt — B 3; 14. Kt × P.

13. Q × B Kt — B 3
14. Q × Q P Kt — K 4
15. Q — R 4 !

The Queen is to be centralised on Q B 2, where it exerts most pressure on the centre and King's wing.

15. ...... Q R — K 1

This is not the best square for the Q R. He should have reserved Kt for his K R and played 15. ....Q R — Q 1.

16. B — Q 5 !

Another fine centralising move which serves many purposes. The Bishop is placed at its position of maximum efficiency on Q 5, whence it attacks K B 7 and protects Q B 4; at the same time, a square is vacated on Kt 2 for the Kt via which this last piece in its turn can be centralised.

Very bad would be 16. Q × P, Kt × P with double attack on White's Pawns.

16. ...... P — K Kt 4
17. Kt — Kt 2 Kt — Kt 3
18. P — K 3 R — K 2

Black would have a lost end-game after 18. ....Q × P; 19. Q × P, Q × R; 20. R × Q, B × R; 21. Q × P, Kt — K 2; 22. Q × R P, etc.

19. Q — B 2

Preventing 19. ....Q × P because of 20. Q × Kt.

19. ......   R — Q 2

Now really threatening 20. ....Q × P, since 21. Q × Kt would be met by R × B.

20. P — Kt 3   Kt — K 2

Black would lose material after 20. ....Q × R; 21. R × Q, B × R; 22. Q × Kt ch.

21. Q R — Q 1   K R — Q 1
22. P — K 4   Q — Kt 3

Marshall persists in trying to bring off one of his well-known swindles. He now threatens to regain a Pawn by 23. .... Kt × B; 24. B P × B, R × P, etc.

It is instructive to observe how Capablanca deals with these traps and at the same time improves his position by clear logical play.

23. P — B 4!   Q — R 4

And not now 23. ....Kt × B; 24. B P × Kt, R × P; 25. R × R, R × R; 26. P — B 5.

24. P × P   Kt × B
25. K P × Kt   P × P
26. Q — B 5   B — Q 5 ch
27. K — R 1   R — K 2
28. Q R — K 1

White must keep the Black Rook off the 7th rank.

28. ......   R × R
29. Kt × R   R — Q 3

If 29. ....R — K 1; 30. Kt — B 3, B — K 6; 31. R — K 1 winning the Kt Pawn.

30. P — K Kt 4!

Forcing the exchange of Queens.

30. ......   Q — Kt 3
31. Kt — B 3   Q × Q
32. P × Q

After which, as Black has no counter-attack, he is completely lost and might as well resign. The finish, however, is quite interesting, Capablanca conjuring up a mating net.

32. ......   B — K 6
33. K — Kt 2

The plausible 33. Kt × P would give Black distinct counter-chances after 33. ....B × Kt; 34. R — K Kt 1, P — Kt 4!

33. ......   P — Kt 4
34. R — K 1   B — B 5
35. K — R 3   P × P
36. P × P   R — R 3
37. R — K 2   R — R 6
38. K — Kt 4   R — B 6
39. Kt × P   R × P
40. R — K 8 ch K — Kt 2
41. Kt — K 4   B × P

Position after 41. ....B × P

42. K — R 5 !

Just when Black has managed to secure material equality there surges up the threat of mate in two moves.

42.	B — B 5
43. P — B 6 ch	K — R 2
44. R — K 7	K — Kt 1
45. P — Q 6	R — Q 5
46. P — Q 7	R — Q 4 ch
47. K — Kt 4	B — B 2
48. Kt — Kt 5	R — Q 5 ch
49. K — R 5	Resigns.

67

SECOND ROUND, BUDAPEST, 1929

Queen's Gambit Declined, Slav Defence

White	Black
CAPABLANCA	A. BRINCKMANN
1. P — Q 4	P — Q 4
2. P — Q B 4	P — Q B 3
3. Kt — K B 3	Kt — B 3
4. Kt — B 3	P × P

This idea of a delayed acceptance of the Gambit was introduced long ago by the Russian master, Alapin, and after a considerable period of neglect became popular again some fifteen year ago, Euwe especially being responsible for its frequent employment. Its advantage over other defences to the Queen's Gambit lies in the early development of the Q Bishop, and it gives rise to complex and interesting struggles in the centre mainly based on the control of White's K 4.

5. P — Q R 4   B — B 4
6. Kt — K 5

The most interesting choice from the three alternatives here; inferior is 6. Kt — R 4, to which Black can simply reply 6. ....B — B 1 after which White has nothing better than 7. Kt — B 3, since 7. P — K 3, P — K 4; 8. P × P, Q × Q ch; 9. Kt × Q, B — Kt 5 ch; 10. B — Q 2, B × B ch; 11. K × B, Kt — K 5 ch; 12. K — K 1, B — K 3; 13. P — B 4, Kt — R 3 is in Black's favour (Alekhine–Euwe, 15th match game, 1935).

The other main line is the more restrained 6. P — K 3, when again the question is who shall control K 4. After 6. ....P — K 3; 7. B × P, B — Q Kt 5; 8. Castles, Castles; 9. Q — K 2, B — Kt 5 the prospects are about even — Black having excellent play for his minor pieces whilst White's central position is to be preferred.

6. ......   Q Kt — Q 2

The less ambitious 6. ....P — K 3 leads to a safer game for Black, as, for example, in the game Flohr–Mikenas, Prague, 1931, which continued 7. P — B 3, B — Q Kt 5; 8. Kt × P (B 4), Castles; 9. B — Kt 5, P — B 4; 10. P × P, Q × Q ch; 11. K × Q, B × P; 12. P — K 4, B — Kt 3; 13. Kt — K 5, K Kt — Q 2; 14. Kt × B, R P × Kt; 15. K — B 2, Kt — Q B 3 with an equal position.

7. Kt × P (B 4)　　Q — B 2
8. P — K Kt 3

A strong move serving a double purpose; the immediate threat is 9. B — B 4 and, in addition, White's K Bishop is developed in a most effective manner on K Kt 2. Poor would be 8. P — B 3 because of 8. ....P — K 4! and still worse would be 8. Q — Kt 3 with the idea of exerting pressure on Black's Q Kt 2, since the second player can profit by the early exposure of the Queen, e.g. 8. ....P — K 4; 9. P × P, Kt — B 4; 10. Q — R 2, Kt — R 3!; 11. P — K 4, Kt × P; 12. Kt × Kt, B × Kt, etc. (Petrov–Capablanca, Semmering, 1937).

8. ......　　P — K 4
9. P × P　　Kt × P
10. B — B 4　　K Kt — Q 2
11. B — Kt 2　　P — B 3

Better than 11. ....B — K 3 which leaves White a clear-cut advantage after 12. Kt × Kt, Kt × Kt; 13. Castles, B — K 2 (bad is 13. ....Q — R 4; 14. Kt — K 4; cf. Game No. 78); 14. Q — B 2, R — Q 1; 15. K R — Q 1, Castles; 16. Kt — Kt 5 (Alekhine–Euwe, 1st match game, 1935).

12. Castles　　B — K 3

Black can score a momentary triumph in driving the Queen off the open file by 12. ....R — Q 1; 13. Q — B 1, B — K 3, but his game is badly hemmed in after 14. Kt — K 4, B — Q Kt 5; 15. P — R 5.

13. Kt × Kt　　P × Kt
14. B — K 3　　B — K 2

Black would do better to relieve his somewhat cramped position by 14. ....B — Q B 4.

15. P — R 5　　P — Q R 3 ?

A nervous reaction which greatly increases the strength of White's last move; it is true White was threatening 16. P — R 6, P — Q Kt 3; 17. Kt — Kt 5, but this would be best met by 15. ....R — Q B 1. Now Black's Q side is permanently fixed and presents an ideal object of attack.

16. Q — B 2　　Castles K
17. K R — Q 1　　Q R — K 1 ?

The final error after which the game is positionally lost, as Capablanca convincingly demonstrates. 17. ....Q R — B 1 was imperative.

Position after 17. ....Q R — K 1 ?

18. Kt — Q 5 !

Obtaining the advantage of two Bishops in an open position. The utilisation of this to force a Rook

on to the 7th rank is most instructive and typical of Capablanca's
consummate technique.

18. ......   B × Kt

18. ....Q — Q 1 would lose
at once because of 19. B — Kt 6
and if Kt × B; 20. Kt — B 6 ch
winning the Queen. Should Black
prefer to give up the K Bishop
rather than the Q Bishop, then he
must play 18. ....Q — B 1;
19. Kt × B ch, R × Kt, though
White's two Bishops would still
give him much the better game,
e.g. 20. B — K 4, P — K R 3;
21. R — Q 2, Q — B 2; 22. P —
Q Kt 4, R (K 2) — B 2; 23. Q R
— Q 1, Kt — B 3; 24. B —
Q Kt 6 winning.

19. B × B ch   K — R 1
20. B — K 6   Kt — B 3

If 20. ....R — Q 1 White will
double Rooks on the Q file, forcing the Kt to move.

21. B — Kt 6   Q — Kt 1
22. B — Q 7   Kt × B
23. R × Kt

Accomplishing the plan commenced on his 18th move, after
which Black loses with startling
rapidity.

23. ......   R — B 3

So great is White's command
of the board that Black has no
plausible chance of counter-attack; he now reorganises his
pieces so as to protect K 4 and
K Kt 2, but fails to find an adequate means of protection for his
weakest point — Q Kt 2.

If 23. ....B — Q 1 then 24.
B — B 5!

24. Q R — Q 1   R — K 3
25. Q — Kt 3   B — B 3
26. P — K 4

Quenching Black's feeble hope
of obtaining some freedom by 26.
....P — K 5.

26. ......   P — R 3

If 26. ....R (K 3) — K 2,
White can win the K Pawn by
27. B — B 7, but would do still
better to maintain the pressure
by 27. R × R, B × R; 28. R —
Q 7, B — B 3; 29. Q — B 7, etc.

27. B — B 5   K — R 2
28. R × P   Q — B 1
29. R (Q 1) — Q 7   Resigns

Black is absolutely helpless;
amongst the many ways to finish
off the game is 30. Q — K B 3
followed by Q × B and R × P ch
with mate in two.

68
SIXTH ROUND,
BUDAPEST, 1929

*Queen's Pawn, Nimzovitch
Defence*

White	Black
K. HAVASI	CAPABLANCA
1. P — Q 4	Kt — K B 3
2. P — Q B 4	P — K 3
3. Kt — Q B 3	B — Kt 5
4. Q — B 2	P — Q 4
5. Kt — B 3	

The most vigorous move here is
5. P × P, when Black's best reply is 5. ....Q × P; 6. P — K 3,
P — B 4, somewhat as in the actual game.

Against Nimzovitch at Bad
Kissingen, 1928, Capablanca tried
5. B — Kt 5, but after 5. ....P
× P; 6. Kt — B 3, P — Kt 4;
7. P — Q R 4, P — B 3; 8. B
× Kt, P × B; 9. P — R 3, P —
Q R 3 Black was able to retain
the Gambit Pawn without ill
effects.

5.	P — B 4
6. B P × P	Q × P
7. P — Q R 3	B × Kt ch
8. P × B	Kt — B 3
9. P — K 3	Castles
10. B — K 2	

Much too timid a move, after
which White justly loses the initiative. White must endeavour to
make his centre mobile by playing 10. P — B 4, Q — Q 3; 11. B
— Kt 2, P × P; 12. P × P, P —
Q Kt 3; 13. B — Q 3, B — Kt 2
as in the 10th game, Alekhine-
Euwe match, 1937. It is true that
he then has to be careful lest his
centre Pawns prove vulnerable to
attack, but this is compensated
by the powerful raking effect of
his two Bishops.

The text move initiates a plan
of attacking the Queen by playing the Bishop to K B 3, but is
too cumbrous and slow. Black
profits by the time consumed to
complete his development satisfactorily.

10.	P × P
11. B P × P	P — Q Kt 3
12. Kt — Q 2	B — Kt 2

Naturally, not 12. ....Q ×
Kt P; 13. B — B 3 winning a
piece.

| 13. B — B 3 | Q — Q 2 |
| 14. Castles | Q R — B 1 |

Already going over to the attack, Black threatens Kt × P.
The one advantage White had in
the position is about to disappear,
for he cannot prevent the exchange of the Bishop he has been
at such pains to develop.

| 15. Q — Kt 1 | Kt — Q R 4 ! |
| 16. B × B | |

If 16. B — K 2, then Kt —
Q 4 followed by Kt — B 6.

| 16. ...... | Q × B |
| 17. B — Kt 2 | |

In the position now reached,
Black has an accumulation of
small positional advantages
which, taken one by one, are not
particularly alarming, however,
by weaving them together, Capablanca is able to obtain a crushing attack on the Q side.

Firstly, Black is rather better
developed, since White has been
too slow in his opening strategy;
next, he possesses the latent endgame advantage of two Pawns to
one on the Q side; finally, owing
to White's Pawn formation, he
will be able to exert considerable
pressure on the white squares.

Position after 17. B — Kt 2

is doomed, but what makes the finish so impressive is the logical and harmonious way in which each move fits in with the theme.

24. P — Q R 4   Kt — R 6!
25. Q — Kt 2

If 25. Q — Q 1, Q — B 5 followed by 26. ....Kt — B 7 and wins.

25. ......   Q × P
26. R — K 2

Or 26. K R — R 1, Q — Kt 4!

26. ......   P — Q Kt 4

The quickest way; White will be unable to stop the advance of this Pawn.

27. P — Q 5	P × P
28. P × P	P — Kt 5
29. Q — Q 2	P — Kt 6
30. R — Kt 2	R — B 7
31. Q — K 3	R × Q R
32. R × R	Kt — B 5
33. Q — B 1	Q — R 6

Resigns. The Rook is lost after 34. R — Kt 1, Q × Q ch; 35. R × Q, P — Kt 7; 36. R — Kt 1, R — Kt 1 followed by 37. ....Kt — R 6.

17. ......   Q — R 3

Threatening Q — K 7 and increasing his control over several important white squares.

18. R — K 1

And not 18. R — B 1, Q — K 7; 19. Kt — B 3, Kt — Kt 6; 20. R × R, R × R; 21. R — R 2, R — B 7, etc.

18. ......   Kt — Q 4

Black can comfortably concentrate all his pieces on the Q side since White has no shadow of a counter on the K wing.

19. R — R 2   R — B 3
20. P — K 4

Otherwise Black simply doubles Rooks on the Q B file, followed by R — B 7.

20.	Kt — B 6
21. B × Kt	R × B
22. Kt — B 3	K R — B 1
23. P — R 3	Kt — B 5

This is the final unleashing of Black's attack. White's Q R Pawn

69

FIRST ROUND,
BARCELONA, 1929

English Opening

White	Black
CAPABLANCA	E. COLLE
1. P — Q B 4	Kt — K B 3
2. Kt — K B 3	P — B 4

A move which is much too committal for Black at this early

stage; more elastic is 2. . . . . P —
K 3 and solid enough is 2. . . . .
P — K Kt 3 then if 3. Kt — B 3,
P — Q 4! (otherwise White plays
4. P — K 4); 4. P × P, Kt × P
with a good game.

The text is an endeavour at
symmetry which unfortunately
depends for its effect on White
falling in with Black's plan.

3. Kt — B 3

Best here is 3. P — Q 4 as
Capablanca played in later games
in this tournament; cf. Game No.
72 v. Torres.

3. . . . . . .   Kt — B 3

Inferior to 3. . . . . P — Q 4; 4.
P × P, Kt × P and now if 5. P
— K 4, Kt × Kt (not 5. . . . . Kt
— Kt 5;   6.   B — B 4,   Kt —
Q 6 ch; 7. K — K 2, Kt × B ch;
8. R × Kt, P — Q R 3; 9. P —
Q 4 with marked advantage to
White);   6.   Kt P × Kt,   P —
K Kt 3 arriving at a line similar
to that in the note above.

4. P — Q 4   P × P
5. Kt × P   Kt × Kt ?

Giving White's Queen a dominating position in the centre; bad
also is 5. . . . . P — K Kt 3; 6. P
— K 4 transposing into a variation of the Sicilian which is strategically won for White.

Still best for Black is 5. . . . .
P — Q 4.

6. Q × Kt   P — K Kt 3
7. P — K 4   P — Q 3
8. B — K 3   B — Kt 2
9. P — B 3   Q — R 4

An ineffectual attempt at counter-play on the Q side which
merely leaves Black's Queen misplaced. Better was simply 9. . . . .
Castles.

10. Q — Q 2   P — Q R 3
11. B — K 2   B — K 3
12. Q R — B 1

Removing the Rook from a
dangerous diagonal to place it on
a file which will be opened eventually. Capablanca's exploitation
of his opening advantage is very
instructive.

A rash inversion of moves by
12. P — Q Kt 3 would dissipate
White's advantage after 12. . . . .
Kt — Kt 5; 13. B — Q 4, B × B;
14. Q × B, Q — K 4; 15. Q ×
Q, Kt × Q and the general exchange would leave White little
to play for.

12. . . . . . .   R — Q B 1
13. P — Q Kt 3   Kt — Q 2

Not quite good enough is the
intriguing move 13. . . . . P —
Q Kt 4; 14. Kt — Q 5 (14. P ×
P leads to disaster after 14. . . . .
Kt × P!); 14. . . . . Q × Q ch;
15. K × Q, P × P; 16. P × P, B
× Kt; 17. B P × B, R — R 1;
18. R — B 7 with a won game for
White.

14. Castles   Castles
15. Kt — Q 5

Forcing the Black Queen to
retire, since 15. . . . . Q × Q loses
a Pawn after 16. Kt × P ch. Now
the point of Black's 13th move
becomes clear, as otherwise White

would have been able to play 16.
B — Kt 6.

15.	Q — Q 1
16. Q — Kt 4 !	B × Kt

White's last move has forced
this exchange, there being no other means of protecting the Kt
Pawn. If 16. ....R — Kt 1 then
17. B — R 7.

17. B P × B	R × R

Bad for Black is 17. ....P —
Q Kt 4; 18. Q — R 3, R — R 1
(or 18. ....Kt — Kt 1; 19. B —
R 7); 19. R — B 2 (and not 19.
R — B 6, Kt — Kt 1; 20. B —
Kt 6, Q — Q 2; 21. R — B 7 ? B
— Q 5 ch) when White obtains
full control of the Q B file.

18. R × R	Q — Kt 1
19. Q — B 4	B — Kt 7

This move not only loses time,
but facilitates White's advance in
the centre. Black, however, has
no adequate defence, since 19.
....Kt — B 4 is met by 20. P —
Q Kt 4 followed by 21. Q — B 7.
After 19. ....Kt — B 4 White
should not allow Black chances
of a draw by 20. B × Kt, R —
B 1; 21. Q — Kt 4, R × B; 22.
R × R, P × R; 23. Q × B P, B
— K 4; 24. P — Kt 3, Q — B 2
coming down to an ending with
Bishops of opposite colour.

20. R — B 2	B — B 3

It would have been better to
admit the waste of time by 20.
....B — Kt 2. Here the Bishop
is exposed to eventual Pawn attack.

21. P — B 4	R — Q 1
22. Q — B 7	Q — R 1

Exchange of Queens only in-
creases White's pressure, e.g. 22.
....Q × Q; 23. R × Q, P —
Q Kt 4; 24. R — R 7, Kt — Kt 1;
25. B — Kt 6, R — Q B 1; 26. R
— R 8, etc.

Interesting, but still more unprofitable for Black is 22. ....
Kt — B 4; 23. Q × Q, R × Q;
24. P — K 5, B — Kt 2; 25. B ×
Kt, R — Q B 1; 26. P — Q Kt 4,
P — Kt 3; 27. B × P, R — B 2;
28. B — Kt 5, Kt P × B; 29.
Kt P × P, P × P; 30. P — Q 6
winning easily.

23. B — Kt 4	Kt — B 4

If 23. ....Kt — B 1 then 24.
B — B 8 (too precipitate is 24. P
— K 5, P × P; 25. P × P, B —
Kt 2; 26. B — B 8, R × P; 27.
B × P, R — Q 8 ch; 28. K —
B 2, Q — Q 1 and Black has
good counter-chances); 24. ....
R — K 1; 25. B × P winning.

24. P — K 5 !	

Taking neat advantage of the
hanging position of Black's Kt.
White is in no hurry to remove
the Pawn, but first increases the
pressure in the centre.

24.	B — Kt 2
25. Q × K P	P — K R 4

A wild attempt to break
White's bind on the position; it
fails against the ensuing elegant
combination. Black had to play
25. ....B — B 1, though he
should still lose after 26.
Q — B 7.

26. P — K 6 !

Position after 26. P — K 6 !

The consequent logic of this combination is much to be admired. Black is forced to pay for the rash Pawn move which weakened his K side.

26. ......   P × B

Or 26. ....P × P; 27. B × P ch, Kt × B; 28. Q × Kt ch, K — R 2; 29. R — B 7, R — K 1; 30. Q — B 7, R — K Kt 1; 31. B — Q 4.

27. P × P ch   K — R 2
28. Q — R 4 ch   B — R 3
29. P — B 5   P — K Kt 4

If 29. ....K — Kt 2; 30. Q × B ch, K × P; 31. Q × P ch, K — K 2; 32. Q — Kt 7 ch, K — K 1; 33. P — B 6 followed by mate.

30. B × P   K — Kt 2
31. Q × B ch   Resigns

After 31. .... K × P; 32. Q — R 7 ch Black is mated in four moves.

70

THIRTEENTH ROUND, BARCELONA, 1929

Réti's Opening

White	Black
CAPABLANCA	F. D. YATES
1. Kt — K B 3	Kt — K B 3
2. P — B 4	P — K Kt 3

A very sound method of countering the slow form of Réti's system adopted by White.

3. P — Q Kt 3

This was quite a favourite type of development with Capablanca in his later period.

3. ......   B — Kt 2
4. B — Kt 2   Castles
5. P — Kt 3   P — Q 3

Solid enough; but a preferable way of treating the problem of the centre is 5. ....P — B 4.

6. B — Kt 2   Kt — B 3

Here again 6. ....P — B 4 is better, but Black has quite another system in mind. He intends to play an eventual P — K 4 and therefore wishes to get as much pressure as possible on the central black squares.

Quite a good alternative is 6. ....Q Kt — Q 2 followed by R — K 1 and P — K 4.

7. Castles   P — K 4
8. P — Q 4   Kt — Q 2

More aggressive was 8. ....P — K 5, with the possible continuation 9. Kt — K 1, R — K 1; 10.

Kt — B 2, P — Q 4 and Black stands quite well.

It would, however, be wrong for Black to abandon the centre by 8. ....P ✕ P; 9. Kt ✕ P, B — Q 2; 10. Kt — Q 2, R — K 1; 11. P — K 4 when White has a strong grip on the position. Black's actual move in the game attempts to steer a middle course between the two lines and meets with the usual unhappy fate attending such compromises.

9. P ✕ P

Simplest and best. It would be bad for White to block the centre by 9. P — Q 5, Kt — K 2; 10. P — K 4, P — K B 4 with an excellent game for Black.

9.	Kt (Q 2) ✕ P
10. Kt — B 3	R — K 1
11. Kt ✕ Kt	

It is remarkable how White, by a series of simple exchanges, increases the power and scope of his pieces; this is, in fact, one of the outstanding characteristics of Capablanca's style and one in which he was supreme amongst all great masters.

| 11. ...... | Kt ✕ Kt |

If 11. ....B ✕ Kt then 12. Q — Q 2 followed by Kt — Q 5 and White will be able to attack the weakened black squares on Black's K side.

| 12. Q — Q 2 | P — Q R 4 ? |

A weak move with the intention of laying a trap, but it only

reacts to Black's disadvantage. Better was 12. ....R — Kt 1 at once, in order to permit development of the Q Bishop.

13. Q R — B 1

Foreshadowing pressure on the Q B file and eliminating the possibility of Black's above-mentioned trap, viz. 13. ....P — R 5; 14. Kt ✕ P, Kt ✕ P !

| 13. ...... | R — Kt 1 |
| 14. P — K R 3 | |

This innocent-looking move not only limits the action of Black's minor pieces, but prepares a K side attack.

| 14. ...... | B — Q 2 |
| 15. Kt — Q 5 ! | |

White's attack is proceeding logically and harmoniously. The incidental attack on the Q R P forces Black to spend a move to defend it, and meanwhile White is able to create weaknesses on Black's K side.

| 15. ...... | P — Kt 3 |

After 15. ....B — Q B 3; 16. Q ✕ P, R — R 1; 17. Q ✕ P, R ✕ P; 18. Q ✕ Q, R ✕ Q; 19. Kt — K 7 ch (not 19. B ✕ Kt, B ✕ B; 20. P — K 3, B ✕ Kt and Black has good drawing chances owing to the Bishops of opposite colour); 19. ....K — B 1; 20. Kt ✕ B, Kt ✕ Kt; 21. B ✕ B ch, K ✕ B; 22. P — K 3 White is a Pawn up and has much the better game.

16. P — B 4	Kt — B 3
17. B × B	K × B
18. Q — Kt 2 ch	P — B 3
19. P — K Kt 4 !	

The threat of P — Kt 5 forces Black's next move, which nevertheless cannot adequately parry the onslaught of White's Pawn attack.

19.	Kt — Kt 5
20. P — Kt 5	Kt × Kt
21. P × Kt	R — Q B 1

Now the virtue of White's Rook move is fully realised; he threatened 22. Q × P ch followed by R × P.

| 22. P — K 4 ! | P — B 3 |

This leads speedily to disaster; there is, however, no really good defence for Black here. If, for example, 22. ....B — Kt 4 then 23. R — B 2, R — B 1; 24. K R — B 2, R — B 2; 25. P — Q R 4, B — Q 2 (not 25. ....B — R 3; 26. P — R 4 followed by B — R 3); 26. P — K 5, Q P × P; 27. P × P forcing the win of the Q B P.

Or, if Black tries to escape from the pin by 22. ....K — B 2, then 23. P × P, Q × P; 24. P — K 5 winning a piece; equally 22. ....R — B 1 loses because of 23. P × P ch, Q × P; 24. P — K 5, etc.

| 23. P × P | R × B P |
| 24. P × P ch | K — B 2 |

The Pawn and the game are lost, since Black cannot play 24. ....Q × P; 25. Q × Q ch, K ×

Q; 26. P — K 5 ch and White wins a piece.

25. P — K 5	R × R
26. R × R	P × P
27. P × P	Q — Kt 1

Or 27. ....B — K 3; 28. Q — B 3, K — B 1; 29. Q — B 7 and wins.

Position after 27. ....Q — Kt 1

28. Q — Q.4 !

A pretty, centralising manœuvre, especially neat when considered in conjunction with White's 30th move.

| 28. ...... | B — B 4 |

If 28. ....B — K 3; 29. R — B 6, R — Q 1; 30. Q — K B 4, R — Q 8 ch; 31. K — B 2 and Black is helpless against the threat of Q — R 6.

29. B — Q 5 ch   K — B 1

Black is mated after 29. .... B — K 3; 30. B × P ch, K × B; 31. R — B 6 ch, K — B 4; 32. Q — Kt 4 ch, K × P; 33. Q — Kt 5 ch, K — K 5; 34. R —

B 4 ch,   K — Q 6;   35.   Q —
Q 5 ch, etc.

30. Q — K B 4   R × P
31. Q — R 6 ch   K — K 1
32. P — B 7 ch   Resigns

After 32. ....K — K 2 White
would win by 33. R — B 7 ch, B
— Q 2; 34. P — B 8 = Q ch, Q
× Q; 35. R × B ch.

The whole game is a fine example of the sparkling clarity of
Capablanca's style.

71
SIXTH ROUND,
BARCELONA, 1929

*Queen's Pawn, Queen's Indian
Defence*

White	Black
M. Monticelli	Capablanca
1. P — Q 4	Kt — K B 3
2. Kt — K B 3	

Not so aggressive as 2. P —
Q B 4, since it allows Black an
immediate Q fianchetto with a
very sound game.

2. ......   P — Q Kt 3
3. P — K Kt 3

After which Black can employ
the Marienbad system, which de-
rives its name from a famous
game,   Rubinstein–Nimzovitch,
Marienbad, 1925. This method
gives Black a fine game, with excellent chances of play against
White's Q side. It is therefore
best to avoid the continuation by
playing 3. P — Q B 4.

3. ......   B — Kt 2
4. B — Kt 2   P — B 4

Taking advantage of the temporarily unguarded nature of
White's K Bishop to strike at the
centre. It is to be noted that had
White played 3. P — Q B 4 this
move would give Black a very
bad game after 5. P — Q 5.

5. P × P

Of the four alternatives at
White's disposal, the text is the
meekest and poorest.

Instead, he can play (a) 5.
Castles, P × P; 6. Kt × P, B ×
B; 7. K × B, P — Kt 3 (also
good for Black is 7. ....Kt —
B 3; 8. P — B 4, Q — B 2); 8.
P — Q B 4, B — Kt 2; 9. Kt —
Q B 3, Q — B 1; 10. P — Kt 3,
Q — Kt 2 ch; 11. P — B 3, P —
Q 4 with a level game (Capa-
blanca–Botvinnik,   Nottingham,
1936).

Or (b) 5. P — B 4, P × P; 6.
Q × P, P — Kt 3; 7. Castles, B
— Kt 2; 8. Kt — B 3, Kt — B 3;
9. Q — Q 1, Kt — Q R 4; 10. Kt
— Q 2, B × B; 11. K × B and
now Black could have obtained
an equal game by 11. ....P —
Q 4 (T. Berg–Alekhine, Kemeri,
1937).

Finally, (c) Tartakower's suggestion, 5. P — B 3, which presents an immediate 5. ....P —
Kt 3 because if 6. Q — Kt 3 with
the unpleasant threats of Kt —
K 5 and P × P, is best met by 5.
....Q — B 1.

5. ......   P × P
6. P — B 4   P — Kt 3

The Bishop is very powerfully placed on the long diagonal, since it is aided in its pressure on the centre by the Pawn in Q B 4.

7. P — Kt 3

Other continuations by White are no better, e.g. 7. Castles, B — Kt 2; 8. Kt — B 3, Castles; 9. B — K 3, P — Q 3; 10. Q — B 1, R — K 1; 11. R — Q 1, Q Kt — Q 2; 12. P — K R 3, R — Q Kt 1; or 7. Kt — B 3, B — Kt 2; 8. Castles, P — Q 3; 9. Q — B 2, Kt — B 3; 10. P — Q R 3, Castles; 11. P — K 4, P — K 4 !

7.	B — Kt 2
8. B — Kt 2	Castles
9. Castles	P — Q 3

Here Nimzovitch in the above-mentioned game at Marienbad, 1925, played 9. ....Kt — B 3; 10. Kt — B 3, P — Q R 4; 11. Q — Q 2, P — Q 3; 12. Kt — K 1, Q — Q 2. Capablanca, however, has quite another method of play in mind.

10. Kt — B 3   Kt — K 5 !

Improvement of position by exchange is a weapon requiring careful handling, since it may often degenerate into a dull drawing technique. In Capablanca's hands, however, it has a subtle power possessed by no other master.

11. Q — B 1	Kt × Kt
12. B × Kt	B × B
13. Q × B	P — Q R 4

A fine move serving a double purpose. The advance at once threatens an attack on White's Q side Pawn structure and provides for the liquidation of Black's isolated Pawn.

14. K R — Q 1   Kt — Q 2

The incautious 14. ....Kt — B 3 would lead to too many exchanges after 15. Kt — K 5, Q — B 2; 16. Kt × Kt, etc., and White's game, though still leaving something to be desired on the Q side, would have good drawing chances.

15. Q — K 3

Threatening Q — R 6 followed by Kt — Kt 5, a threat which is easily parried. As the text and the next moves show, White is obsessed with the idea of a K side attack. But the means at his disposal are not sufficient to carry this out effectively, and he would do better to seek immediate exchange by 15. Kt — K 1.

15.	K — Kt 2
16. P — K R 3	Kt — B 3
17. P — K Kt 4	P — R 3
18. Kt — K 1	Q — B 2
19. Kt — Q 3	

A more energetic and better continuation was 19. B × B, Q × B; 20. Q — B 3, Q — Kt 3; 21. P — K R 4 with some attacking chances.

| 19. ...... | B × B |
| 20. K × B | P — R 5 ! |

The timing of this minority attack is admirable. It reaches its peak of intensity just when White is planning the exchange of the last minor piece and so hoping for good drawing chances.

21. Kt — B 4   K R — Q Kt 1 !

Threatening to win a Pawn by 22. ....P × P; 23. P × P, R × R; 24. R × R, Q — Kt 2 ch.

22. P — B 3	P × P
23. P × P	R × R
24. R × R	P — K 4 !

The unfortunate Kt must now go to Q 5, with a resulting weakening of White's Pawn position.

| 25. Kt — Q 5 | Kt × Kt |
| 26. P × Kt | R — Kt 5 ! |

A beautifully accurate move which quenches any hope White may have entertained of arriving at a drawn endgame after 26. ....Q — Kt 2; 27. Q — Q 3, Q × Kt P; 28. Q × Q, R × Q; 29. R — R 6.

After the text move, however, Black's Q — Kt 2 can no longer be adequately met.

Position after 26. ....R — Kt 5 !

27. Q — Q 3   Q — Kt 2

Rightly refusing to be deflected from his plan by the immediate win of a Pawn by 27. ....R — Q 5, when White would obtain a draw by 28. Q — R 6, R × P; 29. Q — R 8, R — Q 7; 30. R — R 7, Q — Kt 3; 31. R — Kt 7, R × P ch; 32. K — Kt 3, R — Q R 7 (32. ....Q — B 3 ?; 33. R × P ch, etc.); 33. R × Q, R × Q; 34. R × P, R — Q Kt 1; 35. R — Q 5; an excellent illustration of the necessity for the utmost accuracy in finishing off a positionally won game.

| 28. Q — R 6 | Q × P |
| 29. Q — B 8 | Q — Kt 2 |

Mercilessly eliminating any chance of a White counter-attack by 29. ....R × P; 30. R — R 8 when Black's King would be in a mating net.

| 30. Q — Q 8 | Q — Kt 1 |
| 31. Q — Q 7 | |

Hoping to be able to play 32. R — R 7; which hope Black immediately dispels.

31.	R — Kt 2
32. Q — B 6	R × P
33. R — R 6	R — Kt 7

And White resigns, since the endgame is hopeless for him after 34. Q × Q P, R × P ch; 35. K — B 1, Q × Q; 36. R × Q, R — B 7; whilst if 34. K — B 2 then R — Q 7.

72

BARCELONA, 1929

English Opening

White	Black
CAPABLANCA	TORRES
1. Kt — K B 3	Kt — K B 3
2. P — B 4	P — B 4
3. P — Q 4	

Stronger than 3. Kt — B 3, as Capablanca played against Colle in the 1st Round of this tournament.

The resulting open lines are to White's advantage.

3.	P × P
4. Kt × P	P — K 4 ?

The tempo gained in development by this move is not sufficient compensation for the permanently backward Q Pawn; but neither are the alternatives very attractive.

These are (*a*) 4. ....Kt — B 3; 5. Kt — Q B 3, P — K Kt 3; 6. P — K 4 and White has transposed into the Maroczy bind against the Sicilian, which is much in his favour.

Or (*b*) 4. ....P — Q Kt 3; 5. Kt — Q B 3, B — Kt 2; 6. B — Kt 5, Kt — K 5; 7. Kt × Kt, B × Kt; 8. P — B 3, B — Kt 2; 9. P — K 4 and White completely controls the centre (Alekhine–Sämisch, Baden-Baden, 1925). Comparatively best is (*c*) 4. .... P — Q 4; 5. P × P, Kt × P; 6. P — K 4, Kt — Kt 5; 7. Q — R 4 ch, Q Kt — B 3; 8. Kt × Kt, Kt × Kt; 9. Kt — B 3, B — Q 2;

10. B — K 3, and now Black should have played 10. ....P — K Kt 3 followed by B — Kt 2, though White would still have the preferable game. Instead, he played 10. ....P — K 3; 11. R — B 1, B — Q 3; 12. B — K 2, B — K 4; 13. Castles and White's opening advantage was soon turned into a win (Oake–Müller, Folkestone, 1933).

5. Kt — Kt 5	B — Kt 5 ch

5. ....P — Q 4 cannot be played because of 6. P × P, Kt × P; 7. Q × Kt, etc.

6. B — Q 2	

Though plausible, this is not the best move, as it places White's Bishop on a poor diagonal. Correct is 6. Q Kt — B 3, Castles; 7. B — Kt 5, Kt — B 3; 8. P — K Kt 3 with a fine game for White.

6.	B × B ch ?

Missing the chance of obtaining an excellent game by 6. .... B — B 4!; 7. B — B 3, Q — Kt 3; 8. P — K 3, P — Q R 3; 9. K Kt — R 3, Kt — B 3; 10. B — Q 3, Castles; 11. Castles, P — Q 3; 12. Kt — B 2, B — K 3 (Oake–Fine, New York, 1933).

7. Q × B	

White recaptures with the Queen in order to be able to reserve his Q Kt for B 3.

.. ..	Castles
8. Q Kt — B 3	Kt — R 3

This manœuvre is too slow. Best was 8. ....Kt — B 3, though Black's backward Q Pawn would always constitute a terrible positional disadvantage.

9. P — K Kt 3   Kt — B 4
10. B — Kt 2   P — Q R 3
11. Kt — Q 6   Q — R 4

Black has evolved a laborious plan for counter-attack on the Q side. White takes advantage of Black's loss of time to complete his development and institute a strong attack on the Black King.

12. Castles K   R — Kt 1
13. K R — Q 1   P — Q Kt 4
14. P × P   P × P

White has attained an ideal position; his development is complete and he has complete mastery of the long open central lines. It is amazing how rapidly Black's position collapses.

Position after 14. ....P × P

15. Q — Kt 5   Kt — R 5 ?

Black must quietly surrender the K Pawn by 15. ....P — R 3.

After the text move, there comes disaster.

16. Kt — B 5   Kt — K 1
17. Kt — R 6 ch   K — R 1
18. Q — K 7   Resigns

73
BARCELONA, 1929

Queen's Pawn, Queen's Indian Defence

White	Black
A. Ribera	Capablanca

1. P — Q 4   Kt — K B 3
2. Kt — K B 3   P — K 3

Diverging from 2. ....P — Q Kt 3 as he played against Monticelli in this tournament in order to pursue quite another system.

3. P — B 4   P — Q Kt 3
4. Kt — B 3

Somewhat unusual; much more in favour at present is 4. P — K Kt 3 with immediate counter-fianchetto on the K side. The text move announces White's intention to indulge in fluid minor piece play rather than manœuvre on close positional lines. It is instructive to observe how Capablanca nullifies all White's attempts at attack and calmly obtains a decisive positional advantage.

4. ......   B — Kt 2
5. B — Kt 5

Or 5. Q — B 2, B — Kt 5; 6. P — Q R 3, B × Kt ch; 7. Q ×

B, Kt — K 5; 8. Q — B 2, Castles; 9. P — K Kt 3, P — K B 4;
10. B — Kt 2, Kt — B 3; 11. P
— Q Kt 4, B — K 5; 12. Q —
B 3, P — Q R 4; 13. P — Kt 5,
P — Q 3 and Black has a sound
game (Lissitzin–Kan, Moscow,
1935).

5. ......   B — K 2

Sounder than 5. ....B —
Kt 5; 6. Q — B 2, P — K R 3; 7.
B — R 4, Castles; 8. P — K 3, P
— Q 3; 9. B — Q 3, Q Kt —
Q 2; 10. Castles K, K B × Kt;
11. P × B, P — K Kt 4; 12. B
— Kt 3, Kt — R 4; 13. Kt — Q 2,
P — B 4 (Flohr–Botvinnik, Mos-
cow, 1936), and now after 14. P
— B 4, Q Kt — B 3 White could
have obtained the better game by
either 15. P — K 4 or 15. P —
Q 5 instead of B — K 2 as actu-
ally played.

6. P — K 3

6. Q — B 2 would have prevented Black's next freeing manœuvre; and then the threat of
P — K 4 would force Black to
play 6. ....P — Q 4 with an ap-
proximately level game.

6. ......   Kt — K 5!
7. B × B   Q × B
8. Kt × Kt   B × Kt
9. B — Q 3

Humbler but more solid is 9.
B — K 2, Castles; 10. Castles, P
— Q 3; 11. Kt — Q 2, B — Kt 2;
12. B — B 3 with an early draw
in sight.

9. ......   B — Kt 2
10. Castles   P — Q 3
11. R — K 1   Kt — Q 2
12. P — K 4   Castles K
13. P — K 5

Preventing P — K 4 and hoping to obtain more play for his
pieces. Its defect, however, is
that it loosens White's Pawn
structure, and against Black's
compact position little is to be
achieved by violent means. Consequently, White should have continued positionally by 13. Q —
K 2 and 14. Q R — Q 1.

13. ......   Q R — Q 1!

A strong move, with a veiled
threat in the Q file, the seriousness of which White only half
comprehends.

14. Q — K 2?

14. P × P was now necessary
in order to avoid loss in material.

14. ......   P × P

For once, Capablanca fails to
find the accurate continuation.
For now White could have saved
the Pawn by recapturing with the
Kt. Then after 15. ....Q — R 5;
16. Q — K 3 is sufficient.

15. P × P ?   Kt — B 4

By this and his next few moves
Black obtains control of the Q
file and with it the game.

16. B — B 2   B × Kt
17. Q × B   R — Q 7
18. Q — B 3   K R — Q 1

Position after 18. ....K R — Q 1

White is faced with the problem of finding a reasonably good continuation. The move he actually makes leads to the loss of a Pawn; if he plays 19. P — Q Kt 4 then Q — R 5!; 20. P — Kt 3, Q — Q 5; 21. Q × Q, R (Q 1) × Q; 22. Q R — Q 1 (22. B × P ch, K × B; 23. P × Kt, R × Q B P; 24. P × P, R P × P; 25. Q R — B 1, R (B 5) — B 7 leads to a lost Rook and Pawn ending for White); 22. ....R × R; 23. R × R, R × R ch; 24. B × R, Kt — Q 6 and a Pawn is lost.

Or if 19. P — K Kt 3 then Q — Q 2; 20. P — Q Kt 4, Q — Q 5 with variations similar to the above.

In actual fact, since there is no adequate means of challenging Black on the Q file White is lost.

19. Q R — Q 1   Kt — K 5 !
20. Q — K 3

A Pawn is equally lost by 20. Q — Q Kt 3, Q — Q B 4; 21. Q — K 3, Q × B P, etc.

20. ......   R × B
21. Q × Kt   R × Kt P

The rest is a matter of technique — but Capablanca's technique, being impeccable, is interesting and instructive.

22. P—Q R 3   R (Kt 7)—Q 7
23. R × R   R × R
24. P — R 3

Or 24. Q — R 8 ch, Q — Q 1; 25. Q × P, P — R 3; 26. P — R 3, Q — Q 5, etc.

24. ......   P — Q B 4
25. R — K 3   R — Q 5
26. Q — R 8 ch   R — Q 1
27. Q — B 3   Q — Q 2

It is pleasing to observe how Black preserves control of the Q file throughout the game. The exploitation of this control is masterly in the extreme.

28. K — R 2   Q — Q 5
29. R — K 4   Q — Q 6
30. Q — Kt 4   P — K R 3

Black is in no hurry to take the Pawn, his positional superiority being such that he can afford to spend a move to safeguard his King's position.

31. R — K 3   Q — Q 5
32. Q — K 2   Q — Q 8
33. Q — Kt 2   Q — Q 7
34. Q — B 3

After 34. Q × Q, R × Q; 35. K — Kt 3, R — B 7 White must lose either the Q R or the Q B Pawn.

34. ......   Q × P
and White resigned.

CHAPTER EIGHT

Prelude to Retirement

As though losing heart through failure to bring about a return match for the World Championship, Capablanca's appearance in tournaments now became more and more rare until, in 1931, he retired from active chess for some years. Consequently, the games from this pre-retirement phase are not of such high quality as of former years. Errors become more frequent and are present even in his best games; whilst the old, calm, clear harmonious style is no longer to be seen except for brief moments.

We have therefore limited our choice to comparatively few games from this period. The two taken from the Hastings Tournament are each models in their way; Game No. 74 demonstrates how to take advantage of an opponent's lack of aggressive spirit in the most economical way, and the next game is a study in the utilisation of advantage in space. Both the games given from the New York Tournament have most piquant finishes. The two games selected from the match *v.* Euwe suffer from the emergence of the faults and blunders mentioned above, and these errors will mar the purist's enjoyment of them as model games. They are, nevertheless, full of interesting moments and fine positional conceptions; the drawn game being an especially hard-fought struggle in which Capablanca has his opponent to thank for being let off on at least two occasions, whilst the analysts have revelled in the opportunities provided for showing these two great masters where they missed their way.

As a *bonne bouche*, we give a delightful little exhibition game in the old style in which H. Steiner falls victim to a very fine mating combination.

HASTINGS, 1930–31

	Euwe	Capablanca	Sultan Khan	Michell	Yates	Thomas	Winter	Vera Menchik	Tylor	Colle	
1 Euwe	–	½	1	1	1	½	1	0	1	1	7
2 Capablanca	½	–	0	½	1	½	1	1	1	1	6½
3 Sultan Khan	0	1	–	1	½	1	0	1	½	1	6
4 Michell	0	½	0	–	1	1	½	1	0	1	5
5 Yates	0	0	½	0	–	1	1	½	1	½	4½
6 Thomas	½	½	0	0	0	–	1	0	1	1	4
7 Winter	0	0	1	½	0	0	–	1	½	½	3½
8 Vera Menchik	1	0	0	0	½	1	0	–	½	0	3
9 Tylor	0	0	½	1	0	0	½	½	–	½	3
10 Colle	0	0	0	0	½	0	½	1	½	–	2½

NEW YORK, 1931

	Capablanca	Kashdan	Kevitz	Horowitz	Kupchik	Steiner	Santasiere	Turover	Oake	Lasker	Marshall	Fox	
1 Capablanca	–	½	1	1	1	½	1	1	1	1	1	1	10
2 Kashdan	½	–	1	1	½	½	1	½	½	1	1	1	8½
3 Kevitz	0	0	–	0	1	½	1	½	1	1	1	1	7
4 Horowitz	0	0	1	–	½	½	0	1	1	0	1	½	5½
5 Kupchik	0	½	0	½	–	½	0	1	½	½	1	1	5½
6 Steiner	½	½	½	½	½	–	0	1	½	0	½	1	5½
7 Santasiere	0	0	0	1	1	1	–	0	0	0	1	1	5
8 Turover	0	½	½	0	0	0	1	–	1	1	½	0	4½
9 Oake	0	½	0	0	½	½	1	0	–	½	0	1	4
10 Lasker	0	0	0	1	½	1	1	0	½	–	0	0	4
11 Marshall	0	0	0	0	0	½	0	½	1	1	–	1	4
12 Fox	0	0	0	½	0	0	0	1	0	1	0	–	2½

74
HASTINGS, 1930–1

*Queen's Pawn, Queen's Indian
Defence*

White	Black
Miss V. Menchik	Capablanca
1. P — Q 4	Kt — K B 3
2. Kt — K B 3	P — Q Kt 3
3. P — K 3	B — Kt 2
4. B — Q 3	P — B 4
5. Castles	Kt — B 3
6. P — B 3	P — K 3
7. Kt — K 5	

7. Q Kt — Q 2 leads into the normal lines of the Colle formation to which White's opening moves had seemed to be tending. For a fine example of how to deal with this variation, see Game No. 65, in which Capablanca was opposed by the master after whom the opening was named. The text move is a signpost as to White's intentions throughout the game; she is determined to force off as many pieces as possible in the hope of obtaining the draw. This is quite the wrong policy against Capablanca, who excelled in obtaining the advantage by continual exchanges.

7.	P — Q 3
8. Kt × Kt	B × Kt
9. Q — K 2	

Played, not with any idea of advancing in the centre, but solely in order to exchange another piece.

| 9. ...... | B — K 2 |
| 10. B — Kt 5 | |

Logical and noncommittal enough, but White might have tried to put some life into the game by 10. P — K 4.

10.	Q — Q 2
11. B × B	Q × B
12. Kt — Q 2	Castles K
13. P × P	

A miserable decision, but 13. P — K 4 is no longer good on account of 13. ....P × P; 14. P × P, Q — B 7, and 13. Q — B 3 in order to pursue still further the exchanging strategy is foiled by 13. ....P — Q 4.

| 13. ...... | Q P × P |
| 14. P — K 4 | |

White must attempt to develop her Q Bishop; hence the text move, 14. Q — B 3, Q × Q; 15. Kt × Q, Q R — Q 1 would leave Black in command of the Q file.

| 14. ...... | Q R — Q 1 |
| 15. P — K 5 | |

This advance is not to be recommended; its chief result is a weakness on the white squares. A solid method of continuing was 14. P — B 3 and if 14. ....P — Q Kt 4; 15. Kt — Kt 3 followed by 16. B — K 3.

15.	Kt — Q 4
16. Kt — B 3	R — Q 2
17. R — Q 1	K R — Q 1
18. B — Q 2	

A poor square to develop the Q Bishop, but 18. B — K 3, Kt × B; 19. R × R, Q × R leaves

Black in control of the Q file and 18. B — Kt 5, B × B; 19. Kt × B, Kt — B 5 wins for Black.

18. ...... P — Q Kt 4 !

A fine positional move which foreshadows the method of victory; Black's Kt is to be given an outpost on either Q B 5 or Q R 5 from which it will threaten the somewhat weakened white Q side.

19. K — B 1   Kt — Kt 3
20. B — B 4

White has succeeded, at any rate, in contesting Black's pressure on the Q file, but it soon becomes apparent that this move is merely part of White's faulty zeal to exchange.

20. ...... P — K R 3

A strong move of semi-waiting tendencies which also fills the purposes of providing an escape square for the King if necessary and projecting a possible attack by P — K Kt 4.

21. R × R

This and her next move are positively bad. White has nothing to gain by further exchanges, but should play simply B — Kt 3.

21. ...... R × R
22. R — Q 1   R × R ch
23. Q × R   Q — K 5

This move is curiously decisive; White must lose a Pawn.

Position after 23. ....Q — K 5

24. B — Kt 3

If 24. B — K 3 or B — Q 2, Kt — B 5 wins a Pawn, and if 24. B — B 1, Q — B 5 ch; 25. Q — K 2, Q × R P; 26. Q × P ? Q — Kt 8 winning a piece.

24. ...... Q — B 5 ch
25. Q — K 2   Q × Q ch
26. K × Q   Kt — R 5

Owing to White's faulty strategy, her Q side is quite helpless; the win is now a matter of technique.

27. K — Q 2   Kt × Kt P
28. K — B 2   Kt — B 5
29. Kt — Q 2   Kt × Kt
30. K × Kt   P — B 5
31. B — B 4

White recentralises the Bishop, only to find this piece runs into more trouble in the process; however, the game has long been past saving.

31. ...... P — R 3

A bad blunder would be 31. ....B — Kt 4; 32. B × B, P ×

B; 33. K — K 3, K — B 1; 34. K
— Q 4, K — K 2; 35. K — B 5,
etc.

32.	B — K 3	K — B 1
33.	B — Kt 6	K — K 1
34.	K — K 3	K — Q 2
35.	K — Q 4	K — B 3
36.	B — R 7	P — B 4
37.	P — Q R 4	

A desperate move that accelerates the end; 37. P × P e.p., B
× P ch wins a Pawn, and after
other moves Black eventually
wins by zugzwang.

37.	......	P — Kt 3

37. ....P × P; 38. K × P, P
— R 6 also wins; the text is a
more cold-blooded method.

38.	P — B 4	P — K R 4
39.	P × P ch	K × P
40.	P — Kt 3	P — R 4
41.	K — K 3	B — B 4 ch
42.	B × B	K × B

Resigns; an interesting example of how to obtain a whole
point from an opponent whose
heart is set on the draw.

75
HASTINGS, 1930-1

Queen's Gambit Declined

White	Black
CAPABLANCA	T. H. TYLOR
1. P — Q 4	P — Q 4
2. P — Q B 4	P — K 3
3. Kt — K B 3	Kt — K B 3
4. B — Kt 5	P — B 3

This move is not directly bad,
but faulty in so far as it commits

Black to one line of play too early
in the game, and, more important
still, leads to the type of position
of which Capablanca was the
complete master.

5.	Q Kt — Q 2

The move with which Capa-
blanca won his famous game
against Alekhine at St. Petersburg, 1913 (see Game No. 13).

5.	......	Q Kt — Q 2
6.	P — K 3	B — K 2
7.	B — Q 3	Castles
8.	Castles	P × P

Playing into White's hands;
the correct move here is 8. ....
P — B 4, rectifying to some extent the error on the 4th move.

9.	Kt × P

It is instructive to watch how
from now on White's command of
the board increases until Black is
left with very little space in
which to manœuvre.

9.	......	Kt — Q 4
10.	B × B	Kt × B
11.	R — B 1	Kt — Kt 3
12.	B × Kt	

This is the type of position in
which Kts, having such excellent
future outposts as K 5 and Q B 5,
are superior to the Bishops.

12.	......	R P × B
13.	P — K 4	

Not so much with the object of
playing P — K 5 followed by Kt
— Q 6, but in order to deprive
Black's Kt of the square Q 4.

13.	......	Kt — Kt 3

On this poor post the Kt remains out of the game for a considerable period, but if 13. .... Kt — B 3; 14. Q — K 2, followed by 15. K R — Q 1 gives White an ideal attacking position.

14. Kt (B 4) — K 5   B — Q 2
15. Q — Q 2   B — K 1

Black is intent on developing this Bishop via the diagonal K 1 — K R 4, but he would have done better to prevent White's next space-seizing manœuvre by Q — K 2.

16. Q — Kt 4 !   P — B 3
17. Kt — Q 3   P — Kt 4
18. Kt — B 5   Q — K 2
19. P — K R 3

Anticipating Black's B — K R 4 and preparing to drive it back by P — K Kt 4.

19. ......   B — R 4
20. Q — Kt 3   K R — K 1

If 20. ....B — B 2 White plays 21. Q — K 3.

21. K R — K 1

The purpose of this positional move is to build up a hidden attack on Black's K 3.

21. ......   Q R — Q 1

Threatening to win a Pawn by B × Kt and so forcing White's hand.

22. P — Kt 4   B — Kt 3
23. P — Q R 4   R — Kt 1
24. Q — K 3

There is no point in playing P — R 5, since Black will have to play Kt — Q 2 eventually in order to gain breathing space.

24. ......   Kt — Q 2
25. Kt — Q 3

It is hackneyed enough, but none the less true, to say that exchange only benefits the more constricted position.

25. ......   Q R — Q 1
26. K — Kt 2   Kt — B 1
27. R — K R 1

Suddenly a fresh menace arises on the K side; White threatens to gain an overwhelming K side attack by P — K R 4 followed by an eventual Q — K R 3.

27. ......   Q — Q 3

So that now if 28. P — K R 4, P × P and White will have to retake with the Rook owing to the threat on the Q Pawn.

28. Q R — Q 1   P — K B 4

Position after 28. ....P — K B 4

A superficially attractive move which results in a rapid break up; Black should have tried 28. .... K — B 2.

29. Kt (Q 3 — K 5   P × K P

If 29. ....P — B 5; 30. Q — K 2, Q — K 2; 31. P — R 4 with a very strong attack.

30. Kt × Kt P   P — B 4

Desperation; if 30. .... Q — Q 4; 31. Q — B 4, P — K 6 dis ch; 32. P — B 3 and there is no defence against the threatened Kt × B.

31. Q — B 4!   P × P

If 31. ....Q — K 2 White can play simply 32. P × P followed by an eventual Kt × K P winning two Pawns.

32. Kt × B   Q × Q
33. Kt × Q   P — K 4
34. Kt — K 2   Resigns

76
SECOND ROUND, NEW YORK, 1931

Réti's Opening

White	Black
KEVITZ	CAPABLANCA
1. Kt — K B 3	P — Q 4
2. P — B 4	P — Q B 3
3. P — Q Kt 3	B — B 4
4. B — Kt 2	Kt — B 3
5. P — Q 3	P — K 3
6. P — Kt 3	Q Kt — Q 2
7. B — Kt 2	B — Q 3

An interesting reversal of rôles; Capablanca is confronted with a system of play much fa-

voured by himself as first player, and indeed in the 5th Round of this tournament his first 13 moves against Santasiere were identical with those employed by Kevitz here. Very similar too is the opening of his game against Lilienthal, Moscow, 1936; here the latter unnecessarily played 7. .... P — K R 3.

8. Q Kt — Q 2   Q — K 2
9. Castles   Castles K
10. R — K 1

Stronger than 10. R — B 1, since Black after 10. ....P — K 4 will eventually play P — Q R 4 threatening P — R 5, which threat can now be met by P — Q R 3 for White, since the Q Rook is still on R 1.

10. ......   P — K 4
11. P × P!

And not 11. Kt — R 4, B — K 3; 12. P — K 4, P — Q 5 with a fine game for Black.

11. ......   P × P
12. P — K 4!

White is playing the opening with considerable skill; Black must exchange Pawns, since an opening up of the K file will react to his disadvantage with the Queen *vis-à-vis* White's K Rook.

12. ......   P × P
13. P × P   B — K 3
14. Q — K 2

In his game against Santasiere, Capablanca played 14. Kt — R 4 with advantage, but the text move is also very good. It threatens Kt — B 4 when Black has to exchange Bishop for Kt and so give White the marked positional advantage of two Bishops.

14.	Q R — B 1
15. Kt — B 1	B — Q R 6

A dubious sacrifice of a Pawn; the resulting play Black obtains on the Q side should not have been full compensation for the Pawn lost. Best is 15. ....K R — Q 1 when White would have to proceed more slowly with some such attack as P — K R 3, P — K Kt 4 and Kt — Kt 3.

16. Kt × P

And not 16. B × P, Kt × B; 17. Kt × Kt, B — Q Kt 5; 18. K R — B 1, B — B 6, etc.

16.	B × B
17. Q × B	Kt × Kt
18. Q × Kt	Q — R 6

The dust of the exchanges having cleared away, one now has leisure to observe that White is a solid Pawn to the good, with a slight weakness on the Q side. That Black manages to extract sufficient compensating attack from this circumstance is indeed remarkable; he is, however, aided by White's rather feeble and purposeless play hereabouts.

19. Kt — K 3

White must prevent R — B 7.

19.	Kt — Kt 5
20. Kt × Kt	B × Kt
21. P — R 3	B — K 3
22. R — K 2	K R — Q 1
23. Q — Kt 2	

White, now and on the next move, is in too great a haste to offer exchanges. By 23. K — R 2 followed by 24. P — B 4 and P — B 5 he would have not only maintained but increased his advantage. Timidity is out of place when one is a Pawn up with an excellent position.

23.	Q — B 4
24. R — Q 2	R × R
25. Q × R	P — Q Kt 3

This innocent little move is the forerunner of a very powerful Q side attack.

26. R — Q 1	P — Kt 3
27. K — R 2	P — Q R 4!

The present phase of the game is very instructive; with deceptively easy elegance, Black is building an attack out of the straw provided by White.

28. Q — K 2

Otherwise Black will play Q — B 7 followed by P — Q Kt 4 and P — R 5.

28.	P — Q Kt 4
29. P — B 4	P — R 5
30. P × P	P × P

This advanced Pawn is the secret of the violence of Black's attack, since when it reaches R 6, in unison with his major pieces, it will provide an attack on White's Q R 2 followed by queening threats.

31. R — Q 2

This move is not sufficient to hold the game. White must now

try the desperate fling 31. P —
B 5 sacrificing a Pawn, but freeing a diagonal for his Bishop and
breaking up Black's K side.

31. ......   P — R 6 !
32. P — Kt 4

P — B 5 was still his best
chance of saving the game,
though rather a remote one now.
There now occurs a fascinating
and surprising finish.

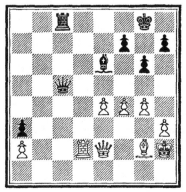

Position after 32. P — Kt 4

32. ......   P — Kt 4 !

The point of this move is that
by threatening to open the diagonal Q Kt 1 — K R 7 it deprives
the White King of its only safe
post on K R 2, and this threat is
intimately bound up with the
presence of a Black Pawn on
Q R 6, as will soon become evident.

33. Q — B 2

For if either 33. P — B 5 or
P × P then 33. ....Q — K 4 ch;
34. K — Kt 1 (or 34. K — R 1,
R — B 8 ch; 35. R — Q 1, Q —

Kt 7; 36. Q — K 1, R — B 7; 37.
B — B 1, B — B 5, etc.); 34.
....R — B 8 ch; 35. R — Q 1
(or 35. B — B 1, B — B 5); 35.
....Q — Q 5 ch. The violence of
the whole attack is truly exceptional in view of the paucity of
material.

33. ......   Q × Q
34. R × Q   P × P
35. R — B 3

Since after 35. R × P, B ×
R P Black's Rook's Pawn cannot
be stopped.

35. ......   R — R 1
36. R — B 2

White now fondly imagines he
has stemmed the attack, but
Black has in store a potent move
that makes the game resemble an
endgame study.

36. ......   P — B 6 !

Very pretty indeed; 37. B × P
cannot be played because of 37.
....R — Kt 1 followed by R —
Kt 7.

37. B — B 1   R — Kt 1
38. R × P   R — Kt 7 ch
39. K — Kt 3   R × P
40. R — B 3   R — R 8

Resigns, there being no way to
stop the Q R P from queening —
a very interesting game with a
fresh and original finish.

77

NINTH ROUND,
NEW YORK, 1931

Queen's Pawn, Queen's Indian
Defence

White	Black
F. MARSHALL	CAPABLANCA
1. Kt — K B 3	Kt — K B 3
2. P — Q 4	P — K 3
3. P — B 4	P — Q Kt 3
4. P — K Kt 3	B — Kt 2
5. B — Kt 2	B — Kt 5 ch
6. B — Q 2	B × B ch
7. Q Kt × B	

Not so good as 7. Q × B, as Euwe played in Game No. 79. The Kt should be reserved for its better post on Q B 3 in order to be able to reply P — Q 5 in answer to an eventual P — Q B 4 by Black.

| 7. ...... | Castles |
| 8. Castles | |

A more vigorous continuation is 8. Q — B 2 as in the game, Sacconi–Colle, Meran, 1926, which ran: 8. .... P — B 4; 9. P — K 4, P — Q 3; 10. Castles K, Kt — B 3; 11. P — Q 5, Kt — Q 5; 12. Kt × Kt, P × Kt; 13. P — K R 3, P — K 4; 14. P — B 4 with chances about equal.

| 8. ...... | P — B 4 |

The freeing move; from now on Black rapidly outplays his opponent, making especial use of his control of the black squares.

| 9. P × P | P × P |
| 10. R — B 1 | |

A routine move which is quite useless here. Against Nimzovitch at Berlin, 1927, Bogoljuboff played 10. Q — B 2, Q — B 2; 11. Q R — Q 1, P — K R 3; 12. P — Q R 3, Kt — B 3 and though Black's position is satisfactory enough, White's game lacks many of the defects of Marshall's.

| 10. ...... | Q — B 2 |

Already Black has the upper hand and is planning to exert pressure on the Q side. If White now plays Q — B 2 followed by P — K 4, Black will be able to establish a Kt on Q 5; such are the evil consequences of a momentary spell of mechanical thinking, as evidenced by White's 10th move.

| 11. Kt — Kt 3 ? | |

And this poor move puts the Kt right out of play. He might have tried 11. P — K 3 followed by Q — K 2 and K R — Q 1.

11.	P — Q 3
12. Q — Q 2	Kt — B 3
13. K R — Q 1	K R — Q 1
14. Kt — R 4	

White's handling of his Knights in this game is distinctly unfortunate. They seem fated to wander to the worst squares. Marshall hopes to create some sort of K side attack, but he is never allowed time for this. Heroic methods of reorganisation are now called for, and he should have recentralised his Q Kt by Kt — R 1 — B 2 — K 3.

14. ......   P — Q R 4 !

Black profits by the position of White's Kt and conducts his Q side attack with gain of tempo.

15. P — R 4

A blunder, after which the game is already past saving. It gives Black's Kt the fine square Q Kt 5 as an outpost and seriously weakens the Q side Pawn structure. The Kt manœuvre given above was still White's best course.

15.	Q R — Kt 1
16. R — B 3	B — R 1
17. P — R 3	

As will be seen later, this is part of a plan for a K side attack that never is allowed to mature. White, however, now has no reasonably good course. If, for example, 17. Kt — R 1, R — Kt 5! and such moves as R — Q 3 have no point, owing to the hanging nature of White's Q Kt.

17.	Kt — Q Kt 5
18. B × B	R × B
19. Q — B 4	Q — B 3 !

This attack on the Q R P admits of no parrying. White hopes to recoup himself for the loss of the Pawn by winning the Q P, but Capablanca has a combination in store to deal with this.

20. R — B 3

Intending an attack on the K B P by P — Kt 4 — Kt 5, an attacking player like Marshall would have shuddered at the thought of 20. R — R 1, and in fact this would have allowed Black to increase his command of the centre by 20. ....P — Q 4 followed by P — Q 5.

20. ......   R — Q 2

Meeting White's eventual threat and also an essential part of the winning combination.

21. P — Kt 4   Q × P
22. R × P

Position after 22. R × P

22. ......   Q Kt — Q 4 !

A neat little combination, winning a Pawn by force. The full import of his 20th move is now apparent; had the Rook been on Q 1, White would have been able to play R × R ch. As it is, the Queen has to leave the Q B P to its fate.

23. Q — K 5	R × R
24. Q × R	Kt — K 5
25. Q — K 5	Q × P

Not only is Black a Pawn up, but his Q side attack still persists; it is a pleasure to observe with what neat logic Capablanca terminates the game.

26. R — Q 3	P — R 5
27. P — B 3	K Kt — B 3
28. Kt — Q 2	Q — B 8 ch
29. K — B 2	P — R 3

A necessary precaution, since the Rook may have to leave the back rank.

| 30. P — B 4 | P — B 5 |
| 31. R — Q 4 | P — B 6! |

A terrible mistake would be 31. ....Q × P ?; 32. R × Kt.

32. P × P	P — R 6
33. P — Kt 5	P — R 7
34. Kt — Kt 3	Q × P
35. P × Kt	Q × Kt
36. R — Q 1	Q × R

Resigns; the final position is most amusing, with Black's Q side attack at its culminating point and White's counterpart on the K side having just passed its embryonic stage.

78
NINTH MATCH GAME, AMSTERDAM, 1931

Queen's Gambit Declined, Slav Defence

White	Black
CAPABLANCA	M. EUWE
1. P — Q 4	P — Q 4
2. Kt — K B 3	Kt — K B 3
3. P — Q B 4	P — B 3
4. Kt — B 3	P × P
5. P — Q R 4	B — B 4
6. Kt — K 5	Q Kt — Q 2
7. Kt × P (B 4)	Q — B 2
8. P — K Kt 3	P — K 4
9. P × P	Kt × P
10. B — B 4	K Kt — Q 2
11. B — Kt 2	

As regards the opening, see Game No. 67, *v.* Brinckmann, which was identical with this game up to Black's 11th move. The move Black plays is inferior to P — B 3, as Brinckmann played.

11.	B — K 3
12. Kt × Kt	Kt × Kt
13. Castles	Q — R 4

Better is 13. ....B — K 2 at once.

| 14. Kt — K 4 | R — Q 1 |
| 15. Q — B 2 | B — K 2 |

And this allows White to play an interesting and surprising combination. Black feared 14. Kt — Kt 5, but without justification, for he could have safely played 15. ....B — Q Kt 5; 16. Kt — Kt 5, B — Q B 1; 17. Q — K 4, B — Q 3; 18. K R — Q 1, P — B 3. 19. Kt × P would now be a mistake because of 19. ....K — B 2.

Position after 15. ....B — K 2

16. P — Q Kt 4 !

A fine diversionary Pawn sacrifice which Black must accept.

16. ......   B × P

Black loses at least a Pawn after 16. ....Q — B 2; 17. Kt — B 5, B — Q B 1 (17. ....B × Kt; 18. Q × B, P — B 3; 19. P — Kt 5, etc.); 18. Q — K 4, P — B 3; 19. Kt — Q 3, B — Q 3; 20. P — Kt 5, P — Q B 4; 21. Q R — B 1, P — Q Kt 3; 22. B × Kt, P × B; 23. P — B 4, etc.

17. Q — Kt 2   P — B 3
18. K R — Kt 1 ?

An unfortunate move, lacking in precision. Correct was 18. Q R — Kt 1, B — K 2; 19. B × Kt, P × B (or 19. ....Q × B; 20. Q × Q, P × Q; 21. R × P winning); 20. Q × Kt P, B — Q 4; 21. K R — Q 1, and now Black has no satisfactory move, e.g. 21. ....K — B 2; 22. Kt — Kt 5 ch, K — B 3; 23. B × B, P × B; 24. R — Kt 5, Q × P; 25. R (K 1) × P, R × R; 26. R × R, P — K R 3; 27. Kt — B 3, P — K 5; 28. Kt — Q 4 and wins.

The defect of the text is that it allows Black to play R — Q 8 ch at the appropriate moment, winning the Queen for Rook and minor piece.

18. ......   Castles ?

Black in his turn misses the most energetic continuation, which was 18. ....Kt — B 5!, and now if 19. Kt × P ch, K — B 2!; 20. Q × B, R — Q 8 ch; 21. R × R, Q × Q; 22. Kt — K 4, P —

K R 3; 23. Q R — Kt 1, Q — K 2; 24. Kt — Q 6 ch, Kt × Kt; 25. B × Kt, Q — Q 2; 26. B — K 5, Q — B 1 and Black, having weathered the storm, should win easily enough.

Once this chance has been neglected, White hastens to remove the offending Kt.

19. B × Kt   P × B
20. Kt — Kt 5   B — B 6

The alternative is 20. ....B — B 2 when, however, White can win by 21. B — K 4!, P — K Kt 3 (or 21. ....B — B 6; 22. B × P ch followed by Q × Kt P); 22. Kt × B, either K or R × Kt; 23. B — B 2, etc.

21. Q — B 2   B — B 4
22. B — K 4!   P — K Kt 3

Position after 22. ....P — K Kt 3

Black is quite without a saving move. If 22. ....B × R; 23. B × B, B — Q 5; 24. B — K 6 ch, etc. If 22. ....P — K R 3; 23. B × B, P × Kt; 24. R — R 3, B — Q 5; 25. P —

Kt 4, R — B 3; 26. R — R 3, R
— R 3; 27. R × R, P × R; 28.
B — K 6 ch, K — R 1; 29. Q —
Kt 6 and wins. And, finally, if 22.
....B × B; 23. Q × B, P —
K Kt 3; 24. Q — B 4 ch, K —
R 1; 25. R × P.

23.	Q — R 2 ch	K — Kt 2
24.	R × P ch	R — Q 2
25.	Q R — Kt 1	Q — R 3
26.	Q — Kt 3	

Rather a quicker win resulted
after 26. R × R ch, B × R; 27.
Q — R 3 winning a clear piece.

26. ......   R × R

Black is forced to exchange into an endgame that is without
hope; for if 26. ....B — Q 5;
27. R × R ch, B × R; 28. Q —
Kt 7, Q × Q; 29. R × Q winning
a piece.

27.	Q × R ch	Q × Q
28.	R × Q ch	K — Kt 1
29.	B × P	R — Q 1
30.	R × Q R P	R — Q 3
31.	B — K 4	B — Q 2
32.	P — K R 4	B — Q 4
33.	R — R 8 ch	K — Kt 2
34.	P — K 3	B — B 6
35.	B — B 3	Resigns

Black cannot prevent 36. Kt —
K 4, for if 35. ....B — B 4; 36.
P — Kt 4, B — Kt 8; 37. R —
R 7 ch, etc.

79

EIGHTH MATCH GAME, AMSTERDAM, 1931

Queen's Pawn, Queen's Indian Defence

White	Black
M. Euwe	Capablanca
1. P — Q 4	Kt — K B 3
2. P — Q B 4	P — K 3
3. Kt — K B 3	P — Q Kt 3
4. P — K Kt 3	B — Kt 2
5. B — Kt 2	B — Kt 5 ch

The other main line of play,
5. ....B — K 2, is safe and solid enough for Black.

6. B — Q 2   B × B ch

Probably the best of the three
alternatives here. 6. ....Q —
K 2; 7. Castles, B × B; 8. Q ×
B, Castles; 9. R — K 1 sets
Black some very awkward prob-
lems to solve. If he plays 9. ....
P — Q 4 as in the match game,
Euwe–Spielmann, 1932, then 10.
Kt — K 5, Kt — K 5; 11. Q —
B 2, P — K B 3; 12. P × P, P
× P; 13. Kt — Q 3 followed by
Q Kt — Q 2 and Q R — B 1 with
a fine game; whilst after 9. ....
P — Q 3; 10. Kt — B 3, Q Kt —
Q 2; 11. Q — B 2 he cannot play
11. ....P — K 4 because of 12.
P × P, P × P; 13. Kt × P, Kt
× Kt; 14. B × B, Q R — Kt 1;
15. Kt — Q 5 winning a Pawn.

6. ....B — K 2, as Alekhine
tried in his match against Euwe
in 1937, leads to a bad game after
7. Kt — B 3, Kt — K 5; 8. Castles, Castles; 9. P — Q 5, Kt ×

B; 10. Kt × Kt, Q — B 1; 11.
P — K 4.

7. Q × B

Stronger than 7. Q Kt × B,
since this Kt is more powerfully
placed on Q B 3.

7. ......　　Castles

If Black defers Castling and
plays 7. ....P — Q 3; 8. Kt —
B 3, Kt — K 5, then White gets
the advantage by 9. Q — B 4!

8. Kt — B 3　　Kt — K 5

A risky move owing to the
latent pin on Black's Q Bishop.
Black can get a solid, if some-
what constricted, position by 8.
....P — Q 3; 9. Q — B 2, Q —
K 2; 10. Castles K, Q Kt — Q 2;
11. P — K 4, Q R — B 1; 12.
K R — K 1, P — K 4; 13. Q R
— Q 1, P — B 3 (Reshevsky-
Keres, Semmering, 1937).

9. Q — B 2　　Kt × Kt

Now Black loses the exchange,
but is not without certain compensations. However, these should
not prove sufficient to save the
game.

Black is committed to this sacrificial line, since 9. ....P —
Q 4; 10. Kt — K 5 would be very
bad for him, whilst 9. ....P —
K B 4, as Flohr played in his
match against Euwe in 1932,
gives White a positional win
after 10. Kt — K 5, P — Q 4; 11.
P × P, P × P; 12. Castles K, Kt
— Q 2; 13. P — B 4, Q Kt —

B 3; 14. Q R — B 1 owing to the
strong pressure on the Q B file.

10. Kt — Kt 5

Position after 10. Kt — Kt 5

10. ......　　Kt — K 5

And not 10. ....Q × Kt; 11.
B × B, Kt × K P; 12. Q × Kt,
Kt — B 3; 13. B × R when Black
receives no compensation at all
for the loss of the exchange.

11. B × Kt	B × B
12. Q × B	Q × Kt
13. Q × R	Kt — B 3
14. Q — Kt 7	Kt × P

Better than 14. ....Q —
R 4 ch; 15. K — B 1, since Black
can now establish his Kt in the
centre with the threat of Kt —
B 7 ch.

15. Q R — Q 1

And not 15. Q — K 4, Q —
R 4 ch; 16. K — B 1, Kt — Kt 6
followed by 17. ....Kt — Q 7 ch.
Better than the text, however, is
15. Castles, Kt × P ch; 16. K —
Kt 2, P — K B 4; 17. P — B 4
with good winning chances.

15. ......   Q — K 4

This blunt threat is easily parried; better is 15. ....P — Q B 4, as Capablanca played in the 10th match game with the continuation 16. P — K 3, Kt — B 7 ch; 17. K — Q 2, Q — B 4; 18. Q — Kt 2, Kt — Kt 5; 19. P — K 4, Q — B 3; 20. K — B 1, Kt × P ch; 21. K — Kt 1, Kt — Kt 5; 22. R × P, Kt — B 3; 23. P — B 4, P — K 4 and Black established a Kt on Q 5 with an early draw.

16. P — K 3   Kt — B 7 ch
17. K — K 2

If 17. K — B 1, P — Q 4; 18. P × P, Q — K 5; 19. R — Kt 1, Kt × P ch; 20. P × Kt, Q — B 6 ch; 21. K — K 1, Q × K P ch with a draw by perpetual check.

17. ......   P — Q 4

Much better than 17. ....Q × Q Kt P; 18. R — Q 2, Q × P; 19. Q × B P, Q — R 5; 20. R — Q B 1, Kt — Kt 5; 21. R × P with a won game for White.

18. R — Q 2

The position of White's King is precarious after 18. P × P, Q — R 4 ch; 19. P — B 3, Q — K 4; 20. R — Q 3, Q × Q Kt P.

18. ......   Q × Q Kt P
19. P × P

Necessary, since 19. Q × B P, P — Q 5!; 20. K R — Q 1, P — K 4! would give Black strong winning chances.

19. ......   Q — Kt 4 ch

It is now White's Q Pawn that has to be watched, for if 19. .... Q × P; 20. Q × B P, Q — R 3 ch; 21. K — B 3, R — B 1; 22. P — Q 6! winning.

20. K — B 3   Kt — Kt 5
21. R — Q B 1

This somewhat elaborate move should also win, but there is a simpler continuation in 21. Q × B P, Kt × Q P; 22. Q — K 5! (and not 22. Q × R P, Kt × P followed by perpetual check).

21. ......   Q — R 4
22. P — Q 6!

The best way of obtaining play for White's Rooks. 22. R × P would give Black a kind of pendulum attack on the Rooks by 22. ....Kt × Q P; 23. R (B 7) — B 2, Kt — Kt 5, etc., and Black gets a strong K side attack by 22. Q × B P, Kt × Q P; 23. Q — B 2, Kt — Kt 5; 24. Q — B 4, Kt — B 3; 25. Q — B 3, Q — R 4 ch; 26. K — Kt 2, Kt — K 4.

22. ......   P × P
23. R — B 8   P — Kt 3

Black must keep the Queens on the board, for after 23. ....P — Q 4; 24. Q — Kt 8, Q — B 4; 25. R × Q, R × Q; 26. R — B 7 White's win of the ending is merely a matter of technique.

24. R × R ch ?

Here White misses a clear win by 24. Q — Kt 8, R × R; 25. Q × R ch, K — Kt 2; 26. Q —

B 3 ch, K — R 3; 27. R — Q 4.
A narrow escape for Black, who
now fights back strongly.

Position after 23. ....P — Kt 3

24.	K × R
25. Q — B 8 ch	K — K 2

And not 25. ....K — Kt 2;
26. Q — B 3 ch transposing into
the winning variation for White
given above.

26. Q — B 7 ch	K — B 3
27. Q — B 3 ch	K — K 2
28. Q — B 7 ch	K — B 3
29. Q — Q 8 ch	K — Kt 2
30. Q × Q P	Kt × P

Black now has two united
passed Pawns for the exchange,
but White's Rook is very powerful in this open position.

31. Q — Q 4 ch	P — K 4
32. Q — Q 5	Q × Q
33. R × Q	P — K 5 ch

Capablanca spent 40 minutes
thinking about this move. He
rightly preferred to block the
Pawns on the K side rather than
to launch out on the tempting

venture of advancing his Q side
Pawns by 33. ....Kt — B 6; 34.
R × P, P — Q R 4; 35. R — K 7,
P — Q Kt 4; 36. R — B 7, P —
Kt 5; 37. R — Kt 7, after which
Black's Q side Pawns and piece
are paralysed.

34. K — B 4	Kt — Kt 5
35. R — Q Kt 5	Kt — Q 6 ch
36. K × P	Kt × P ch
37. K — Q 4	P — B 4
38. R — Kt 2	Kt — Kt 5
39. P — R 3	Kt — B 3
40. R — Q B 2	Kt — K 5

The endgame is highly dramatic; just when it looks as
though Black's Q side Pawns are
about to fall, Capablanca attacks
White's weakened K side Pawns.

41. P — Kt 4	K — B 3
42. P × P	K × P
43. R — B 7	Kt — Kt 4
44. R × Q R P	P — R 4

Position after 44. ....P — R 4

45. R — R 3

A neat way of protecting the
R Pawn, but nevertheless not the
best. Takacs has demonstrated

that White can win here by 45.
P — R 4! Kt — B 6 ch; 46. K —
Q 5, P — K Kt 4 (or 46. .... Kt
× P; 47. R — B 7 ch, K — Kt 5;
48. P — K 4, P — K Kt 4; 49. P
— K 5, Kt — Kt 3; 50. P — K 6,
P — R 5;   51. R — B 6 and
wins); 47. P × P, K × P (if 47.
.... Kt × P; 47. R — R 4!); 48.
K — K 4, Kt — Q 7 ch; 49. K —
Q 3, Kt — B 6; 50. K — K 2, Kt
— K 4; 51. R — Kt 7 with a sim-
ple win.

45. ......   Kt — B 6 ch

And not 45. .... Kt × P; 46.
P — K 4 ch, K — Kt 5; 47. R ×
Kt, K × R; 48. P — K 5, K —
Kt 7; 49. P — K 6, P — R 5; 50.
P — K 7, P — R 6; 51. P — K 8
= Q, P — R 7; 52. Q — K 5 ch,
K — Kt 8; 53. Q — Kt 4 ch, K —
B 7; 54. Q — R 3, K — Kt 8; 55.
Q — Kt 3 ch, K — R 8; 56. Q —
B 2 followed by 57. Q — B 1
mate.

46. K — Q 3

Again not the best. A win was
still to be obtained by 46. K —
Q 5, P — K Kt 4; 47. R — R 8,
P — Kt 5; 48. P × P ch, P × P;
49. R — B 8 ch, K — Kt 4; 50.
K — K 4, Kt — R 5; 51. R —
Kt 8 ch, Kt — Kt 3; 52. K — Q 3,
K — B 4; 53. P — K 4 ch, K —
Kt 4; 54. K — K 3, P — Kt 4;
55. R — Kt 8, P — Kt 5; 56. R
× P, K — R 5; 57. R — Kt 6, K
— Kt 4, 58. K — B 2, etc.

46. ......   Kt — Kt 8

The ensuing last 11 moves had
to be made very quickly, since

Capablanca had got into great
time trouble. However, he now
plays with his customary accuracy to secure the draw.

	White	Black
47.	K — Q 2	P — K Kt 4!
48.	R — Kt 3	P — R 5
49.	R × P	Kt × P
50.	K — K 2	P — Kt 5
51.	R — Kt 5 ch	K — K 5
52.	R — Kt 4 ch	K — B 4
53.	K — B 1	K — Kt 4
54.	R — Kt 5 ch	K — Kt 3
55.	R — Kt 4	K — R 4
56.	R — Kt 7	Kt — Kt 4

Drawn.

Black has established a small
but impregnable fortress, and
White dare not move his King
away from the K side to assist
the advance of his K Pawn for
fear that Black's Pawns may go
on to Queen; an extremely hard-
fought game.

80

EXHIBITION GAME,
LOS ANGELES, 1933

Four Knights' Game

White	Black
CAPABLANCA	H. STEINER
1. P — K 4	P — K 4
2. Kt — K B 3	Kt — Q B 3
3. Kt — B 3	Kt — B 3
4. B — Kt 5	

This game was played with
living pieces before a numerous
audience. Capablanca adopted a
time-honoured opening, in which,
however, he soon managed to in-
fuse fresh life.

4.	B — Kt 5
5. Castles	Castles
6. P — Q 3	P — Q 3
7. B — Kt 5	B × Kt

Black has now to deal with the threat of 8. Kt — Q 5. An excellent alternative to the text is Tarrasch's suggestion 7. . . . . B — K 3; 8. P — Q 4, P × P; 9. Kt × P, P — K R 3; 10. B — K R 4, Kt — K 4; 11. P — B 4, B — Q B 4; 12. K — R 1, Kt — Kt 3; 13. B × Kt, Q × B with equality.

| 8. P × B | Kt — K 2 |

Once very popular, this variation has rightly faded out of master chess. The illogicality of inviting White to break up Black's K side Pawn formation after having exchanged off a Bishop for a Knight to avoid this is sufficient to condemn it; Capablanca demonstrates the weakness of Black's K side in sparkling fashion.

There are many sound alternatives here, e.g. 8. . . . . B — Q 2 or 8. . . . . Q — K 2 or, finally, 8. . . . . P — K R 3, as in a famous game, Capablanca–Lasker, St. Petersburg, 1914, which went on: 9. B — K R 4, B — Kt 5; 10. P — K R 3, B × Kt; 11. Q × B, P — Kt 4; 12. B — Kt 3, Kt — Q 2; 13. P — Q 4, P — B 3 with a solid game for Black.

| 9. Kt — R 4 ! |

Strongest; it prepares P — K B 4 and counters Black's threatened Kt — Kt 3.

| 9. . . . . . . | P — B 3 |

If 9. . . . . Kt — Kt 3; 10. Kt × Kt, R P × Kt; 11. P — K B 4 with a strong attack on the K B file.

| 10. B — Q B 4 | B — K 3 |

If 10. . . . . Kt — K 1; 11. P — B 4 is very strong, and after the natural-looking 10. . . . . P — Q 4 an analysis by Yates has shown Black gets a very bad game by 11. B — Kt 3, P × P; 12. P × P, Q × Q; 13. Q R × Q, Kt — Kt 3; 14. Kt × Kt, P × Kt; 15. B × Kt, P × B; 16. P — K B 4. This last move is the thematic continuation which occurs again and again in the Four Knights, as can be seen in the present game. Black hopes to blunt White's attack by the double exchange that results after the text move.

11. B × Kt	P × B
12. B × B	P × B
13. Q — Kt 4 ch	

Forcing the King on to the K B file before opening up the attack on that line.

| 13. . . . . . . | K — B 2 |
| 14. P — K B 4 | K R — Kt 1 |

This attempt at counter-attack fails against White's 17th move, which Black has obviously not foreseen. But he now has no good move at his disposal. If, for example, 14. . . . . Kt — Kt 3 then 15. P — B 5 ! or 14. . . . . P × P; 15. Q × P, Kt — Kt 3; 16. Q — R 6 !

15. Q — R 5 ch   K — Kt 2
16. P × P   Q P × P

Position after 16. ....Q P × P

17. R × P!

A fine mating combination with an especially neat point on the 19th move.

17. ......   K × R
18. R — B 1 ch   Kt — B 4
19. Kt × Kt!

19. P × Kt would allow the Black King to escape to the Q side via K 2.

19. ......   P × Kt
20. R × P ch   K — K 2
21. Q — B 7 ch   K — Q 3
22. R — B 6 ch   K — B 4

Or 22. ....Q × R; 23. Q × Q ch, K — Q 2; 24. Q × K P and the extra Pawns win easily.

23. Q × Kt P

Threatening Q — Kt 4 mate as well as Q × B P mate.

23. ......   Q — Kt 3

Apparently guarding against both threats, but now, with a nice symmetry of sacrifice, the remaining White Rook delivers the *coup de grâce.*

24. R × P ch   Q × R
25. Q — Kt 4 mate

CHAPTER NINE

Triumphant Return

In 1935 Capablanca returned to the international chess arena, and soon demonstrated that he was by no means a spent force by his play in the Moscow Tournament of that year. It is true he had to be content with fourth prize, but he produced a large number of fine games, of which we here give five. In Game No. 81, Alatorzeff meets with early disaster through the mistaken notion that a draw would be easy to obtain by frequent exchanges — just the type of play which Capablanca delighted in confuting. The Ragosin game is a masterly example of far-flung attack on both wings, and in the next game Kan succumbs to a slashing K side assault, as does Miss Menchik in Game No. 84. There is a little story attached to Capablanca's classic win against the Meran Defence in the next game. The previous day, Capablanca was having dinner with Stahlberg, the Swedish master, and during the meal he said plaintively that the next day he was due to play the great Russian analyst, Löwenfisch, a famous opening theoretician, especially as regards the Meran Defence to the Queen's. What was he to play against him? Stahlberg then told him of his innovation against Spielmann at Stockholm, and Capablanca, very much taken with the move, played it for the first time in the following round, with devastating effect.

The Margate games that follow are all in Capablanca's best positional vein, especially the last game against Milner-Barry, where Black's K side is cunningly and irresistibly destroyed.

Moscow, 1936, marked a definite return to Capablanca's supreme style; the two games given were won against two of the strongest representatives of the younger school, and are well worthy of the contestants. There follows a little-known consultation game containing a remarkable and instructive endgame, and an interesting positional game from Nottingham, where Capablanca again scored a success by tieing for first prize with Botvinnik in a very strong tournament indeed.

HASTINGS, 1934–35

				Thomas	Euwe	Flohr	Capablanca	Botvinnik	Lilienthal	Michell	Vera Menchik	Milner-Barry	Norman	
1	Thomas	..	..	–	0	½	1	1	1	0	1	1	1	6½
2	Euwe	..	..	1	–	½	½	1	½	1	½	1	½	6½
3	Flohr	..	..	½	½	–	½	½	½	1	1	1	1	6½
4	Capablanca	..	..	0	½	½	–	½	0	1	1	1	1	5½
5	Botvinnik	..	..	0	0	½	½	–	½	½	1	1	1	5
6	Lilienthal	..	..	0	½	½	1	½	–	1	½	½	½	5
7	Michell	..	..	1	0	0	0	½	0	–	½	1	1	4
8	Vera Menchik	..	..	0	½	0	0	0	½	½	–	1	½	3
9	Milner-Barry	..	..	0	0	0	0	0	½	0	0	–	1	1½
10	Norman	..	..	0	½	0	0	0	½	0	½	0	–	1½

MARGATE, 1935

				Reshevsky	Capablanca	Thomas	Klein	Reilly	Sergeant	Fairhurst	Milner-Barry	Vera Menchik	Mieses	
1	Reshevsky	..	..	–	1	½	½	1	1	1	½	1	1	7½
2	Capablanca	..		0	–	1	½	1	1	½	1	1	1	7
3	Thomas	..	..	½	0	–	½	½	1	½	1	½	½	5
4	Klein	..	..	½	½	½	–	0	½	1	0	1	½	4½
5	Reilly	..	..	0	0	½	1	–	½	1	½	0	1	4½
6	Sergeant	..	..	0	0	0	½	½	–	½	1	1	1	4½
7	Fairhurst	..	..	0	½	½	0	0	½	–	½	1	1	4
8	Milner-Barry	..	..	½	0	0	1	½	0	½	–	0	1	3½
9	Vera Menchik	..	..	0	0	½	0	1	0	0	1	–	0	2½
10	Mieses	..	..	0	0	½	½	0	0	0	0	1	–	2

MARGATE, 1936

				Flohr	Capablanca	Stahlberg	Lundin	Milner-Barry	Tylor	Vera Menchik	Thomas	Sergeant	Reilly	
1	Flohr	..	..	–	½	½	1	1	1	½	1	1	1	7½
2	Capablanca	..	..	½	–	½	½	1	½	1	1	1	1	7
3	Stahlberg	..	..	½	½	–	0	½	½	1	½	1	1	5½
4	Lundin	..	..	0	½	1	–	½	½	1	½	0	1	5
5	Milner-Barry	..	..	0	0	½	½	–	0	1	1	½	1	4½
6	Tylor	..	..	0	½	½	½	1	–	½	0	½	1	4½
7	Vera Menchik	..	..	½	0	0	0	0	½	–	½	1	1	3½
8	Thomas	..	..	0	0	½	½	0	1	½	–	½	0	3
9	Sergeant	..	..	0	0	0	1	½	½	0	½	–	½	3
10	Reilly	..	..	0	0	0	0	0	0	0	1	½	–	1½

MOSCOW, 1935

	Botvinnik	Flohr	Lasker	Capablanca	Spielmann	Kan	Löwenfisch	Lilienthal	Ragosin	Romanovsky	Alatorzeff	Goglidse	Rabinovich	Riumin	Lissitzin	Bogatyrchuk	Stahlberg	Pirc	Tschejover	Vera Menchik	
1 Botvinnik	–	½	½	½	1	0	1	½	1	1	½	1	½	1	½	0	1	½	1	1	13
2 Flohr	½	–	½	½	½	½	½	½	½	1	½	1	1	½	1	1	1	1	½	½	13
3 Lasker	½	½	–	1	½	1	½	½	½	½	½	1	½	½	½	½	½	1	1	1	12½
4 Capablanca	½	½	0	–	½	1	1	½	1	½	1	½	½	0	1	½	½	½	1	1	12
5 Spielmann	0	½	½	½	–	½	½	½	0	1	1	½	0	½	½	½	1	1	1	1	11
6 Kan	1	½	0	0	½	–	½	0	1	0	½	½	1	1	0	1	1	½	½	1	10½
7 Löwenfisch	0	½	½	0	½	½	–	½	½	½	1	½	0	1	1	1	1	½	0	1	10½
8 Lilienthal	½	½	½	½	½	1	½	–	0	½	½	½	0	1	½	½	0	1	1	½	10
9 Ragosin	0	½	½	0	1	0	½	1	–	0	0	½	½	1	½	½	1	1	½	1	10
10 Romanovsky	0	0	½	½	0	1	½	½	1	–	½	½	1	0	½	½	1	0	1	1	10
11 Alatorzeff	½	½	½	0	0	½	0	½	1	½	–	0	0	1	1	½	½	½	1	1	9½
12 Goglidse	0	0	0	½	½	½	½	½	½	½	1	–	½	½	½	½	0	1	1	1	9½
13 Rabinovich	½	0	½	½	1	0	1	1	½	0	1	½	–	½	0	½	0	½	1	1	9½
14 Riumin	0	½	½	1	½	0	0	0	0	1	0	½	1	–	0	1	1	1	½	1	9½
15 Lissitzin	½	0	½	0	½	1	0	½	½	½	0	½	1	1	–	0	½	½	½	1	9
16 Bogatyrchuk	1	0	½	½	½	0	0	½	½	½	½	½	½	0	1	–	½	½	0	½	8
17 Stahlberg	0	0	½	½	0	0	0	1	0	0	½	1	1	0	½	½	–	½	1	1	8
18 Pirc	½	0	0	½	0	½	½	0	0	1	½	0	½	0	½	½	½	–	1	1	7½
19 Tschejover	0	½	0	0	0	½	1	0	½	0	0	0	0	½	½	1	0	0	–	1	5½
20 Vera Menchik	0	½	0	0	0	0	0	½	0	0	0	0	0	0	0	½	0	0	0	–	1½

MOSCOW, 1936

	Capablanca	Botvinnik	Flohr	Lilienthal	Ragosin	Lasker	Eliskases	Kan	Löwenfisch	Riumin	
1 Capablanca ..	—	1 ½	½ ½	1 ½	1 ½	½ 1	½ 1	½ 1	½ ½	1 1	13
2 Botvinnik ..	0 ½	—	½ 1	1 ½	½ 1	½ 1	½ ½	1 1	½ ½	½ 1	12
3 Flohr ..	½ ½	½ 0	—	½ 1	0 ½	½ 1	1 1	0 ½	½ 0	½ 1	9½
4 Lilienthal ..	0 ½	0 ½	½ 0	—	½ ½	½ 1	½ ½	½ 1	½ 1	½ ½	9
5 Ragosin ..	0 ½	½ 0	1 ½	½ ½	—	1 ½	½ 0	0 ½	1 ½	½ ½	8½
6 Lasker ..	½ 0	½ 0	½ 0	½ 0	0 ½	—	1 ½	½ ½	½ 1	1 ½	8
7 Eliskases ..	½ 0	½ 0	0 0	½ ½	½ 1	0 ½	—	½ ½	0 1	½ ½	7½
8 Kan ..	½ 0	0 0	1 ½	½ 0	1 ½	½ ½	½ ½	—	½ ½	0 ½	7½
9 Löwenfisch	½ ½	½ ½	½ 1	½ 0	0 ½	½ 0	1 0	½ ½	—	½ 0	7½
10 Riumin ..	0 0	½ 0	½ 0	½ ½	½ ½	0 ½	½ ½	1 ½	½ 1	—	7½

NOTTINGHAM, 1936

	Botvinnik	Capablanca	Euwe	Fine	Reshevsky	Alekhine	Flohr	Lasker	Vidmar	Bogoljuboff	Tartakower	Tylor	Alexander	Thomas	Winter	
1 Botvinnik	–	½	½	½	½	½	½	½	1	1	1	1	1	1	½	10
2 Capablanca ..	½	–	½	½	1	1	0	½	1	½	½	1	1	1	1	10
3 Euwe	½	½	–	½	1	0	½	0	1	½	1	1	1	1	1	9½
4 Fine	½	½	½	–	½	½	½	1	½	1	½	1	1	½	1	9½
5 Reshevsky	½	0	0	½	–	1	½	1	1	1	½	1	1	1	½	9½
6 Alekhine	½	0	1	½	0	–	1	½	½	1	1	½	1	½	1	9
7 Flohr	½	1	½	½	½	0	–	1	1	1	½	0	0	1	1	8½
8 Lasker	½	½	1	0	0	½	0	–	½	1	½	1	1	1	1	8½
9 Vidmar	0	0	0	½	0	½	0	½	–	1	½	½	1	½	1	6
10 Bogoljuboff ..	0	½	½	0	0	0	0	0	0	–	½	1	1	1	1	5½
11 Tartakower ..	0	½	0	½	½	0	½	½	½	½	–	0	0	1	1	5½
12 Tylor	0	0	0	0	0	½	1	0	½	0	1	–	½	½	½	4½
13 Alexander	0	0	0	0	0	0	1	0	0	0	1	½	–	½	½	3½
14 Thomas	0	0	0	½	0	½	0	0	½	0	0	½	½	–	½	3
15 Winter	½	0	0	0	½	0	0	0	0	0	0	½	½	½	–	2½

81
THIRD ROUND,
MOSCOW, 1935

Queen's Gambit Declined,
Orthodox Defence

White	Black
ALATORZEFF	CAPABLANCA
1. P — Q 4	Kt — K B 3
2. P — Q B 4	P — K 3
3. Kt — Q B 3	P — Q 4
4. B — Kt 5	B — K 2
5. P — K 3	Castles
6. P × P	

White has determined to exchange off pieces at every opportunity in the hope of securing an easy draw. This was a very unwise policy against such a player as Capablanca, whose special *forte* lay in the accumulation and exploitation of a series of small advantages obtained by profitable exchanges. Best is the normal 6. Kt — B 3.

6.	Kt × P

Not so good would be 6. .... P × P; 7. B — Q 3, Q Kt — Q 2; 8. K Kt — K 2 and White's game has superior elasticity in manœuvring possibilities with chances of attack on both wings.

7. B × B	Q × B
8. Kt — B 3	

An automatic type of move which is symptomatic of White's lack of fighting spirit in this game. Better would have been 8. Q — B 2 so as to be able to re-capture with the Q on B 3, thereby preventing Black's P — Q B 4.

8.	Kt × Kt

An excellent move, showing a true understanding of the nature of the position. Black plans to obtain the advantage on the Q side by an eventual P — Q B 4 followed by P × Q P; this will serve the double purpose of giving him play along the Q B file and the latent advantage of two Pawns to one on the Q side.

9. P × Kt	P — Q Kt 3
10. B — K 2	

This, in combination with his 12th and 14th moves, achieves the wished for exchanges of two pieces, but at the cost of both time and position. There was still time to obtain some counter-play by 10. B — Q 3, B — Kt 2; 11. Castles, P — Q B 4; 12. Q — K 2.

10.	B — Kt 2
11. Castles	P — Q B 4
12. Kt — K 5	Kt — B 3
13. Kt × Kt	

Part of the above-mentioned plan; the alternative of 13. P — K B 4 would be too belated a form of counter-attack. Black could play 13. ....Q R — B 1 followed by P × P and Kt — Kt 5 (after White had played B P × P); for 14. P — B 5 would fail against 14. ....Kt × Kt followed by 15. Q — Kt 4.

13.	B × Kt
14. B — B 3	Q R — B 1
15. P — Q R 4	

Not so much with the intention of obtaining play on the Q R file by P — R 5, but more in the hope of exchanging off another Pawn by this move.

15.	P × P
16. B P × P	P — Kt 3

A quiet positional move which proves extremely useful later on, when it gives the Black King a flight square and so permits Black's major pieces to leave the back rank.

17. B × B

Otherwise Black will himself force this exchange by Q — Kt 2.

17.	R × B
18. Q — Q 3	

Intending P — R 5, which would not have been advisable at once on account of 18. ....P — Q Kt 4.

18.	Q — Kt 2

A strong move which facilitates the co-operation of Black's major pieces and again prevents P — R 5 on account of P — Q Kt 4.

19. K R — Kt 1

White cannot successfully dispute control of the Q B file; for if 19. K R — B 1, K R — B 1; 20. Q — Q 2, Q — B 2.

19.	K R — B 1
20. P — R 3	

And not 20. P — R 5, P — Q Kt 4; 21. R × P, R — B 8 ch. Now P — R 5 is again threatened.

20.	P — Q R 3 !

Once and for all disposing of White's only counter-stroke, P — R 5, which would now be worse than useless because of 21. .... P — Q Kt 4.

21. Q — R 3.

This, and his next move, precipitate the disaster for White by removing the Queen from the scene of action just when Black is preparing the final onslaught. White is, however, positionally lost, and quiet moves will only put off the inevitable end.

He cannot prevent Black from occupying the 7th rank by 21. R — Kt 2 because of 21. ....Q — B 2 !

21.	R — B 7
22. Q — Q 6 ?	

This loses at once. White is, however, without any really good continuation. 22. R — Q B 1, R × R ch; 23. R × R, R × R ch; 24. Q × R, P — Q Kt 4 leads to a won endgame for Black. And if 22. R — R 2, R (B 1) — B 6; 23. R — Kt 3, Q — B 2; 24. R × R (B 2), R × R; 25. P — Kt 3, R — B 8 ch; 26. K — R 2, Q — B 3 and wins.

Finally, if 22. Q — Kt 3, R (B 1) — B 6; 23. Q × Kt P ? R — B 8 ch.

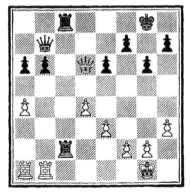

Position after 22. Q — Q 6 ?

22. ......   R × P !
23. Q — Kt 3

If 23. K × R, R — B 7 ch; 24.
K — K 1,   Q × P;   25.   Q —
Kt 8 ch,   K — Kt 2;   26.   Q —
K 5 ch,   K — B 1;   27.   Q —
Q 6 ch,   K — K 1;   28.   Q —
Kt 8 ch,   K — K 2;   29.   Q —
R 7 ch, K — B 3.

23. ......   R — K 7

Resigns; for White must prevent R (B 1) — B 7 by 24. R —
Q B 1,   R × R ch;   25.   R × R
when Q — K 5 is crushing. If
then 26. R — B 3, R — R 7, etc.

82

SIXTH ROUND,
MOSCOW, 1935

Queen's Pawn, Nimzovitch
Defence

White	Black
CAPABLANCA	V. RAGOSIN
1. P — Q 4	Kt — K B 3
2. P — Q B 4	P — K 3
3. Kt — Q B 3	B — Kt 5
4. P — Q R 3	

An unusual choice for Capablanca, who usually preferred Q
— B 2 against the Nimzovitch
Defence. The present game, however, is a masterly illustration
of the subtlety and power of
the Sämisch variation. In truly
majestic style, Capablanca demonstrates how to attack on
both wings when the centre is
closed.

4. ......   B × Kt ch
5. P × B   P — Q 3

Black has an almost bewilder-
ing profusion of moves to choose
from here: apart from the text,
he can play 5. ....Castles or P
— Q 4 or P — Q Kt 3 or P —
B 4 or even Kt — K 5. Each
move implies a somewhat different system and each is well playable. Capablanca himself tried 5.
....P — Q Kt 3 against Lilienthal at Hastings, 1934, but after
6.   P — B 3,   P — Q 4;   7.   B —
Kt 5,   B — R 3;   8.   P — K 4 his
game was much inferior.

Probably best is 5. ....P —
B 4, as Botvinnik played in a
later round against Lilienthal at
Moscow; for after 6. P — B 3, P
— Q 4;   7.   P — K 3, Castles;   8.
B P × P, Kt × P;   9.   B — Q 2,
Kt — Q B 3;   10.   B — Q 3, P ×
P;   11   B P × P,   P — K 4 the
game opens up to Black's ad-
vantage.

6. Q — B 2

An interesting variation from
the usual 6. P — B 3 in this line.

White wishes to occupy the centre at once by P — K 4.

6.	Castles
7. P — K 4	P — K 4
8. B — Q 3	P — B 4

Black wishes to enforce P — Q 5 in order to be able to fix White's Q B Pawns as objects for attack.

9. Kt — K 2	Kt — B 3
10. B — Q 3	Kt — K 2 ?

Much too defensively played; Black must concentrate on White's weak spot with 10. .... Kt — Q R 4 followed by P — Q Kt 3 and B — R 3. After the text, White can build up his attack without any possibility of interference from Black.

11. P — B 3	Kt — Q 2

If 11. ....Kt — K 1 (threatening P — B 4) then 12. P — Kt 4.

12. P — K R 4

This initiates a powerful attack on the K side. Black decides to move his King over to the other wing and so averts immediate disaster. But as a result of the time consumed in this King flight White gains more and more control of the board and establishes his Kt in a commanding position.

12.	Kt — Q Kt 3
13. P — Kt 4	P — B 3
14. Kt — Kt 3	K — B 2

15. P — Kt 5	Kt — Kt 1
16. P — B 4	K — K 1
17. P — B 5	Q — K 2

An attempt to break open the position by P — Kt 3 only reacts to Black's disadvantage, e.g. 17. ......P — Kt 3; 18. B P × P, R P × P; 19. P — R 5, Kt P × P (19. ....B P × P; 20. P — R 6); 20. Kt × P, P × P; 21. Kt — Kt 7 ch, K — B 2; 22. R — R 7 and wins.

18. Q — K Kt 2	K — Q 1
19. Kt — R 5	

Now the Kt will reach Kt 7, whence, after due preparation, it will go to K 6 with a stifling effect on Black's game.

19.	K — B 2
20. P × P	P × P
21. Kt — Kt 1	B — Q 2
22. P — R 5	Q R — B 1
23. P — R 6	K — Kt 1

Black now hopes that his King is tucked away safely, but White also has an open file on the Q wing and soon starts an attack on this side too.

24. R — K Kt 1	R — K B 2
25. R — Kt 1	Q — B 1
26. B — K 2	K — R 1
27. B — R 5	R — K 2
28. Q — Q R 2	Q — Q 1
29. B — Q 2	Kt — R 5
30. Q — Kt 3	Kt — Kt 3

And not 30. ....P — Kt 3; 31. Kt — K 6.

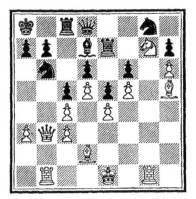

Position after 30. ....Kt — Kt 3

31. P — R 4 !

After due preparation, White delivers another onslaught on the unfortunate Black King. The immediate threat is the win of a piece by P — R 5, and if Black now plays 31. ....B × R P, then 32. Q — R 2, B — Q 2 (or 32. ....Q — Q 2; 33. R × Kt followed by 34. B — Q 1); 33. Kt — K 6, B × Kt; 34. Q P × B and, since Black cannot play 34. ....K R — Q B 2 because of R × Kt, he is helpless against the threat of B — B 7.

It should be noted that Capablanca defers playing Kt — K 6 until the move can be played with the utmost effect, thereby using it as a final threat to destroy the Black position. This faculty of restraint is one of Capablanca's most marked attributes and is an essential quality of his greatness as a player.

31. ......   R — Kt 1
32. P — R 5   Kt — B 1

32. ....Kt — R 5 would be met by 33. Kt — K 6.

33. Q — R 2   Q — B 1
34. B — K 3   P — Kt 3
35. P — R 6

Black's plight is now pitiable. With the exception of the Queen, none of his pieces can move at all, and he must move this piece up and down the back rank until White chooses to deliver the *coup de grâce.*

35. ......   Q — Q 1
36. K — Q 2   Q — B 1
37. R — Q Kt 2   Q — Q 1
38. Q — Kt 1   P — Kt 4

A desperate attempt to gain breathing space. If he continues his passive policy by 38. ....Q — B 1 then 39. Q — K B 1, Q — Q 1; 40. Kt — K 6, B × Kt; 41. B P × B, R — Q B 2; 42. B — B 7, Q Kt — K 2; 43. R — Kt 7, Q — K B 1; 44. R × R P followed by R — R 8 and P — R 7.

39. P × P   Kt — Kt 3
40. Q — R 2   P — B 5

Creating another weakness on Q 3, of which White soon takes advantage. But against any passive move White plays P — B 4 followed by K — Q 3, and a leisurely regrouping of his major pieces on the K side, with a final Kt — K 6 to clinch matters.

41. Q — R 3   Q — B 2
42. K — B 1   R — K B 1
43. R (Kt 2)—Kt 2

Again threatening Kt — K 6 followed by B — B 7.

43.	Q — Kt 1
44. Q — Kt 4	R — Q 1
45. R — Kt 3	R — K B 1
46. Kt — K 6	B × Kt

If Black does not capture, he loses his Kt, e.g. 46. ....R — Q B 1; 47. B × Kt, P × B; 48. P — R 7.

47. Q P × B	R — Q B 2

Forced because of the threat of B — B 7.

48. Q × Q P	Kt — K 2

If 48. ....R — Q 1; 49. Q × R, Q × Q; 50. R × Kt.

49. R — Q 1	Resigns

Black prefers not to wait for 49. ....Kt (Kt 3) — B 1; 50. Q — Kt 4, Kt — Q Kt 3; 51. R — Kt 7, Kt (Kt 3) — B 1; 52. R — Q 7, etc. A fine example of Capablanca's enveloping art and the inevitable feeling of increasing paralysis which this induces in his opponent.

83
EIGHTH ROUND, MOSCOW, 1935

Queen's Gambit Declined, Orthodox Defence

White	Black
CAPABLANCA	I. KAN
1. P — Q 4	Kt — K B 3
2. P — Q B 4	P — K 3
3. Kt — Q B 3	P — Q 4
4. Kt — B 3	Q Kt — Q 2

Black prefers to transpose into the orthodox defence. An excellent alternative is 4. ....P —

B 4; 5. B P × P, Kt × P; 6. P — K 4, Kt × Kt; 7. P × Kt, P × P; 8. P × P, B — Kt 5 ch; 9. B — Q 2, B × B ch; 10. Q × B, Castles with a level game.

5. B — Kt 5	B — K 2
6. P — K 3	Castles
7. R — B 1	P — B 3
8. B — Q 3	P × P
9. B × P	Kt — Q 4
10. B × B	Q × B
11. Castles	Kt(Q 4)—Kt 3

Inferior to the normal equalising continuation, 11. ....Kt × Kt; 12. R × Kt, P — K 4. The text puts the Kt on a poor square, where it is out of play, and leaves White's Kts in control of the centre.

12. B — Kt 3	P — K 4

If 12. ....P — Q B 4 then 13. Kt — K 4! is still stronger than in the actual game.

13. Kt — K 4

A strong move, the theme of which resembles the semi-waiter in chess problems. The Kt is brought over to the attack on the K side and meanwhile Black has to find a reasonable noncommittal continuation. If he plays 13. ....P × P, then 14. Q × P gives White considerable command in the centre and makes it very difficult for Black to complete his development. 13. ....R — K 1 fails against 14. Kt — Kt 5 and 13. ....P — Kt 3, though preventing White from attacking along the Q Kt 1 — K R 7 diagonal, leaves some holes on Black's K side.

13. ......   P — K R 3

Black chooses this move so as to prevent Kt — Kt 5, but a marked weakness is created on the diagonal mentioned in the last note.

14. Q — Q 3 !

White sets about the immediate exploitation of this weakness and commences a most persistent and formidable K side attack.

14. ......   K — R 1

Unpinning the B Pawn so as to threaten P — B 4 and P — K 5. White must prevent Black from achieving this.

15. Kt — Kt 3   P × P

Forced because of the threat of 16. Kt — B 5, Q — B 3; 17. B — B 2.

16. B — B 2   Kt — B 3

If at once 16. ....P — Kt 3 then 17. P — K R 4! with P — R 5 to follow gives White a very strong attack.

Position after 16. ....Kt — B 3

17. P — K 4 !

A subtle finesse which forces Black to weaken his K side by P — Kt 3 because of the threat of P — K 5.

17. ......   P — Kt 3
18. Q × P   B — K 3

The Bishop must be used to block this square; if, instead, 18. ....B — Kt 5; 19. P — K 5, Kt (B) — Q 4; 20. P — K 6 dis ch and wins.

19. P — K R 4 Q R — Q 1
20. Q — B 3

Better than Q — K 3, which would allow Black chances of eventual counter-attack on White's Pawns by Q — Kt 5.

20. ......   K — R 2
21. K R — K 1 Kt(Kt 3)—Q 2
22. B — Kt 1

Now White proceeds to round off his own position and deprive Black of possible counter-chances before delivering the final onslaught. The text guards R 2 and prevents Black from playing Q — B 4; it also threatens Kt — B 5.

22. ......   K R — K 1

Now, if 23. Kt — B 5, Q — B 1 and White has to retreat with the Kt.

23. P — Q R 3

So as to be able to move the Queen without having to reckon with Black's Q — Kt 5.

23. ......   B — Kt 5

An impatient move, which only
accelerates White's attack. He
cannot play 23. ....Kt — B 1
because of 24. Kt — B 5, but a
better scheme of defence was 23.
....Q — B 1 followed by 24.
....Q — Kt 2.

24. Kt — R 2   P — K R 4
25. P — B 3   B — K 3
26. P — B 4

Capablanca conducts this part
of the attack in his best style.
The threat of P — B 5 forces the
return of the Bishop, after which
Black's K side is broken up.

26. ......   B — Kt 5
27. Q — K 3

The Queen is manœuvred over
to the K side in order to enforce
the attack on that wing.

27. ......   P — R 3
28. Q — B 2   Kt — K 2
29. P — K 5   Kt — Q 4
30. Kt × B   P × Kt
31. P — R 5   R — K R 1

Or 31. ....Kt — B 1; 32. P —
B 5.

32. P × P   P × P
33. P — K 6 !

This energetic move is the prelude to a brilliantly decisive sacrifice entirely demolishing Black's
K side. With the possible exception of Black's 23rd move, Black
has found the best possible defence, but to no avail against the
masterly demolishing tactics employed by White.

33. ......   Kt — B 1

Position after 33. ....Kt — B 1

34. B × P !   K × B
35. Q — B 2 ch   K — B 3

Other K moves are met by
Kt — B 5 ch.

36. Q — B 5 ch   K — Kt 2
37. Q × P ch   K — R 2
38. K — B 2 ?

Overlooking Black's next move,
which forces exchange of Queens
and enables him to prolong
though not save the game. The
finish would have come about
much sooner after 38. R — K 5,
when if 38. ....Kt — B 3; 39.
Q — R 4 ch, K — Kt 1; 40. R —
Kt 5 ch, etc.

38. ......   Q — Kt 2
39. Q × Q ch

This leads to an easily won
endgame with two united passed
Pawns. White cannot play to win
the Rook by 39. Q — R 4 ch, K
— Kt 1; 40. Q × R because of
40. ....Q — Q 5 ch; 41. K —
B 3, Q × P ch and it is Black
who has the winning attack !

39. ......   K × Q
40. P — K 7

Regaining the piece with an easy technical win.

40. ......   R — K 1
41. P×Kt=Q ch   R(K 1)×Q
42. P — B 5   R — R 5
43. Q R — Q 1   R — B 5 ch
44. K — Kt 1   R — K Kt 5
45. R — Q 3   K — B 2
46. K — B 2   R — K R 1
47. R — Kt 3   P — Kt 3
48. Kt — K 4   R — R 3
49. P — Kt 3   R — Kt 1
50. K — B 3   P — R 4
51. R — Q 3   P — R 5
52. R — Q 2

And Black lost on the time limit, but in any case his position is clearly lost.

84

SEVENTEENTH ROUND, MOSCOW, 1935

Queen's Pawn, King's Indian Defence

Black   White
CAPABLANCA   MISS V. MENCHIK

1. P — Q 4   Kt — K B 3
2. P — Q B 4   P — K Kt 3
3. Kt — Q B 3   B — Kt 2

Wrongly rejecting the chance of using the Grünfeld Defence, which is much the best variation for Black in the K Indian. Miss Menchik, however, was a great believer in the close form of the K Fianchetto Defence which she handled with considerable virtuosity.

4. P — K 4   P — Q 3
5. P — B 3

White first strengthens his centre and then prepares to attack on the K wing very much as in his game in an earlier round against Ragosin.

5. ......   Castles
6. B — K 3   P — K 4
7. K Kt — K 2

An immediate 7. P — Q 5 could well be met by 7. ....P — B 3 with good counter-play.

7. ......   P — Q R 3 ?

An unduly defensive move which leaves White free to build up his attack unmolested by any counter on Black's part. More in the nature of the K Indian Defence would be 7. ....Kt — B 3; 8. Q — Q 2, Kt — Q 2; 9. P — Q 5, Kt — K 2; 10. P — K Kt 3, P — K B 4; and also interesting is 7. ....Q Kt — Q 2; 8. Q — Q 2, Kt — K 1; 9. P × P, Kt × P; 10. Kt — Q 4, B — K 3; 11. P — Q Kt 3, P — Q B 3; 12. B — K 2, P — Q 4; 13. B P × P, P × P with a good game for Black (Fine-Tartakower, Warsaw, 1935).

8. Q — Q 2   B — Q 2

And here again both 8. ....Kt — B 3 and Q Kt — Q 2 were to be preferred.

9. P — Q 5 !

Now Black's Q Kt will take a great deal of time to develop.

9. ......   Kt — K 1

Threatening to counter-attack on White's centre by P — K B 4.

10. P — K Kt 4

Preventing P — K B 4, since 11. Kt P × P would open up the K Kt's file and lead to a most dangerous attack.

10. ......   P — R 3

An ingenious little trap which also serves a positional purpose. If 11. B × P, Q — R 5 ch wins a piece, and now after White has played P — K R 4 and P — Kt 5 Black will be able to avoid the attack by P — K R 4.

11. P — K R 4   K — R 2
12. Kt — Kt 3   P — Q B 4

A good move which must be played sooner or later; otherwise White will obtain an attack on the Q wing as well by P — Q B 5.

13. B — Q 3   Q — R 4

Threatening P—Q Kt 4, which is at once prevented by White's next move.

14. Q — K 2   R — R 1
15. P — R 3

Depriving Black's Queen of the valuable attacking square, Q Kt 4.

15. ......   Q — Q 1

Black has to regroup his pieces in order to develop his Q Kt — this loss of time being a direct consequence of the unhappy 7th move.

16. P — Kt 4

White takes advantage of Black's constricted position to attack his Pawn structure on the Q wing; Black will be forced to permit the closing up of all lines on this side, thereby allowing White to carry on his attack on the K wing without any distractions caused by possible counter-attacks.

16. ......   P — Kt 3
17. Q — Q Kt 2

Now 18. P × P, Kt P × P ?; 19. Q — Kt 7 is threatened.

17. ......   B — Q B 1
18. K — K 2   Kt — Q 2
19. Q R—K Kt 1   R—Q Kt 1
20. P — Q Kt 5   P—Q R 4

If 20. ....P × P; 21. Kt × P, B — R 3; 22. P — R 5, P — Kt 4; 23. Kt — B 5 with a further gain in space for White.

21. K — Q 1   K — Kt 1
22. Q — Q 2   Kt — B 1
23. K — B 2   P — B 3 ?

Up to this move, Black has defended herself well, but now, overlooking White's 26th move, she gives Capablanca just the object of attack he desires. The text is prompted by a wish to get the King into safety via K B 2. Black must not, however, meddle further with her Pawn position, but should continue regrouping her pieces by Q — K 2 and Kt — B 2.

24. P — Kt 5 !   B P × P
25. P × P   P — R 4

Thus far Black seems to have warded off White's attack satisfactorily, but now comes a surprise move which reveals the insecure nature of her position.

Position after 25. ....P — R 4

26. Kt — B 5 !   K — B 2

If 26. ....P × Kt; 27. P × P, Kt — Q 2; 28. P — B 6, B — B 1; 29. B — B 5 followed by B — K 6 ch.

27. Kt — K R 4   Q — K 2
28. Q — K R 2

Preparing the final breakthrough on the K side.

28. ......   Kt — B 2
29. R — K B 1   K — K 1
30. P — B 4   P × P

Black is equally lost after 30. ....K — Q 1; 31. P — B 5 followed by either P — B 6 or P × P.

31. B × K B P   K — Q 2
32. B × P !   Resigns

For if 32. ....Q × B; 33. R — B 7 ch. This game is a fine illustration of Capablanca's technical skill in exploiting the advantage of space.

85
EIGHTEENTH ROUND, MOSCOW, 1935

Queen's Gambit Declined, Slav Defence

White	Black
CAPABLANCA	G. LÖWENFISCH
1. P — Q 4	P — Q 4
2. P — Q B 4	P — Q B 3
3. Kt — K B 3	Kt — B 3
4. P — K 3	P — K 3
5. Kt — B 3	Q Kt — Q 2
6. B — Q 3	P × P

Leading to the Meran Defence, by which Black hopes to obtain an attack on the Q wing. Experience of recent years shows that Black's Pawn position on the Q wing becomes very insecure. The safest line for the second player here is 6. ....B — K 2.

7. B × B P   P — Q Kt 4
8. B — Q 3   P — Q R 3

8. ....P — Kt 5 gives White the advantage after 9. Kt — K 4, B — K 2; 10. Kt × Kt ch, Kt × Kt; 11. P — K 4, B — Kt 2; 12. B — K Kt 5, Castles; 13. R — Q B 1 (Botvinnik–Lissitzin, Leningrad, 1933).

9. P — K 4

More vigorous than 9. Castles, P — B 4; 10. P — Q R 4, P — Kt 5; 11. Kt — K 4, B — Kt 2; 12. Kt × P, Kt × Kt; 13. P × Kt, B × P with an excellent game for Black.

9. . . . . . .   P — B 4

In the 9th round of this tournament, Löwenfisch tried 9. . . . . P — Kt 5 against Ragosin, but after 10. Kt — Q R 4, P — B 4; 11. P — K 5, Kt — Q 4; 12. Castles, P × P; 13. R — K 1, Kt — B 4; 14. B — K Kt 5, Q — R 4; 15. Kt × Kt, B × Kt; 16. R — Q B 1, P — R 3; 17. B — R 4, B — K 2; 18. B × B, Kt × B; 19. Kt × P, Castles; 20. Q — Kt 4 White obtained a strong K side attack.

10. P — K 5   P × P
11. Kt × Kt P !

This move, first introduced in an analysis by the Russian master, Blumenfeld, gives rise to very interesting play in which White tries to exploit the weakness of Black's Q Kt Pawn.

11. . . . . . .   Kt × P !

Tournament praxis has shown this is the best continuation. For if 11. . . . . P × Kt; 12. P × Kt, P — K 4; 13. P × P, B × P; 14. Q — K 2, Q — K 2; 15. Castles, B — Kt 2; 16. R — K 1, Q — Q 3; 17. Kt — R 4 and Black's position is most insecure (Bogoljuboff–Sir George Thomas, Baden-Baden, 1925); at Noordwijk, in 1938, Spielmann tried 11. . . . . Kt — Kt 5 against Eliskases, but after 12. Q Kt × P, K Kt × K P; 13. B — K 4, B — Kt 5 ch; 14. B — Q 2, R — Q Kt 1; 15. Castles, B × B; 16. Q × B his position was much inferior.

12. Kt × Kt   P × Kt
13. Q — B 3 !

Stahlberg's move, first played by him in a match against Spielmann at Stockholm, 1933. It is much stronger than either 13. B × P ch, B — Q 2; 14. Kt × B, Q — R 4 ch or 13. Castles, Q — Q 4; 14. Q — K 2, B — R 3; 15. B — Kt 5, B — K 2; 16. P — Q R 4, Castles; 17. P × P, B — Kt 2; 18. P — B 4, P — R 3 (Alekhine–Bogoljuboff, 12th match game, 1934).

13. . . . . . .   R — R 4 ?

Löwenfisch, previously unacquainted with White's 13th move, thought for nearly an hour before he played this awkward-looking Rook manœuvre. It gives Black a very poor game indeed. If Black plays instead 13. . . . . Q — Q 4; 14. Q × Q, Kt × Q; 15. B × P ch, K — K 2; 16. Kt — B 6 ch wins a Pawn. His best move is 13. . . . . B — Kt 5 ch; 14. K — K 2, R — Q Kt 1; 15. Q — Kt 3, Q — Q 3; 16. Kt — B 3, Q × Q; 17. R P × Q, B — Q 2 and, though White is left with a clear advantage, Black has some counter-play.

14. Castles

And not 16. Kt — B 6, B — Kt 2.

14. . . . . . .   P — Kt 5
15. B — K B 4   B — K 2
16. K R — B 1   Castles
17. Q — R 3 !

With lightning rapidity, Capablanca has conjured up an attack on the Black King. His immediate threat is Kt — B 6, but his pieces are concentrating on K R 7.

17. ......   R — B 4

Forced; for if 17. ....B — Kt 2; 18. Kt — Kt 4 threatening either mate or B — B 7.

18. R × R   B × R
19. B — K Kt 5   P — R 3

If 19. ....P — Kt 3; 20. Kt — B 6, Q — B 2; 21. B × Kt, Q × Kt; 22. Q — R 6.

Position after 19. ....P — R 3

20. Kt — Kt 4 !

Capablanca concludes the game with an elegant final combination. The Bishop cannot be taken because of mate in two, and the immediate threat is Kt × R P ch.

20. ......   B — K 2
21. B × Kt !

It is interesting to note that the move mentioned in the last note would not now be so deci-

sive, for if 21. Kt × R P ch, P × Kt; 22. Q × R P, Kt — K 5; 23. B × B, Q × B; 24. B × Kt, P — B 4 and Black is still alive.

21. ......   P × B

Mate follows after 21. ....B × B; 22. Kt × P ch, P × Kt; 23. Q × R P, R — K 1; 24. B — R 7 ch, etc.

22. Kt × R P ch   K — Kt 2
23. Q — Kt 4 ch !   K — R 1

If 23. ....K × Kt; 24. Q — R 4 ch and mate next move.

24. Q — R 5   K — Kt 2
25. Kt × P   R — R 1

Or 25. ....R × Kt; 26. Q — R 7 ch, K — B 1; 27. Q — R 8 mate.

26. Q — Kt 6 ch   Resigns

86
THIRD ROUND, MARGATE, 1935

Queen's Gambit Declined, Slav Defence

White	Black
CAPABLANCA	J. MIESES
1. P — Q 4	P — Q 4
2. P — Q B 4	P — Q B 3
3. Kt — K B 3	Kt — B 3
4. P — K 3	P — K 3
5. Kt — B 3	Q Kt — Q 2
6. B — Q 3	P × P
7. B × B P	

So far as in the Meran Defence, but Black now embarks on an interesting and original variation, out of which he does not emerge at all badly.

7. ......   P — Q R 3
8. P — K 4   P — B 4

8. ....P — Q Kt 4 would transpose back into the Meran Defence.

9. P — K 5   Kt — Kt 5

Mieses thought for half an hour before making this ingenious move and Capablanca took the same time to find a reply. After the game he said: " I'm nearly dead with fatigue. He made what appeared to be a silly move — but it wasn't." And indeed the move has considerable point, since it threatens 10. .... P × P; 11. Q × P, Q Kt × P!

10. Kt — K Kt 5

This is the only satisfactory continuation; 10. P — K R 3 or 10. Castles fail against the variation given in the last note, whilst 10. B — B 4, P × P; 11. Q × P, B — B 4 loses for White.

10. ......   Kt — R 3

And not 10. ....P × P; 11. Q × Kt, P × Kt; 12. Kt × B P!

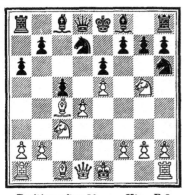

Position after 10. ....Kt — R 3

11. B × K P !

A move which deserves to be known as the Capablanca sacrifice; it occurs before in very similar circumstances in two of his best games. See Game No. 40, *v.* Bogoljuboff at Moscow, 1925, and Game No. 56, *v.* Havasi at Budapest, 1928.

11. ......   P × P

Black cannot accept the sacrifice, for if 11. ....P × B; 12. Kt × P, Q — R 4; 13. B — Q 2, P × P; 14. Kt — Q 5!

12. B × Kt ch   Q × B
13. Q Kt — K 4   Q — Kt 4!

Black rightly seeks to solve the problem of defence by counterattack. If now 14. Q × P, Kt — B 4 winning back the K P with an excellent game.

14. P — Q R 4!

White is in no hurry to capture the Q Pawn, but prefers to complete his development; he has to dislodge the Black Queen in order to Castle.

14. ......   B — Kt 5 ch
15. B — Q 2   B × B ch
16. Q × B   Q × K P
17. Castles K   Castles
18. K R — K 1

Threatening 19. Kt × R P, K × Kt; 20. Kt — Kt 5 ch.

18. ......   Q — Q 4
19. Kt — K B 3

And now he threatens Kt — B 6 ch breaking up Black's K side.

19. ......   Kt — B 4
20. Q R — Q 1   R — Q 1

It soon becomes apparent that, owing to White's superior development and his centralised attacking position, Black cannot hope to retain his extra Pawn, and attempts to do so only worsen his game. Black should therefore abandon the Q Pawn and play 20. ....B — Q 2, as Capablanca subsequently recommended. If then 21. Kt — B 3, Q — R 4; 22. Kt × P, Kt × Kt; 23. Q × Kt, B — B 3 with equality.

21. Q — Kt 5   P — R 3

If 21. ....K — B 1; 22. Kt — B 3, Q — Q 3; 23. Kt × P, Kt × Kt; 24. R × Kt, Q × R; 25. Q — K 7 ch followed by mate in two, and 21. ....K — R 1 is very bad for Black after 22. P — K Kt 4!

22. Kt — B 6 ch   K — B 1

Mieses, now in great time trouble, offered a draw under the impression that White would continue 23. Kt — R 7 ch, K — Kt 1; 24. Kt — B 6 ch, etc., but Capablanca rightly declined, since he regains the Pawn and still retains some attack.

23. Kt × Q   P × Q
24. Kt — Kt 6

Best if he wishes to play for a win. 24. Kt — B 7, R — Kt 1; 25. Kt × P, B — Q 2 leads only to equality.

24. ......   R — Kt 1
25. Kt × Kt P   B — Q 2
26. P — K Kt 4   Kt — R 5

An attractive-looking attacking move, which relies upon the threat of P — B 3 followed by Kt — B 6 ch to preserve the Q P. Capablanca is undeterred by this and proceeds to take the Pawn without any qualms. The best move was 26. ....Kt — R 3 and if 27. P — R 3, B — B 3.

27. R × P   B — B 3
28. R — K B 4   P — B 3

Position after 28. ....P — B 3

29. Kt — K 6 ch   K — Kt 1
30. Kt × R   R × Kt
31. R — Q B 1   R — K 1

Black cannot regain the exchange by 31. ....Kt — B 6 ch; 32. K — Kt 2, Kt — K 8 db ch; 33. K — Kt 3, Kt — Q 6 because of 34. R — Q 1.

32. P — R 3   R — K 7

Now, however, he could have put up much more resistance by 32. ....Kt — B 6 ch, when White would have had to return the exchange. Black's game would still be lost eventually after 33. K — Kt 2, Kt — K 8 db ch; 34. K —

Kt 3, Kt — Q 6; 35. R × B !, P ×
R (or 35. .... Kt × R; 36. R —
B 7); 36. R — Q 4! since Black
cannot play 36. .... Kt × Kt P;
37. R — Q 2 winning the Kt.

33. Kt — B 4	Kt — B 6 ch
34. K — B 1	R — K 2
35. Kt — K 3	Resigns

White is now the safe ex-
change and a Pawn up and Black
has nothing further to play for; a
game with many exciting moments.

87
NINTH ROUND,
MARGATE, 1935

*Queen's Pawn, Bogoljuboff
Defence*

White	Black
CAPABLANCA	SIR G. THOMAS
1. P — Q 4	Kt — K B 3
2. P — Q B 4	P — K 3
3. Kt — K B 3	B — Kt 5 ch

This is the Bogoljuboff variation of the Q Pawn, a highly so-
phisticated form of defence demanding the utmost accuracy in
its conducting.

| 4. B — Q 2 | Q — K 2 |

Simpler is 4. .... B × B ch
and if 5. Q × B, P — Q 4 or 5.
Q Kt × B, P — Q 3; 6. P — K 3,
Castles; 7. B — Q 3, Kt — B 3;
8. Castles, P — K 4 with a level
game.

5. P — K Kt 3	P — Q Kt 3
6. B — Kt 2	B — Kt 2
7. Castles	B × B
8. Q Kt × B	P — Q 3
9. Q — R 4 ch	

An interesting deviation from
the normal line, 9. Q — B 2,
whereby White concentrates on
forcing P — K 4 by direct means.
The text achieves P — K 4 by a
more indirect fashion.

| 9. ...... | P — B 3 ? |

A bad move, which allows
White to play P — K 4 at once
and also seriously weakens
Black's Q side Pawn structure.
Correct was 9. .... Q Kt — Q 2.
White could then proceed with
10. Kt — R 4, B × B; 11. K ×
B, Castles K; 12. P — K 4 with
some pressure on the Q side,
though Black has a solid position.

| 10. P — K 4 | Castles |
| 11. P — K 5 | |

White plays this part of the
game with great vigour, and
Black's pieces are rapidly deprived of their best squares.

| 11. ...... | Kt — K 1 |

Played with illogical patience.
It is true that after 11. .... P ×
P; 12. Kt × P, P — B 4; 13. B ×
B, Q × B; 14. P × P, P × P; 15.
Kt — Kt 3 White gets some attack
on Black's weak Q B P, but he
gets this, anyway, in the actual
game, and Black then has a worse
development than in the variation
given in the note.

| 12. K R — K 1 | |

A positional alignment of the
Rook opposite Black's Queen, the
value of which becomes apparent
on White's 20th move.

12. ......   P — Q B 4

Black attempts to gain some freedom at the cost of weakening his Pawn position. The alternative of 12. ....Kt — Q 2; 13. Kt — K 4, P — Q 4; 14. P × P, B P × P; 15. Kt — B 3 still leaves him very much penned in.

13. P × Q P   Kt × P

If 13. ....Q × P; 14. Kt — K 4! Now White isolates the Q B P and proceeds to concentrate his forces on it in typically elegant style.

14. P × P   P × P
15. Q — R 5   Kt — Q 2
16. P — Kt 3   K R — Q 1
17. Q R — Q 1   Q R — B 1
18. Kt — B 1

Naturally, not 18. Q × R P, R — R 1.

18. ......   P — Q R 3

Creating a fresh weakness on Q Kt 3, of which White subsequently takes advantage; but he wishes to clear his position a little by moving his Q Kt, and cannot do this whilst his Q R P is *en prise*.

19. Kt — K 3   Kt — K 1

A pitiful move to have to play, but Black's Q side Pawns are too weak to permit him the slightest aggression. If, for example, 19. ....Kt — B 3; 20. Kt — Q 5, Kt × Kt; 21. P × Kt, P — B 5; 22. Kt — Q 4 winning.

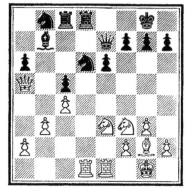

Position after 19. ....Kt — Kt 1

20. Kt — Q 5   Q — B 1
21. Kt — Kt 6   R — B 2
22. Kt — R 4

The Kt has made a most effective tour of the board via Q 2, B 1, K 3, Q 5, Kt 6, to land up finally on a square whence it attacks Black's weakest point. For a very similar Kt manœuvre, compare Game No. 31, *v.* Yates at New York, 1924.

22. ......   R (Q 1) — B 1
23. Kt — K 5   B × B
24. K × B   Kt — B 4

If 24. ....Kt — Kt 2; 25. Q — Kt 6 and Black is paralysed.

25. Kt — Q 3   Q — Q 3

Giving up the wretched Q B P in the vain hope of obtaining a counter-attack. The beautiful accuracy of Capablanca's style, however, nullifies all Black's attempts.

26. Kt (Q 3) × P   Q — B 3 ch
27. K — Kt 1   P — R 4
28. Kt — Q 3   P — R 5

29. Kt — K 5   Q — Kt 2
30. Q — Kt 6 !

White's command of the board is now too great for Black to fashion the faintest vestige of an attack.

30. ......   P × P
31. R P × P   Q — R 1
32. R — Q 8 ch   R × R

This loses immediately but 32. ....K — R 2; 33. R × R, R × R; 34. Kt × P leaves Black quite helpless.

33. Q × R   R — K B 1
34. Kt — Q Kt 6 !   Resigns

A very amusing finish; the Queen is trapped, although rejoicing in the longest diagonal on the board!

88
FIRST ROUND,
MARGATE, 1936

English Opening

White   Black
CAPABLANCA P. S. MILNER-BARRY

1. P — Q B 4   P — K 4
2. Kt — Q B 3   Kt — Q B 3
3. P — K Kt 3   P — K Kt 3
4. B — Kt 2   B — Kt 2
5. P — Q 3   K Kt — K 2
6. P — K R 4

Against Alexander at Nottingham, 1936, Capablanca preceded this with Kt — Q 5, without, however, obtaining more than an equal game. The text, though attacking on the K side, does not commit White to the one line of attack, since, as will be seen later on, he is also able to advance on the Q side and Castle K with equanimity.

6. ......   P — K R 3

Symptomatic of Black's attitude throughout the game — one of dour defence. The idea is to play P — K Kt 4 when and if White advances his Pawn to R 5. An alternative worthy of consideration was 6. ....P — Q 3 followed by B — K 3 and Q — B 1.

7. B — Q 2   P — Q 3
8. R — Q Kt 1

This manœuvre illustrates the main theme in the English — exploitation and enhancement of the power of the fianchettoed K Bishop. White plans to aid his Bishop's attack by P — Q Kt 4–5.

8. ......   Castles
9. P — Q Kt 5   Kt — Q 5

This, and the succeeding moves, are an attempt to muffle the strength of White's attack on the long diagonal, K R 1 — Q R 8. Its over-defensive nature results eventually in complete destruction. It would have been better to have played for a counter-attack by 9. ....P — B 4.

10. P — K 3   Kt — K 3
11. K Kt — K 2   P — Q B 3
12. Q — Kt 3

A subtle move played to deter Black from an immediate P — K B 4 and also with the idea of exerting pressure on the Q side (see move 16).

12.	B — Q 2
13. Castles	Q — B 2
14. K R — B 1	K R — B 1

Again too defensive; 14. ....
P — K B 4 was still best.

| 15. P — R 4 | Q R — Kt 1 |
| 16. Q — R 3 | B — B 1 |

Now if 16. ....P — K B 4;
17. Kt — Q 5 ! is bad for Black.

17. Kt — K 4.

By means of this move, White
gains the latent positional advantage of two Bishops, an advantage which he exploits to perfection later on by opening up the
game as much as possible.

| 17. ...... | P — K B 4 |

If 17. ....B — Kt 2; 18. P —
Kt 5, P — Q B 4; 19. P — Q R 5
followed by 20. P — Kt 6 with
very strong pressure on the Q
wing.

18. Kt — B 6 ch	K — B 2
19. Kt × B	Q × Kt
20. B — Q B 3	

White's Bishops begin to menace the K side.

| 20. ...... | B — Kt 2 |
| 21. Q — Kt 2 | Q — Q B 2 |

A stronger defence would have
been provided by 21. ....P —
B 4. The text allows White to
break open the centre and thereby increase the scope of his Bishops.

| 22. P — Q 4 | Kt — B 1 |

So as to be able to reply to 23.
P — Q 5, P — B 4 blocking the
position.

| 23. P × P | B × P |

If 23. ....P × P; 24. P —
B 4, Kt — Q 2; 25. P — K 4 !
weakening Black's K side considerably.

24. Kt — Q 4 !

The exchange of Bishops would
obviously slacken White's attack.

| 24. ...... | Kt — Q 2 |

Black would lose material after
24. ....P — B 4; 25. Kt — Kt 5.

25. P — K 4 !

Forcing Black to give up his
Bishop, the key to his defence, by
the threat to isolate Black's
K B P.

25.	B × Kt
26. B × B	Kt — K 4
27. Q — Q 2	P × P
28. B × K P	

This concentration of strength
on the unfortunate King leads to
rapid victory; not so conclusive is
28. Q × P, Kt — B 4; 29. Q —
R 7 ch, K — B 3 and Black has
escaped disaster.

| 28. ...... | Kt — B 4 |

Gaining a temporary respite
from the fact that 29. B ×
Kt (B 5) loses the Queen after
Kt — B 6 ch.

| 29. B — Q R 1 | K R — Kt 1 |
| 30. P — K R 5 ! | |

The prelude to an elegant and
incisive finish.

| 30. ...... | Q R — K B 1 |
| 31. P — B 5 | |

Especially to be admired is the tactical skill with which the position of both Kts is undermined.

31. ......   P — Q 4

Position after 31. ....P — Q 4

32.	B × P ch!	P × B
33.	Q × P ch	K — B 3
34.	P — B 4	Q — B 3
35.	B × Kt ch	K — K 2
36.	B — Q 6 ch	Resigns

Because of 36. ....Kt × B; 37. P × Kt ch, Q × P; 38. R — K 1 ch, K — Q 2; 39. Q × P ch, etc.

89
EIGHTH ROUND, MOSCOW, 1936
Réti's Opening

White	Black
CAPABLANCA	A. LILIENTHAL
1. Kt — K B 3	P — Q 4
2. P — B 4	P — Q B 3

This, in conjunction with the early development of the Q Bishop, is a solid system of defence much favoured by the late Em-

manuel Lasker, who won an impressive game with it against Réti at New York, 1924.

3.	P — Q Kt 3	B — B 4
4.	B — Kt 2	P — K 3
5.	P — Kt 3	Kt — B 3
6.	B — Kt 2	Q Kt — Q 2
7.	Castles	P — K R 3

Played to avoid the forced exchange of Kt for Bishop, but hardly necessary at this stage, since White is not likely to open up a line of attack for Black on the K R file by 8. Kt — R 4, B — Kt 3; 9. Kt × B, R P × Kt.

Black's most vigorous line is that employed by Lasker in the above-mentioned game at New York: 7. ....B — Q 3; 8. P — Q 3, Castles; 9. Q Kt — Q 2, P — K 4; 10. P × P, P × P; 11. R — B 1, Q — K 2; 12. R — B 2, P — Q R 4; 13. P — Q R 4, P — R 3; 14. Q — R 1, K R — K 1; 15. K R — B 1, B — R 2; 16. Kt — B 1, Kt — B 4 with a fine game.

8. P — Q 3

White can obtain a stronger hold on the position by 8. P — Q 4, B — K 2; 9. Kt — B 3, Castles; 10. Kt — Q 2 threatening 11. P — K 4.

8. ......   B — K 2
9. Q Kt — Q 2

Simpler play, leading to a more open position, gives White no advantage, e.g. 9. Kt — B 3. Castles; 10. Q — B 2, B — R 2; 11. P — K 4, P × K P; 12. P ×

P, Kt — B 4; 13. Q R — Q 1, Q
— B 2; 14. Kt — Q 4, Q R —
Q 1 with an equal game (Euwe-
Kmoch, Leningrad, 1934).

9. ......   Castles
10. R — B 1   P — Q R 4

Lasker's method for obtaining
a counter-attack on the Q side by
the threat of P — R 5. White's
next move meets this by preparing to play P — Q Kt 4 if the R
Pawn advances.

11. P — Q R 3   R — K 1
12. R — B 2   B — R 2
13. Q — R 1   B — B 1

Black is content with his solid
position and leaves the onus with
White as to how to open up the
position. A more aggressive and
logical continuation was 13. ....
B — Q 3 followed by 14. ....
P — K 4.

14. R — K 1

For the next six moves both
players indulge in a kind of spar-
ring for position with a distinct
reluctance to make any move compromising either on a definite line.
With this move, White dallies
with the idea of a thrust in the
centre by P — K 4.

14. ......   Q — Kt 3
15. B — R 3

15. P — K 4 would make 15.
....B — Q B 4 still more powerful than in the actual game.

15. ......   B — Q B 4
16. R — K B 1   B — B 1
17. R(B 2)—B 1   Q R — Q 1

18. K R — K 1   B — Q B 4
19. R — B 1   B — B 1
20. B — Kt 2   B — Q 3

White now commits himself to
a partial clearance in the centre.

21. Kt — K 5   B × Kt
22. B × B   Kt × B
23. Q × Kt   Kt — Q 2

Any attempt at blocking the
centre by P — Q 5 reacts to
Black's disadvantage, since it
yields White the important square
on Q B 4, e.g. 23. ....P — Q 5;
24. P — B 5, Q — Kt 4; 25. R —
B 4, etc. Or 23. ....Kt — Kt 5;
24. Q — Kt 2, P — Q 5; 25. P —
B 5, Q — Kt 4; 26. P — Q Kt 4
followed by Kt — B 4 and Kt —
Q 6.

24. Q — Kt 2   Kt — B 3 ?

Black is still intent — over intent — on preserving the sound
structure of his position. Now
was the right time to advance in
the centre by 24. ....P — K 4.
As played, he permits White to
dictate a type of endgame very
much to the first player's advantage.

25. P — Q Kt 4 !

White now threatens R —
Q Kt 1, with a latent double attack on the Q Kt Pawn.

25. ......   R P × P
26. Q × P   Q × Q

If 26. ....Q — R 2 or B 2
then 27. R — Kt 1, R — Kt 1; 28.
P — B 5 followed by R — Kt 2
and K R — Kt 1.

27. P × Q   R — R 1
28. R — R 1

In this seemingly innocuous position, Black is at a definite disadvantage on the Q side, where White has an attacking Pawn formation with the possibility of two fine outposts for his Kt on Q B 5 or Q R 5.

28. ......   Kt — Q 2

Anticipating that White will attempt to establish his pieces on Q B 5 and Q R 5 and hastening either to prevent or nullify such manœuvres.

29. Kt — Kt 3   K — B 1
30. R — R 5   P × P ?

This inconsequent move opens up fresh lines of attack for White. Black should bring his King into the game by 30. ....K — K 2. White's advantage would still persist after 31. K R — R 1, R × R (not 31. ....Kt — Kt 3; 32. P — B 5 winning a Pawn); 32. R × R with control of the Q R file and prospects of attack on Black's Q Kt Pawn.

31. P × P   Kt — Kt 3
32. R × R   R × R
33. Kt — R 5

White now exerts such strong pressure on the Q wing that Black cannot escape the loss of a Pawn.

33. ......   R — R 2
34. R — Q 1

Threatening 35. B × P, P × B; 36. R — Q 8 ch, K — K 2; 37. Kt × P ch, etc.

34. ......   K — K 1

If 34. ....K — K 2; 35. B × P wins a Pawn.

Position after 34. ....K — K 1

35. Kt × Kt P !

The Q side is demolished and White's fianchettoed Bishop springs to life.

35. ......   R × Kt
36. B × P ch   R — Q 2
37. P — B 5   K — K 2

This is the best move if further resistance is contemplated, since it enables Black to obtain two minor pieces for the Rook, with chances for stopping the advance of White's Q side Pawns. However, the endgame is clearly lost for Black owing to the strength of White's Pawns and the power of his Rook in an open position.

To a much speedier loss leads 37. ....Kt — Q 4; 38. P — Kt 5, K — K 2; 39. B × R, K × B; 40. R — R 1 followed by R — R 7 ch; and if 37. ....B — K 5; 38. R × R, B × B; 39. R — Q 6.

38.	B $\times$ R	Kt $\times$ B
39.	P — B 6	Kt — Kt 3
40.	P — B 7	B — B 4
41.	R — Q 8	

White has evolved a simple and clear winning process; Black's pieces will first be fixed to prevent White's Pawns from queening, and then his Rook will be switched to attack Black's K side Pawns.

41.	......	P — K 4
42.	R — Q Kt 8	Kt — B 1
43.	P — Kt 5	K — Q 3
44.	P — Kt 6	Kt — K 2
45.	R — K B 8	

A massacre now takes place.

45.	......	B — B 1
46.	R $\times$ P	Kt — Q 4
47.	R $\times$ P	Kt $\times$ Kt P
48.	R — R 7	Kt — Q 4
49.	R $\times$ P ch	K $\times$ P
50.	P — K 4	Kt — K 2
51.	P — B 3	K — Q 2
52.	P — R 4	K — K 1
53.	R — K B 6	Kt — Kt 1
54.	R — Q B 6	Resigns.

90
EIGHTEENTH ROUND, MOSCOW, 1936

Giuoco Piano

White	Black
CAPABLANCA	E. ELISKASES
1. P — K 4	P — K 4
2. Kt — K B 3	Kt — Q B 3
3. B — B 4	B — B 4
4. Kt — B 3	Kt — B 3
5. P — Q 3	P — Q 3
6. B — K Kt 5	

The Canal variation, so named after the Peruvian master, who introduced it into master chess in the late 1920's. White gives up his Q Bishop for a Knight in order to obtain control of the centre.

| 6. | ...... | P — K R 3 |

The usual reply in this variation, but, in view of Capablanca's innovation on move 10, one cannot believe it to be the best. At Carlsbad in 1929 Bogoljuboff played the simplifying 6. ....Kt — Q R 4; 7. Kt — Q 5, P — B 3 and equalised. Another good alternative is 6. ....B — K 3.

7.	B $\times$ Kt	Q $\times$ B
8.	Kt — Q 5	Q — Q 1
9.	P — B 3	Kt — K 2

Capablanca himself played 9. ....Castles against Canal at Carlsbad in 1929 with the continuation 10. P — Q R 4, P — Q R 4; 11. Castles, Kt — K 2; 12. P — Q 4 (12. Kt — K 3 is preferable on the model of the present game); 12. ....P $\times$ P; 13. Kt $\times$ Q P, Kt $\times$ Kt; 14. B $\times$ Kt, Q — B 3 with an equal game.

A trap into which Black must take care not to fall is 9. ....B — K 3; 10. P — Q 4, P $\times$ P; 11. P $\times$ P, B — Kt 5 ch; 12. K — B 1, B — Q 2; 13. Kt $\times$ B, Kt $\times$ Kt; 14. Q — Kt 3 and wins.

| 10. | Kt — K 3 | |

Stronger than the old 10. P — Q 4, when Black can equalise by 10. ....P $\times$ P; 11. P $\times$ P, B —

Kt 3; 12. Castles, Kt × Kt; 13.
B × Kt, Castles; 14. P — K R 3,
P — B 3 (Golombek–Michell,
Hastings, 1935).

10. ...... B — K 3

This move, usually a sound and
workmanlike method of blunting
the edge of White's attack in the
Giuoco, is here a positive error,
since it gives White fresh objects
of attack. Safest for Black is 10.
....Castles; 11. Castles, B —
Kt 3; 12. P — Q 4, Kt — Kt 3,
though White still retains an attack by Q — Kt 3 followed by
Q R — Q 1 and K R — K 1.

11. B × B	P × B
12. Q — Kt 3	Q — B 1
13. P — Q 4	

With this move White gains
space in the centre.

13.	P × P
14. Kt × P	B × Kt
15. P × B	Castles
16. Castles K R	Q — Q 2
17. Q R — B 1	

And not 17. Q × P, K R —
Kt 1; 18. Q — R 6, R × P; 19.
Q R — Kt 1, R — Kt 3 when
Black has freed his position.

17. ...... Q R — Kt 1

Now necessary, since White
would be threatening the Q B
Pawn after Q × Kt P.

18. R — B 3

More vigorous was 18. P —
B 4 threatening P — B 5.

18.	P — Q 4
19. Q — B 2	P — B 3

Black hereby deprives his Kt
of the attacking square Q B 3 and
allows White to call the tune.
Correct was 19. ....Kt — B 3;
20. R — Q 1 (or 20. P × P, P ×
P; 21. R — B 5, Kt × P; 22. Q
— Q 3, Kt — K 3; 23. R × P, Q
— R 5 in favour of Black); 20.
....P × P; 21. Q × P, Q R —
Q 1 and White's attack on the
K P is compensated by Black's
on the Q P.

20. P — K 5	R — B 5
21. Q — Q 1	

White protects the Q Pawn in
this way in order to have the
square on Q B 2 free for the Kt
if further protection of the Pawn
should become necessary.

21.	Q R — K B 1
22. P — B 3	Q — Q 1 ?

Black is under the misapprehension that his position is quite
secure and that waiting moves are
his best policy. But White has
formed the plan of advancing his
Pawns on the K side in order to
attack the slight weakness in
Black's Pawn structure on that
side.

Black can anticipate and nullify this by 22. ....R (B 5) —
B 2; 23. P — K Kt 3, Kt — B 4;
24. Kt × Kt, R × Kt; 25. P —
B 4, P — K Kt 4 with the better
game. Therefore White would
have to abandon his King side
plan and play 23. P — Q Kt 4
with pressure on the Q wing.

23. P — K Kt 3	K R — B 2
24. P — B 4	Kt — B 4

25. Kt × Kt   R × Kt
26. P — K R 4 !

A strong move which prevents
26. ....P — K Kt 4 because of
27. Q — R 5 and if 27. ....Q —
K 1; 27. Q × Q, R × Q; 29. B P
× P, R × R ch; 30. K × R, R —
B 1 ch; 31. K — Kt 2, P × P;
32. P × P, R — B 4; 33. R —
Kt 3 winning a Pawn. Black's
waste of a tempo on move No. 22
has provided White just sufficient
time to carry out his plan.

26. ......   P — K Kt 3
27. K — Kt 2   Q — K 2
28. P — Q R 3 !

A necessary precaution; White
eliminates Black's possible counter by Q — Kt 5 and prepares an
eventual P — Q Kt 4. He must not
rush the attack on the K side by
28. R (B 3) — B 3 because of 28.
....P — B 4 with fresh chances
for Black.

28. ......   Q — Kt 2 ?

This was Black's last chance
for P — K Kt 4. If, then, 29.
R P × P, P × P; 30. Q — Kt 4,
Q — Kt 2; 31. R (B 3) — B 3, P
× P; 32. R × P, R × R and now
after 33. R × R, Q × Q; 34. R
× Q ch, K — R 2 the ending is
clearly drawn. So that White, in
order to preserve any winning
chances, must play 33. Q × Q ch,
K × Q; 34. P × R and Black has
to play with great care to secure
the draw, e.g. 34. ....K — Kt 3;
35. K — B 3, R — B 2 and not
35. ....R — K R 1; 36. R —

Kt 1 ch, K — B 2; 37. P — B 5 !,
P × P;   38.   K — B 4,   R —
R 5 ch; 39. K × P, R × P; 40.
P — K 6 ch, K — B 1; 41. K —
K 5, R — K 5 ch; 42. K — Q 6,
P — Q 5; 43. R — B 1 ch, K —
K 1; 44. R — K R 1, K — B 1;
45. K — Q 7 followed by R —
B 1 ch and wins.

Position after 28. ....Q — Kt 2 ?

29. Q R — B 3   Q — K 2
30. Q — B 2

At once preventing Black's P
— Q B 4 and threatening 31. P
— K Kt 4.

30. ......   K — Kt 2

If Black prevents White's K
side advance by 30. ....P —
K R 4, White switches his attack
over to the Q side by P — Q Kt 4,
R — Kt 3 and R — B 1 followed
by P — Q R 4 and P — Q Kt 5
and meanwhile Black has a permanent weakness to defend on
K Kt 3.

31. P—K Kt 4   R (B 4)—B 2
32. K — R 3   Q — Q 2

In order to prevent 33. P — B 5.

33. P — Kt 4	R — K Kt 1
34. R — K Kt 1	

P — B 5 would no longer be good, since it would give Black a lasting pin on White's Rook after 34. P — B 5, Kt P × P; 35. P × P, P × P; 36. R × P, R (Kt 1) — K B 1.

34.	K — R 1
35. Q — Q 2	

P — B 5 is now back in favour, since it would be followed by Q × R P ch.

35.	R — R 2
36. Q — K B 2	P — K R 4

Black endeavours to obtain counter-play on White's K R Pawn.

37. P × P	R × P

And not 37. .... P × P; 38. R — Kt 5.

38. R — Kt 5	Q — R 2
39. Q — Kt 3	Q — R 3
40. Q — Kt 4	R — Kt 2
41. R — Kt 3	K — R 2

A remarkable position in which all the available pieces are concentrated on the two right-hand files. Black has defended himself well and it is difficult for White to break through.

42. R — Kt 2	K — R 1
43. K — Kt 3	K — R 2
44. R — K R 2	

White has now regrouped his pieces so as to force Black to move his Rook off the K Kt file to defend his K Pawn.

44.	R — K 2
45. R — R 3	K — Kt 2

Position after 45. ....K — Kt 2

Black's last move leads to a speedily lost Rook and Pawn ending. Eliskases afterwards thought he could have made the ending much more difficult for White to win by playing waiting moves, such as R — K 1 and R — K 2. For then, after 46. R × R, Black would be able to recapture with the Pawn and retain the Queens on the board.

White's winning process would then be as follows: 45. .... R — K 1; 46. K — B 3, R — K 2; 47. R (R 3) — Kt 3, R × P; 48. R × P, R × Q; 49. R × Q ch, K × R; 50. R × R, R — Kt 2; 51. R — R 4 ch, K — Kt 3; 52. R — R 8, R — K 2; 53. K — Kt 3, K — Kt 2; 54. R — R 8, P — R 3; 55. K — Kt 5 and gradually Black's available good moves will be exhausted.

46. R × R	Q × R
47. Q × Q	P × Q
48. P — B 5 !	

By this temporary sacrifice, White forces a passed Pawn and, what is even more important, penetrates into the Black position with his King.

48.	P × P
49. K — B 4	R — K 3

Or 49. . . . . R — K B 2 ; 50. R — Kt 3 ch followed by R — Kt 5.

50. K × P	R — Kt 3

Again if 50. . . . . K — B 2 ; 51. R — Kt 3 — Kt 5.

51. P — K 6	R — Kt 5
52. K — K 5	R — K 5 ch
53. K — Q 6	R × Q P
54. R — K 3	Resigns

By winning this game, Capablanca made sure of the first prize, and the play from move 29 onwards is a fine example of involved middle and endgame strategy.

91
CONSULTATION GAME, LENINGRAD, 1936

Queen's Pawn, Queen's Indian Defence

White	Black
ILJIN-GENEVSKY	CAPABLANCA
and	
I. L. RABINOVITCH	

1. P — Q 4	Kt — K B 3
2. Kt — K B 3	P — Q Kt 3
3. P — K Kt 3	B — Kt 2
4. B — Kt 2	P — B 4

5. Castles	P × P
6. Kt × P	B × B
7. K × B	P — Q 4

Strangely enough, Capablanca is following the 3rd game of his match against Alekhine in 1927 — a game which he won for White (see Game No. 47) ; as pointed out there, 7. . . . . P — K Kt 3 is good for Black. The game Capablanca–Botvinnik, Nottingham, 1936, continued 7. . . . . P — K Kt 3 ; 8. P — Q B 4, B — Kt 2 ; 9. Kt — Q B 3, Q — B 1 ; 10. P — Kt 3, Q — Kt 2 ch ; 11. P — B 3, P — Q 4 ; 12. P × P, Kt × P with a level position.

8. P — Q B 4	Q — Q 2

Better than 8. . . . . P — K 3 as Alekhine played when White got a marked advantage by 9. Q — R 4 ch, Q — Q 2 ; 10. Kt — Kt 5.

9. P × P	

The order in which Black has played his moves has made a great difference, for now if 9. Kt — Kt 5, P — Q R 3 ; 10. Q — R 4, R — R 2 ! ; 11. Kt (Kt 5) — B 3, P — K 3 with a good game for Black, since 12. P × P, Q × Q ; 13. Kt × Q, Kt × P ; 14. P — K 4, Kt — Kt 5 is in his favour.

9.	Kt × P

Black must keep his Queen on Q 2 ; if he plays 9. . . . . Q × P ch ; 10. K — Kt 1, P — K 4 ; 11. Q — R 4 ch, Q — Q 2 ; 12. Kt — Kt 5 White has a won game.

10. P — K 4	Kt — B 2

This is the best square for the Kt, since Black's weakest point is Q Kt 4. If 10. .... Kt — B 3; 11. Kt — Q B 3, P — K 4; 12. Kt (Q 4) — Kt 5, Kt — R 3; 13. Q — R 4 and wins.

11. Kt — Q B 3 P — K 4
12. Kt — B 5   Q × Q
13. R × Q   Q Kt — R 3
14. B — K 3   R — Q 1
15. R × R ch K × R
16. P — Q R 4

The White players have evolved a plan for forcing Kt — Kt 5, followed by the gain of the Q R P. But this allows Black just sufficient time to remedy his defective development. White could have maintained the pressure by 16. R — Q 1 ch, K — B 1; 17. P — Q R 3, P — Kt 3; 18. Kt — R 6, B × Kt; 19. B × B, R — K 1 (not 19. .... R — Q 1; 20. R × R ch, K × R; 21. B — Kt 7); 20. P — Q Kt 4.

16. ......   K — Q 2

And now 17. R — Q 1 ch, K — K 3; 18. R — Q 8, P — Kt 3; 19. Kt — R 6, B — Kt 2 would lead to nothing for White.

17. Kt — Kt 5

There was still time to change the plan and obtain a satisfactory enough game by 17. P — R 5. It is true that the text move gains a Pawn, but only at the cost of destroying White's own Pawn structure, with fatal consequences in the endgame.

17. ......   P — Kt 3
18. Kt — R 4

White's Kt manœuvres are not very happy; the piece is badly out of play on the R file. An equal game was to be obtained by 18. R — Q 1 ch, K — K 3; 19. Kt (B 5) — Q 6, Kt × Kt; 20. Kt × Kt, B — B 4!; 21. B — R 6.

18. ......   B — B 4
19. Kt × R P B × B

Forcing the first pair of isolated Pawns.

20. P × B   Kt — B 4!

With this Black compels White to isolate his second pair of Pawns, since, apart from the mild threat of 21. .... Kt × K P, he has the much more violent 21. .... R — R 1.

21. Kt — Kt 5 Kt × Kt
22. P × Kt   K — K 3

An instructive position has been reached. In material, White is a Pawn up, but his Pawn position is shocking and his pieces (unlike Black's) are decentralised. Capablanca's conduct of the rest of the game is an object lesson in precision.

Position after 22. .... K — K 3

23. K — B 3

If White gives up the K P and plays R — Q 1 in order to prevent Black's Rook from occupying this file, Black simply takes the K P and follows this by R — R 1, when White will lose one of his pathetically helpless Q side Pawns.

23. ......   R — Q 1
24. P — Q Kt 4   Kt — Kt 6
25. R — R 7

If 25. R — R 6, Kt — Q 7 ch; 26. K — K 2, R — Q 3; 27. Kt — B 3, Kt × P followed by P — R 3 with the threats of Kt — B 6 ch and also P — Kt 4 — Kt 5.

25. ......   Kt — Q 7 ch
26. K — Kt 2   Kt × P
27. Kt — B 3   R — Q 4

White's weak Pawns continue to fall; he now attempts to gain some counter-play on the K side.

28. R — R 8   R × P
29. R — K 8 ch   K — B 3
30. P — Kt 4   Kt — Kt 4
31. Kt × Kt   K × Kt
32. K — Kt 3   K — B 3
33. R — K R 8   K — Kt 2
34. R — K 8   P — R 3
35. P — R 4   K — B 3
36. R — Q B 8

Giving up his brief hope of attack on the K side; for if now 36. R — K R 8, R × P; 37. R × P, K — Kt 2 and his Rook will be out of play for the rest of the game.

36. ......   R × P
37. R — B 6 ch   K — Kt 2
38. P — Kt 5   P — R 4
39. R — B 8   R — Kt 5 ch
40. K — R 3   R — K 5
41. R — B 3   P — Kt 4

Resigns, since after 42. .... P — Kt 5; 43. R — Kt 3 Black can win quite simply by bringing his King to the centre.

92
THIRTEENTH ROUND, NOTTINGHAM, 1936

English Opening

White	Black
CAPABLANCA	C. H. O'D. ALEXANDER

1. P — Q B 4   P — K 4
2. Kt — Q B 3   Kt — Q B 3
3. P — K Kt 3   P — K Kt 3
4. B — Kt 2   B — Kt 2
5. P — Q 3   K Kt — K 2
6. Kt — Q 5

A somewhat artificial manœuvre intended to weaken Black's K side by forcing him to advance his K B P (see move 8); a more solid line of development with opportunities of lasting attack is 6. Kt — R 3 followed by 7. P — B 4.

6. ......   Castles
7. P — K R 4

A method of play greatly favoured by Capablanca in the English and Réti Openings (see Games Nos. 35 and 88). It is an illustration of the theories of Steinitz by which the centre is kept blocked as far as possible whilst an attack is developed on the wing. With correct play on Black's part, it should not succeed, but Capablanca's virtuosity in seizing upon slight defects in his opponent's play made the variation very profitable for him.

7. ...... Kt — Q 5

A good move which prepares to open up the centre by P — Q B 3 and P — Q 4.

8. B — Kt 5   P — K B 3

Black cannot permit 9. B — B 6 which would eliminate his extremely important fianchettoed Bishop.

9. B — Q 2   P — B 3
10. Kt × Kt ch

And not either 10. Kt — B 3 or 10. Kt — K 3 allowing Black to play P — Q 4.

10. ......   Q × Kt
11. P — K 3   Kt — K 3
12. Kt — K 2   P — K B 4

It is easily understandable that Black wishes to round off his Pawn structure and increase the scope of his K Bishop, but this move has two defects: the positive one of giving White an object of attack on the K side and the negative fault of doing nothing towards solving the problem of the central advance by P — Q 4. Best was 12. ....P — Kt 3 at once followed by B — Kt 2 and P — Q 4.

13. Q — B 2   P — Kt 3
14. P — B 4 !

This move has great thematic value in the English Opening; Black is forced to exchange a centre Pawn for a flank Pawn and lines of attack are opened up for the major pieces.

14. ......   B — Kt 2

Black dare not exchange Pawns himself as White would obtain a strong attack by recapturing with the Kt Pawn followed by P — R 5 and Castles Q.

15. P × P   B × P
16. Castles Q   P — Q 4

This move is no longer the strongest; best was 16. .... Q R — B 1, after which, should White proceed along the same lines as in the actual game with 17. P — Q 4, B — Kt 2; 18. K — Kt 1, then Black gets excellent counter-chances by 18. ....P — Q Kt 4!; 19. P — B 5, P — Q 3.

The text move only temporarily embarrasses White's King, after which the isolated Q Pawn remains a lasting weakness; it is, however, instructive to observe how Capablanca manœuvres to take advantage of this.

17. P — Q 4   B — Kt 2
18. P × P   P × P
19. K — Kt 1   Q R — B 1
20. Kt — B 3   Q — Q 2
21. R — Q B 1   Kt — B 2

Alekhine suggests as more prudent the following line in his

notes in the book of the tournament: 21. ....P — K R 4; 22. Q — Kt 3, K R — Q 1, but White can then maintain pressure by doubling Rooks on the Q B file, e.g. 23. R — B 2, Q — Q 3; 24. K R — Q B 1, Q × P; 25. B × P, B × B; 26. Kt × B, R × R; 27. R × R, K — R 2 (27. ....Q × P loses a piece after 28. Kt — B 4); 28. Kt — B 6 ch, B × Kt; 29. Q × Kt, B — Kt 2 (29. .... B × R P ?; 30. Q — B 7 ch and wins); 30. Q — K 7 followed by R — B 7. It may be seen from this variation that the position holds more dangerous possibilities than appear on the surface.

Position after 21. ....Kt — B 2

22. Q — Kt 3   K — R 1
23. P — R 5

Now that the King has been induced to go to the corner on account of the pin on the Q Pawn, this move in turn forces a weakening of the K side Pawn structure.

23. ......   P — K Kt 4
24. P — R 6   B — K B 3
25. K R — B 1   B — K 2
26. Q — Q 1

Threatening Q — R 5 followed by P — K 4 with a combined attack on the K Kt Pawn.

26. ......   Q — K 1
27. P — K Kt 4

The process of exchanging flank for centre Pawns is admirably carried out to its logical conclusion; as a result, the weakness of Black's Pawn position becomes more and more apparent.

27. ......   Q — Kt 3
28. P × P   R × P

And not 28. ....Q × R P; 29. P — K 4!

29. R × R   Q × R ch
30. K — R 1   R — B 1
31. Q — R 1

Concentrating on the all-important square K 4; once White can play P — K 4 the game is won.

31. ......   Q — Q 6

Temporarily preventing P — K 4; if this is allowed, as, for example, after 31. ....Q — Kt 3, then 32. P — K 4, P × P; 33. B × P, B × B; 34. Kt × B, Kt — Q 4; 35. R — K Kt 1, Kt — B 5; 36. B × Kt, R × B; 37. Kt × P winning a Pawn, since 37. ....B × Kt loses at once by 38. Q — R 8 ch.

32. Kt — Kt 1   B — Q 3
33. B — K B 3   Q — B 4

34. R — B 1   Q — Kt 3
35. R — Kt 1

Threatening Kt — B 3 and P
— K 4 with a concentrated attack
on the K Kt Pawn; therefore the
K Bishop has to retire to defend
it.

35. ......   B — K 2
36. Kt — B 3   Q — Kt 1

If 36. ....Q — K 3, then 37.
R — K 1 again forcing an eventual P — K 4.

37. P — K 4

This long-dreaded move comes
in with stunning effect.

37. ......   Q — B 2
38. B — Kt 2   Q — B 7

38. ....P × P; 39. B × K P,
B × B; 40. Kt × B wins very
much as in the note indicated
after Black's 36th move. Now
Black must lose material.

Position after 38. ....Q — B 7

39. B × P !   B × B

Losing the Q for Rook and minor piece, after which Black's
case is hopeless. If he wished to
continue, he should have played
39. ....B — Kt 5, though the
game would still be eventually
won for White after 40. R —
K B 1, Q × P; 41. R × R ch, B
× R; 42. Kt × P.

40. R — K B 1   Q × R ch
41. B × Q   P × P
42. B — Kt 2   Kt — K 3
43. B × P   B — R 3
44. B — Kt 1   Resigns

Black has no adequate means
of fending off 45. Q — K 4.

CHAPTER TEN

The Final Phase

With the year 1937, Capablanca's chess career inclines on the downward grade. He no longer has the stamina for long, arduous tournaments, and his former great style only returns to him in flashes and at intervals. But for the one fine game given here against Ragosin, his results in the Semmering-Baden Tournament of this year were unrelievedly bad. It is true that he won a tournament in Paris in the next year in overwhelming fashion, but this was against inferior opposition. Not that the two games given from that tournament are less pleasing to play through; for they both have great value from the æsthetic and instructive points of view.

In the great A.V.R.O. Tournament of 1938, Capablanca again failed badly and produced few good games, the best being the one we give against Flohr, the opening of which is of especial interest. There follows a neat, calm game from Margate, in which Capablanca achieves a strategical purpose with great economy of effort.

Finally, we come to his last tournament, the International Team Tournament at Buenos Aires, where Capablanca represented Cuba for the first time. This resulted in some extremely good games, though, on the whole, again not opposed by the former formidable opposition. Games Nos. 98 and 99 belong to the same tranquil class of high classic simplicity that constitutes the mastery of Capablanca's style; whilst the last game against Czerniak is a fascinating example of cut and thrust.

SEMMERING–BADEN, 1937

	Keres	Fine	Capablanca	Reshevsky	Flohr	Eliskases	Ragosin	Petrov			
1 Keres	—	½ ½	½ ½	1 0	½ 1	1 0	½ 1	1 1	5	4	9
2 Fine	½ ½	—	½ ½	½ ½	½ ½	½ ½	1 ½	1 ½	4½	3½	8
3 Capablanca ..	½ ½	½ ½	—	½ ½	1 ½	½ 0	½ 1	½ ½	4	3½	7½
4 Reshevsky ..	0 1	½ ½	½ ½	—	½ ½	1 1	½ 0	1 0	4	3½	7½
5 Flohr	½ 0	½ ½	0 ½	½ ½	—	1 ½	½ ½	1 ½	4	3	7
6 Eliskases ..	0 1	½ ½	½ 1	0 0	0 ½	—	½ 1	0 ½	1½	4½	6
7 Ragosin.. ..	½ 0	0 ½	½ 0	½ 1	½ ½	½ 0	—	1 ½	3½	2½	6
8 Petrov	0 0	0 ½	½ ½	0 1	0 ½	1 ½	0 ½	—	1½	3½	5

A.V.R.O., 1938

	Keres	Fine	Botvinnik	Alekhine	Euwe	Reshevsky	Capablanca	Flohr	
1 Keres	—	1 ½	½ ½	½ ½	½ ½	1 ½	1 ½	½ ½	8½
2 Fine	0 ½	—	1 ½	1 1	1 0	1 0	½ ½	1 ½	8½
3 Botvinnik ..	½ ½	0 ½	—	1 ½	½ 0	1 ½	½ 1	½ ½	7½
4 Alekhine	½ ½	0 0	0 ½	—	1 ½	½ ½	½ 1	½ 1	7
5 Euwe	½ ½	0 1	½ 1	0 ½	—	0 ½	0 1	1 ½	7
6 Reshevsky ..	0 ½	0 1	0 ½	½ ½	1 ½	—	½ ½	1 ½	7
7 Capablanca ..	0 ½	½ ½	½ 0	½ 0	1 0	½ ½	—	1 ½	6
8 Flohr	½ ½	0 ½	½ ½	½ 0	0 ½	0 ½	0 ½	—	4½

PARIS, 1938

		Capablanca		Rossolimo		Cuhierman		Znosko-Borowski		Romi		Anglarés		
1	Capablanca	—		1	½	1	½	1	½	½	1	1	1	8
2	Rossolimo	0	½	—		1	1	½	1	1	1	1	½	7½
3	Cuhierman	0	½	0	0	—		½	1	1	1	1	1	5½
4	Znosko-Borowski	0	½	½	0	½	½	—		½	0	½	1	4
5	Romi	½	0	0	0	0	0	½	1	—		1	1	4
6	Anglarés	0	0	½	0	0	0	½	0	0	0	—		1

MARGATE, 1939

		Keres	Capablanca	Flohr	Thomas	Milner-Barry	Najdorf	Golombek	Sergeant	Vera Menchik	Wheatcroft	
1	Keres	-	½	½	1	½	1	1	1	1	1	7½
2	Capablanca	½	-	½	1	½	½	1	½	1	1	6½
3	Flohr	½	½	-	0	½	1	1	1	1	1	6½
4	Thomas	0	0	1	-	½	1	½	½	½	1	5
5	Milner-Barry	½	½	½	½	-	0	1	½	½	½	4½
6	Najdorf	0	½	0	0	1	-	0	1	½	1	4
7	Golombek	0	0	0	½	0	1	-	½	½	1	3½
8	Sergeant	0	½	0	½	½	0	½	-	1	0	3
9	Vera Menchik	0	0	0	½	½	½	½	0	-	½	2½
10	Wheatcroft	0	0	0	0	½	0	0	1	½	-	2

BUENOS AIRES, 1939

	Capablanca	Petrov	Alekhine	Eliskases	Stahlberg	Keres	Mikenas	Tartakower	Van Scheltinga	Czerniak	Opocensky	Trompovski	Enevoldsen	Grau	Castillo	Played	Pts.
1 Capablanca (Cuba)	–	–	½	–	–	½	1	1	½	1	1	1	1	½	–	10	8
2 Petrov (Latvia)	½	–	–	–	½	½	½	1	1	½	1	1	1	1	–	11	8½
3 Alekhine (France)	–	–	–	–	½	½	–	½	–	½	1	½	1	–	1	8	5½
4 Eliskases (Germany)	–	–	–	–	1	½	0	½	–	½	–	1	–	1	1	8	5½
5 Stahlberg (Sweden)	½	½	½	½	½	–	–	1	½	1	–	½	1	–	1	11	7½
6 Keres (Estonia)	–	½	½	0	–	½	1	1	½	–	–	1	–	–	–	8	5
7 Mikenas (Lithuania)	0	½	0	½	0	0	1	–	0	½	1	–	1	1	1	13	6½
8 Tartakower (Poland)	½	–	0	–	½	½	–	1	–	0	0	½	1	–	1	10	5
9 Van Scheltinga (Holland)	0	½	½	½	–	0	0	½	1	–	0	½	1	1	–	12	5½
10 Czerniak (Palestine)	0	0	0	–	–	–	1	0	1	1	–	–	0	–	–	8	3
11 Opocensky (Czechoslovakia)	0	–	½	1	0	–	–	0	–	1	0	–	–	–	1	8	3½
12 Trompovski (Brazil)	0	½	0	0	0	½	–	–	½	½	–	–	1	–	0	10	3
13 Enevoldsen (Denmark)	0	0	0	–	0	0	–	0	0	0	1	0	–	½	1	12	2½
14 Grau (Argentina)	½	–	0	0	–	–	–	0	–	0	–	–	½	–	½	7	1½
15 Castillo (Chile)	–	0	–	0	–	0	0	0	0	–	–	1	0	½	–	9	1½

93
TWELFTH ROUND, SEMMERING–BADEN, 1937

Queen's Gambit Declined, Slav Defence

White	Black
V. Ragosin	Capablanca
1. P — Q 4	P — Q 4
2. P — Q B 4	P — Q B 3
3. Kt — K B 3	Kt — B 3
4. Kt — B 3	P × P
5. P — Q R 4	B — B 4
6. P — K 3	

For 6. Kt — K 5 see Games Nos. 67 and 78.

6.	P — K 3
7. B × P	B — Q Kt 5

This is the modern method of playing the Slav Defence, by which Black tries to prevent White from obtaining control of K 4.

8. Castles	Castles
9. Q — Kt 3	

With the idea of exerting pressure on Black's Q Kt Pawn and taking temporary advantage of Black's unprotected Bishop on Kt 5. Against Euwe at Nottingham in 1936 Capablanca tried 9. Kt — K 5, P — B 4; 10. Kt — R 2, B — R 4; 11. P × P, Q × Q; 12. R × Q, B — B 7; 13. R — Q 4, B — B 2; 14. Kt — B 3, Kt — B 3; 15. R — Q 2, B — K Kt 3; 16. P — Q Kt 4, P — Q R 4 and Black had the better game.

White can eventually force P — K 4 by 9. Q — K 2, which is the logical method of procedure, but meanwhile Black can complete his development unhindered, as, for example, in the game Flohr–Reshevsky, Semmering-Baden, 1937, which continued: 9. ....B — Kt 5; 10. R — Q 1, Q Kt — Q 2; 11. P — R 3, B — K R 4; 12. P — K 4, Q — K 2; 13. P — K 5, Kt — Q 4; 14. Kt — K 4, P — K R 3; 15. Kt — Kt 3, B — Kt 3; 16. Kt — K 1, P — B 3 and after a hard-fought struggle lasting 116 moves a draw was agreed.

9.	Q — K 2
10. Kt — K 5	P — B 4
11. Kt — R 2	B — R 4
12. Q — Kt 5	

Embarking on an adventure, which eventually results in Black gaining command of the centre. Preferable is 12. P × P, R — B 1; 13. Kt — Q 3 with a level game.

12.	P — Q Kt 3
13. P — B 3	

Now, if 13. P × P, P — Q R 3! is to Black's advantage. The sacrifice of a Pawn gives White an attack which lasts, however, for a short time only.

13.	P × P
14. P — K 4	

14. P × P is playable, but leaves White with a poor game after 14. ....R — Q 1 owing to the weakness of his isolated Pawn.

14.	B — Kt 3
15. B — Kt 5	P — Q R 3
16. Q — Kt 3	Q — B 4 !

Forcing the exchange of White's Q Bishop, after which White is noticeably weak on the black squares.

17. B × Kt	P × B
18. Kt — Q 3	Q — Q 3
19. Q — Q 1	

An ignominious confession that his Q excursion has failed.

| 19. ...... | R — B 1 |
| 20. P — Q Kt 3 | |

This creates a weakness on Q B 3 of which Black takes full advantage. He refrains from playing R — Q B 1, since he wishes to bring the Q Kt into play via B 1. Nevertheless, this was his best course, followed by Q — K 2 and B — Kt 3.

20.	Kt — Q 2
21. Q — K 2	Kt — B 4
22. Kt × Kt	Q × Kt
23. B — Q 3	

Not 23. B × R P, P — Q 6 dis ch.

| 23. ...... | P — B 4 ! |

Black profits from the fact that White's Bishop has to remain on guard on Q 3 to exchange off a doubled Pawn and further weaken White's Pawn structure.

| 24. Q R — Kt 1 | |

With the threat of P — Q Kt 4, but Black's Bishop does not stay to be shut in on R 4.

| 24. ...... | P × P |
| 25. P × P | |

If 25. B × K P, P — Q 6 dis ch; 26. Q — B 2, B × B; 27. P × B, Q × Q ch; 28. R × Q, B — B 6 leaves Black with a won ending.

| 25. ...... | B — B 6 |

It is interesting to observe how in the next phase of the game Black dominates the black squares and conducts all his manœuvres on them.

26. P — Q Kt 4	Q — K 4
27. Kt — B 1	P — Q R 4
28. P × P	

If P — Kt 5 Black will first double Rooks on the Q B file and then play B — Kt 5 followed by B — Q 3 with an overwhelming attack.

28.	B × P
29. R — Kt 5	R — B 4
30. Q — B 3	

30. R × R, P × R gives Black two united passed Pawns and an easily won game.

| 30. ...... | R × R |
| 31. P × R | |

Owing to the necessity of retaking with the Pawn, White now has to open up the Q R file, along which the Black Rook penetrates with decisive effect.

31.	B — Q 7
32. Kt — K 2	B — K 6 ch
33. K — R 1	R — B 6
34. R — Q 1	P — R 4 !

A necessary preliminary to Black's next crushing manœuvre.

35. P — R 3

Which White either overlooks or despairs of meeting adequately. He is, however, so tied up that there is no good move at his disposal. The most innocuous seems to be 35. Kt — Kt 3, but Black can then play 35. .... R — B 7; 36. Kt — B 1, R — K B 7; 37. Q — R 3, B × P winning easily.

Position after 35. P — R 3

35.	R × B !
36. R × R	B × P
37. R × B	

Now the point of Black's 34th move is clear; but for this White could now play Q — Kt 4 ch.

| 37. ...... | P × R |
| 38. Q — B 1 | |

And not 38. Q × K P, B × Kt P ch.

| 38. ...... | Q × P |
| 39. Q — B 4 | |

Loses another Pawn, but the game is hopeless, anyway.

39.	B × P ch
40. K × B	Q × Kt ch
Resigns.	

94
THIRD ROUND, PARIS, 1938

Queen's Gambit Declined, Orthodox Defence

White	Black
CAPABLANCA	ROSSOLIMO
1. P — Q 4	Kt — K B 3
2. P — Q B 4	P — K 3
3. Kt — Q B 3	P — Q 4
4. B — Kt 5	B — K 2
5. P — K 3	Castles
6. Kt — B 3	Q Kt — Q 2
7. R — B 1	P — B 3
8. B — Q 3	P — K R 3

The normal continuation, 8. ....P × P; 9. B × P, Kt — Q 4, is better.

9. B — R 4

A very satisfactory alternative is 9. B — B 4, and if Kt — R 4; 10. B — K 5, Kt × B; 11. P × Kt, as was played in the game Fine–Maroczy, Zandvoort, 1936.

| 9. ...... | P × P |
| 10. B × P | P — Q Kt 4 |

To 10. ....Kt — Q 4 now White would reply 11. B — K Kt 3 !

| 11. B — Q 3 | P — Q R 3 |
| 12. P — Q R 4 ! | P — Kt 5 ? |

This leaves the Q B Pawn extremely weak. Better for Black is 12. ....P × P, and now if 13. Q × P, R — Q Kt 1 and pressure on the White Q Kt Pawn will enable Black to eliminate his weakness on the Q B file by P — Q B 4. 13. Kt × P, Q — R 4 ch leads to interesting play: 14. Kt — Q 2, B — Kt 5; 15. Kt — B 3, P — B 4; 16. Kt — Kt 3, Q — Q 1; 17. Castles, B — Kt 2; 18. Kt — K 4, P — Kt 4; 19. Kt × Kt ch, Kt × Kt; 20. B — Kt 3, P × P and Black's position, though somewhat loose, is tenable enough!

13. Kt — K 4   Kt × Kt
14. B × B   Kt × P
15. B × Q

Bad for White would be 15. K × Kt, Q × B; 16. R × P, P — K 4 and Black has a strong attack.

15. ......   Kt × Q
16. K × Kt   R × B
17. R × P   B — Kt 2 ?

Position after 17. .... B — Kt 2 ?

Black misses the opportunity of freeing his game by 17. .... P

— K 4! White could not then reply P × P because of 18. .... B — Kt 2; 19. R — B 7, B × Kt; 20. P × B, Kt × P winning a piece. White's best reply to P — K 4 would be 18. R — Q 6 and if B — Kt 2; 19. B — B 5.

18. R — B 7   B × Kt ch
If 18. .... B — Q 4; 19. K — K 2 followed by K R — Q B 1 and P — K 4.

19. P × B   Kt — Kt 3
Now, if 19. .... P — K 4; 20. B — K 4, Q R — B 1; 21. R × R, R × R; 22. B — Kt 7, etc.

20. R — B 6   Kt × P
21. K — B 2   K R — Kt 1
To ensure a retreating square for the Kt.

22. R — Q R 1   P — Kt 6 ch
23. K — B 1   R — Kt 5
24. B × P   Kt — Kt 3
25. K — Q 2   P — K 4

A combination which has a flaw, as Capablanca ably demonstrates. However, the endgame after 25. .... R — R 5; 26. R × R, Kt × R; 27. K — B 1 is quite lost for Black, who will soon lose his Q Kt Pawn. In addition, White's Bishop is much stronger than Black's Kt in this open position.

26. P × P   Kt — B 5 ch
27. K — B 3   Kt × P (K 4)
28. R — B 5   R — Kt 3

Position after 28. ....R — Kt 3

29. B — Q 3 !   Resigns

Black must lose a piece, however he plays.

95
FIFTH ROUND, PARIS, 1938

Queen's Gambit Declined, Tarrasch Defence

White	Black
CAPABLANCA	E. ZNOSKO-BOROWSKI

1. P — Q 4	P — Q 4
2. P — Q B 4	P — K 3
3. Kt — Q B 3	P — Q B 4

Not the right defence to choose against Capablanca, who delighted in the exploitation of just such positional advantages as can be obtained by White in this variation.

4. B P × P	K P × P

Lively play results after 4. ....B P × P, which rejoices in the colourful name of the Von Henrig-Schara Gambit, but Black

gets no adequate compensation for the Pawn after 5. Q — R 4 ch, B — Q 2; 6. Q × Q P, P × P; 7. Q × Q P, Kt — K B 3; 8. Q — Kt 3, Kt — B 3; 9. P — K 3, B — Q Kt 5; 10. B — Q 2, Castles; 11. Kt — B 3, Q — K 2; 12. B — K 2.

5. Kt — B 3	Kt — Q B 3
6. P — K Kt 3	Kt — B 3

Here the Swedish master, G. Stoltz, has introduced 6. .... P — B 5, to be followed up by 7. ....B — Q Kt 5 and 8. .... K Kt — K 2, but White can obtain an overwhelming game by the combinational 7. P — K 4, P × P; 8. Kt — K Kt 5, Q × P; 9. B — B 4, P — K R 3; 10. K Kt × K P, Q × Q ch; 11. R × Q, B — K 3; 12. Kt — Kt 5, B — Kt 5 ch; 13. K — K 2, R — Q 1; 14. K Kt — Q 6 ch, etc.

As for 6. ....B — K 3, see Game No. 6, in which Capablanca himself was playing the Black pieces against Marshall.

7. B — Kt 2	B — K 2
8. Castles	Castles
9. P × P	B × P

The Gambit 9. ....P — Q 5, though dangerous, is to White's advantage after 10. Kt — Q R 4, B — B 4; 11. B — B 4, Kt — K 5; 12. P — Q Kt 4, Kt × Kt P; 13. Kt × P.

10. Kt — Q R 4 !

Réti's move, and very strong, since hereby White gains control of the important central squares Q 4 and Q B 5.

Not so good is 10. B — Kt 5, with which Capablanca experimented in some other games (notably against Euwe and Lasker in his matches); for Black can then reply 10. ....P — Q 5!; 11. Kt — K 4, B — K 2; 12. Kt × Kt ch, B × Kt with a good game.

10.	B — K 2
11. B — K 3	Kt — K 5
12. Kt — Q 4	

Better than 12. R — B 1, Q — R 4; 13. Kt — Q 4, B — Q 2 with counter-chances for Black.

12.	Kt — K 4 ?

A weak move from which Black is not allowed to recover. White's next two moves show that Black has merely moved this piece from a good to a bad square. Best for Black is 12. ....Kt × Kt; 13. Q B × Kt, B — K 3; 14. Kt — B 3, Kt × Kt; 15. B × Kt, B — B 3, though White still preserves a positional plus after 16. B — Q 4!

13. R — B 1

This strong positional move also has the tactical advantage of preventing 13. ....Kt — B 5, which would now be met by 14. R × Kt.

13.	Q — R 4

Threatening P—Q Kt 4, which White at once prevents by his Bishop manœuvre.

14. B — B 4!

Forcing the Kt on to its weakest position on K Kt 3, where it remains out of play for the rest of the game.

14.	Kt — Kt 3

Black cannot successfully maintain the Kt in the centre, for if 14. ....B — B 3; 15. K B × Kt, P × B; 16. R — B 5 winning a piece and if 14. ....B — Q 3; 15. Q B × Kt, B × B; 16. B × Kt, B × Kt; 17. B × P ch, whilst after 14. ....P — B 3; 15. Q — Kt 3, K — R 1; 16. K R — Q 1 Black has a very bad game.

15. B — B 7   Q — R 3

The only square. 15. ....Q — Q 7; 16. Q × Q, Kt × Q; 17. K R — Q 1 loses time and merely aids White's development.

16. P — Q R 3

The necessary prelude to playing Kt — Q B 3 and thereby removing Black's best placed piece, but also with the idea of further circumscribing the Black Queen by an eventual P — Q Kt 4.

16.	B — Q 2
17. Kt — Q B 3	Kt × Kt
18. R × Kt	B — K 3

There is no other means to protect the Q Pawn; if 18. ....B — Q B 3; 19. Kt × B, P × Kt; 20. Q — B 2 winning the Q B Pawn.

19. P — Q Kt 4

Threatening to win the Queen by P — Kt 5, and thereby provoking a further weakness on the long diagonal.

19.	P — Kt 3

Position after 19. ....P — Kt 3

20. P — K 4

Capablanca pursues the logical course of breaking open the position in order to expose the many weaknesses in Black's game. Another very strong continuation was 20. P — B 4, after which Black has nothing better than the extremely miserable 20. ....Kt — R 1.

| 20. ...... | P × P |
| 21. B × K P | Q R — K 1 |

A Pawn is lost after 21. .... Q R — B 1; 22. Kt × B, P × Kt; 23. Q — Q 7.

22. Kt × B	P × Kt
23. B — B 6	B — B 3
24. P — Kt 5	Q — B 1

Less passive, but equally leading to disaster, is 24. ....Q — R 4; 25. R — B 4, R — K 2; 26. R — R 4, Q — B 6; 27. R × P, Q — Q 5; 28. Q — R 5, R — B 1; 29. R — Q 1, etc.

25. R — B 2	R — K 2
26. B — Q 6	R — Q 1
27. P — B 4	

Threatening 28. P — B 5, P × P; 29. B — Q 5 ch.

27.	K — R 1
28. K R — B 2	R — K B 2
29. K R — Q 2	

Position after 29. K R — Q 2

A remarkable position, with White's Rooks and Bishops sweeping the board in impressive style. The threat of 30. B — K 8 now drives Black's Rook into the corner.

29.	R — K Kt 1
30. Q — R 5	Q — Q 1
31. B — K 4	Resigns

A piece is lost after 31. .... R — Q 2; 32. B × Kt, P — K R 3; 33. Q — Q 1.

96
EIGHTH ROUND,
A.V.R.O., 1938

*Queen's Pawn, Grünfeld
Defence*

White	Black
CAPABLANCA	S. FLOHR
1. P — Q 4	Kt — K B 3
2. P — Q B 4	P — K Kt 3
3. Kt — Q B 3	P — Q 4

The Grünfeld Defence is one
of the most interesting and better
defences to the Queen's Pawn. It
is based on the strategic theme of
counter-attack on White's centre
in which the power of Black's
fianchettoed Bishop is used to the
full. In the present game, Flohr
employs a complicated variation
much analysed and used by the
Russians of recent years.

4. B — B 4

This is the most solid method
of development. The experience
of tournament play has shown
that 4. P × P, Kt × P; 5. P —
K 4, Kt × Kt; 6. P × Kt, P —
Q B 4 gives Black too great a
pressure on White's centre.

4.	B — Kt 2
5. P — K 3	Castles
6. Q — Kt 3	

Acceptance of the Gambit
Pawn is not good for White, as
was shown in another game of
the Avro Tournament, between
Flohr and Botvinnik, which ran
6. P × P, Kt × P; 7. Kt × Kt,
Q × Kt; 8. B × P, Kt — R 3; 9.
B × Kt, Q × Kt P; 10. Q — B 3,

Q × Q; 11. Kt × Q, P × B; 12.
Castles K, B — Kt 2 and the possession of two Bishops more than
compensates Black for his inferior Pawn formation.

| 6. ...... | P — B 4 |

A good and sound alternative
is 6. ....P — B 3, as Flohr himself played against Capablanca
in the 1937 Semmering Tournament. This continued 7. Kt —
B 3, P × P; 8. B × P, Q Kt —
Q 2; 9. Castles K, Kt — Kt 3;
10. B — K 2, B — K 3; 11. Q —
B 2, Q Kt — Q 4; 12. B — K 5,
B — B 4; 13. Q — Kt 3, Q —
Kt 3 with complete equality.

7. Q P × P

A risky capture which, however, makes for an extremely interesting game. The strongest
method of play is that used by
Löwenfisch in his 13th match
game against Botvinnik in 1937;
7. B P × P, P × P; 8. P × P,
Q Kt — Q 2; 9. B — K 2, Kt —
Kt 3; 10. B — B 3.

The main defect of the text
move is that it opens up the long
diagonal to Black's K Bishop.

| 7. ...... | Kt — K 5! |
| 8. P × P | |

White's position is now very
difficult. If 8. Kt × P, Q —
R 4 ch; 9. Q — Kt 4, Q × Q ch;
10. Kt × Q, B × P and Black
has the advantage. Whilst to cling
on to the Pawn by 8. Kt × Kt, P
× Kt; 9. Q — R 3 puts White too
far behind in development.

8.	Q — R 4
9. Kt — K 2	Kt × Q B P
10. Q — B 4	

The best move here is 10. Q — Q 1 since on R 4 White's Queen is liable to be attacked by Black's pawns and minor pieces.

| 10. ...... | Q Kt — R 3 |

Not the strongest way of continuing the attack. Flohr himself advises 10. ....P — K 4 and also very effective is 10. ....P — Kt 3; for then if 11. P — Q Kt 4, Q × Kt P; 12. Q × Q, Kt — Q 6 ch and if 11. Kt — Q 4, B — Q R 3; 12. P — Q Kt 4, B × Q; 13. P × Q, B × B; 14. K × B, P × P in both cases with the better game for Black.

11. Kt — Q 4

This is aimed at preventing Black's threat of P — Q Kt 4.

| 11. ...... | B — Q 2 |

11. ....Kt — Kt 5 fails against 12. P — Q R 3, B × Kt; 13. Q × Kt (Kt 4).

12. R — Q Kt 1

Position after 12. R — Q Kt 1

| 12. ...... | K R — B 1 ? |

This is the really crucial point; Flohr misses a most promising continuation in 12. ....P — Q Kt 4!, e.g. 13. P — Q Kt 4, P × Q; 14. P × Q, P — K 4; 15. P × P e.p., Kt × P; 16. B × P, Kt × B; 17. B × Kt, Kt × P ch and Black has the better game.

13. P — Q Kt 4	Q — Q 1
14. P × Kt	R × P
15. Q — Kt 3	Q — R 4
16. B × Kt!	

Better than an attempt to retain the piece, which would only end in disaster, as follows: 16. K — Q 2, Q R — Q B 1; 17. R — B 1, Kt — Kt 5 followed by 18. ....Kt × Q P.

| 16. ...... | R × Kt |
| 17. Q — Kt 4 | Q × Q |

Not 17. ....R — B 8 ch; 18. K — Q 2, Q × Q ch; 19. R × Q, R × R; 20. B × P, R — K 1; 21. B — B 6 and White wins.

| 18. R × Q | P × B |
| 19. K — K 2 | R — B 4 ? |

A final mistake, after which the game is not to be saved, since the White Rooks get going on the 7th rank. White would still have the superior game, but Black should be able to hold it by 19. ....B × Kt; 20. R × B, B — Kt 4 ch.

20. K R—Q Kt 1	P — R 3
21. P — K 4	Q R—Q B 1
22. B — K 3	R — R 4

Somewhat better is 22. ....B
× Kt followed by R — B 7 ch.

23. R — Kt 7   R × P ch
24. K — B 3   B — R 5

If 24. ....R — Q 1; 25. R ×
P followed by R (Kt 1) — Kt 7
and wins.

25. R × K P   R — R 6
26. Kt — B 6

Simplest and decisive; now
both White's Rooks will operate
on the 7th rank.

26. ......   B × Kt
27. P × B   R — B 6

If 27. ....R × P; 28. R —
Kt 8 ch followed by R × B P
after Black's enforced K — R 2.

28. R(Kt1)—Kt7   R(B1)×P

Or 28. ....R — B 1; 29. P —
B 7, R — B 1; 30. B — B 4, etc.

29. R × B P   R — B 3 ch
30. R × R   B × R
31. R × P   R — R 6
32. K — K 2   B — Kt 2
33. P — B 4   P — K R 4
34. P — K 5   B — B 1
35. R — R 8   R — R 7 ch
36. K — B 3   K — Kt 2
37. B — Q 4

And Black lost by exceeding
the time limit. His game is, of
course, quite lost, as after 37. R
— R 5; 38. K — K 3 he has no
reply to the threatened P — K 6
dis ch.

Final Position

97
SEVENTH ROUND, MARGATE, 1939

Queen's Pawn, Nimzovitch Defence

White	Black
CAPABLANCA	H. GOLOMBEK

1. P — Q 4   Kt — K B 3
2. P — Q B 4   P — K 3
3. Kt — Q B 3   B — Kt 5
4. Q — B 2   P — Q 4
5. P × P   P × P

Tried in rather an experimen-
tal mood, since I knew that Capablanca was fully versed in the
variations resulting from 5. ....
Q × P. The text had been out of
fashion for some time, and rightly so, since Black gets little
chance for counter-attack with
this variation.

6. B — Kt 5   P — B 3

The once popular 6. ....Q —
Q 3 has been discredited by numerous tournament games, and
leads to a poor game for Black,

e.g. 6. .... Q — Q 3; 7. P — K 3, Kt — K 5; 8. B — K B 4, Q — K 2; 9. B — Q 3, P — K B 4; 10. Kt — K 2, Castles; 11. Castles K, P — B 3; 12. P — B 3, Kt × Kt; 13. P × Kt and White is well ahead in development.

7. P — K 3   Q Kt — Q 2

A somewhat mechanical, routine-like move which allows White to dictate the scheme of things. Better and leading to a more lively game for Black is 7. .... B — Kt 5.

8. B — Q 3	P — K R 3
9. B — R 4	Castles
10. Kt — B 3	R — K 1
11. Castles K	B — K 2

The Bishop no longer serves any useful purpose on Kt 5, and rather than facilitate White's Q side advance by P — Q R 3 and P — Q Kt 4, I resolved to retire the piece to a more useful square.

12. B — Kt 3

Preventing Black's threatened Kt — K 5.

12. ......   Kt — B 1

I now formed a plan for exchanging my rather useless Q Bishop for White's active piece on Q 3. The drawback to the scheme is that it demands a great deal of time, and meanwhile White gets on with his Q side attack.

Unfortunately for Black, there does not seem any good line at his disposal. Bad is 12. .... Kt — R 4; 13. B — K 5, Kt × B; 14. P × B and Black's Kt on R 4 is in great danger.

13. P — K R 3   B — K 3
14. Q R — Kt 1

Now commences the famous and formidable minority attack on the Q side, against which Black is helpless unless he can manage to create sufficient compensating counter-attack on the K side.

14.	Kt — R 4
15. B — R 2	P — K Kt 3
16. Kt — K 5	Kt — Kt 2
17. P — Q Kt 4	B — K B 4

I have achieved my purpose, but meanwhile White has brought his Kts to bear on the Q side Pawn position.

18. Kt — R 4

Holding the ever-harassing threat of Kt — B 5 over Black's head.

18.	B × B
19. Q × B	Kt — 2
20. K R — B 1	Kt × Kt
21. B × Kt	B — Q 3
22. B × B	Q × B

One might have thought that Black, by his numerous exchanges, had eased his position, but in reality White, by extremely economical means, has been able to bring his minority attack to a rapid climax, as is demonstrated by the next powerful blow.

Position after 22. ....Q × B

23. P — Kt 5 !   P × P

Forced, since 23. ....K R — B 1; 24. P × P, P × P would leave Black with a hopeless Pawn position.

24. Q × Q Kt P   Kt — K 3

No better is any attempt at direct defence of the Q Kt P. For if 24. ....R — K 2; 25. R — B 5, R — Q 1; 26. Kt — B 3 and the Q P falls; whilst 24. ....P — Kt 3; 25. R — B 6, Q — Q 2; 26. R × Kt P wins the Q Kt P or 25. ....Q — Q 1; 26. Kt — B 3 wins the Q P.

25. Kt — B 3 !

Better than 25. Q × Kt P, which gives Black chances by 25. ....K R — Kt 1; 26. Q — B 6, Q × Q; 27. R × R ch, R × R; 28. R × Q, R — Kt 8 ch, etc., though even then White should win. The text allows Black no possible counter.

25. ......   K R — Q 1
26. Q × Kt P   Q — R 6

I had hoped to obtain a glimmer of a counter-attack by this Queen sortie, but was merely drawing the noose tighter round my own neck.

27. Kt × P   Q × R P
28. Kt — Kt 4   Q — R 5
29. Kt — B 6 !   Resigns

For White not only threatens to take the Rook, but also to win the Queen by 30. R — R 1; an impeccably played game by White, typical of his seeming effortless simplicity.

98
BUENOS AIRES, 1939

Queen's Pawn, Nimzovitch Defence

White	Black
CAPABLANCA	V. MIKENAS
1. P — Q 4	Kt — K B 3
2. P — Q B 4	P — K 3
3. Kt — Q B 3	B — Kt 5
4. Q — B 2	Kt — B 3

This, the Milner–Barry or Zürich Variation, should lead to most interesting strategic play. Black endeavours to force P — K 4, whilst White seeks compensation in play on the Q side with, very often, the additional advantage of two Bishops against Bishop and Knight.

5. Kt — B 3

Better than 5. P — K 3, which allows Black to play P — K 4 at once, as in the game Keres–Alekhine, Dresden, 1936, which continued: 5. P — K 3, P — K 4; 6.

P — Q 5, Kt — K 2; 7. Kt — B 3, B × Kt ch; 8. Q × B, P — Q 3; 9. B — K 2, Castles; 10. Castles, Kt — K 5; 11. Q — B 2, P — K B 4 with an excellent game for Black.

5. ......   P — Q 4 ?

This is quite against the theme of the defence, which is based on an eventual P — K 4. Black should play 5. .... P — Q 3, when he can obtain an equal game after 6. P — Q R 3, B × Kt ch; 7. Q × B, P — Q R 4 (it is important to prevent White from playing the cramping move, 8. P — Q Kt 4); 8. B — Kt 5, P — K R 3; 9. B × Kt, Q × B; 10. P — K 3, Castles; 11. B — K 2, P — K 4 (Lasker–Alekhine, Nottingham, 1936).

6. P — Q R 3   B × Kt ch
7. Q × B

As a result of his 5th move, Black now suffers, not only from the normal disadvantages that would attend the orthodox defence to the Queen's Gambit Declined, but also some others in addition. He can never play P — K 4 freeing the Bishop, and his Q Kt is misplaced, thereby preventing the advance of his Q B Pawn.

7. ......   P — Q R 4

Restraining P — Q Kt 4 and threatening P — R 5 followed by Kt — Q R 4 — Kt 6.

8. P — Q Kt 3   Castles
9. B — Kt 5   P — R 3
10. B × Kt

Capablanca chooses the simplest line, by which he obtains control of the centre with continued pressure on the Q side; 10. B — R 4 also offered good prospects, but would have produced a different and more complicated type of game.

10. ......   Q × B
11. P — K 3   B — Q 2
12. B — Q 3   K R — B 1

Preparing a counter-attack which is doomed to failure in view of the awkward positions of the Black pieces. Unfortunately, Black is unable to play for the normal freeing move P — K 4, since his Q Pawn must always be protected.

13. Castles K   P — R 5
14. P — Q Kt 4   P × P
15. B × P   Kt — R 2
16. Kt — K 5   B — K 1

Black would do better to exchange off this Bishop by 16. .... B — Kt 4.

17. P — B 4   P — Q Kt 3

And now Black should centralise the Kt by 17. .... Kt — Kt 4 followed by Kt — Q 3. His remorseful preparations for P — Q B 4 are too slow and come too late.

18. Q — Q 3   R — Q 1
19. P — B 5

A strong move which takes advantage of Black's dislocated position to institute a decisive attack.

19. ......   P — Q Kt 4

Mikenas has prepared a trap; if now 20. B — R 2, Q × Kt, or 20. Kt — Kt 4, Q — Kt 4.

Position after 19. ....P — Q Kt 4

20. P × P!

Capablanca ignores Black's trap and wins material by a fine combination.

20. ......   P × B
21. R × Q   P × Q
22. P × P ch   B × P
23. R × B   Kt — Kt 4

No better is 23. .... Kt — B 3; 24. R × P, Kt × Kt; 25. P × Kt, P — Q 7; 26. R — Q 1 and the Q Pawn soon falls.

24. R — B 2   R — Q 4
25. Kt × P   R — K 1
26. R — B 3   Resigns

Black is two Pawns down, with a hopeless game.

99
BUENOS AIRES, 1939
Queen's Gambit Declined, Slav Defence

White	Black
CAPABLANCA	VASSAUX

1. Kt — K B 3   P — Q 4
2. P — K 3   Kt — K B 3
3. P — B 4   P — B 3

Black commits himself to one line too early in the game. Better here are both 3. ....P — K 3 and 3. ....P — K Kt 3.

4. Kt — B 3   P — K 3
5. P — Q 4   Q Kt — Q 2
6. B — Q 3   P × P

As pointed out in earlier games in this book, the safest move for Black here is B — K 2.

7. B × B P   B — Kt 5

Not liking the Meran Defence, (7. ....P — Q Kt 4), Black decides to depart from theory, but the move is a poor one, since the Bishop serves no strategic purpose on Kt 5.

8. Castles   Castles
9. Q — K 2   Q — K 2
10. Kt — K 5   P — B 4

As a result of Black's 7th move, White can establish his Kt on K 5 without Black being able either to repel the piece or remove it by exchange. For if he plays 10. ....Kt × Kt; 11. P × Kt, Kt — Q 4 (or 11. ....Kt — Q 2; 12. P — B 4 with much the better game); 12. Kt — K 4 and Black has a very bad position.

Vassaux therefore tries to undermine White's central position by indirect means.

| 11. P — B 4 | Kt — Kt 3 |
| 12. B — Kt 3 | Q Kt — Q 4 |

Black wastes time with this manœuvre, which merely succeeds in strengthening White's centre. Best here is 12. ....P × P; 13. P × P, B — Q 2 followed by Q R — Q B 1.

| 13. B — Q 2 | B × Kt |

Under the misapprehension that he can force further exchanges, Black allows White to obtain the advantage of two Bishops against Bishop and Knight. He now has, however, a badly compromised position. If he plays 13. ....Kt × Kt; 14. P × Kt, B — R 4; 15. B — B 2 followed by P — K Kt 4 and P — K Kt 5 gives White a very strong K side attack.

| 14. P × B | Kt — K 5 |
| 15. B — K 1 ! | P — B 3 |

The Q B Pawn cannot be taken; for if 15. .... Kt (K 5) × P; 16. Q — Q 3, P × P; 17. P × P, Q — B 2; 18. R — B 3, P — B 3; 19. B — Q B 2, P — K Kt 3; 20. Kt × P, etc., and 15. .... Kt (Q 4) × B P; 16. Q — Q 3, P × P; 17. P × P, Q — B 2; 18. B × Kt, Kt × B; 19. Q R — B 1 wins a piece.

| 16. Q — Q 3 | P — B 4 |

If 16. ....P × Kt; 17. Q × Kt wins a Pawn, since 17. .... P

× P loses a piece after 18. B × Kt.

| 17. P — Q R 4 | K — R 1 |

Black fears 18. P — R 5 followed by 19. P — B 4 and P — Q 5 with threats on the diagonal Q R 2 — K Kt 8; hence he puts his King into what he hopes is a safe corner. He is, however, still not completely developed, and White is able to take advantage of this to deliver a decisive K side attack.

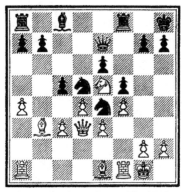

Position after 17. ....K — R 1

18. P — Kt 4 !

Threatening to win a Pawn by 19. P × P and thereby forcing one of the Kts to move.

18.	Kt (Q 4) — B 3
19. B — R 4	B — Q 2
20. R — B 3	

With the idea of playing R — R 3 followed by Kt — Kt 6 ch winning the Queen; Black's reply is directed against this manœuvre.

20.	B — K 1
21. R — K R 3	Q — Q 3
22. P × K B P	P × P
23. R — Q 1	

White consolidates his position and centralises his pieces before he embarks on the final attack — a manœuvre that marks Capablanca's style throughout his career.

23.	P × P

With this and the next move, Black despairs too soon; his game, though bad, was still tenable by 23. ....R — B 1 threatening P × P followed by R — B 6. White would then have to abandon his K side attack temporarily for the positional line, 24. P — Q 5 followed by Kt — B 4.

24. K P × P	Q — R 6

Again R — B 1 was preferable; rapid disaster results after the text move.

25. B — K 6	P — K Kt 3
26. B — Kt 5	

Threatening 27. B — R 6.

26.	Kt × B

If 26. ....B × P; 27. B — R 6, B × R; 28. Kt × P ch, P × Kt; 29. B × R dis ch.

27. P × Kt	Kt — K 5

Allowing a mating finish; if 27. ....Kt — R 4; 28. P — Q 5, Q × R P (White threatened Q — Q 4); 29. P — B 4, Kt — Kt 2;

30. Q — Q 4, R — Q 1; 31. R — R 4 and Black is helpless against the manœuvre R — Q 3, Q R — K R 3.

28. R × P ch	Resigns.

100
BUENOS AIRES, 1939

Caro-Kann Defence

White	Black
CAPABLANCA	M. CZERNIAK
1. P — K 4	P — Q B 3
2. P — Q 4	P — Q 4
3. P × P	P × P
4. P — Q B 4	Kt — Q B 3

More usual is 4. ....Kt — K B 3, in order to be able to retake with the Kt after White exchanges Pawns in the centre and so avoiding bringing the Queen prematurely into the game.

5. Kt — K B 3	B — Kt 5

The safest line here is 5. .... P — K 3 with a solid if somewhat constricted position.

6. P × P !	

White takes advantage of Black's neglect to support the centre to lure the Black Queen into play and gain tempi by attacking it.

6.	Q × P
7. B — K 2	P — K 3
8. Castles	

Stronger than the immediate 8. Kt — B 3, to which Black could reply 8. ....B — Kt 5.

8. . . . . . .   Kt — B 3
9. Kt — B 3   Q — Q R 4

Played on a parallel with similar positions arising out of the
Centre Counter Defence and hoping to be able to obtain pressure
on White's isolated Q Pawn. But
here, as in the Centre Counter,
White's greater freedom of pieces
and command of more space assure him the better game.

If, instead, Black plays 9.
. . . .Q — Q 2; 10. Kt — Kt 5, Kt
× Kt (or 10. . . . .B × B; 11. Q
× B, Kt × P; 12. Q — Q 3, Q
— Q 3; 13. B — B 4, Kt — R 4;
14. Kt — Kt 5, Kt × Kt; 15. Q
× Kt ch and wins); 11. P × Kt,
Q × Q; 12. B × Q, B × B; 13.
R × B, Kt — Q 2; 14. Kt —
Kt 5, K — Q 1; 15. B — K 3 with
a winning position, since Black
cannot play 15. . . . .P — Q R 3
because of 16. B — Kt 6 ch.
So Black should content him-
self with the humble 9. . . . .Q —
Q 1; 10. B — Kt 5, B — K 2,
when he is indeed behind in de-
velopment but has nothing radi-
cally wrong with his position.

10. P — K R 3   B — R 4
11. P — Q R 3   R — Q 1

Pursuing his policy of attack
on the isolated Pawn; more prudent would have been 11. . . . .B
— K 2 so as to Castle as soon as
possible.

12. P — K Kt 4

White is playing with great
vigour and succeeds in completely
disproving Black's opening strategy.

12. . . . . . .   B — Kt 3
13. P — Kt 4

The start of a fine combination by which White gains a
piece for three Pawns whilst re-
taining the attack.

Position after 13. P — Kt 4

13. . . . . . .   B × P

Black goes in for the complica-
tions; the alternative is to sub-
mit to being driven back and play
13. . . . .Q — B 2, when the lost
time will tell very badly on
Black's game, e.g. 14. B — K 3,
Kt — Q 4; 15. Kt × Kt, R ×
Kt; 16. R — B 1, Q — Kt 1; 17.
B — B 4, R — Q 1; 18. B —
Q Kt 5, B — K 5; 19. Kt — K 5,
R — B 1; 20. Q — R 4 with an
overwhelming game.

14. P × B   Q × R
15. Q — Kt 3

Threatening to win the Queen
by B — Kt 2.

15. ......   R × P

An ingenious counter, which, in combination with his next move, suffices to extract his Queen from danger.

16. B — R 3

Bad for White would be both 16. Kt × R, Kt × Kt; 17. Q — B 4, Q × Kt; 18. Q × Q, Kt × B ch and 16. B — Kt 2, R × P; 17. Q × R, Q × R ch.

16. ......   B — B 7

The only move to save the Queen.

17. Q × B   Q × B
18. Kt — Q Kt 5

Again he cannot play 18. Kt × R, Kt × Kt followed by 19. .... Q × Kt.

18. ......   Q × P

Black misses an important finesse which would have given him excellent drawing chances; he should have played 18. .... R × P ch; 19. P × R, Q × P and now if 20. Kt — K 5, Castles; 21. Kt × Kt, P × Kt; 22. Q × P, Kt × P; 23. Kt × P, Q — K B 5; 24. Q — Kt 2, Kt — K 4 and White's attack, in contradistinction to the actual game, is nonexistent.

19. K Kt × R   Kt × Kt
20. Kt × Kt   Castles

If 20. .... Q × Kt; 21. Q — B 8 ch, Q — Q 1; 22. B — Kt 5 ch, K — K 2; 23. Q × P ch, K — B 1; 24. R — B 1 winning

the Queen. But, as White proceeds to demonstrate, in the present position a piece is worth more than the three Pawns.

Position after 20. .... Castles

21. R — Q 1   Kt — Q 4
22. B — B 3   Kt — B 5
23. K — R 2   P — K 4

This eventually allows White to establish his Kt on Q 5, but 23. .... R — Q 1 is met by 24. Kt — B 6, and meanwhile Black must do something against the threat of 24. Q — K 4, since if he plays some such passive move as 23. .... P — K R 3 then 24. Q — K 4, Kt — Q 4; 25. Q — K 5 threatening either B × Kt or Kt × P or Kt — B 5.

24. Kt — B 5   P — K Kt 3
25. Kt — K 3   Kt — K 3
26. Kt — Q 5   Q — R 6
27. R — Q 3   Q — R 8
28. Q — Q 2   K — Kt 2

And not 28. .... P — K 5; 29. B × P, Q — K 4 ch; 30. K — Kt 1, Q × B; 31. Kt — B 6 ch.

29. Q — K 2   P — B 3
30. Q — K 3

Threatening R — R 3.

30. ......   P — Q R 3
31. R — Q 1   Q — Kt 7
32. Kt — B 3   Kt — Q 5

If Black tries to prevent the entry of the Rook on his 7th rank by 32. ....R — B 2 then 33. B — Q 5 is decisive.

33. R — Q Kt 1   Q — B 7
34. B — K 4   Resigns.

INDEX OF OPENINGS

(All references are to game numbers)

Caro-Kann Defence 46, 100

English Opening 69, 72, 88, 92

Four Knights' Game 80

Giuoco Piano 90

King's Gambit Accepted 36

Petroff Defence 24

Queen's Gambit Accepted 38, 40, 56
Queen's Gambit Declined:
    Cambridge Springs Defence 48, 49
    Irregular Defences 10, 16, 23, 42, 75
    Orthodox Defence 20, 26, 27, 29, 51, 58, 64, 81, 83, 94
    Queen's Fianchetto Defence 14
    Slav Defence 7, 13, 21, 25, 34, 67, 78, 85, 86, 93, 99
    Stonewall Defence 63
    Tarrasch Defence 6, 95
    Westphalia Variation 45, 62
Queen's Pawn Opening 2, 32, 41, 54
    Bogoljuboff Defence 87
    Budapest Defence 50
    Colle System 65
    Dutch Defence 30
    Grünfeld Defence 96
    Irregular Defence 11
    King's Indian Defence 31, 84
    Nimzovitch Defence 59, 60, 61, 68, 82, 97, 98
    Queen's Indian Defence 39, 43, 47, 53, 66, 71, 73, 74, 77, 79, 91
    Rubinstein Variation 55

Réti's Opening 35, 37, 70, 76, 89
Ruy Lopez:
    Bird's Defence 17
    Close Opening 9
    Morphy Defence 12, 18, 19, 22, 28, 33, 44
    Steinitz Defence 3, 4, 5, 8, 15

Sicilian Defence 52, 57

Vienna Gambit 1

LIST OF OPPONENTS

(All references are to game numbers)

Alatorzeff, 81
Alekhine, 13, 15, 43, 47, 48, 49
Alexander, 92
Allies, 91

Becker, 62
Bernstein, 8, 14, 16
Blackburne, 17
Bogoljuboff, 28, 32, 40, 53
Brinckmann, 67
Burn, 9

Chajes, 19
Colle, 65, 69
Corzo, 1, 2, 11
Czerniak, 100

Dus-Chotimirski, 12

Eliskases, 90
Euwe, 78, 79

Flohr, 96
Fox, 3

Golombek, 97
Gotthilf, 39

Havasi, 56, 68

Jaffe, 7
Janowski, 21, 23, 35

Kan, 83
Kevitz, 76
Kostich, 24
Kupchik, 18

Lasker, Ed., 41
Lasker, Em., 26, 27, 34
Lilienthal, 89
Löwenfisch, 85

Maroczy, 33, 64
Marshall, 4, 5, 6, 22, 37, 66, 77
Mattison, 61
Menchik, 74, 84
Merényi, 57
Mieses, 51, 86
Mikenas, 98
Milner-Barry, 88
Molina, 10
Monticelli, 71

Nimzovitch, 42, 46

Ragosin, 82, 93
Ribera, 73
Rossolimo, 94
Rubinstein, 54, 55

Schroeder, 20
Scott, 25
Spielmann, 45
Steiner, H., 58, 80
Subarew, 38

Tartakower, 30, 36, 50
Thomas, Sir George, 87
Torres, 72
Treybal, 63
Tylor, 75

Vassaux, 99
Vidmar, 29, 44
von Balla, 59

Winter, 60

Yates, 31, 52, 70

Znosko-Borowski, 95

Made in the USA
Las Vegas, NV
05 January 2022

40436184R00193